1848

The British state and

the Chartist movement

Cronto

JOHN SAVILLE

Emeritus Professor of Economic and
Social History, University of Hull

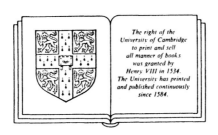

The right of the
University of Cambridge
to print and sell
all manner of books
was granted by
Henry VIII in 1534.
The University has printed
and published continuously
since 1584.

CAMBRIDGE UNIVERSITY PRESS

Cambridge

New York   Port Chester   Melbourne   Sydney

Published by the Press Syndicate of the University of Cambridge
The Pitt Building, Trumpington Street, Cambridge CB2 1RP
40 West 20th Street, New York, NY 10011, USA
10 Stamford Road, Oakleigh, Melbourne 3166, Australia

First published 1987
First paperback edition 1990

British Library cataloguing in publication data
Saville, John
1848: the British state and the
Chartist movement.
1. Chartism
1. Title
322.4′4′0941   HD8396

Library of Congress cataloguing in publication data
Saville, John.
1848: the British state and the Chartist movement.
Bibliography.
Includes index.
1. Chartism. 2. Great Britain – Politics and
government – 1837–1901.1. Title.
HD8396.S28 1987   322′.2′0941   86–29975

ISBN 0 521 33341 5 hardback
ISBN 0 521 39656 5 paperback

Transferred to digital printing 1999

SE

Contents

TO VICTOR KIERNAN

Preface

All authors of historical works incur intellectual debts of many kinds and to many different people. In the early stages of research on this present volume I was especially grateful for guidance to F. C. Mather's meticulously learned *Public Order in the Age of the Chartists* and to Dr David Goodway's manuscript on London Chartism, finally published in 1982. For a close reading of my penultimate draft I am deeply obliged to my colleague Dr Barbara English; to Mr Brian Pearce of London; and to Professor Ralph Miliband. To the last named I owe a long-standing debt for the many discussions we have had over the past three decades, and which for me have been a continuous source of intellectual stimulation. Cambridge University Press sent my manuscript to two outside readers who read my draft with great care and sympathy, although it was clear in both cases that neither shared my own intellectual assumptions. Let me record my gratitude to both – they have remained anonymous, as is the custom – and offer the assurance that I have tried seriously to meet their more critical comments.

Among others to whom I have the pleasure of expressing my thanks for their help are Mlle Marie-Thérèse Bodin, University of Poitiers; Ruth and Edmund Frow, Working Class Movement Library, Manchester; Dr Douglas Hay, Faculty of Law, York University, Toronto; Mr Monty Johnstone, London; Mrs Dorothy Thompson, University of Birmingham; Dr Noel Thompson, University College, Swansea.

Parts of this book have been read as seminar papers, and I gained much from the discussions which followed. These have included sessions at the University of Illinois; the Centre for European Studies, Harvard University; York University, Toronto; Institute of Historical Research, London; Institute of Advanced Studies, Canberra.

Librarians and Record Offices provide the main tools of the trade for historians. My greatest obligation is to the Brynmor Jones Library, University of Hull. For many years now I have used its considerable resources, and consulted its always helpful librarians. With them I mourn the recent death of Philip Larkin, its chief librarian, a personal friend who gave much support to the subject area within which I have spent a good deal of my academic life although his own interests were very different. He was a man some of us loved, and all respected. Among the other institutions in which I have worked for this present volume are the Royal Archives, and all the MS material quoted in the text or notes is by the gracious permission of Her Majesty The Queen. Miss Jane Langton and her colleagues at Windsor Castle were most kind and helpful. I have further to record my appreciation to the staffs of the British Library, at Bloomsbury and Colindale; Public Record Office, Chancery Lane and Kew; Scottish Record Office, Edinburgh; National Library of Scotland, Edinburgh; Manchester Record Office; Trinity College, Dublin; the central reference libraries at Manchester, Liverpool, Bradford, Barnsley, Hull, Birmingham; the Working Class Movement Library, Manchester; Marx Memorial Library, London; British Library of Political and Economic Science (LSE); Institute of Historical Research, London; Bodleian Library, Oxford; Bibliothèque Nationale, Paris; International Institute of Social History, Amsterdam.

I am under particular obligation to my colleague, Dr Joyce Bellamy for her constant helpfulness; and above all, a special note of appreciation to my wife for her gentle encouragement and unswerving and consistent support. The volume is dedicated to Victor Kiernan, emeritus professor of history at the University of Edinburgh. My intellectual debts to him through all our many years of friendship are beyond any simple or straightforward statement of affirmation.

University of Hull   JOHN SAVILLE

Abbreviations

DLB	*Dictionary of Labour Biography*
DNB	*Dictionary of National Biography*
GOC	General Officer Commanding
HO	Home Office
NCA	National Charter Association
PRO	Public Record Office
Rev.	Reverend
Rev.	*Review*
RA	Royal Archives
SC	Select Committee
TS	Treasury Solicitor

1

PROLEGOMENA

Chartist studies in Britain have developed remarkably in range and sophistication during the past three decades, and yet there remains a large number of unanswered questions. We now have Dr Epstein's detailed study of Feargus O'Connor in the years up to 1842, but a full-scale biography is lacking; and until that is produced we shall continue to read the political history of the movement in an incomplete way. Much of the work in recent years has been concerned with regional and local studies, admirably summarised in Dorothy Thompson's volume published in 1985, but we still do not have that overall view of Chartism within the political history of the nineteenth century the assessment of which would be so rewarding. In particular the relationship of the Chartist movement to other political developments is still too perfunctory, and the interaction of Chartism, as the centre of political radicalism, with the administrative and coercive powers of the early Victorian state has been seriously neglected. F. C. Mather published his excellent pioneering study in 1959, and there was the later writing of Radzinowicz and others, but it is only in the fairly recent past that younger scholars have begun to enquire into the themes of political and social control.

It is to help remedy some of these deficiencies that the present volume has been written, but it is concerned with one year only and much remains to be quarried for other years and for other themes. The year 1848 is often treated in history texts as an example of a revolutionary period whose turbulence reverberated round Europe with the exception of Britain and Russia: societies at the extreme ends respectively of the political spectrum. This volume takes the contrary view of Britain, and locates British domestic politics within the triangle of revolutionary Paris, insurgent Ireland, and a revitalised native Chartist movement in London and the industrial North. The approach has been through official records; and the long prolegomena with which this study begins are not intended to provide a comprehensive history of the preceding years, but rather to emphasise those parts of the political structures of Britain and Ireland that offer an understanding of the

1

events of the year itself. This is not then a history of Chartism in 1848, although inevitably much of the detail of that history has to be provided; nor is it a narrative account of the Whig administration whose prime minister was Lord John Russell. It is rather the story of the interrelationships between those directing the various organs of state power, and those in Britain and Ireland who were regarded as actually or potentially dangerous to the stability of the established order. What makes 1848 unusual, and in certain respects unique, in nineteenth-century history, is the extraordinary impact and influence of revolutionary Paris upon the whole of the United Kingdom, and the beginnings of the *rapprochement*, as a result of the French events, between the radicals on both sides of the Irish Channel.

ENGLAND

Sir Robert Peel, Prime Minister since 1841, resigned on 27 June 1846, and the Queen sent for Lord John Russell the next day. An offer to the Peelites came to nothing and Russell set about appointing his Cabinet of sixteen members, eight in each House.[1] The leading personalities in the new government, in addition to Lord John himself, were Palmerston, who took the Foreign Office, and the Marquis of Lansdowne, Lord President of the Council and leader of the House of Lords. Both Palmerston and Lansdowne were Irish landlords and in domestic affairs both were conservatively minded Whigs, facts of considerable import for the five and a half years of Whig government that was about to begin. The general election in July 1847 returned a House of Commons that was difficult to identify precisely in political terms, but with the support of the Peelites – which in fact was always to be given in sufficient numbers – Russell considered he could expect an effective working majority, or so he told the Queen in August.[2] He was right. The new session opened on 18 November 1847 with a Cabinet almost the same as that of 1846, the only major change being the appointment of the Earl of Clarendon, formerly president of the Board of Trade, to the Lord Lieutenancy of Ireland. Lord Bessborough, the previous Viceroy, had died in May 1847, and Clarendon was acceptable to both Houses, to the Court and in the country at large. It was an appointment that was accompanied with none of the bitterness that had attached to Lord Normanby's tenure of the Irish office between 1835 and 1839 during the Melbourne administration,[3] and the Whigs and Tories were to be satisfied with the consensus they achieved in the most difficult domestic situation with which they were to be confronted. Labouchere took Clarendon's place at the Board of Trade – a more congenial position for him than the Irish office – and Sir William Somerville, an Irishman, replaced Labouchere as Chief Secretary for Ireland, but unlike Labouchere he was not in the Cabinet.

The Constitution, so the House of Commons confirmed in 1851, did not recognise the Cabinet as a constitutional entity, nor was the office of Prime Minister defined as such.[4] Russell, like most, but not all prime ministers in the nineteenth century, took the office of First Lord of the Treasury, a position which gave him an official salary, and an official residence at 10 Downing Street.[5] The Cabinet, of course, had long been part of the structure of government in Britain, as had the position of First Minister. When Bagehot wrote *The English Constitution* in 1867 his opening chapter was devoted to the Cabinet: 'a combining committee – a *hyphen* which joins, a *buckle* which fastens, the legislative part of the State to the executive part of the State'. As he had remarked several paragraphs earlier,

The efficient secret of the English Constitution may be described as the close union, the nearly complete fusion, of the executive and legislative powers. No doubt by the traditional theory, as it exists in all the books, the goodness of our constitution consists in the entire separation of the legislature and executive authorities, but in truth its merit consists in their singular approximation. The connecting link is *the Cabinet*.[6]

It was accepted that membership of previous Cabinets was normally the rule for a position in future administrations. In Russell's 1846 Cabinet thirteen of its sixteen members had previously served in the Melbourne government; the collective experience of office was formidable, much aided by the close personal relationships between the Whig leaders. Russell had first entered the Commons in 1813 by which time Lansdowne, at the age of twenty-five, had already been Chancellor of the Exchequer in the government of 'All the Talents'; and Palmerston had been Secretary at War for four years. Russell's family connections hurried him along. He was Paymaster-General in 1830, in the Cabinet in 1831, and a leading figure in the Reform Bill agitation. In Melbourne's administration he was Home Secretary and then, at his own wish, he moved in 1839 to the Colonial Office, mainly because of the problems associated with Canada. Palmerston, eight years older than Russell and less well connected socially, was Secretary at War from 1809 until 1827: a junior ministerial position usually without a seat in the Cabinet, its affairs being mainly of a routine kind except for the presentation each year of the Army estimates in the Commons. He was a Tory until 1829 when he joined the Whigs, and during the 1830s was almost continuously at the Foreign Office where he began to exhibit his aggressive patriotism, as well as a notable waywardness in dealing with colleagues that became more marked as he got older. Radicals abroad, and conservatives at home such as the young Queen Victoria, often misunderstood Palmerston's political position in foreign affairs. He was a passionate adherent of constitutional monarchy, was never unwilling to denounce those foreign rulers whom he regarded as despots, and was always ready to offer the example of the British way of political life as that most suited to the needs of the contemporary world. There was no contradiction, it must be stressed, between Palmerston's foreign policies and his domestic outlook. He took for granted the central importance of property rights as the essential basis of social stability, and he was a firm believer in the rule of law provided the interests of a propertied society were in no way threatened.[7] He had inherited about 6,000 acres in Ireland, and probably half his income for much of his life must have come from Irish rents.[8] The third of the Whig leaders, the Marquis of Lansdowne, was one of the largest Irish landowners although he also had considerable estates in England and Scotland. Lansdowne was a Whig all his life, more liberal in his younger days than he later became, but always a man of moderate outlook. This was especially true of his attitude towards Irish affairs, summed up rather tactfully by the author of the entry in the *Dictionary of National Biography* (*DNB*) as 'inclined to temper a very firm support of the existing government with generosity'. He had great experience of public affairs over many decades and after Wellington's death he took on the position of informal adviser to the Crown on political and constitutional questions.[9] One interesting coincidence in the early lives of these three Whig leaders was their attendance at the University of Edinburgh where Dugald Stewart seems to have been an influence upon each of them. It was not uncommon for aristocratic families, particularly Whig, to send their sons, especially those marked out for political careers, to the University of Edinburgh: an equivalent during the French wars of the Grand Tour. Palmerston, who left Harrow in 1800, actually lodged with Dugald Stewart and was contemporary with Francis Horner, Henry Brougham, Sydney Smith and Henry Petty (Lansdowne). Both Palmerston and Lansdowne then went on to Cambridge, also a more favoured educational institution for Whigs than Oxford. John Russell, being younger, arrived in Edinburgh in October 1809 and he too heard Dugald Stewart lecture. Stewart, who had a considerable influence upon the young men who founded the *Edinburgh Review*, mostly followed Adam Smith in political economy, and although Palmerston remained a Tory during and after his Edinburgh days, he absorbed many of the elements of what was to become the economic 'commonsense' of middle-class Britain, and much of aristocratic Britain, in the coming decades.[10]

Russell was the most liberal of the three Whig leaders, imbued with a sense of political principle that stemmed from the 'self-confident, casual and cosmopolitan grandees' who made up the great Whig families.[11] His liberalism was to be severely tested during the years of his own government, and it proved a fragile construction, vulnerable to the Whig sense of political realities and much weakened by the advice of his fellow grandees. In particular, liberal ideas and liberal ideals over Irish affairs, so often vigorously expressed in opposition, easily fell to pieces during periods of office. As Mather has noted, no leading nineteenth-century politician ever confused the problems of coercion, or of personal liberty, in Ireland with those in the rest of the Kingdom.[12] In English politics by the second quarter of the century Whigs and most Tories had been 'civilised' by the experience of history and, most recently, by the fears of turbulence and unrest from below since the time of the French revolutionary wars.[13] Although Ireland was different, by the 1830s even the Orange peers in the House of Lords, whose outlook was more primitive than any other group, were no longer to be compared with their predecessors, so grimly delineated by Bishop Berkeley as 'vultures with iron bowels'.[14]

Russell and his ministers always appeared preoccupied with their majority in the House of Commons, although the bitterness of the Peelites and anti-Peelites towards each other meant that the government's position was usually more secure than its own leaders believed. It was the clear intention of Peel himself to keep the Whig administration in office. The Whigs, too, during the troubled year of 1848 often underestimated the support in the Commons for their coercive measures, and they were sometimes surprised by the range of approval that was forthcoming. They had considerably more problems with the House of Lords, although not in matters of internal security.

Until the accession of George III in 1760 the number of peers constitutionally permitted to sit in the House of Lords had increased only slightly since 1688, and the majority of its members were Whigs, or Whiggish. To assist the transformation of the Lords into a reliable support of his own version of Toryism, George III began creating peerages in considerable numbers. Between 1760 and 1784 forty-three new peers were introduced into the House of Lords in addition to fifty-nine new Irish peers who by definition were excluded from taking their seat at Westminster. Pitt the Younger subsequently continued peerage creation on a more extended scale, and large numbers of new peers were raised during the years of the French wars.[15] After 1815 the process slowed down, but between 1783 and 1833 the total number of peers allowed to sit in the House of Lords nearly doubled, from 230 to 423. In 1847 the number was 450 and in 1867 it was 464.[16] There were interesting differences in the social background of the new peerage between the closing decades of the eighteenth century and the first Reform Bill. What had formerly been the privilege of mainly the great landowners was now being extended to those who had distinguished themselves in the public service: diplomats, soldiers, judges and politicians. Most were still connected with land or with families with a landed background and were not yet representatives of commerce and industry; more immediately important the new creations did not alter but rather enhanced the now permanent Tory majority in the Lords: the political consequences of which were far-reaching.

There was, moreover, a result of the Union with Ireland in 1801 that further increased the reactionary character of the House of Lords and enhanced its conservative role in the affairs of government. It may be noted as a preliminary observation that owning property rights in Ireland, given the nature of Irish society, tended to encourage more extreme political attitudes. The Union added twenty-eight representative Irish peers to the House of Lords at Westminster together with four spiritual peers. The Irish lay peers were elected for life, and by the 1830s the choice of new representatives was virtually in the control of the Conservative leader in the Lords. The consequences of this direct Irish representation was the consolidation of a specifically Orange group in the Lords, who were bigoted reactionaries in Irish affairs and just as unpleasant elsewhere; and the general political atmosphere in the Lords could only have been worsened by these latter-day representatives of the Protestant Ascendancy. It is sometimes argued[17] that while such groups could be politically embarrassing to their party leaders, their effective influence was minimal and they would always be outvoted by the solid mass of mainstream Conservative opinion at the disposal of the leadership. However, this kind of reasoning ignores the direct and indirect influence upon the processes of decision-making of articulate minority groups within political organisations. The propensity of party leaderships to trim or to tergiversate was never likely to be discouraged by the presence of interest groups, such as the ennobled representatives of the Orange order, whose arrogant narrow-mindedness was sustained by a deep sense of historic destiny, and whose tenacity of opposition to the Catholic majority in Ireland was unyielding.

The increase in the Irish influence in the Lords was not, moreover, limited to the direct consequences of the Union but was also an indirect product of the increase in the number of peers sitting at Westminster. In the middle of the eighteenth century and down to about the 1780s about one-eighth of all peers owned Irish land or held Irish mortgages. By 1833 almost one peer in four possessed an Irish 'interest': 105 out of a total of 423. Dr David Large, from whom these figures are taken, added that a further twenty-two peers in 1833 may have owned land in Ireland.[18] This increase in the Irish interest had come about partly because of the Union but also because with the general increase in the number of peers some Irish peers acquired English titles, and some titles were also conferred upon commoners or knights who held land in Ireland. The political consequences within the House of Lords were obviously significant at a time when the first mass political movement in Ireland, under the leadership of Daniel O'Connell, was getting under way.

In the decades which followed 1832 the elements of political democracy were slowly and very unevenly introduced into the daily workings of middle-class political life, and then, much later, into the working-class constituency. The House of Commons began to reflect in hesitant and partial fashion these changes whereby the expressed will of interest groups and sections of public opinion among these new strata affected parliamentary debate and legislative action. There were spectacular episodes such as the repeal of the Corn Laws, but normally change was an incomplete recasting of traditional institutions at any one particular time. The House of Lords always presented a more formidable obstacle to reforming measures. As Halévy remarked, it was a general rule that 'the House of Lords defended established abuses with greater obstinacy than the Commons';[19] and while Bagehot emphasised that the Lords used their power, for the most part, with prudence – as in the crises of Catholic emancipation and the first Reform Bill – he also well appreciated the delaying power that resided in the conservatism of the upper House. In the last resort the Lords would be overruled, but the last resort, like the long run, was often distant in time. Here is his summing up:

In fact the House of Lords, as a House, is not a bulwark that will keep out revolution, but an index that revolution is unlikely. Resting as it does upon the old deference, and inveterate homage, it shows that the spasm of new forces, the outbreak of new agencies, which we call revolution, is for the time simply impossible. So long as many old leaves linger on the November trees, you know that there has been little frost and no wind; just so, while the House of Lords retains much power, you may know that there is no desperate discontent in the country, no wild agency likely to cause a great demolition.[20]

Bagehot was highly conscious of the ways in which the old ruling groups were deeply embedded within the power and political structures of Britain, although he may have underestimated the economic power that was represented in the House of Lords; but his comments reinforced the argument that the Lords exercised a constant and continuous check upon reforming legislation.

John Bright caused a satirical laugh in the House of Commons towards the end of 1847 when he was reported in *Hansard* as saying:

The present Parliament contains a larger number of men of business and Members representing the middle classes than any former Parliament. The present Government is essentially of the middle classes – [A Laugh] – and its members have on many occasions shown their sympathy with it. Let the hon. gentleman laugh; but he will not deny that no Government can long have a majority in this House which does not sympathise with the great middle class of this country.[21]

Bright had half the truth about the alignment of political forces, and the more important half, for the Reform Bill of 1832 had begun the political recognition of the shift of economic power within Britain. What Bright failed to emphasise was the compromise which 1832 involved, although in his daily political life he was acutely conscious of the position and power of the landed interest. The Reform Bill had ensured that the landed aristocracy continued to exercise dominant control in most of the different parts of the state apparatus while pursuing economic and social policies broadly consonant with the interests of the bourgeoisie. A European contemporary of John Bright who lived in England – Karl Marx – showed a more perceptive understanding of the relationship between the different sections of the propertied classes although he, too, suggested certain formulations that are no longer acceptable. In an article published in the *Neue Oder-Zeitung*, 6 March 1855, Marx wrote:

The British Constitution is, in fact, only an antiquated and obsolete compromise made between the bourgeoisie, which rules in actual practice, although *not officially*, in all the decisive spheres of bourgeois society, and the landed aristocracy, which forms the *official government* . . . Legislative history since 1831 is the history of concessions made to the industrial bourgeoisie; from the Poor Law Amendment Act to the repeal of the Corn Laws, and from the repeal of the Corn Laws to the Succession Duty on landed property.[22]

Although the bourgeoisie – itself the highest social stratum of the middle classes – thus gained general *political* recognition as the *ruling class*, this only happened on one condition, namely:

that the whole business of government in all its details – including even the executive branch of the legislature, that is, the actual making of laws in both Houses of Parliament – remained the guaranteed domain of the landed aristocracy. In 1830 the bourgeoisie preferred a renewal of the compromise with the landed aristocracy to a compromise with the mass of English people. Now, subjected to certain principles laid down by the bourgeoisie, the aristocracy (which enjoys exclusive power in the Cabinet, in Parliament, in the Civil Service, in the Army and Navy and which is thus one half, and comparatively the most important one, of the British nation) is being forced at this very moment to sign its own death warrant and to admit before the whole world that it is no longer destined to govern England.[23]

This passage from Marx illustrates both his insight and understanding of the British power structure as well as the mistakes that even the most perceptive can make about their contemporary world. The generalisation that Marx offered in the opening lines of the quotation just given: 'an antiquated and obsolete compromise' failed to recognise that the landed aristocracy were not only enormously wealthy from past accumulations and present rentals, but that the growing urbanisation of society would greatly enhance their rent rolls as well as maintain the prosperity of agriculture for several decades to come, given the protectionist barrier of distance. The statement further played down the ways in which sections of the landed aristocracy had become increasingly involved with industrial and mining enterprise.[24] As for his closing remarks concerning the rapidly diminishing political role of the aristocracy in the year 1853, Marx was here mistaking the realignments of party politics that occupied the 1850s for the elimination of the landed groups from the political scene. The economic strength and resilience of the landed aristocracy were indeed formidable; and their implantation in the political and social institutions of British society, from the Court downwards, was too pervasive to permit of any easy dislodgement.

With these qualifications Marx nevertheless had the heart of the matter. Between 1830 and 1850 the bourgeois state established itself as the dominant mode of political relations. It had been a long time in the making, and there was certainly no clean break with the past following the passing of the 1832 Reform Act.[25] What has been less appreciated, however, was the political complement of 1832 whereby political control in the great provincial towns was made over to the wealthier sections of the middle classes. The municipal reform of 1835 is often mistakenly discussed as a codicil to the Reform Bill of 1832,[26] and its importance is often underestimated. The greater part of the industrial and commercial bourgeoisie lived outside London in or near the rapidly growing urban centres; and following the spectacular demonstration of their political strength in 1832 they could now insist upon self-government in their own cities. The changes proposed by the Commission on Municipal Corporations were far-reaching. The old closed corporations, dominated in many places by the Tory-Anglican establishments, were to be abolished, and the Commission actually proposed household suffrage and the ballot. For many Tories at the time, these proposals for municipal reform were more sinister in their political implications than the 1832 Reform Bill; and the House of Lords effectively reduced certain of the more democratic elements of the original bill but without destroying the shift in political power that was its object. The Act which emerged was in a 'much chastened form' from that first proposed by the Whig administration[27] and it included a property qualification for councillors who were to hold office for three years, and the introduction of aldermen, elected by the councillors, whose tenure was for six years. Incorporation under the new Act was not automatic, and the timing was a matter of the balance of local political forces; but the first municipal elections after their incorporation, whichever date it was, produced Liberal majorities in Leeds, Liverpool, Leicester, Nottingham, Manchester, Birmingham, Salford and Bradford. In Manchester and Birmingham at their first elections in 1838 not a single Tory was returned.[28] In the year 1848 the northern towns beset by problems of riot and turbulence – Manchester, Bradford, Leeds, with Birmingham in the Midlands – all had Liberal mayors. Only Liverpool was the exception. The Whig aristocracy ruled at Westminster, and their provincial middle-class allies dominated the great town halls.

The large cities of the 1830s and 1840s, now controlled by middle-class

wealth, developed into regional capitals after 1850; and the great expansion
of municipal buildings - libraries, museums and above all town halls –
together with their own increasing personal wealth, steadily enlarged the
bourgeois sense of pride and achievement. The civic pomp and mummery of
local government office provided status and distinction of a kind that was
not obtainable outside their municipal boundaries until Westminster was
reached. Wealthy bourgeois often acquired country mansions and small
estates but they rarely became part of gentry society and their focus of social
and political power remained in local government and, especially after the
second reform bill, at Westminster.[29]

The restructuring of the administrative apparatus of the British state,
including the reluctant but inevitable acceptance of increasing administrative obligations, owed something to Benthamite vigour, but as much to the
ad hoc response to the imperatives of a rapidly industrialising and urbanising
society. The two are much less easily separated than some historians have
allowed;[30] but what was crucial for the bourgeois state that became
increasingly defined after the political changes of 1832 and 1835 was a
clear and, as far as possible, an unambiguous economic policy: one that
offered no obstacles to the pursuit of profit.

The mid-Victorian bourgeois, in an ideal society of his making, asked for
no restraint upon the exploitation of resources available to capital; for the
absence of any but minimal claims by the state upon his income and capital;
for an enforceable commercial law which provided for the sanctity of
contracts and adequate safeguards against fraud; for the physical inviolability of persons and property; and, in general, for the proper weight and
expression of bourgeois interests in the political decision-making of
government.[31] With the establishment of free trade in the forties there were
no further issues of economic policy that the industrial and commercial
classes felt strongly about; and the removal of any serious restrictions or
limitations upon profit-making encouraged attitudes of conservatism
among the wealthier middle class. There were still matters upon which they
felt deeply, but none was fundamental, and there was no issue which could
encourage the kind of passionate commitment that had made the Anti-Corn
Law League into such a formidable movement of political agitation. It was
not the presence of many vestiges of the old political order or their failure to
be recognised; it was rather the fact that no single issue, or combination of
issues, was capable of rousing sufficient numbers of the propertied members
of the middle classes to urgent political action. They campaigned for
financial reform; for a reduction in military expenditure; for a decrease in the
burden of colonies; and for the elimination of the many financial privileges
which the old landed classes still enjoyed, including the considerable claims
exercised by the Established Church; but while these were matters of import,

they were not the stuff of which radical movements were made at a time when profits, capital growth and personal wealth were increasing remarkably. The same year that the Reform Act was passed John Wade published the last edition of *The Extraordinary Black Book: An Exposition of Abuses in Church and State, Courts of Law, Representation, Municipal and Corporate Bodies.* It was a closely packed volume of nearly seven hundred pages, and it included an alphabetical list of 'places, Pensions, Sinecures, Grants and Compensations' which ran to eighty-five pages. But this represented the ending of 'Old Corruption', not its heyday, and the next half century was to witness the suppression of many pockets of jobbery and nepotism that Wade had publicised. Many, but by no means all, for mid-Victorian radicalism was unable to eliminate completely the old-style patronage and the distribution of largesse from the public purse. In 1848, for example, two books were published by W. Strange: one, the *Black Book of the Aristocracy,* and the other, *Sketches of Her Majesty's Household,* which provided generous examples of the legalised malversation enjoyed by the traditional ruling groups. The subject is one much neglected by historians, as is the delineation of the new, more sophisticated forms of bourgeois venality that emerged during the half century after 1850.[32]

There are two aspects of the political economy of the middle decades that illuminate the particular configuration of the bourgeois state in Britain. The first was land, a factor of production that in large part was not responsive to the workings of the free market. 'If I were five-and-twenty or thirty', said Richard Cobden in his last speech in public, 'instead of, unhappily, twice that number of years, I would take Adam Smith in hand, and I would have a League for free trade in land just as we had a League for free trade in Corn'.[33] What was at issue was the elimination of all legal restrictions upon the ownership and sale of real property. The real source of the 'evil', the *Economist* wrote on 24 November 1855, was to be found 'in the system of settlements and entails by which men continue to regulate the ownership of land in the hands of a future generation'. The demand for free trade in land, that land should become, like capital, a factor of production answering to the economy of the market, was an important minor political issue in the third quarter of the nineteenth century; but it never gained unanimous support from among the middle classes, and was never central to the concerns of the business and the mercantile classes. To the cotton and iron masters, the shipbuilders and the engineering employers the land question could never be elevated into a political issue of the first rank; while at the same time it was land, and the terms on which it was held, that underwrote the compromise of 1832. Whatever their other business and commercial interests, it was the ownership of land that gave economic power and social status to the aristocracy and gentry, and provided them with the foundations upon which their political power was sustained. The consequences of a direct assault upon the bastions of landed wealth and the associated political structures could not seriously be contemplated.

Middle-class attitudes and approach to the working population were quite different: inevitably so, as the source of surplus value and accumulation; and it was during the second quarter of the century that the economic policies appropriate to the labour market of a rapidly industrialising society became defined and made workable. There could be no compromise, for example, with Fielden's attempt to establish minimum wages in 1833.[34] That went so contrary to the logic of orthodox political economy as to be inconceivable of acceptance. At the same period the reform of the Poor Law had become an urgent necessity, partly because of the abuses that were so widely publicised, but much more because the arguments of the political economists and the 'commonsense' of the businessmen (and many landlords) demanded that the labourers must operate within the economy of the free market. It was not practical politics, as Nassau Senior would have wished in his younger days, to abolish public relief altogether;[35] but to provide public relief for those unwilling or unable to make provision for themselves on terms less favourable than those obtainable by the lowest paid worker in employment was the nearest that could be expected by those who understood poverty as the result of some defect of character. Edwin Chadwick's belief, expressed in the early 1830s, that the old Poor Law provided bounties on 'Indolence and vice' had become the commonplace wisdom among the middle classes and many of the upper class, especially those who were Whigs; and the report of the Commission of Enquiry into the workings of the old Poor Law, probably the most prejudiced public investigation of the century, confirmed what the Commissioners had set out to prove. The Poor Law Amendment Act of 1834 quickly passed into law and was expeditiously implemented, meeting with fierce opposition only when it began to be applied to the industrial districts of the North.

Interpretations of the new Poor Law by later historians have often misunderstood its central significance. An American historian wrote of the new Poor Law that 'though harsh by modern standards it was a step towards a more rational and more national and a more practical system of caring for the unemployed', and more recently, and just as inaccurately, it has been suggested that the new Poor Law was 'a non-partisan remedy for the long-standing burden of heavy poor rate and the evils publicised by the recent agricultural riots in southern England'.[36] It is agreed that there were abuses, although they were much exaggerated by the Commission of Enquiry, and Blaug has shown that the economic consequences of the old Poor Law were not understood by contemporaries or by later historians.[37] There was, however, no misunderstanding on the part of those who framed the terms of the new Poor Law as to its purposes. 'One of the most encouraging of the results of our enquiry', the Report said, 'is the degree to which the existing pauperism arises from fraud, indolence and improvidence'.[38] It was indolence and improvidence with which the authors of the new Poor Law were most concerned: the elimination of fraud would more or less automatically follow. Pauperism was a defect of character, and there was always work to be had at the prevailing market price if energetically sought. Hard work and thrift would always ensure a competence, however modest the level at which the individual was working and living. These values, encapsulated in the practices of the new Poor Law, exercised a deep and lasting impression upon Victorian society, and shaped not only the Victorian attitudes to poverty but also those of the twentieth century. Middle-class opinion in Victorian England widely reflected the basic principles of 1834; they provided the intellectual framework for the Charity Organisation Society, the most influential body in the policies of social work in the half century before 1914;[39] and even more striking, these attitudes towards poverty deeply influenced many among the respectable groupings of working people. A sense of shame at the acceptance of public relief developed – the dread of a pauper's funeral was only the most dramatic of working-class attitudes in this context – and 'respectability' in these general matters extended much further down the income scale than the skilled worker stratum.

The new Poor Law was an institutional complement to what Marx called the 'dull compulsion' of economic relations in society: the crucial fact that the worker in a capitalist economy has only labour power to sell; and that in this economy there was work for wages, or starvation. The problems of the labour market for industrial capitalism, however, went much beyond the elementary compulsion to work inherent in the position of workers divorced from the means of production. What was required was a labour force that could respond positively to the economic incentives the system offered, in order to realise the high productivity of which it was capable. The adaptation of labour involved not only the coercive forces whereby the labourer was compelled to work, but, in the long run, the transformation of social consciousness by which some of the basic assumptions of middle-class society would be accepted, in more or less degree, by the working population. In particular what was required was a response to the material incentives the industrial system had to offer. Over a very long period of time, this transformation has been largely accomplished, although never completely; but during the first century of industrialisation in Britain the adaptation of labour was only partially effected, and for those below the privileged stratum of the skilled, the processes of adjustment and accommodation – the transformation of the peasant or the labourer into an efficient factory hand – remained, in large though varying degree, coercive.[40] It was necessary, for example, to prohibit or, at the very least, to limit the collective power of workers to enforce their own working conditions or to attempt to raise wages. The formal legal freedom of the trade unions had been established by the Act of 1825 (6 Geo. IV c. 26), although very considerable difficulties continued to be experienced by trade unions until the legislation of the seventies. The Tolpuddle Martyrs were convicted for administering illegal oaths, but much more commonly used against trade unions was the general law of conspiracy which was stretched to include many different kinds of action and organisation. Trade unions were in fact only viable, except as very short-lived groupings, where the workers had a modicum of monopoly power through their skills.[41] Although it is difficult to be precise in quantitative terms, it is probable that most workers were subject to the operations of the Master and Servant laws whose statutory provisions treated masters and men on an entirely unequal basis. A workman who broke his contract could be punished as a criminal and sentenced to hard labour for up to three months on a summary conviction, while the master who could be proved to have broken his contract was liable only in a civil action for damages or wages owing. In the twenty years before the Master and Servant laws were abolished with the passing of the Conspiracy and Protection of Property Act of 1875, there was an average of 10,000 prosecutions a year in England and Wales under the Master and Servant laws. The Acts used for conviction were from both eighteenth and nineteenth centuries although the most common was that of 1823 (4 Geo. IV c. 34); and it was in the 'small master' trades that this particular measure of coercion was most applied. The correlation between trades, size of enterprise and application of the Acts is, however, a complicated question that still requires investigation.[42]

The 'dull compulsion' of labour, the wide-ranging material impact and social influence of the new Poor Law – the most important single item of social legislation passed in the nineteenth century – the legal frailty of trade unions, the active use of the Master and Servant laws, together provided the components of the 'free' labour market of the political economists.[43] The bourgeois state thus responded positively to the demands of its most important group of constituents: the owners of capital. This reordering of British society after 1832 to conform more closely with the requirements of a bourgeois order proceeded steadily but unevenly. By 1850 there were no important obstacles to the unhindered pursuit of profit, and the misappropriation of public funds, while not eliminated, was being slowly reduced. Factory legislation, while seriously questioned by contemporaries in its early years, proved no barrier to increasing levels of profitability and the growth of accumulation.[44] It was different in other parts of the social formation. The strength of the entrenched interests in matters affecting landed property, positions of political power and status generally was such that while change in the long term could not be denied it was often obstructed and delayed, and when it was effected it was invariably piecemeal. The young Robert Cecil summed up the essentials of conservative opposition to any change which affected power and privilege: 'There were left to them the chances of war, and it might be of victory, but at any rate they had obtained delay, and delay was life.' He was speaking in 1861 on the Church Rates Abolition Bill in the House of Commons.[45] No better guide to political practice could have been offered to his fellow aristocrats: delay was indeed life.

There were three outstanding issues that came to confront the Russell government in 1848, and none could have been predicted in its full significance and intensity at the beginning of the year; not even the issue of Ireland, England's perennial problem, which was still passing through the agonies of the famine. The other two were the political consequences in England and Europe of the Paris revolution of February 1848, and the domestic problems of Chartism and the *rapprochement* with Irish Repealers. The Radical movement was not moribund at the beginning of 1848, but in spite of the economic and financial crisis of 1847 it had maintained a fairly low level of activity; and, although the number of rural outrages in Ireland increased quite rapidly throughout 1847 and potential insurgency was always present, there was little to indicate in the early days of 1848 the turbulent character of the year that was to follow. The connecting link was France. With the beginning of the revolutionary days in Paris, and above all because of the speed with which the revolution developed, Europe began to explode; and within the United Kingdom both the Chartist movement in Britain and the left nationalist groups in Ireland were quickly stirred into fiery speech-making and political action. Once brought to vigorous life, the momentum of past movements carried them forward.

The departments of state mostly involved with these developments during 1848 were the Home Office, responsible for all matters of internal security within the kingdom, and the Foreign Office, always important, but in a year of European revolutions, of major significance. Both departments, in constitutional theory and usually in practice, were in the final analysis responsible to the Prime Minister and the Cabinet for the general principles informing their actions and for the results of these actions. The Prime Minister was assumed to be involved with all his main departments although there were quite significant differences between different administrations. Peel had concerned himself with the whole range of government business, and he described his burdens to Gladstone in 1846:

He said he had been twice prime minister, and nothing should induce him again to take part in the formation of a government; the labour and anxiety were too great . . . Then he spoke of the immense accumulation. 'There is the whole correspondence with the Queen, several times a day, and all requiring to be in my own hand, and to be carefully done; the whole correspondence with peers and members of parliament, in my own hand, as well as other persons of consequences; the sitting seven or eight hours a day to listen in the House of Commons. Then I must, of course, have my mind in the principal subjects connected with the various departments. . . .' And he spoke of the defects of the Melbourne government as a mere government of departments without a centre of unity, and of the possibility that the new ministers might experience difficulty in the same respect.[46]

Peel was right in expecting the Russell administration to exercise a less centralised control than his own government of 1841–6. Russell had never been as businesslike as Peel, and there were innumerable examples of official boxes remaining unopened, of letters not being answered or wrongly addressed and of appointments being forgotten.[47] As for Peel's care in the matter of his obligations to the Queen, Russell by contrast was inclined at times to display an aristocratic nonchalance that no doubt infuriated Albert and Victoria. 'The Transportation Bill', he wrote to the Queen on 23 June 1849, 'was then committed, and the usual nonsense was spoken upon it till past one in the morning'.[48] Russell also had some strong-minded colleagues, above all Palmerston; and for the years of his administration one of Russell's minor burdens was to keep the Queen soothed and appeased when Palmerston was more than usually arbitrary in his conduct of foreign affairs. The Crown had traditionally claimed special privileges in matters of foreign policy.[49] The Queen stated her side of the case, after many complaints against Palmerston, in a letter to Russell dated 12 August 1850:

She expects to be kept informed of what passes between him and the Foreign Ministers before important decisions are taken, based upon that intercourse; to receive the Foreign Despatches in good time, and to have the drafts for approval sent to her in sufficient time to make herself acquainted with their contents before they must be sent off. The Queen thinks it best that Lord John Russell should show this letter to Lord Palmerston.[50]

Palmerston's dismissal at the end of 1851 was much welcomed by the Queen, although she was certainly not responsible. Without the Cabinet's vigorous opposition to Palmerston, it is unlikely he would have gone at this time, for the monarchy was by now always kept firmly in its constitutional place.[51]

The Home Secretary was Sir George Grey, a highly competent administrator who remained calm and steady under pressure. According to Spencer Walpole, Whig Prime Ministers regarded the Home Office as among their closest responsibilities, and Russell had himself been Home Secretary for four years in the Melbourne government. In his own administration, however, Russell appears to have been content to leave the conduct of affairs to Grey and his senior officials. There was, no doubt, close personal contact between the Prime Minister and Sir George Grey but exactly how close it is not possible to say from the records available. There is little guide in the Russell papers or the Home Office files, which are in this regard disappointing, and from the documentary evidence available it was especially the internal security problems of Ireland in which Russell took a continuing interest: the correspondence in the Clarendon papers provides abundant evidence of his concern.[52] For most of March 1848, when the patterns and policies of control and coercion in Britain were being worked out by the Home Office, Russell was unwell and this was undoubtedly a contributing factor to the independence that Sir George Grey seems to have enjoyed. He inherited a department that had been acquiring a great deal of experience during the Chartist years.[53] His predecessor, Sir James Graham, in office between 1841 and 1846, was a close colleague of Sir Robert Peel and was immensely hardworking and competent. Graham, however, was inclined to take a conspiratorial view of most rioting and disturbance while both Russell and Grey had a somewhat more relaxed approach. Grey was also a more effective performer than Graham in the House of Commons, an important matter for the Whig administration given the volatility of voting in the Commons. He was personally much liked and respected, and throughout the difficulties of 1848 commanded the confidence of the House of Commons with his calm and well-ordered statements.[54]

The Home Office was established in 1782 although its historical roots lie in earlier centuries. There were various changes between 1782 and 1848 the results of which were to establish more firmly a small bureaucracy. After 1832, with the growth of state intervention in certain areas of social life – factory legislation, for example – new responsibilities were added to the work of the Home Office but for the first half of the century the overriding commitment was the maintenance of public order throughout the United Kingdom. The keeping of the King's Peace ('the legal name of the normal state of society')[55] was the general responsibility of the King's Ministers, but in practice it was the Secretary of State at the Home Office who was answerable.[56] There was a separate administration for Ireland with the Lieutenant-General appointed by patent.[57] He represented the sovereign, and was always a peer. He was the official leader of social life in Ireland, and was surrounded with considerable state ceremonial. While the Viceroy had very wide powers in his own right, including the prerogative of mercy, he was subject in the last resort to the government in London. Sir Robert Peel, in the House of Commons on 9 May 1844, stated the constitutional position:

It will be remembered that the Lord Lieutenant was a subordinate officer, although certainly he held a high office of great dignity, and he was bound to act upon the instructions which he received from the Secretary of State for the Home Department.[58]

There were two Under-Secretaries of State at the Home Office – one parliamentary, and usually a member of Parliament,[59] and the other a permanent civil servant – both on fixed salaries. In addition there was a private secretary to the Secretary of State, usually a political appointment, and a legal counsel. This small group of men, working under the direction of the Home Secretary, made all the decisions of any importance, although all major questions would first have been discussed with the Prime Minister and some of his colleagues: more rarely in full Cabinet. Sir George Grey followed the clear precedent of his predecessors in making a sharp distinction between those who took decisions and the clerks in the office, however experienced, who put them into practice. This was the division detailed precisely in the Trevelyan-Northcote report on the Civil Service in 1854, but both Graham and Grey, among others, had stated earlier the broad principles involved. Examined before a Select Committee in 1848 Grey was asked questions about the Home Office clerks:

Is there anything in the duties which requires more than habit and practice and a knowledge of precedents in the office? Is it one of those offices for which a person should be selected of superior intelligence and education? I should think an average degree of intelligence would qualify a gentleman for that office, but it requires great accuracy and great care and attention.[60]

Two years later Graham was specific on this division of labour:

I am most anxious to prevent the delegation of effective duties by the heads of departments to the Chief Clerks. No head of department, who really does his duty to the public, permits any such delegation; he keeps the reins of his department in his own hands, and allows nothing that is important to be done without his knowledge.[61]

There were fourteen clerks in the Home Office in 1848, presided over by a Chief Clerk. In addition, there was a small group of four clerks concerned with criminal business, a librarian and a précis writer whose functions were combined in one person, and a clerk for aliens' business. The total number of permanent officials in 1848, excluding doorkeepers and the like, was twenty-two. In March 1782 when the Home Office came formally into existence, the clerks had numbered eleven with the two Under-Secretaries: it was hardly a bureaucratic explosion that had taken place in the sixty or so years to 1848. What is striking about the personnel of the Home Office in the 1840s is the length of service and the breadth of experience that was represented. The Permanent Under-Secretary had been in the department since 1827, the Chief Clerk since 1816, and the four senior clerks had been appointed to this grade in 1834, 1835, 1837 and 1841, all four having been in the department since at least 1822.[62] Such longevity of service inevitably made for conservatism in policy matters and a reliance upon predecedent; but in matters of public order it also meant that among other benefits the quite complicated ladder of authority in the country at large was fully understood.

The distribution of work within the Home Office was not wholly rigid, but as normal daily practice the Parliamentary Under-Secretary dealt with matters concerned with Parliament, Ireland, Scotland and the Channel Islands. Since Ireland had a separate administration, and was the most consistently 'troublesome' of any part of the United Kingdom, there was inevitably a close liaison between the Parliamentary Under-Secretary and the Irish Chief Secretary who, during the parliamentary session, was always in London. The Permanent Under-Secretary, who was always a barrister, was responsible for legal questions, criminal work and the general correspondence coming into the department.

Sir George Grey's first Parliamentary Under-Secretary was Sir W. M. Somerville who was succeeded in July 1847 by Sir Denis Le Marchant, now without the parliamentary seat he had held for about a year. He moved back to the Board of Trade in May 1848, and his place was taken by George Cornewall Lewis.[63] The Permanent Under-Secretary was Samuel Mark Phillipps, in office since 1827 and whose health was now becoming precarious. He too retired in May 1848, being succeeded by Horatio Waddington. Phillipps was the son of a landowner, had been educated at Charterhouse and Cambridge, and then entered the legal profession. His *Treatise on the Law of Evidence* (1814) became a standard text. His successor, Waddington, was also educated at Charterhouse and Cambridge before becoming a barrister, and at the time of his appointment to the Home Office he was Recorder of Warwick and Litchfield and forty-nine years old.

The Law Officers of the Crown for England and Wales, the Attorney-General and the Solicitor General, and for Scotland the Lord Advocate and the Solicitor General, acted in both advisory and judicial capacities. It was they whom the Home Office often consulted in the matter of prosecutions, either of persons or journals. These were important questions where politics were involved, and there was often much debate, once the legal position had been established, as to whether prosecutions would be successful or not, or whether it was desirable to prosecute at this or that particular time. The Lord Advocate and the Scottish Solicitor General were used in a more administrative capacity than their colleagues in England.[64]

In mainland Britain the institutional arrangements for controlling disorder had improved strikingly since the mid 1830s, although as late as 1842 there were still many problems that were to be absent six years later. The basic structure of authority in rural areas did not alter in any significant way. The Lords Lieutenant of counties were appointed by the Crown on the

recommendation of the Home Secretary. They were always chosen from the
aristocracy and were usually prominent in the social life of their counties.
The appointments of Deputy Lieutenants and county magistrates were
made on their recommendation, and even by 1848 the latter had hardly as
yet been infiltrated by those from the commercial or industrial classes,
although there were marked differences between different regions. When
there was an outbreak of disturbances the Lord Lieutenant was expected to
give a lead to his county. The Yeomanry could be called out on his authority,
and it was assumed that he would encourage positive action on the part of
the local magistrates. Mather noted that in the early years of Chartism some
Lords Lieutenant were absent from their counties during periods of riot and
unrest.[65]Lords Lieutenant did not, of course, always live in the counties they
represented; they might have estates in other parts of the country, or they
might be in residence at their London house. There is an interesting letter
from Sir George Grey to the Viceroy in Ireland dated 19 July 1848, which not
only makes the point concerning their constitutional relationship, but
suggests that matters in England might have improved by this year. After
complaining that in a particularly troubled area of Ireland neither the Lord
Lieutenant nor his Deputy was present in the county, Grey continued:

Here in the event of disturbances we order Lords Lieutenant of counties to repair to
their counties and to take measures in concert with the magistrates for the
maintenance of peace. And why should not Irish Lords Lieutenant be required to do
their duty also?[66]

Whether Sir George Grey was representing faithfully the situation in Britain,
it is impossible to say; but it is likely. Clarendon often needed comforting, and
at times cajoling, and Grey might have been writing just to encourage him in
a situation that everyone recognised was always much more difficult than
anywhere on the mainland. It would further not be unreasonable to accept
Grey's letter as an additional proof of the all-round improvement in security
arrangements in England. It must be remarked in general, however, that
Chartist activity was hardly noticeable in rural areas during 1848, and little
work was required of Lords Lieutenant in the agricultural counties, whether
they were resident or not.

Scotland had a different structure of authority. At the top of the hierarchy
there was the Sheriff Principal, the equivalent of the Lord Lieutenant and
who, like his English counterpart, was usually an aristocrat of high
standing. Their functions were broadly the same. Below the Sheriff Principal
came the salaried Sheriff Deputy, normally known as the Sheriff. It was not a
full-time position and the Sheriff Deputy could live outside the area of his
jurisdiction. The third category of official, the Sheriff Substitute, was also
salaried and was required to reside in the county he represented. It was the
Sheriff Deputy who was usually in command during periods of unrest; the

most famous during the Chartist years was Archibald Alison, Sheriff Deputy of Lanarkshire. Alison had been a contemporary of Palmerston at the University of Edinburgh and during the Chartist years displayed remarkable energy and courage in confronting angry multitudes and pacifying potentially riotous crowds.[67]

The county magistrates in England were appointed on the recommendation of the Lord Lieutenant. There were property qualifications to be met, set low enough for small landowners to be eligible, but the problems of recruitment were often serious. The county nobility often showed a marked reluctance to sit on the bench. One consequence of the selectiveness of Lords Lieutenant in their choice of magistrates and of the unwillingness of many of the gentry to serve was the large number of Anglican clergymen as Justices of the Peace;[68] although by the 1840s the situation in most areas was beginning to change. Whig politicians were always concerned to reduce the Anglican element among the county magistracy and to increase middle-class representation. For one thing, the traditional authorities in rural areas were often troublesome to Whitehall, whatever the politics of the government. County magistrates fell easily into panic and just as easily allowed their political prejudices to bias their magisterial judgements. Governments, especially Whig administrations, were constantly apprehensive in times of trouble about the reactions of the backwoods gentry and their Church allies, and they were conscious always of the social damage that could be inflicted. These local magistrates in the shires were the equivalent of what Bagehot quoted, referring to the Tory back-benchers, as 'the finest brute votes in Europe'.[69] In 1848, however, it was not the rural areas but the industrial regions of the North, together with London, that were the main centres of radical agitation and unrest; and it was here that the most important structural changes in the character of authority had taken place. Outside London, the crucial legislation for the great towns of the provinces was the Municipal Corporations Act of 1835. The incorporated towns were now free from the petty tyranny as well as the inconveniences of the county bench. The new places on the borough commissions were filled, in most places, by Liberals and Whigs who formed the majority parties. These magistrates were much superior to their predecessors who had often lived outside the town boundaries. They demonstrated an energy and a vigour that was in sharp contrast with what was still the lethargy of magisterial practices in many of the unincorporated towns. These new justices, of course, had a direct interest in the preservation of law and order in their own urban areas: it was they who owned the mills and the warehouses and the shops. And they were also more sensitive to the social problems of their rapidly growing towns than the traditional county bench. Sympathy did not affect the toughness of their attitude towards disorder and turbulence, but many

among the business classes understood that repression was a beginning and
not an end: an appreciation that was certainly not pervasive among the old
order of magistrates, whether lay or clerical.

The most important single consequence of the 1835 Act was the
obligation it imposed upon the incorporated towns to establish a Watch
Committee whose responsibility it was to appoint and maintain an
adequately sized police force – the phrase was 'a sufficient number' of
constables – to be financed out of local rates. Progress in the country at large
was uneven for there were many vested interests to be overcome and much
opposition to professional policemen of the new type, but in most large
towns by 1848 the size and the competence of the police forces proved to be
more or less adequate for the special problems of that year. This was
certainly true of Manchester and Liverpool. The metropolitan police of
London, who came directly under the control of the Home Office, were by far
the most efficient in the country; and their aid was at times requested by
local authorities in other parts of the country. By contrast the Home Office in
London, except in times of crisis, had almost no influence over local police
forces in the incorporated boroughs. The 1835 Act obliged Watch
Committees to send quarterly reports, with quite minimal information, to
the Home Office, but these were not apparently used to improve those police
forces that were backward.[70] It was in the rural areas that the development
of professional forces was most uneven. The Rural Police Act of 1839 was
permissive, and the most important element in the many strands of
opposition or reluctance to its adoption was the expense involved and the
future burdens on the rates. It was to the Home Office that magistrates
reported or requested advice, and it was the Home Office which issued
instructions: either local, to a particular individual or bench, or, in times of
national crisis, by means of circulars throughout the country. In times of
stress the closeness of contact was impressive, and the Home Office was
never slow to remind local benches and commissioners of the peace of their
duties, including the obligation to keep Whitehall fully informed. There were
occasions, in very critical periods, when a town mayor would write three
times in one day to the Home Office, and daily correspondence, both ways,
was quite usual.[71]

The magistrates had the responsibility of maintaining public order in the
area of their jurisdiction. A disturbance that involved three or more people
was in common law a riot, and if it led to an arrest, the prisoner would be
charged with a misdemeanour, punishable by imprisonment or a fine. If,
however, more than twelve persons were involved in a disturbance and
refused to disperse, the Riot Act of 1715 could be read, and once read, the
riot became a felony, allowing the authorities concerned to use force
including the use of firearms. These matters were the responsibility of the

magistracy. It was the duty of the local magistrates to gather a sufficient force and to lead it in person to the scene of the disturbance; and it was their decision whether the Riot Act was read and they alone could give the order to open fire. The magistrates had to rely in the first instance upon the local police force and if this proved insufficient, two or more magistrates were entitled to swear in special constables; or, if a disturbance was feared at some time in the future, special constables could be sworn in against that contingency. The magistrates could also require aid from the local military, or they could call out, on their own authority, the local Yeomanry. By 1848 they also had the power to summon a detachment of the Enrolled Military Pensioners and request the Home Office to issue a warrant retrospectively to legalise their action. The police in Britain were not armed, but the magistracy could, and often did, apply to the Home Office for arms to be distributed. In almost all cases their requests were refused, but in the summer of 1848 sections of the metropolitan police, and the police forces in selected industrial towns of the North, were issued with cutlasses. Special constables, in spite of a good many requests, were never allowed arms by the Home Secretary at any time during the Chartist years.[72]

When the military acted in support of the civil power they were in theory, and in some important matters in practice, under the control of the civil authorities. At the Whitehall level, it was the Home Secretary who was responsible for the distribution of troops throughout the United Kingdom, although there was consultation with the Horse Guards, and with the commanders of the military districts. When the Lord Lieutenant of Ireland requested another regiment, the decision would be taken by the Home Secretary, usually in consultation with the Prime Minister, sometimes with the Cabinet, and it was the Home Department which issued the instructions. There would normally always be consultations with the Commander-in-Chief or, in 1848, more likely with the Military Secretary, since the Duke of Wellington seems often to have been by-passed.

At the local level it has often been assumed that the magistracy had the power to requisition the military forces that were within reach of the actual or threatened disorder. The practice had grown up during the eighteenth century of the Secretary of State issuing a general order authorising military commanders to give aid to the civil power; and magistrates became accustomed to call upon the military without a previous application to the central government. This precedent was accepted during the first half of the nineteenth century, but it was always possible for the officer in command to refuse a request if he considered the call for assistance had been made on insufficient grounds, or he could refer the request to a superior officer. Most of Britain was divided into military districts. London, including Windsor, was directed from the Horse Guards, and there were quite a large number of rural counties not included in any military district which were also administered from Whitehall.[73] The largest district was the Northern and Midland which from 1842 took in the whole of the north of England, from the Scottish border south through Durham, Yorkshire and Lancashire down to Birmingham and the counties of Leicestershire and Northamptonshire. The headquarters of the district were in Manchester, and the General Officer Commanding was Lieutenant-General Sir Thomas Arbuthnot. He had taken command in mid August 1842.[74] His senior officers were Major General Sir Willaim Warre, with headquarters at Chester, and responsibility for the North-West including the key town of Liverpool; and Major-General Thorn with his headquarters at York. The other districts were the South-West (Portsmouth); the Western (Devonport); Monmouth and South Wales (Carmarthen); Scotland (Edinburgh); and the Channel Islands, Jersey being separately administered from Guernsey and Alderney.

The military commanders were mostly Peninsular veterans, and in the main were able and efficient men. Sir Thomas Arbuthnot seems to have been quite outstanding, as interesting, although not so radical in political outlook, as Sir Charles Napier, but much less well known. He died in 1849 at the age of seventy-three. Both Graham and Sir George Grey used Arbuthnot for many services for which they judged the civilian authorities less competent; and his long reports to Grey during the troubled months of 1848 were intelligent, markedly shrewd and very informative. He was probably the most useful single source of intelligence during the spring and summer months of 1848 for the whole of the industrial North.

The military forces stationed in the United Kingdom were divided broadly between mainland Britain and Ireland; and the respective levels of order and disorder largely determined their distribution between these two main parts of the kingdom. In the late 1830s, for example, the Litchfield House compact between the Whigs and O'Connell, together with a Whig administration in Dublin Castle meant relative tranquility in Ireland[75] and the practicability of withdrawal of troops from Ireland to the mainland: a matter of considerable importance in the years 1839–40. In 1840 there were 26,845 troops (excluding officers and NCOs) in Britain and 13,112 in Ireland. It was indeed O'Connell's boast that he had saved Britain from the Chartists.[76] In 1848 the situation was quite different and the figures were 33,738 in Britain and 28,942 in Ireland. A large part of the army, it must be remembered, was overseas, and one of the favourable factors for the government in 1848 was the return of several regiments from overseas service. What helped the situation even more was the rapid extension of the railway network. The Quartermaster-General emphasised in evidence before a committee in 1844 how the railways had enabled the army 'to do the work of a very large one; you send a battalion of 1,000 men from London to Manchester in nine hours; that same battalion marching would take 17 days; and they arrive at the end of nine hours just as fresh, or nearly so, as when they started'.[77]

In addition to the police, the special constables and the army there were two other groups that could be used by those responsible for maintaining public order. The Yeomanry had been in existence since the 1790s. It was a volunteer force, made up in most counties from the better-off farmers and the lesser gentry. Certain of the metropolitan counties by the second quarter of the century were served by Yeomanry drawn from business and professional groups; but most of the Yeomanry forces were rural. They were the equivalent of a regular cavalry force, armed and to some extent trained. They had a standard six-day training each year and were inspected annually by a Field Officer of the regular army. On active service, under an Act of 1804, they were subject to military discipline, but their control was by the civil authorities. The Yeomanry were called out by the Lord Lieutenant or by the local magistrate but, as always in a period of crisis, the chain of command could be superseded by Whitehall. The Home Secretary could authorise the Commanders of military districts to call out the Yeomanry and retain them under their command.[78]

Governments never forgot Peterloo or the consequences of making martyrs; and during the Chartist years there was considerable reluctance to use the Yeomanry in the control of riot and disturbance. The Yeomanry were exceedingly unpopular, much more disliked than the army, and their presence might often exacerbate and worsen a difficult situation. The Whigs especially were critical of what Sir Charles Napier in his *Memoirs* described as the over-zealousness of the Yeomanry 'for cutting and slashing'; and during his period as Home Secretary, Lord John Russell carried through a reduction in the numbers of the Yeomanry: 'for his part he would rather that any force should be employed in case of local disturbance than the local corps of Yeomanry'.[79] The cost of the Yeomanry was also a consideration, for they were paid during their days of service. They were mostly agriculturalists and farmers of one kind and another, and the seasonal round, especially harvesting, could be seriously interrupted. It was a matter that governments always tried to take into account. Opposition to the use of Yeomanry must not, however, be exaggerated. The Tories used the Yeomanry extensively in the difficult years of 1841 and 1842, and Whig scruples were never pushed beyond the real needs of internal security, as the events of the summer of 1848 clearly demonstrated.

The last auxiliary group at the disposal of the law and order enforcers were the Enrolled Pensioners. Army pensioners had long been used in times of social unrest as special constables: indeed, in many places they were often the only auxiliaries available. In 1843, as a result of the massive turbulence of the previous year, retired soldiers were enrolled into local uniformed corps (6 and 7 Vict. c. 95). They were given eight days training each year. The total number enrolled was not to exceed 10,000 and the normal age of retirement from the new corps was 55, although volunteers could be taken up to the age of 58. In 1846 a further Act brought in the naval pensioners. When called out on active service the Pensioners were armed with muskets and bayonets. The total number of Enrolled Pensioners in Britain in 1848 was 8,720; and a War Office memorandum listed the following numbers for certain towns in the industrial North: Bolton 211; Preston 141; Stockport 87; Liverpool 350; Manchester, First Division 378, Second Division 378; Halifax 157; Sheffield 175; Hull and York 130.[80] The authority to call out the Enrolled Pensioners was vested in the Home Secretary, but he could, and often did, issue general warrants to selected persons which enabled Pensioners to be called out on local initiative. Warrants were normally issued to Lords Lieutenant and to the Mayors of incorporated boroughs. Again, as with the Yeomanry, in times of crisis the Enrolled Pensioners could be put directly under the commanders of the military districts. Enrolled Pensioners could be called out for twelve days in any one year under warrant; thereafter, only volunteers were available. In practice, because of the 'high rates of pay', there was never any difficulty in assembling sufficient numbers. The Enrolled Pensioners were highly cost-effective. In evidence before an 1850 Select Committee Fox Maule, Secretary at War, reported that the cost of Pensioners for a normal year was about two pounds and ten shillings per head, exclusive of clothing which was issued once every five years.[81]

By 1848 the coercive forces at the disposal of those acting on behalf of the Crown, and the administrative machinery of central and local government for their direction and control, were more efficiently organised than at any previous period. The growth of the great urban areas which went with industrialisation had created qualitatively new problems of social and political control for the governing classes. The definition of adequate security measures had become inextricably intertwined with the political problems of power sharing between the landed groups and the rapidly growing numbers of the middle class in the towns; and given that Ireland was always on a quite different level of social tension than the rest of Britain, it became the laboratory for experiment and exploration of new ways of dealing with insurgency. The much more urgent problems of law and order in Ireland provided patterns of control and coercion that could be applied, suitably adjusted and modified, to the rest of the United Kingdom. It was the emergence of mass movements, in both Ireland and Britain in the two decades before 1850, that forced Dublin Castle and the Home Office in Whitehall to improve the chain of command and increase the weight of coercive power that could quickly be applied to the areas of unrest and turbulence. In England the years 1839 to 1842 were crucial in these matters. What was new in 1848, compared with all previous years, was the stimulus to revolutionary action by the events in France at the same time as Ireland was apparently moving in parallel with the radical movement in Britain. For the first time the seemingly intractable problem of internal security in Ireland had now close links with radical activity in Britain. The coming together of Irish nationalists with English Chartists provided new dimensions to the security problem overall, and to contemporaries the conjuncture looked alarming and potentially highly dangerous. Revolutionary Paris, Irish insurgency and the Chartist mobilisation all came together to produce a situation in which the ranks of the propertied – the large and the small and the high and the low – joined in a striking demonstration of unity against what was felt to be a serious threat to the foundations of social life. The impressive response to the call for special constables in 1848 all over Britain exhibited the determination of the middle strata to preserve their economic and social positions. It was, for middle-class Britain, a *levée en masse* of quite remarkable proportions.

IRELAND

Four hundred years of savage hostility, culminating in the wars of the first Elizabeth, completed the conquest of Ireland by England and the imposition of English law over more or less the whole island. The cruelties of the wars of the sixteenth century were compared by Lecky with those of Alva in the Netherlands.[82] In the next century the Cromwellian Settlement ended years of butchery, on both sides, in which Petty estimated that over six hundred thousand, out of a total population of one and a half million, had died from war and famine, the greater part of the dead being native Irish. There was a further period of killing, destruction and death in the reign of James II and the early years of William; and at the beginning of the eighteenth century the Irish Catholics were in possession of only some 14 per cent of the productive land of their country: a third less than when James II had come to the throne.[83] The now dominant Protestant Ascendancy began to consolidate their superiority by proceeding to introduce the Penal Laws against Catholics. These were begun in 1695, assumed their 'worst features' in the reign of Anne, and were more or less completed in the 1720s. Large numbers of Irish emigrated, especially from among the upper classes: removing what an Irish historian described as the 'last barrier between the Irish people and their foreign rulers'.[84] The overwhelming mass of the peasantry who remained lived in bitter, degrading poverty. During the first half of the eighteenth century the Penal Laws were vigorously applied, but from the middle decades their impact became less although the range of proscriptions and prohibitions which continued explains the unyielding and ineradicable hostility of the Irish towards the imperial power of Britain. No understanding of Anglo-Irish relations in the modern era, from the eighteenth century to our own day, is comprehensible except in terms of the fierce hatred engendered within the hearts and minds of the Catholic Irish by the centuries of English occupation. When, to take an extreme example, the Irish Privy Council in 1719 attempted, unsuccessfully, to substitute castration for branding as the penalty for unregistered Catholic priests, it must be understood as a commonplace manifestation of the rancorous virulence and brutality with which the Protestant Ascendancy and the Catholic masses acted towards each other: one small part of the historical record which helped to inculcate the pervasive sense of history as injustice which has been such a marked characteristic of Irish consciousness in the period of nationalism.[85]

Ireland during the eighteenth century, and especially from about 1750, gradually became more prosperous although the mutilating poverty of the greater part of the labouring classes was only slowly remedied. Anglo-Irish trade expanded tenfold between 1700 and 1800, mostly the result of the growth in the output of the linen industry; agricultural rents probably increased threefold by 1780; and the economic differences between Ulster and the rest of the country, which were to play such an important part in the history of the nineteenth and twentieth centuries, were already pronounced by the end of the eighteenth century. But even in Ulster the living standards bore no comparison with those of contemporary England. The Irish remained locked in poverty, rack-rented by many landlords and within the commercial framework of a restrictive, mercantilist policy which seriously stifled the growth of employment opportunities other than those in the agricultural sector; although by 1800 some development of manufacturing had taken place, it was organised almost everywhere on a domestic basis.[86] There were many other evils in the eighteenth century attributable to English rule, among them an alien church which through tithe, pluralist holdings and high incomes for those in the top levels of hierarchy, insisted upon the full monetary settlement of what was owed to the representatives of a Protestant God on Irish earth. The serious drain of capital from Ireland, of which part of the revenues of the Anglican church must be included, came from various other sources including many sinecures with generous emoluments, a swollen bureaucracy often staffed by the English and a very large pension list. For Catholics there were almost insuperable problems to personal advancement before the 1780s: 'Apostasy', Lecky wrote, 'was the first step in the path of ambition'.[87] These were all matters that were grievous and harmful to the development of Irish society and to the moulding of the national character of the Irish people; but the central problem, the condition of conditions, was land and the terms on which it was held. The oppression of the mass of the tenants by their landlords, or increasingly by the middlemen who came in growing numbers between the cultivator and the owner, was a major component of the nationalist politics which took shape in the nineteenth century.

When the Union with England was brought about in 1800 the contrast was striking compared with the earlier union which had taken place with Scotland in 1707. Scotland kept its own legal system, its native educational institutions and its own (Protestant) churches. The timing of the Union, at the beginning of the eighteenth century, was an important element in the cluster of factors that were to Scotland's advantage: England's manufacturing capacity was much less powerful than it later became and the establishment of a free trade area included access to colonial markets which assisted Scottish economic growth.[88] There were problems for Scotland, inevitably, for the Celtic lands have been subject to the centripetal forces of the English economy and English political structures, and within Scotland the Highlands and Islands have been vulnerable to a form of 'internal colonialism'. But the case of Scotland cannot in most respects be compared with that of Ireland for the problems of the latter were qualitatively different, and worse. Ireland was a subject country ruled from Dublin on behalf of a metropolitan imperialism, much complicated by the difference in religion which was similar to that of England's main enemies, of which France was much the most important. The Irish looked steadily towards their fellow-Catholics in Europe for sympathy and for material help; and again France was the country from which most was expected. A considerable part of the emigration of the upper classes between 1690 and 1720 was to France, and the Irish Brigade (the 'wild geese') in the French army was present throughout the eighteenth century. When Smith O'Brien presented an address on behalf of the people of Ireland to the Provisional Government in Paris in early April 1848, the *Moniteur* (4 April) reported him in one passage which especially angered the British ambassador:

Dans les temps passés, au moment le plus extrême de l'Irlande, vos pères ont accueilli avec hospitalité nos guerriers exilés; et les champs de Fontenoy peuvent dire comment cette hospitalité a été acquittée par l'effusion du sang irlandais, coulant pour soutenir la gloire de la France.[89]

The battle of Fontenoy was fought in May 1745.[90] There was inevitably an important strategic factor in the English attitudes towards Ireland. It was the gateway to the Atlantic; in the control of a hostile power, or as an independent country capable of making foreign alliances, Ireland could offer a continuous threat to Britain. It was always France that was in mind and, during the French wars of the eighteenth century and especially the events of the year 1798, as well as in the decades after Waterloo, these strategic considerations were confirmed as a major premise of British policy.

The Union with England in 1800 was achieved by a shrewd combination of hard-nosed political bargaining, lying promises and massive corruption. Castlereagh was one of its prime movers.[91] Three major reforms outside the terms of the agreement had been agreed by Pitt in return for Irish support: Catholic emancipation, tithe commutation and the endowment of the Catholic priesthood. None was in fact carried out in the immediate aftermath of the Union and they remained for years unfulfilled, encouraging movements of discontent which helped to shape the pattterns of protest for many decades to come. Catholic emancipation was achieved only in 1829 and the first effective Tithe Act was in 1838.

The Union of 1800 took place when English industrialisation was well under way. A rapidly advancing industrialism was therefore joined with a largely agricultural economy whose domestic manufacturing sectors would be overwhelmed once a common market was established. There had been some considerable progress in Irish economic life after the mid eighteenth century and Grattan's parliament was protectionist, although not as stringently as many interests were demanding. Free trade was not immediately introduced once the Union was agreed, but phased; a 10 per cent *ad valorem* duty on a range of articles, eighteen in all, was to last until 1821, which in the event became 1824. Rapid decline in most domestic industries followed, with Belfast and the Lagan valley as the main exceptions; and Ireland became a country supplying cheap food, mainly to Britain, and cheap labour to the industrialising world on both sides of the Atlantic. The decline of handicrafts, the elimination of alternative employment to agriculture and the consequent loss to family income reinforced the growing problems in the rural areas. In this context, there are some interesting and important parallels with India.[92]

The historical symbiosis between Ireland and Britain had profound consequences for both. The interactions between a colonial country and the dominant imperial power are too often discussed in restricted economic terms, important though these are; but the politics of control are significant for both the ruled and those who rule. The techniques of management learned in colonial countries usually influence the behaviour of ruling groups and elites in their own homeland but in ways that are modified and adapted by their own domestic history. Coercive action of the kind that was possible in Ireland during the first half of the nineteenth century was mostly not politically feasible on the British mainland. Ireland was different and was to remain different until the separation of 1922. There were always aristocratic, Anglican, English pressure on the Celtic lands of Wales and Scotland, but there was nothing to compare with the governing practices in Ireland where the majority of the population practised an alien religion, where rural unrest was endemic and where the levels of violence were of an order not to be found elsewhere in the kingdom.

The Union of 1800 meant, theoretically, assimilation, and the constitutional interest of Ireland resides in the ways in which the slow evolution of parliamentary democracy in Britain was modified and bowdlerised in Ireland. The colonial relationship, inherited from before 1800, was only slowly and never completely altered, but in a number of respects the colonial–imperial relationship had special characteristics not found elsewhere in the Empire. Ireland was now an integral part of the United Kingdom, which meant that the Westminster parliament was the supreme legislative body. The Union had been directly and indirectly responsible for the strengthening of the Irish landed interest in the House of Lords, and it had also given one hundred Irish MPs to the Commons: a considerable under-representation in terms of population in 1800 and a significant over-representation by 1900. Elsewhere in the Empire colonial territories always had representatives of their interests at Westminster, and some pressure groups, such as that of the West Indies, were powerful; but no other country approached the special relationships of Ireland with England, where so many of the owners of large properties in Ireland exercised executive functions at Westminster. Of the three leading Whig ministers in 1848 only Russell had no direct economic interest in Ireland.

Irish political structures changed only slowly during the early decades of the Union. Dublin Castle remained the centre of power, as it always had been, and although the Viceroy, as noted earlier, was in the final analysis subject to the direction of the Home Secretary in Whitehall, his powers were wide-ranging. The Viceroy was always an aristocrat, his salary was £20,000 a year at a time when the English Prime Minister received £5,000 a year, and the Viceroy assumed a style of living that was felt to be fitting for a representative of the Crown. The ravages of the famine made no difference to the way the Viceroy's court displayed itself, as the household accounts of Lord Clarendon make abundantly clear.[93]

Ireland was for many British statesmen in the nineteenth century a staging post in their political careers;[94] and this was true both of the positions of Lord Lieutenant and of his second-in-command, the Chief Secretary. The position of the latter, notably subordinate in the eighteenth century, developed new powers after the Union. The Chief Secretary now spent all the parliamentary session in London and was the Irish administration's main spokesman in the Commons. The third leading official was the Under-Secretary who was resident the whole year in Dublin, responsible for the daily work of the administration and the official channel through which officials and the public made their ideas known to the Viceroy.[95] It was a cumbrous, highly centralised structure, and there were a number of attempts at reform, including the abolition of the office of the Lord Lieutenant. There was, however, never any possibility of a serious decentralisation of power for the economic and social structure of Ireland was fundamentally different from that of England where the various grades of the middle-class strata were such an important feature of the rapidly expanding industrial society. In Ireland, as all visitors commented, society was sharply and distinctly divided. 'Only magnificent chateaux and miserable cabins are to be seen in Ireland', de Beaumont wrote in 1839; and de Tocqueville's diary of the journey from Carlow to Waterford recorded the same contrasts:

We travelled along the sides of two or three very well-kept and magnificent parks. All the rest merely tells of the life of the poor. In the villages, no small tradesmen – but such as there were, were almost as poor as the peasants themselves. No signs of work except on the land. Farm labourers in rags. There is an upper class and a lower class. The middle class evidently does not exist, or else is confined to the towns as in the Middle Ages.[96]

The structure of local government reflected the social configuration of Irish society which so much depressed de Tocqueville and de Beaumont. They had both been full of admiration for the English aristocracy and the civil responsibilities they assumed in their own counties. The middle strata of rural society in England – the gentry, well-to-do farmers, professional people down to the lowest levels of the petty-bourgeoisie – which they had also warmly commended, were also absent from the Irish countryside. There were two separate but related problems in Irish local government: one was the small size of the middling groups of society and the second was the tardy response to the call for service. There was much absenteeism, and for those who remained there was intimidation. 'I hardly ever get a grand jury', said the chairman of the magistrates of the county of Limerick in 1874, and throughout the whole of the nineteenth century the attendance of magistrates was always irregular, many attending only for the granting of liquor licences.[97]

Centralisation, which had grown with the English administration before 1800, had produced by the time of the Union a swollen bureaucracy with almost no checks upon its malpractices. Corruption in all parts of the administration was endemic. 'I am quite tired of this shameful corruption which every Irish enquiry brings to light', Peel summed up after five years as Chief Secretary.[98] Ireland had a reputation as a land of corruption, jobbery and extravagance: an exemplar of the consequences of underdevelopment in a dependent economy.

There were, of course, a series of attempts at reform during the nineteenth century alongside the more considerable efforts in England. But Ireland, an economy dominated from the outside by an alien power, was never susceptible to the rationality which at least in part effected administrative change in the rest of the United Kingdom. The two Treasuries were amalgamated in 1816, and by 1835, of the twenty-two departments which existed at the time of Union, eighteen had been absorbed into a British department or a new Irish department had been created or had been eliminated. The county administration remained unsatisfactory until the end of the century. Urban reform, much obstructed by the Lords, was less complete than in England; only ten cities were given elected councils in 1840, and the franchise was markedly more restrictive than on the mainland. As Ireland moved away from the debilitating poverty of the first half of the century, the passions of nationalism slowly accumulated within increasing numbers of the Irish people, and government by devolution and decentralisation was never practicable on any serious scale. Dublin Castle remained the centre of a centralised bureaucracy.[99]

There are two aspects of the political situation in Ireland in the years leading up to 1848 that require special emphasis. One is the extent and impact of violence, unrest and endemic discontent that sharply distinguished Ireland from the rest of the United Kingdom, and the second followed from the roughness and destructiveness of social life in Ireland: the administration of the law, the nature and character of the coercive powers at the disposal of those in authority and the particular problems of law enforcement in a society large parts of which disregarded the rule of law as practised in the rest of the kingdom.

Crime statistics are always difficult to evaluate and assess, and the official data available will only be discussed in broad and general terms.[100] The years before 1850 were, of course, years in which there were periods of acute distress and serious political unrest in many parts of the kingdom. The upper classes, in the decades between 1789 and the late 1840s, often felt themselves to be sitting on a powder barrel of social discontent and bitterness.[101] But in Britain there was no comparison with the situation prevailing in Ireland where in many areas violence was a matter of daily occurrence, and the degree of brutality practised by both the forces of law and the masses they confronted had no counterpart elsewhere. The metropolitan police introduced by Peel in 1829 were intensely disliked by the London masses, but there was nothing comparable with the hatred between the constabulary in Ireland and the rural population. Between 1826 and 1830 12 constables were killed in Ireland and 449 wounded while 84 of the civilian population died and 112 were wounded in clashes and affrays with the police.[102] In the early 1830s, Broeker noted, there occurred some of the bloodiest encounters between soldiers and police and

Table 1 *Persons committed for trial or bailed for appearance at the Assizes and Sessions*

	1841	1842	1843	1844	1845	1846	1847	1848	1849	1850	1851
England and Wales	27,760	31,309	29,591	26,542	24,303	25,107	28,833	30,349	27,816	26,813	27,960
Ireland	20,796	21,186	20,126	19,448	16,696	18,492	31,209	38,522	41,989	31,326	24,684

Source: *Accounts and Papers*, 1852–3, LXXXXI (338). *Tabular Returns of the Numbers of Committals for Crime in Ireland* [and] . . . *in England and Wales*

the peasantry than at any time during the nineteenth century. A published answer to a House of Commons question from Smith O'Brien showed that in affrays between 1831 and April 1846 102 civilians had been killed and 87 severely wounded, while on the police side 35 had been killed and 207 wounded.[103] Such figures were beyond the comprehension of anyone living in the rest of the kingdom, although they still represented a decline in the mortality and injury rate of the late twenties and early thirties: the result of the new national police force in Ireland after 1836 and the lower levels of tension generally in the later years of the thirties under Melbourne's administration.

The published crime statistics offer a broad comparative guide to the relative levels of crime and the categories into which crimes were classified. Table 1 sets out the data. For the second half of the 1830s and for most of the 1840s the absolute totals of committals for trial at the Assizes and Quarter Sessions were lower for Ireland than for the rest of the United Kingdom as would be expected given their respective populations, although the number of committals per head of population was always much higher in Ireland. What is striking is the extraordinary rise in the number of Irish committals in the years 1847 to 1850 at a time when the Irish population was declining, either from death by starvation or from emigration. In 1846, the first year of the famine, the increase in committals was only modest and still well below the figures for England and Wales; and then in 1847 and 1848 there was a remarkable rise, with a total that more than doubled in the two years. 1849 was the peak year, with Irish committals at 41,989 against the figure of 27,816 for England and Wales. Thereafter the Irish totals fall away. The sharp increase in the 1847 committals was commented on officially as the result of 'moral and social disorganisation' attributable to the 'general dearth' and the further large increase in 1848 was put down to the same causes together with 'the evils arising from political agitation'.[104]

The official returns from which these data were extracted divided the committal figures into six main categories, and identified specific offences under each class heading (Table 2). In both Ireland and England the largest

Table 2 Committals (Assizes and Sessions) by categories

	1842	1843	1844	1845	1846	1847	1848
Class 1 (against the person) England and Wales	2127	2431	2306	1906	2249	2023	2234
Ireland	5191	5442	5482	4827	5110	4549	5966
Class 6 (misc.) Riot, breach of peace, pound breach England and Wales	595	543	567	363	302	373	387
Ireland	2890	3343	3018	2574	3471	2437	3222
Rescue and refusing to aid peace officers England and Wales	12	18	13	14	11	2	9
Ireland	1594	2330	1944	1119	983	2251	4131
Total (class 6) England and Wales	2174	1385	1157	773	701	796	1158
Ireland	6053	6966	6197	4769	5192	6443	9320

Note: Several categories of Class 6 have been omitted from the Table.
Sources: Accounts and Papers, 1849, XLIV (1067), Ireland. Tables Showing the Numbers of Criminal Offenders committed for Trial or Bailed for Appearance at the Assizes and Sessions in each County, in the Year 1848, and the Results of the Proceedings, p. 98.
Accounts and Papers, 1849, XLIV (1081), England and Wales. Tables Showing the Numbers of Criminal Offenders committed for Trial or Bailed for Appearance at the Assizes and Sessions in each County, in the Year 1848, and the Results of the Proceedings, p. 64.

class of all was Class 3, crimes against property without violence, including cattle stealing, although it must be added that the figures varied widely from year to year. The figures for which Irish crimes were significantly higher than those for England and Wales – absolutely higher and not only relative to population – were in Class 1, defined as crimes against persons, including murder and violent assault, and Class 6, a miscellaneous category which included most, but not all, the crimes which could be classified as political:

riot, sedition, breach of the peace, pound breach, rescue and refusing to aid the Peace Officers, high treason and felony.

The comparative data were suggestive, and some of the figures for Ireland were astonishing when put against those for England and Wales. Those relating to riot and breach of the peace in the 1840s were about ten times higher than the totals for England and Wales; but the most remarkable column was that headed 'Rescue and refusing to aid peace officers'. On the British mainland the figures declined to single numbers, while in Ireland, during the years 1847 to 1850, they were the largest single item under the miscellaneous Class 6 category. Most of the riot and rescue committals, it needs to be remarked, must have been connected with some form of rural protest – evictions, ejectments, forced sale of goods – and not with directly political objectives.

These crime statistics confirm the general point that the problems of law enforcement were of a quite different order than those for the rest of the United Kingdom. It was not only that Ireland was a country ruled, and felt to be ruled, by an alien power, towards which the greater part of the native inhabitants felt intense hatred; it was also that the moral assumptions in the consciousness of the rural poor were quite different from those encountered elsewhere: the belief was that 'landlords should not levy unjust rents and that no man should take over a farm from which another had been evicted'.[105] Given these premises the law as applied by the English administration had no validity in those areas where social morality was breached. The moral economy of the poor continued to be sustained by the poverty of the poor, and it was poverty which was the central cause of violence, although naturally there were other contributory reasons, including national traditions and the social characteristics of the Irish masses. English contemporaries were not ignorant of the facts of the Irish economic situation, although their remedies were almost always drawn from the postulates of a dogmatically held political economy incapable of comprehending the problems of an underdeveloped society. Among those who provided interesting and perceptive analyses of the Irish problem was George Cornewall Lewis who held many other public offices including the position of Under-Secretary at the Home Department in May 1848. Lewis, who spent much time in the 1830s on Irish questions, achieved a judicious assessment in his book of 1836: *On Local Disturbances in Ireland: and on the Irish Church Question.* Part of his analysis is worth quoting at some length:

It is not the *low rate of wages*, but the *inconsistency of employment* which depresses the Irish labourer, and sends his family begging through the country during the summer months; and which makes him dependent on his potato-ground, and thus sets all his sympathies on the side of Whiteboyism. We should probably exceed the truth if we said that a third part of the Irish labouring population were employed all the year round. The remaining two-thirds obtain work at the seasons of extraordinary demand viz at the potato-digging, and during the harvest. At other times of the year they trust to the produce of their own potato ground for food, or temporarily in the form of conacre. It is this irregularity of employment for hire, and not the low rate of his wages, which is the true cause both of the poverty and turbulence of the Irish peasant. If every labourer in Ireland could earn 8d a day for 310 days in the year, we should probably never hear of Whiteboy disturbances. It is the impossibility of living by wages, which throws him upon the land (x); and it is the liability of being ejected from the land and the consciousness that he has no other resource, which makes him a Whiteboy. If the Irish peasant was as utterly reckless and improvident as he is said to be, he would not commit crimes in order to protect the occupant of the soil; he would not see that his own interest was bound up with that of his class in preventing the ejection of tenants. It is his foresight which prompts him to crime; it is his wish to obtain some guarantee for his future subsistence which drives him to Whiteboy outrage. In these disturbances it it not a question of more or less gain; his very existence is at stake'.[106]

The landlord classes have been somewhat more tenderly treated by modern Irish historians than they were by earlier nationalist writers or by those, like John Stuart Mill, who were observers from the outside. Certainly, neither in the eighteenth century nor in the nineteenth century were all landlords oblivious of the public good; though the more common argument in recent literature appears to be that the landlords were victims within the same framework of dilemmas as their tenants: notably, the large increases in population after 1800, and the absence of alternative employment in the countryside. 'The most important aspect of [recent] Irish agrarian history', Dr Clarkson has written in a general review of the subject, 'has been concerned with rescuing landlords from their reputation for unrestrained rapacity, and seeing them, instead, as trapped by the same social system as their tenants':[107] an anodyne enough platitude except, of course, that one group received rents which the majority paid. There have been relatively few detailed histories of Irish landed estates, and even fewer which show the relationship between Irish rents and English capital accumulation. Maguire's study of the large Downshire properties, most of which were located within the Belfast region, and which were almost certainly better managed than many in other parts of the country, illustrated certain trends which were probably not very different from the rest of the country, whatever the absolute levels involved or the differences between varying rates of return on capital. During the Napoleonic wars the Downshire rent rolls rose steeply, from a gross income of £30,000 in 1801 to £55,000 in 1815; and in spite of the depression which accompanied peace, gross rentals were £58,000 in 1831, £66,800 in 1839 and £72,000 in 1844. A small part of these increases came from additional lands purchased, but the greater part of rise in total income was the result of the rise in rents as leases fell in and their renewal at considerably higher levels. Moreover, it must be recalled, Irish landowners differed from their English counterparts in spending very little, often nothing, on farm buildings or general repairs to the estate. As a result Maguire noted that 'the Irish landowner could expect to enjoy ten per cent more of his gross income than his English contemporary . . . Even on the least favourable comparison'.[108] What is relevant in the context of the present discussion is the remoteness of many landlords from their tenants, the insecurity in the countryside, the feeling of all classes of being beleagured, the hatred of the peasants for their landlords, or sub-landlords, and the reciprocal sentiments by the landed classes against the mass of the rural population. These were characteristics of rural Ireland to which all contemporary observers bore witness.

The Irish question came to increasing prominence in English politics in the quarter century before 1848. The growth of the Irish population and the decline of industrial employment after the Union; the increasing flood of emigrant Irish into Britain; and the more common expression of Irish matters in the House of Commons all contributed to a growing awareness of Ireland and the Irish. The expansion of the press, national and local, meant that Irish news, especially news of Irish violence, became more widely known and commented on; and as anti-Irish sentiment developed more widely, to which the growing numbers of Irish resident in Britain contributed substantially, so the specifically racist component of that prejudice increased steadily. There was now added to the long historical description of the Irish Celts as uncivilised barbarians, the dismissal of the Irish by the political economists as incapable of rational economic behaviour[109] and there was the further development of an appreciation of the Irish as physically and psychologically different from other racial groups within the United Kingdom. During the first thirty years or so of the nineteenth century the Irish peasant was depicted in English literature and political prints as feckless, brutish and slovenly, but not yet as he was to be portrayed in Victorian caricature: as more ape-like than man. It had long been accepted that the Irish were incapable of managing their own affairs; now, from the 1840s on the explanation was seen increasingly to lie in the racial characteristics of the Irish Celt, so clearly delineated in their physical appearance. The tendency among cartoonists and caricaturists was to emphasise the prognathous features of the Irish labouring class: a bulge in the lower part of the face, the chin prominent, the mouth big, the forehead receding, a short nose, often upturned and with yawning nostrils: the simianising of the Irish. It was Tenniel, who joined the staff of *Punch* in 1851, who was probably more responsible than anyone for making Paddy 'look like the offspring liaison between a gorilla father and a prognathous Irish mother'.[110] There was, further, it would seem, a positive correlation between the level of violence at any one particular time, and the bitterness of the cartoonists' drawings.

By the middle of the century there existed in Britain a widespread conviction, a matter of belief and faith, that the English and the Irish, the Saxon and the Celt, were divided by clear-cut racial characteristics as well as by religious and cultural factors. The greater part of the middle and upper classes in Britain had never been in doubt about the savagery of Irish society and the inferiority of the Irish people, and only the radicals, in their speeches and in their limited circulation press, had begun to understand the reasons for the hatred of the Irish for the English. With the decline of a vigorous radicalism among the advanced groups of working people after 1850 the way was open to a more aggressive discrimination against the Irish communities in England. There had always been social tensions and friction; the Irish railway navvies had often been a target for native violence, but now a more generalised racialism was going to be possible. That had been present at all periods in some sectors of British society. *The Times*, always an interesting indicator of sophisticated political opinion, had many different humours in its writing about Ireland: it moved along the spectrum from a degree of patronising sympathy to straightforward racism. On 1 April 1848, in a lengthy editorial apologia *The Times* wrote that Ireland 'is our reproach; and with Ireland are the interested sympathies of foreign liberalism'. But to what or to whom did Ireland owe her position among civilised nations? Why, to the English connection:

Instead of degradation [Ireland] has found equality and union. That which depressed other nations has elevated her. If she talks of privileges, she has none but what England gave her and England shares with her. Law she had none but that which she owes to England. The vices and graces of her institutions are equally hers and Englands. Language? You must plod your way to the more bare and desolate traces of her rugged coast to find a remnant of the tongue, for which she has substituted the language of her repudiated co-parcener. It is English law that she tries against her English government; it is the English tongue in which she courts a French alliance; it is English liberty which she perverts to licence; and English institutions which she would parody to extravagance; and English eloquence which she sublimates to Irish rhetoric.

Two days later, on 3 April, *The Times* returned to its apologia for what it was prepared on this occasion to describe as Irish wrongs; and it offered historical comfort to Irish readers: 'If CROMWELL was a savage in Ireland, he was also a despot in England'. It was, however, more common for *The Times*, and almost standard for the greater part of the English press, to engage in bitter recriminations against the lack of understanding, the absence of generous feeling and the habitual acrimony that the Irish consistently displayed towards the English and their governments. The weekly *Birmingham Journal* for example, a moderate Whiggish paper which would have welcomed the fusion of the Whigs with the Peelites, fell into theatrical rant whenever it discussed Ireland during the year 1848. Here is a sample, following the abortive cabbage-patch rising of Smith O'Brien:

The Irish insurrection is not yet subdued – a peasantry thoroughly demoralised by twenty years of continued agitation, deliberately deceived and designedly deluded – from whose altars sedition was preached, by whose guides disaffection was inculcated, cannot easily be induced to abandon their hopes of confiscation, massacre and revenge, especially when there is a hope that perjury may give impunity to treason as well as sedition. Partial risings, frequent robberies, occasional assassinations, frantic menaces, sulky spite, still demonstrate how deeply rooted is that hatred of law and order which the Irish agitators of every class and profession have sedulously laboured to instill into the minds of the people. (19 August 1848)

The central problem of internal security in Ireland was the need to establish an efficient system of civil policing. The army was always at the disposal of the governing powers, and although it was used in Ireland regularly, and it was assumed that it would be so used, it was equally understood that the equivalent of a military occupation was not practicable. Robert Peel wrote to Leveson Gower in August 1829:

Call it by what name you please, police or constabulary force – this is certain – that the reduction of Ireland to peaceful habits and obedience to the law must be effected by the agency of an organised – stipendiary – civil force whose exclusive province and profession it shall be to execute the law.[111]

The evolution of the Irish police force through the first half of the nineteenth century, its relations with the other arms of the security forces and the special difficulties of law enforcement through an English-type judicial system illustrate vividly the problems of controlling, which often meant coercing, a society the majority of whose people were alienated from the central government and its local representatives. The Act of Union was achieved two years after the rebellion of 1798, and must be understood as one of the ways in which the Irish version of Jacobinism could be put down. There followed years, decades, of agrarian turbulence. At the beginning of the century Irish counties had a small police force, badly paid and mostly part-time. Peel became Chief Secretary in 1812, and two years later he decided to supplement the baronial police by a mobile force under the direction of Dublin Castle. The Lord Lieutenant was empowered to 'proclaim' an area and send in a chief magistrate who during the period of the emergency would take precedence over all other magistrates. He would have at his command a body of specially selected constables known as the Peace Preservation Force. Chief magistrates received £700 a year, and sub-constables £50, salaries for the latter which were considerably in excess of the meagre pay of the baronial police. The costs of the Peace Preservation Fund had to be met by the district they were stationed in; and from the outset the new Force was planned to be organised on military lines.[112] This major reform was an important step towards the complete centralisation of the Irish police forces, finally achieved in 1836. The Dublin police were also reorganised in the same year, and although they had an independence from the rest of the country's police, they too were subject to the political control of the Viceroy's administration.

The Constabulary Bill had first been introduced in 1835 but it was rejected by the Lords, almost all the Irish peers voting against the new proposals. One of their main objections was the transfer of power from the existing magistrates: 'a most excellent and fearless body of men' said the Earl of Roden, one of the most ferocious of the Orange peers; and the Marquis of Londonderry suggested that the effect of the Bill would be to hand over the control of police to Daniel O'Connell.[113] The Bill was reintroduced in the following session. Peel supported it in the Commons, and it became known that Colonel Shaw Kennedy, a Peninsular veteran, was to be the first Inspector-General. The Bill passed the Lords. All the senior posts in the new police force were staffed by Army veterans.

With the legislation of 1836 Ireland obtained its highly centralised national police force, organised on military lines as a paramilitary force. Constables and sergeants lived in barracks and were drilled on army style; and they were armed with carbines. In 1840 the total number of police in the whole country, including officers, was 8,590 with 56 stipendiary magistrates. By 1847 the total had increased to 10,639 with 67 magistrates, and by 1849, the peak year for the decade, there were 12,828 police and 70 stipendiary magistrates. Further, in the middle of the decade there was established a new mobile reserve force, stationed in Dublin, which could be sent to any troubled area or town to reinforce local resources. The new reserve was just over 200 in 1844 and it reached 400 by 1848. An Act of 9 and 10 Vict. c. 37 allowed this force to be increased to 600, but Major-General Sir Duncan MacGregor, who had been fifteen years as Inspector-General, explained in 1854 that the reserve force had never reached its permitted total, and that it rose and fell in numbers according to circumstances. MacGregor went on to describe some of the characteristics of policing as they had developed since the late 1830s. There were between 1,500 and 1,600 police stations throughout the country with an average of seven to eight men in each, although in the more disturbed regions – Tipperary for example – the number of men in each barrack could be much higher. Constables were never employed in their own home district: 'it was formerly tried, and found to be pernicious'. Regular patrolling, mostly at night, was emphasised by MacGregor as one of the main preventive duties the police undertook; only in very quiet conditions did two men go out together. Normally the patrol would be larger. MacGregor was emphatic that people in general had a 'good disposition' towards the constabulary.[114]

To the visitor from the outside world Ireland seemed to be saturated with policemen. Engels wrote to Marx in 1856 that he 'had never seen so many gendarmes in any country, and the sodden look of the bibulous Prussian gendarme is developed to its highest perfection here among the constabulary, who are armed with carbine, bayonets and handcuffs'.[115] A few years earlier, in 1847, another commentator had been equally impressed:

One of the first things which attract the eye of a stranger in Ireland, at least such a stranger as I am, and make him halt in his steps and turn around and look is the police whom he meets in every part of the island, on every road, in every village, even on the farm land, and on the seashore, and on the little islands which lie out in the sea. These policemen wear a dark green uniform and are armed; this is what makes them remarkable, armed from the heel to the head. They have belts and pouches, ball cartridges in the pouches, short guns called carbines, and bayonets, and pistols, and swords. The only difference between them and the regular military is, that the military do not always carry guns and pistols primed and loaded, not always bayonets in their belts, not always swords sharpened. The Irish police never go on duty without some of these.

In the Phoenix Park at Dublin, a barrack of large size, with drill ground, is devoted to the training of these armed police, from which barrack they are drafted into the provinces, as soon as they are trained to prime, load, and fire; to fix bayonets and charge; to march, countermarch, and so forth; these to be distributed and shaken out upon the land in half dozens or dozens.[116]

The Irish Constabulary Act of 1836 is often discussed in terms of Thomas Drummond's liberal contribution to the problems of internal security. Drummond was Under-Secretary from 1835 until his early death in 1840. His insistence upon the non-sectarian character of the constabulary is always counted as among his most useful reforms which seriously assisted the lessening of tensions between Protestants and Catholics; and there is certainly no reason to deny his liberal views and intentions. The commonly accepted account must, however, be modified in certain respects. For one thing, Drummond would not have been able to achieve what he did in fact accomplish had it not been for the firm support he received from Mulgrave, the Viceroy and Morpeth, the Chief Secretary; and Mulgrave (who later became Lord Normanby) was the object of much abuse from Orange elements. The evidence and the cross-questioning during the House of Lords Select Committee of 1839 make it abundantly clear that Mulgrave was as much the liberal villain in the minds of the Orange peers as was Drummond.[117] Symbolic gestures such as the discontinuation of the hoisting the flag on the Castle on the anniversaries of the battles of Aughrim and the Boyne; the appointment of Catholic office holders in the counties; the Viceroy's visit to Sligo and the way it was carried out[118] are all part of the general approach of these years. Without a clear-sighted and firm Viceroy the reforming zeal of the Under-Secretary would have been impossible.

There is a further matter which must be briefly touched upon, and this concerns the social composition of the police. It is true that Drummond did all he could to end the Protestant monopoly of the officer class; but his success was only partial. John O'Connell, in general an ineffective shadow of his father, offered an instructive comment in the House of Commons at the time of the debate on the Crime and Outrages Bill in December 1847:

it should be borne in mind that the police in Ireland were a peculiarly constituted body. Originally, they were taken from the Orange portion of the population; and although that element of evil was somewhat mitigated of late years, at least three-fourths of the officers of that force were to this day among the most embittered Orangemen in Ireland.[119]

An interesting clause in the 1836 Constabulary Act which has been little commented on was the prohibition of all membership of secret societies on the part of the personnel of the police force: with one exception, the Masons, who were excluded from the prohibition because Freemasonry was 'largely charitable'.[120] Now this has always been the claim of Freemasons in Britain, and certainly there has never been the political sectarianism of so many of the Masonic lodges in parts of Europe. The first Grand Lodge in England was organised in 1717 and the Grand Lodge of Ireland was established in 1725. Protestants and Catholics were members, and in 1730 the Catholic Duke of Norfolk became the English Grand Master. In April 1738, however, in the bull In Ementi Clement XII condemned Freemasonry, and the ban was subsequently reiterated on a number of occasions. In Ireland, for reasons that are not clear, the Papal bull was not promulgated until very late in the eighteenth century, or it may have been the early nineteenth century. Daniel O'Connell himself was initiated in 1799, and served as master of his Dublin Lodge; only renouncing his masonic ties when the attitude of the Catholic Church became understood. By the 1830s it is inconceivable that any practising Catholic could still have been a member of a Masonic lodge anywhere in Britain, and certainly not in Ireland where the power of the Church was so pervasive. The effect of the prohibition clause therefore was that the Masonic lodges which the officer class of the police force joined would be wholly Protestant; and it is not straining any argument, given the sectarian passions in Ireland, to suggest that Masonic lodges in Ireland would be a good deal more strongly anti-Catholic than their fellows in the rest of the United Kingdom. Many Masonic lodges tend to attract members of the same social stratum or occupation, so that it could be expected that police officers would often be members of the same lodges.[121] The political sociology of the nineteenth-century police forces in Ireland has not yet been written, but it would offer some interesting comparisons with the police forces in the rest of Britain. Since it was a paramilitary body, the social values were similar to those of the army; and this was noticeably true of the officer class who, in the Irish police, were expected to be gentlemen in social origin and background. There was an enquiry in 1866 into the pay and qualifications of the Irish constabulary which provided revealing details of the service. The report, arguing the case for improved pay and conditions, remarked:

On the one hand it is stated that it is essential that this force should be officered in a large degree by gentlemen, that the sub-inspectors are thrown much into contact with the gentry of their counties, both socially and in the performance of their duties – that it is desirable they should be of a position which would enable them to associate upon equal terms with the gentry (which is one great basis of their complaints as to the inadequacy of their pay) and that the men of the Force pay greater respect to and have greater confidence in, the young gentlemen officer than in the comrade who has been promoted from their ranks. This latter feeling is stated by some witnesses to be peculiarly cherished by the Irish people.[122]

The Report went on to note that it was not possible to compare the social standing of ranks with those in England since the equivalent of sub-inspectors were rarely taken from the ranks of the gentry. In Ireland the comparison could only be with the officer class in the army 'who are, with few exceptions, of gentle birth'.[123]

There was undoubtedly an improvement in the internal situation during the years of the Whig administration of the later 1830s, but the factors which contributed to the reduction in the levels of violence were regrettably short term. One factor was the dissolution of the Orange Lodge in April 1836, although it must also be added that county lodges, for example in Armagh, immediately re-established themselves;[124] another was the un-doubted efficiency of the new constabulary in sharply diminishing faction fighting;[125] and a third was the passing of the Tithe Bill in 1838. But what the reform of 1836 had done was to bring into being a very effective police force, highly centralised and in many respects as efficient as any in Europe, including the metropolitan police in London. Since the Whig government did nothing to alleviate the serious economic problems of the rural areas, a liberal approach to the problems of internal security would always be under very heavy strain and stress; and when the Conservatives returned under Peel in 1841, and with the growing mass movement of Repeal, the police became an essential instrument of coercion. The onset of famine in 1846 multiplied the problems and in the absence of a serious reforming programme – which was never practicable politics – a dozen Drummonds would not have been able to control or remedy the situation.

There was provision for the enrolment of special constables, but given the small number in general of the middle class who could be expected to be friendly to the government, their role was not important. By an Act of 1832 (2 and 3 Wm IV c. 108) special constables were entitled to enjoy all the privileges of ordinary constables, including the carrying of arms, which had to be returned to store after their period of duty was completed. They were also to be allowed reasonable monetary compensation for their services, and on the instructions of Dublin they could be sent to any part of the country where there was unrest. Refusal to act as special constables could be subject to a fine of £5. An Act of 1848 (11 and 12 Vict. c. 72) reaffirmed the legality of payment to special constables.

As on mainland Britain the army was used in a variety of roles in matters of internal security, but as always Ireland had special problems and some special difficulties. The British army had a high proportion of Irishmen in its ranks, and probably a higher proportion of Irish Protestants among its officers than in the population at large. It is estimated that from the 1830s about one-third of the annual intake into the British army came from Ireland, and this did cause some fear for morale and discipline in times of unrest in Ireland itself, where there would almost certainly be some Irish regiments. In fact, apart from isolated cases, there does not appear to have been any reason for unease.[126] The size of the army in Ireland was always greater, often very much greater, than would be expected on a basis of comparative populations, and there were times when there were nearly as many troops in Ireland as in the remainder of the United Kingdom. While, however, the actual numbers of troops fluctuated in different parts of the kingdom according to the local and regional incidence of turbulence and disorder, there was a larger permanent commitment of the army to Ireland than elsewhere. Although there were no specifically Irish regiments on the establishment, there was a large permanent military staff whose offices and duties went on from year to year. At the head was the commander-in-chief, assisted by an adjutant-general, a quarter master-general, a judge-advocate general and an army medical board. There was a military branch in the Chief Secretary's office, and a number of departments classified as civilian also did work for the army. All these were in addition to the Staffs of the military districts of Belfast, Dublin, Athlone, Cork and Limerick, each of which had a major-general as commanding officer. The army estimates for the United Kingdom for April 1848 to April 1849 listed the pay and expenses of all General Staff officers in the United Kingdom. There were thirteen at headquarters in London; twenty-five in the rest of England and Wales plus seven non-combatants, including two chaplains and one veterinary surgeon. In Scotland there were six, but in Ireland there were thirty-five, together with four aides-de-camp of the Viceroy.[127]

The military presence in Ireland was disposed almost entirely in barrack accommodation. Politicians as well as the army command had always preferred barrack accommodation for their troops. Palmerston, when Secretary at War, had been much influenced by the argument that it was important to remove the ordinary soldier from contact with local populations, since the army in its role of assisting to keep the peace required to be kept away from contact with possible sources of disaffection. The same arguments were stronger in Ireland, because of religious and nationalist reasons; and in fact almost all the army in Ireland was in barrack accommodation. In 1849 there were 118 barracks in Britain of which 102 were permanent, 16 temporary; the comparable figures for Ireland were 98 and 11. Major-General Sir J. F. Burgoyne who provided these figures, commented further: 'You will find that the construction of barracks in Ireland and their occupation, vary very much less than they do in England; nearly every barrack is occupied in Ireland; there are barracks in Ireland for 27,500 and there are 26,500 in them.'[128] Cork had 14 barracks, Dublin 11 and Tipperary 15.

In his study of leaders of public opinion in Ireland, Lecky wrote that in 1833, some four years after Catholic emancipation, there was not in Ireland a single Catholic judge or stipendiary magistrate. All the high sheriffs with one exception, the overwhelming majority of the unpaid magistrates and of the grand jurors, the five inspector-generals, and the thirty-two sub-inspectors of police, were Protestant.[129] There is a considerable literature on the legal structures of Ireland in the nineteenth century, both official and secondary. Between 1815 and 1831 there was an official commission to enquire into the working of 'all the temporal and ecclesiastical courts in Ireland'. Twenty-two reports were published, and all the many nooks and crannies as well as the larger edifices, were thoroughly explored and documented.[130] There were reforms after 1815 at many levels of the law-making processes, but the problems remained, whereby judicial decisions were broadly the result of centuries of Irish history and the great divide between the Protestant rulers and the Catholic majority. It is not possible, even by the most detailed description of the formal machinery of the law, to offer any kind of realistic account of how the law actually worked. The gap between formal statement and legal reality was too wide to permit a straightforward elucidation of how justice, and injustice, was achieved.

All judges were appointed by the government of the day. The majority of cases which came before the courts were those involving the ordinary people of the country, and these courts were presided over by the unpaid magistracy. The crucial components of the system at the level of petty sessions and Assizes were the selection and quality of the justices of the peace, the composition of panels of jurors, and the right of challenge of jurors. Jurors were also, of course, of crucial importance in political trials in the higher courts.

The Irish magistracy at the time of the Union was venal, inefficient and politically prejudiced. A government enquiry in 1815, at a time when there were 4,175 magistrates on the rolls, revealed 557 dead, 1,355 no longer resident in Ireland and 311 no longer acting as magistrates. 'I wish to God,' Peel wrote to Saurin in 1816, 'it was possible to revise the magistracy, for half our disorders and disturbances arise from the negligence of some, and corruption and party spirit of others. But what other local authorities can you trust to?'[131] The answer to Peel's question was that there were no other local personalities available for service: except those of the Roman Catholic faith. Even when emancipation came in 1829 it was not until the Whig administration from 1835 that Catholics began to be appointed in noticeable numbers; and right through the nineteenth century there was always a marked discrepancy between the totals of Protestants and Catholics on the magisterial benches compared with their respective ratios in the total population.[132] The only change that caught the public headlines seemed to be the periodic removal of certain of the more blatant Orange adherents from their position as justices of the peace. It came to be taken for granted that local magistrates were more likely to be Protestants than Catholics. It was a variation of an old English custom: in Wales, before the County Council's Act of 1888 almost all the justices of the peace were Anglican, in a country which was overwhelmingly non-conformist.[133]

In 1833 an important piece of legislation was passed which was at least intended to simplify the existing laws relating to the selection of jurors and of juries. This was an Act of 3 and 4 Wm IV c. 91 'for consolidating and amending the Laws relating to jurors and juries in Ireland'. Henceforth, jurors were to be between twenty-one and sixty years old and to possess a £10 household or lease of £20 a year; and those qualified were liable to serve on Petty Sessions or Grand Juries.[134] The list of those qualified were to be made out by the county cess (i.e. tax) collectors, then checked and if necessary revised, by the magistrates. The general list was then to be copied into a book – the jurors book of that particular year – and handed over to the sheriff who selected the jury list for any one court or trial. For the superior courts of Assize, Nisi Prius, Oyer and Terminer the qualifications were £100 in land or personal estate. The highest courts in the land – Kings Bench, Common Pleas and Exchequer – could order a special jury; and the qualifications for special juries, as specified in this Act of 1833, were peers, baronets, knights, magistrates, sheriffs and grand jurors, 'all bankers and wholesale merchants who do not exercise retail trades and of all trades who are possessed of Personal Property of the value of 5000 Pounds or the eldest sons of such Persons respectively'. Grand jurors were regulated by an Act of 1836 (6 and 7 Wm IV c. 116). The Grand Jury which had administrative functions as well as legal were constituted at the discretion of the sheriff, and they had to include at least one representative of each barony in the county who had to be either a £50 freeholder or a £100 leaseholder. The members of a Grand Jury were taken from a list of the hundred highest tax payers in the returns according to the numbers required for the session. The conditions laid down by the Act were capable of being interpreted in different ways, but as a general rule Grand Juries normally consisted of the principal landlords of the county, and although they were a necessary part of the county administration, it was by no means common for Grand Juries to have a full complement of numbers.[135]

One of the many problems of law enforcement in Ireland compared with other parts of the United Kingdom was the greater difficulty of obtaining a conviction. It was the threat of intimidation, or the fact, rather than the refusal of Catholics to pass judgement upon their fellow religionists, that was responsible for the phenomenon of a high rate of acquittal. The proportion of persons tried and acquitted at the Assizes and Sessions in England and Wales in 1847 was 25.1 per cent, and 24.4 per cent in 1848. In Scotland it was even lower although the data are not strictly comparable because of the different judicial procedures in the latter country. But in Ireland intimidation of jurors produced much higher figures of those acquitted. Throughout the 1840s the rate of acquittals was never below the 50 per cent level, in other words double the rate elsewhere; but even more striking was the much higher acquittal rate for the more serious offences. As the 1849 Return summed up:

While the acquittals, of course, vary as the nature of the offence increases or diminishes the difficulty of proof, they appear also to be affected by 'the magnitude of the punishment'. Thus, in Class 1, containing crimes of the gravest description, and involving, in many cases, the extreme penalty of the law, the Acquittals amount to 66.52 per cent.

The same was true of Class 6 which included the categories of 'Riot' and 'Rescue from custody'; these, too, had acquittal rates of about two-thirds.[136]

The jury system was examined in detail on a number of occasions in the second half of the nineteenth century, and each time was found wanting. One was the Select Committee on Outrages in 1852, which had John Bright as a member, and a more comprehensive analysis was provided in 1873 and 1874 by the Select Committee on the Jury System. What the latter showed in considerable detail was not so much the intimidation of jurors which had occupied the 1852 committee, and which still existed, but that the system had never worked in the way set out by the legislation of 1833. It was evidently very difficult to ascertain leasehold qualifications for the common jurors, and difficult, too, to discover the levels of personal property for special jurors. Common jurors had mostly been selected from leaseholders in the years since the Act was passed or even occupiers with no title[137] and their selection was an 'absolute discretion' on the part of the sheriff or, rather, the sub-sheriff who always in practice did the choosing. The sub-sheriffs were usually solicitors who had originally practised in the county 'and, of course, like most people in Ireland, they had their political biases, both on one side and on the other'.[138] There was, it was clear from the evidence, massive abstention from jury service by those who were called, and there was also considerable dereliction of duty by local magistrates, many of whom, so one witness averred, attended only for the granting of liquor licences.[139] The same witness, who was chairman of the Bench in the County of Limerick, further stated that he 'hardly ever' assembled a complete Grand Jury, and when asked, at the end of his evidence, 'In fact, under the previous Act [of 1833] there was no legal jury at all, was there?' – he replied, 'Not the least'.[140]

These problems of jury service, which developed out of the particular forms of the Irish social structure and the associated tensions, were greatly complicated, and worsened, by the practice commonly known as jury packing, whereby membership of juries was chosen in ways which eliminated Roman Catholics or liberal-minded Protestants. It was the former, the elimination of Catholics, which was by far the more serious; and it was achieved in two main ways. The first was the preparation of lists of jurors by the sheriff or those who acted for him; and, during the political trials of 1848, a great deal of evidence was produced to show how the lists were tampered with by lowering the proportion of Catholics. The details are set out more fully below, in Chapter 6. The second was by reducing substantially, or totally eliminating, the jurors who were Catholic by exercising the right of challenge. The rights of challenge were laid down by statute. By 6 Geo. IV c. 50, in cases of murder or felony, the defendant or his counsel had the right of peremptory challenge of up to twenty jurors without showing cause; and by the same statute the Crown had no right of challenge without showing cause. In English law, and its interpretation by the judges, jurors could be interrogated to show want of qualification; but the English courts were reluctant to allow examination on the *voir dire*, or at the most only a very brief one. In Ireland, however, the courts had allowed the practice whereby the Crown could ask jurors to 'stand by' which in effect permitted the Crown to exercise the right of peremptory challenge to a more or less unlimited extent. An example will illustrate the practices involved. It was given by Sir Michael O'Loghlen who had been Solicitor General, then Attorney General, and at the time he gave the evidence below he was Master of the Rolls.[141] He was being interviewed by the House of Lords Select Committee in June 1839, the majority of whom were exceedingly hostile to all that O'Loghlen represented. He had been appointed a Law Officer of the Crown when the Melbourne administration took office in 1835, and early in 1836 he had issued a famous letter about jury challenging which instructed Crown prosecuting counsel not to set jurors aside unless there was a proved connection with the case being tried.[142] The instruction infuriated Protestant Ireland and this Lords Select Committee gave considerable opportunity for conservative and Orange Ireland to state their opposition at length. O'Loghlen, who was a liberal Catholic, and a very able lawyer, stood up to unpleasant and hostile questioning very well; and the example below was part of his attempt to put together a reasoned case against rigging juries. He explained that in the summer of 1834 he had been a King's Sergeant on the Munster circuit. There were 251 persons on the panel returned by the Sheriff and 123 answered their name for jury service. In Court, the main prisoner challenged twenty, which was his limit; the other prisoner, whom O'Loghlen represented, challenged fourteen. The Crown told forty-three to 'stand by'. 'Of the 43 put by by the Crown, three were magistrates of the county, the rest were freeholders of the County, and leaseholders, men of very great respectability . . . There were seven Protestants and 36 Catholics put by by the Crown'.[143] The prisoners were Catholics.

Sir Michael O'Loghlen then continued the argument that his instruction concerning the setting aside of jurors had 'a most beneficial effect upon the administration of justice', and he proceeded to deny the legal right of the Crown to peremptory challenge and in particular to deny the construction the judges in the past had put upon the law. In his support he quoted a summary of the *obiter dicta* of Chief Justice Eyre in the Horne Tooke case regarding the very improper advantage the Crown obtained from the practice of setting jurors aside, without any restriction on numbers. This emphatic statement of O'Loghlen was important, and it encouraged an immediate reaction from the conservative majority of his senior colleagues. The House of Lords Committee finished their deliberations by the end of June 1839, and on 5 July Mr Brady, who later became Chief Baron, set out in a letter of some length the position of the Crown in the matter of challenge. The status of the letter at this particular time is not clear. Lord Normanby had retired from the Lord Lieutenancy and moved back to London as Colonial Secretary, but the administration was still Whig, and why Brady wrote this letter and for what administrative purpose remains uncertain. It was to be used later, as will be indicated below.

Brady's letter was an interesting specimen of legal sophistry although it introduced no new principles into a practice that had been accepted before O'Loghlen's intervention. Naturally, Brady argued, jurors must not be set aside because of religious or political opinions, but:

these instructions were not intended to have the effect and, rightly understood, they cannot be interpreted to mean, that the Crown should altogether abandon the privilege of setting jurors aside, or the right of challenging them on fair and legitimate grounds. The Crown, it is true, has not, as some persons erroneously suppose, the right of peremptory challenge; this right, though given to the prisoner in certain cases, and to a limited extent, has been expressly prohibited by statute in the cause of the Crown . . . In practice, however, the privilege of setting jurors aside at the instance of the Crown has been admitted, as consistent with the true construction of the statute which abolished the right of peremptory challenge.

Brady then proceeded to list the categories of persons whom he thought could properly be set aside. These were: members of secret societies; those who could not speak English, jurors who came from an area or town that was currently 'excited' and, finally, any trade unionist in cases which referred to trade combinations. He added an important rider: that it was legitimate for counsel to receive information on jurors from interested parties.

This letter by Brady must presumably have been circulated when it was first written, but exactly to whom is not clear. It was, however, published in an official paper in 1842, in a collection of documents referring to the problems of jury challenge. This collection included the letter sent out by Sir Michael O'Loghlen in 1836 and Brady's letter of 5 July 1839. It was made clear that the new Attorney General in Peel's administration, Francis Blackburne (who was to be the senior judge in the political trials of 1848 in Ireland), had requested of Crown solicitors that in future the practices laid down by Brady should be followed; that, in other words, the Crown should revert to the practice, if required, of wholesale use of the privilege of setting jurors aside.

The liberal tendencies of the Normanby-Drummond period of office were not to be repeated when the Whigs returned to office during the middle of 1846; and when Lord Clarendon assumed the office of Viceroy a consistently hard line in security matters was the rule. The famine was ravaging the country and the total number of committals was increasing sharply. But Normanby had also taken office during a sharp rise in the number of outrages and outbreaks connected with the tithe war, and there was also a great deal of faction fighting. It was not historically inevitable that Ireland should move into an illiberal administration during 1848 although it would have taken a more intelligent, more sympathetic and more flexible Lord Lieutenant than Clarendon was to prevent it: a fact which throws Normanby's achievements in sharper light. One of Clarendon's problems was that he did not like Catholics and soon came totally to mistrust them. The evidence for his attitudes is abundantly demonstrated through his correspondence during office; and they were known to contemporaries and later historians. Herbert Paul wrote in 1904: 'Lord Clarendon was a much abler administrator than Lord Bessborough (his predecessor as Viceroy). He was a statesman of the good old Whig type, high-minded, public-spirited, and supercilious. He liked Catholics the better the more they resembled Protestants, and his idea of an Irish patriot was an Anglicised Irishman.'[144]

FRANCE

Richard Cobden asked Palmerston in 1850 why the British Ambassador to France had a salary of £20,000 with a further sum of £4,000 for outfit and the upkeep of a furnished house. The occasion was a Select Committee on

Official Salaries. Palmerston replied that the Paris Embassy inevitably had a great deal of hospitality to dispense, and he continued:

I think our relations with France may be considered the keystone of our foreign policy. France is the country among the great powers that is nearest to us, with which we have the most important relations, and with which we are most likely to come into collision if pains are not taken to avoid it, and with which a collision must inevitably be attended with the gravest consequences. I, therefore, think that a perfectly good understanding with France, as long as it can be maintained without any sacrifice of interest and of honour, is the first object at which, in regard to foreign relations, the British Government should aim . . .

A foreign country ought not to mix itself up with the internal concerns of friendly powers; neither has the English Government ever pretended to mix itself up with the internal administrations of France. But the foreign policy of France is a matter of too great importance to the interests of this country for the English Government not to have the means of most confidential communication with the Government of France upon all matters of common interest between them.[145]

What Palmerston omitted from his summary of Britain's attitude towards France was recognition of the traditional rivalry between the two countries, and his own efforts to do all he could to hinder French territorial ambitions and expansion.[146] In this, Palmerston was following the majority trend of opinion although the methods he used were different from his predecessor in the Peel administration. Aberdeen undoubtedly tried very hard to establish co-operation between France and England on a basis of friendly understanding: it 'was a continuous struggle which drove Aberdeen near to distraction';[147] and Cunningham summed up his discussion of the years of Tory foreign policy in the 1840s as: 'The very existence of the *entente* was highly problematical at times, and it was hardly ever cordial.'[148] The years before the revolution of 1848 were full of crises and near crises involving the two countries. It is difficult to evaluate which people were more prejudiced than the other. The growing respectability of Victorian England began to be expressed in an especial disapproval of what was regarded as the looseness and laxity of moral standards in France but this was only an additional gloss on the dislike of French attitudes and customs which had deep roots in history. Thackeray's *Paris Sketch Book* of 1840 was typical of the moralistic comments that regularly appeared in the public prints; but it also summarised the common English approach to what the French were really like, and how they viewed their neighbours across the Channel:

In the first place, and don't let us endeavour to disguise it, they hate us. Not all the protestations of friendship, not all the wisdom of Lord Palmerston, not all the diplomacy of our distinguished plenipotentiary, Mr Henry Lytton Bulwer – and let us add, not all the benefit which both countries would derive from the alliance – can make it, in our times at least, permanent and cordial. They hate us. The Carlist organs revile us with a querulous fury that never sleeps; the moderate party, if they admit the utility of our alliance, are continually pointing out our treachery, our insolence, and our monstrous infractions of it; and for the Republicans, as sure as the morning comes, the columns of their journals thunder out volleys of fierce denunciations against our unfortunate country. They live by feeding the national hatred against England, by keeping old wounds open, by recurring ceaselessly to the history of old quarrels, and as in these we, by God's help, by land and sea, in old times and late, have had the uppermost, they perpetuate the shame and mortification of the losing party, the bitterness of past defeats, and the eager desire to avenge them.[149]

The vulgarity and philistinism of Thackeray suited the commonalty, as well as the upper classes, of England, and in the 1840s there were large and small issues of difference between France and Britain which much encouraged the distrust of France. These included the controversies surrounding the search of shipping on the high seas for slaves and the failure to ratify the new Treaty of 1842 – an episode which was long remembered.[150] 1844 was a year of especially hostile incidents. There was already the Tahiti affair which had begun in the previous year and which made its main impact upon British public opinion from the end of July 1844 when news arrived of the imprisonment and deportation by the French of George Pritchard, a representative of the London Missionary Society who had also become British Consul. Peel made a vigorous speech in the Commons; hysteria on both sides of the Channel increased rapidly; the news that the song 'The English shall never reign in France' had been encored four times at the Paris Opera swelled jingoistic sentiments in England; and the London Missionary Society held a packed meeting at Exeter Hall in mid-August at which there was talk of war.[151] The affair dragged on. Lord Shaftesbury was not exaggerating the state of evangelical feeling, including his own, when he wrote in his diary under the date 4 October:

Grief and indignation cannot go beyond what I feel against the French aggressions in Tahiti. A peaceable and helpless people, a State presenting, as such, the only Christian model in the world, are subjugated by savages and powerful Europeans, and inundated with bloodshed, devastation, profligacy, and crime. God gave the regeneration of our people as a triumph of the Cross; and so it was a thing without parallel in the history of the Gospel. The missionaries made it Christian; they made it English in laws and Constitution. It had, by God's blessing, under their administration, everything but power and commerce . . . What a disgusting and cowardly attitude for England, to stand by and raise not a hand in defence of this merciful gift of Providence! God grant that the Tahitian people may endure and triumph over this fraud and violence.[152]

There was, no doubt, a small element of strategic consideration in the Tahiti affair; for the rest, it was an instance of the stupidities and not least the religious bigotry of the Europeans. There were other instances in this year, of which the de Joinville pamphlet was the most notorious.

In May 1844 there was published in Paris an anonymous pamphlet *Notes sur l'état des forces navales de France*. Its authorship was known: the Prince de Joinville, son of Louis Philippe, who was high in the command of the French navy. The message of the pamphlet was to underline the present weaknesses of the French fleets, and to suggest ways in which the naval supremacy of the British might be reduced. The point seized on by the British press was Joinville's prediction that steam power would seriously redress the unequal balance between the two navies by permitting the rapid transport of troops across the Channel, and elsewhere. He argued that had Napoleon I possessed a few steamers he might have been able to land 15,000 to 20,000 troops on British soil in 1805. There were several English versions of the pamphlet which somewhat naturally caused an immense sensation in Britain and press reactions bordered on the hysterical.[153] In France, too, the pamphlet was received in exhibitionist ways, although Guizot and Louis Philippe hastened to disavow any official connections. Joinville had suggested that with her existing steam power Britain could raid the coasts of France, and in the Mediterranean cut Algeria off from France. The traditional fears of both countries were easily aroused, and all this at the time of the Tahiti episode. In Britain, much of the public, and a great part of the military and naval establishments, began seriously to believe in the possibility of a French descent on the Channel coasts.[154] It was certainly a year of aggravating incidents. The Tsar visited Britain in June 1844, reviving memories for the French of Anglo–Russian action against them in Syria. In July Peel sent a naval squadron to Gibraltar – the issue was Morocco – and France retaliated with an expedition to Tangiers under the command of Joinville himself: a notably tactless gesture. The *entente cordiale* of these years was a very fragile construction, but the peace was kept.

Relations with France continued to be difficult right up to the February Revolution. The affair of the Spanish marriages, inflated by both France and Britain into a serious diplomatic problem at a time when Spain counted for so little; the return of Palmerston to office in mid-1846; and the divisions of opinion over the Swiss crisis, when France aligned with Austria in support of the Sonderbund while Palmerston was openly behind the Federal Diet[155] – all contributed to a continued tension between the two countries. On the eve of 1848 the leading groups of Tories and government Whigs were agreed in their general approach of suspicion and hostility, steadily increasing because of growing doubts about the viability of the French government.[156]

British opinion was not, however, unanimous in these matters of foreign affairs. There was a vigorous minority among the radical middle classes – who themselves differed a good deal in their degrees of radicalism – of whom Cobden and Bright were the best-known leaders. Their support in the country came from diverse groups who derived their ideas from varying mixtures of pacifism, anti-aristocratic sentiment, orthodox political economy with an emphasis upon the need to curb government profligacy in spending and parasitic appointments, the universal solvent of free trade for the evil of militarism, and the diminution of tensions between the countries of the world. In 1862 Cobden published his famous pamphlet *The Three Panics* in which he analysed the occasions in his political lifetime when the supposed threat of a French invasion had led to war scares and actual or demanded increases in military expenditure. The two periods when there was a considerable groundswell of middle-class opinion against increased military spending, because it involved either a rise in the income tax or the continuation of existing high levels of tax were 1848 and 1860; and in both years the middle-class radicals got wide support for their more generalised criticism of the absurdities and follies of militarism. But support was not consistent, and pelf, rather than principle, was too often the basis for opposition, as the years of the Crimean War and the Indian Mutiny so clearly showed; but anti-militarism and opposition to colonial wars remained a minority theme of middle-class radicalism throughout the nineteenth century.[157]

More consistent before 1850, and of a qualitatively different kind of radicalism, were the internationalists of the Chartist movement drawing upon traditions which went back to the 1790s. There were a number of different causes available for the expression of their sentiments of international solidarity: that of the Polish people, for example, in the twenty years before 1850; but it was France, and especially revolutionary Paris, that provided the examples of equality and fraternity which found sympathetic echoes among the political radicals of the National Union of Working Classes and of the Chartist movement. On 1 August 1831 there had been celebrated by a mass meeting in the Copenhagen Fields in London the anniversary of the Revolution of the previous year: the 'three glorious days' of July. An address 'To the Brave People of France' began by offering congratulations of 'your immortal triumph over fraud, cunning and military despotism'; regretted the demise of 'the principle of the Sovereignty of the People, for which you fought and bled, and which you neglected to see consolidated before you suffered yourselves to be dispossessed of the means'; and further regretted 'not only on your own account, but on that of the oppressed of all nations, that you did not take the wise and necessary steps in the great social progress of Universal Liberty – *The Declaration of a Republic!*, in which all men's rights would be recognised and protected ... Your noble triumphs and great sacrifices have yet received no compensation. You, the working people, who effected the revolution and carried it to a successful issue, what have you got? More poverty and less sympathy.' And the address ended: 'Citizens of France, farewell, our hopes are in you. May you continue to deserve our love and affection.'[158]

The flow of French ideas into England continued through the next two decades. Bronterre O'Brien, influential as a journalist in the 1830s, read French fluently and published a translation of Buonarroti's *Conspiration pour*

L'Égalité, dite de Babeuf in 1836, together with an introduction in which he commented trenchantly upon the treachery of the French middle and upper classes. He recommended Buonarroti's work as 'one of the best expositions ... of those great and social principles' which he and others had been advocating in the previous half dozen years.[159] Two years later, after visiting Paris to collect materials, O'Brien published the first (and only) volume of a Life of Robespierre; and it was O'Brien whom the young George Julian Harney took as his mentor. For O'Brien Robespierre was the ideal type while Harney turned to Marat, signing himself for much of his Chartist career with Marat's own adopted L'Ami du Peuple.

Harney, in his Chartist period, was a Jacobin in an English setting.[160] He became sub-editor of the *Northern Star* in the summer of 1843 and formally editor in October 1845; and it was under his influence that the *Northern Star* gave increasing attention to the international movement in the second half of the forties. He had become friendly with Engels soon after the latter first arrived in England, and by November 1843 was already publishing long articles by Engels on Continental socialism.[161] When the *Northern Star* moved to London in late 1844 the opportunities soon developed for organisational links between the Chartist left and European radicals and revolutionaries. There was a considerable foreign community in London, mainly German, French and Italian with a sizeable number of Poles; and an important minority were political refugees. Their numbers, especially of Poles, were not to be compared with those in Paris during these years, and there were significant political differences within national groups and between the nationals of different countries: the Germans and the French, for example, standing for the democratic and social republic; while the Italians, under the influence of Mazzini, were mostly opposed to socialist aims and objectives. Political contacts in London soon grew into firmer organisational forms. The Germans already had their *Deutsche Arbeiterbildungsverein*[162] which Karl Schapper, Heinrich Bauer and Joseph Moll had founded in 1840. Schapper and Bauer were members of the Bund der Gerechten (League of the Just), formed in 1836 as a breakaway from a moderate German emigré organisation. After the failure of the Paris uprising in May 1839 in which members of the Bund fought alongside Blanqui and Barbès, Schapper and Bauer came to London, and within the *Deutsche Arbeiterbildungsverein*, the Bund continued to operate as a secret group. Later the Bund merged into the Communist League.[163] The Poles in Britain were organised in the Polish Democratic Committee following the Polish emigration of 1831, and there was also a little-known grouping around Lud Polski. In September 1845 there was formed the Democratic Committee for Poland's Regeneration which in effect was a sub-committee of the Fraternal Democrats, established in the same month. It was on 22

September, at a banquet held to celebrate the French Republic's constitution of 1792, that the Society of Fraternal Democrats was founded, brought together by Harney from the left-wing groups in London: a forerunner by twenty years of the First International. The Fraternal Democrats was not a political party; indeed, it took some pains to indicate that it was not a party within a party.[164] During the two years before the February events in Paris in 1848 the tide of internationalism was running strongly within the London radical movement. The high point of Harney's internationalism, and an episode which attracted national attention, was his candidature against Palmerston at Tiverton, in Devon, in the general election of mid-1847. In a closely reasoned two-hour speech Harney reviewed Palmerston's foreign policy; and Palmerston replied with a speech that occupied five columns in the pages of *The Times*.[165]

Harney first met Marx when the latter came to London in November 1847 to speak at a meeting arranged by the Fraternal Democrats and the Polish Committee; and also to take part in the second Congress of the Communist League. It was at the secret conference of the latter that it was decided to prepare a statement of aims for revolutionary socialists that appeared in February 1848 as the *Communist Manifesto*. Towards the end of 1847 and the early weeks of 1848 political contacts between the revolutionary movements of different countries in Western Europe were noticeably quickening. Engels was one of the important links through his journalistic work. He had become correspondent of the Paris socialist paper *La Réforme* in October 1847, and he was already contributing to *L'Atelier* which had connections with the Chartist movement. He was also French correspondent of the *Northern Star*, and was sending English and French news to the *Deutsche Brüsseler Zeitung* which was now taking a great deal of material from Marx himself.[166] When the February Revolution broke out in Paris, its influence naturally reverberated round Europe, and for the revolutionaries, democrats and radicals, it seemed the consummation of all they had been working for. In England the reaction was wildly enthusiastic among the Chartists well beyond the Left, and inevitably among the foreign emigrés; and when Harney, Philip McGrath and Ernest Jones went to Paris to deliver a congratulatory address to the Provisional Government, it was a dawn that was indeed blissful, the apparent fulfilment of the hopes that radicals all over Europe had been dreaming about for so many years.

2

JANUARY–FEBRUARY

The year opened with little flourish. There was still gloom about the economy but the worst was over. Failures of import houses had been extensive throughout 1847, especially in the last six months, and most parts of the textile sector had suffered quite severe declines in output and employment. But the rest of the economy for the first nine months of 1847 could be described as prosperous or at least as doing moderately well; and over the country as a whole income and consumption had been well maintained. It was the last few months of 1847, following the financial crisis of October, that witnessed a more widespread depression, and the normal improvement that might have occurred during the first half of 1848 was checked or reversed by the economic effects of the revolutions in France and elsewhere in Europe. During the second half of 1848, however, almost all sections of the British economy, except railways, were showing upward movements in employment, output and exports; and throughout 1849 all indices continued to show increases, leading forward to the vigorous boom of the early years of the 1850s. On the first day of 1848 the *Economist* reported from Manchester: 'The expectations of our spinners and manufacturers for 1848, as far as we can learn, are very moderate, being no higher than that they will be able to get over it without being poorer at the end than they are at present.' They were, in fact, to do better than this prediction, but in general there was no sense at the beginning of this year of any series of events likely to disrupt the economic growth of the wealthiest manufacturing country in Europe. Ireland cannot be included in these generalisations. The extent of Ireland's miseries was grimly evident, but, apart from the effects of the famine upon the import figures and therefore upon the balance of payments, the devastation in Ireland had remarkably little effect upon the course of economic change in mainland Britain. In economic terms Ireland could be, and was, ignored.[1]

It is now possible to appreciate that the turning point in the British economy was not the late forties but 1840–2, and 'turning point' may be too dogmatic a phrase for what was taking place. Certainly the economic depression of the early years was exceptionally severe, but the remainder of the decade after 1842 exhibited quite remarkable growth, broken only during the closing months of 1847 and the early part of 1848. Dr Boot has argued that the growth factors from 1843 remained sufficiently strong and powerful to carry the British economy through the crisis of 1847 and on to the high levels of activity of the late forties and early fifties. These included the changes in commercial policy and the banking reforms as well as the strong impulses generated by the high levels of railway investment in the middle years.[2] At the same time, and an important matter for social historians, the economy continued to grow in a markedly uneven way between different industries and within individual industries. The pressures upon the small-scale producers and the independent craftsmen and artisans, were continuous and in the end irresistible, and pools of misery were constantly being created or deepened. It is a familiar story and throughout the nineteenth century the British economy exhibited many of the characteristics that Clapham described of the first fifty years of industrialisation: of a country which 'abounded in ancient types of industrial organisation and in transitional types of every variety'.[3] It was the differing pace of economic change and industrial transition in the different sectors of the economy that occasioned so much misery in nineteenth-century Britain; and this uneven rate of change affected both industries and regions.[4]

The matter which most newspapers and journals concerned themselves with during the early weeks of 1848 was the state of the revenue, the discussion of which was the prelude to the budget which the Whig government would introduce soon after Parliament reassembled. All the national papers published the revenue accounts in great detail. The *Economist*, in a leading article on 8 January which surveyed the general prospects for the coming year, argued that 'the state of the public revenue ... is really much more unfavourable than a more superficial and cursory review has led the public to believe'. The question of the deficit, which the figures revealed, could not be divorced from one of the main domestic issues of the opening weeks of the year: the alleged deficiencies in the state of the national defences. The story goes back to the furore in 1844 which the Joinville pamphlet had raised, and which has been discussed above. The invasion scare and the public debate of that year had died away, only to be revived when a private letter written to Sir John Burgoyne, Inspector-General of Defences, by the Duke of Wellington was made public. Wellington's letter was in answer to one from Burgoyne in which the latter had set out certain of the military problems in the event of a war with France. The 'Great Captain', as he was often called, replied with an alarmist document in which he first adverted to the new problems that steam had

created and in particular to the greater ease the French would now have in
making a descent upon the southern parts of the British coast. He then went
on to suggest that it would be easy for a French army both to land, and then
to march north upon London. Wellington had personally reconnoitred the
south coast from Dover to Portsmouth, and he had convinced himself that,
with the exception of the beach directly within range of Dover Castle, 'there
is not a spot on the coast on which infantry might not be thrown on shore, at
any time of tide, with any wind and in any weather'; and that there were not
less than twelve great roads from the coast leading to London. Wellington
further insisted that as it was unlikely the regular army would be increased
in numbers a militia force of about 150,000 men should be organised; and
he concluded with the hope 'that the Almighty may protect me from being
the witness of the tragedy which I cannot persuade my contemporaries to
take measures to avert'.[5] This was a private communication to Burgoyne
who, however, was so impressed with the Duke's answer and argument that
he decided to have it copied. This was done by his wife and daughter who no
doubt fell upon their task with enthusiasm. The ladies then showed copies to
close acquaintances, including Lady Shelley, an old friend of Wellington,
who in turn showed it to Lord Ellesmere with the information that the Duke
would be glad to have it published. It appeared in *The Times* and other papers
around the New Year and inevitably created a major sensation. Wellington
was unjustly accused of embarrassing a Whig government, and naturally
he never trusted Burgoyne again.[6] There had been a considerable debate
inside the Peel Cabinet after the Joinville affair, with Aberdeen, the Foreign
Secretary, and Wellington taking opposed positions; and when the Whigs
returned in July 1846 Palmerston was to prove the most determined
advocate of increased defence expenditures.[7] Against a background of
worsening diplomatic relations with France, the publication of the Wellington letter and the consequent public outcry meant that defence expenditure
could not be cut in the 1848 budget and some increase would have to be
accepted. Without defence increases a deficit of around two million pounds
had been forecast in the financial figures made public during January. In the
Russell Cabinet a number of ideas were being floated, including a large
militia recruited by ballot. Palmerston was among those who approved the
idea, providing, Palmerston wrote, that substitution was allowed.[8] The
reaction in the country at large, however, was by no means uniform. *Punch*
made fun of the threatened invasion and its article on the occupation of
London by the French was reprinted in *The Times*.[9] The *Economist* (8
January) ridiculed the Duke's idea of an easy invasion and spoke of his
'mistaken apprehensions'. The trade with France, the *Economist* continued,
had grown faster than with any other country, and it warned that the panic
could lead to a demand for increased taxes. The *Illustrated London News* of the

same date was specific: 'We shall watch the development of the invasion controversy with much interest; and we predict it will culminate in a demand for new taxes, or the retention of former ones, to a heavy amount, and that before the New Year is much older . . .'. The weekly *Nonconformist* of 5 January was a good deal more outspoken, suggesting that the alarm was really a matter of English domestic politics, developed by 'a decrepit oligarchy against the further progress of the people of England' and that the Whig government has followed 'the scribbling of a lucky soldier in his dotage'. The *Nonconformist*, later in the same month, republished from *Howitt's Journal* an anti-war statement whose language was vigorous even for its time:

But the danger is not from without, but from within – not from the French but from the Normans. There is need of war, but war of another kind, and directed into a different quarter. The enemy is already in the camp; the plunder is going on. The rats are in the stack – the old Aristoc – rats who, since the Norman invasion, in increasing numbers, and ever growing audacity, have been tugging at the vitals of John Bull.[10]

In the provinces the reaction of most Whig and all the liberal papers was much the same; and a letter of Richard Cobden, dated 12 January 1848, published in *The Times* and widely reprinted, totally denied that there was any suggestion of France considering an invasion. Nor was there, of course.[11]

The Whig ministers decided on increases in defence spending, and to meet the now enlarged deficit they proposed a dramatic rise in the rate of income tax: from seven pence in the pound to one shilling. The new session had begun on 3 February, with a long debate on the West Indian sugar duties, but on 17 February Lord John Russell rose in the Commons to introduce the financial proposals for the coming year. The income tax decision produced uproar in the House, and vigorous denunciation throughout middle-class Britain. Meetings of protest multiplied, petitions against the increase flowed into the Commons: as the *Annual Register* wrote a year later, it became evident 'from a variety of symptoms, that a formidable agitation was rising up in the country, which if resisted might sweep away the Income Tax and the Ministry altogether'.[12]

The British government and the British press had other concerns with France in these early weeks of 1848. One was the health of Louis-Philippe. It had been much commented on for several years and there was anxious speculation about the succession. In 1847 and early 1848 there was also growing concern about the performance and the viability of the Guizot administration, and the increasing strength of the reform movement was recognised as a serious threat to the regime. Normanby, the British ambassador to Paris, had been sending back critical appraisals of the Guizot ministry throughout 1847;[13] and on 20 January 1848 he wrote a long letter

to Palmerston, mostly on electoral matters, but also indicating the
contemporary position of the Guizot government:

the present situation in France is to maintain the personal government of the King
through the corruption exercised by every class of public functionaries.

For the first time this principle is about to be boldly and unscrupulously attacked in
the Chamber of Deputies, and the next few weeks must shew how far it can stand the
action upon public opinion caused by the vigorous attacks that will be made from the
Tribune.[14]

On 7 February Normanby provided a further detailed analysis of current
political prospects. He doubted whether the 'public mind' would accept
further delays in reform, and he then proceeded to list what he regarded as
the indisputable facts of the political situation in France: that the
government was losing every by-election; that a general election at this time
would 'without doubt return a very hostile majority'; and that the loyalty of
the National Guard was in doubt. This last was a matter he rightly thought
important, and throughout his commentaries on the course of the
Revolution, at the time and later, he often came back to this particular issue.
In this letter of 7 February he wrote that the government did not dare to
assemble the National Guard for fear of popular demonstrations of feeling
against the regime; and in a series of letters in the next fortnight he
constantly expressed his belief that the National Guard, or important
sections of the National Guard, would prove unreliable if called upon to
support the King.[15] Normanby was remarkably well informed, and the
British government were efficiently served by his intelligence reports. So too
were the British public by the newspaper despatches from Paris.

British papers always carried a great deal of material on France in normal
times, and the parliamentary discussion on the King's speech was reported
at length in the London press and copied by many provincial papers. On 13
January 1848 there was a long despatch in The Times from a Paris
correspondent underlining the fears and anxiety that were being felt in the
French capital. The writer had the highest regard for Guizot and his abilities,
but noted that 'his course of government is alarming the best friends of the
State'. Similar statements appeared in a number of journals and papers in
England during the next few weeks, and there was an especial emphasis
upon the failure of Guizot to counter the increasing accusations of
corruption that were being made. This 'increasing spirit of the opposition'
was noted by The Times on 27 January, as the debate on the King's speech
proceeded in the Assembly.

It is interesting that only in one or two places was de Tocqueville's famous
speech of 29 January reported in brief comment in the British press; and
Normanby made only passing references in his despatches. This was the
remarkable prophesy which de Tocqueville offered to his fellow parliamen-

tarians. It was published in full in *Le Moniteur* on 30 January and in large part in his own *Recollections*. The most celebrated passage read:

Have you no intuitive instinct, incapable of being analysed but certain, that tells you the ground is trembling once more in Europe? Do you not feel – how should I say it – a revolutionary wind in the air? We do not know whence it comes, or whither it goes, or what it will carry away; and at such a time you remain calm in face of the degradation of public mores – for the expression is not too strong.

I am bound to disclose to my country my deep and firm conviction. And that profound and fixed conviction is that public mores are becoming degraded, and that this degradation will lead you shortly, very shortly perhaps, into new revolutions. Are the lives of kings supported by stronger threads, which are harder to snap, than the lives of other men? Have you at this very moment any certainty of the morrow? Do you know what may happen in France a year, a month, or perhaps a day from now? You do not know that, but you do know that there is a tempest on the horizon, and it is moving towards you. Will you let it take you by surprise?[16]

It was not, then, a failure to appreciate what forces there were in France working towards some kind of change. Normanby was as clear as de Tocqueville, and Palmerston and his colleagues were fully apprised of the dangerous currents that were moving within the streams of French politics. What no one foresaw was the suddenness of the change when it came and the ease with which the regime was overthrown. As de Tocqueville noted in his *Recollections*, when looking back on his January speech, he had understood the general causes that 'tilted the July Monarchy to its ruin. But I did not see the accidents that were to topple it'.[17]

Until the revolutionary days in Paris in late February Ireland probably occupied more columns in the national press than any other subject, except for the debate on income tax which got under way in the week before 22 February. Throughout 1847, as the consequences of the catastrophic failure of the 1845 and 1846 harvests began to be expressed in scenes of horror all over peasant Ireland except the North, the number of reported crimes and outrages began to rise sharply. Evictions had not ceased, and there was desperation everywhere. Clarendon had become Lord Lieutenant following the death of Lord Bessborough in May 1847. His Chief Secretary was Sir William Somerville, an Irishman, and his Under-Secretary, Thomas Redington, was also an Irishman and a Catholic; and this new administration was confronted with a surge of outrages and lawlessness which were on a scale larger than anything in Ireland since the early 1830s.

Clarendon, born in 1800, was fourth Earl. His younger brother, C. P. Villiers (1802–98) was noted for his advocacy of Corn Law repeal. It was a liberal Whig family, although Clarendon's own liberalism was not evident during his five years as Viceroy. He had accepted his new position with some reluctance. The suggestion that he only took the office on the understanding that it would soon be abolished and absorbed into central government in England has some documentary backing, but it was never a serious proposition, above all in these years of crises. Clarendon was not an unreasonable choice. He had the correct aristocratic background always necessary for the Viceroy, he had entered the diplomatic service in 1820 and his later career exhibited his considerable political abilities. His own knowledge of the country he was to administer at the time of his appointment was limited, and certainly not as extensive as that of Bessborough who was an Irish landlord; but all English politicians were familiar with the general problems of Ireland. In Clarendon's case he was also a close friend of Cornewall Lewis who had written an intelligent appraisal of the Irish question in 1836, and who was also Clarendon's brother-in-law.[18] Quite early, Clarendon was making cautious suggestions to Russell in a reforming direction, urging him to consider once again the relations between landlord and tenant, but the proposals he suggested foundered – after long struggles within the Cabinet – in parliamentary procedure: an indication itself of how lacking in agreement the Cabinet was.[19] Clarendon's very moderate proposals during his period of office – for relief works for example – all failed to win support in London, and he soon came to rely upon the traditional methods of coercion as the sure way of controlling the Irish situation. Throughout the years of his office as Viceroy, Clarendon was always being congratulated by some part or other of the British press for his firmness of stance and policy. The Orange peers in the House of Lords – as useful a touchstone as any for assessing reactionary policies in Ireland – were only marginally critical of Clarendon in 1847–8.[20] Clarendon was also an intimate friend of Henry Reeve who had been on *The Times* since 1840 and who by 1847 was responsible for foreign policy on the paper; *The Times* was always respectful and often warmly supportive of the Clarendon administration.

By the autumn of 1847 agrarian outrages had reached frightening levels. 'The oldest inhabitant', Clarendon wrote to Cornewall Lewis on 21 November 1847, 'cannot remember Tipperary, Clare and Limerick in such a state of disorganisation as now. There never was so open or so widely extended a conspiracy for shooting landlords and agents.'[21] Clarendon had already asked Russell for extraordinary powers. He himself considered the suspension of habeas corpus as the most effective procedure for a limited period while the situation was brought under 'control', and he added other requests including an Arms Act and the power to impose fines on districts where crimes had been committed. Russell's problems in the context of Irish coercion have been much discussed by historians. He had, after all, helped to bring Peel down over an Irish coercion bill, and while his liberal principles were never allowed to obstruct the requirements of internal security, Russell also had to think of his majority in the Commons. In fact, during these

Table 3 *Selected Crimes – Ireland:*
May–October 1846 and
May–October 1847

	1846	1847
Homicides	68	96
Attempts on life by firing at the person	55	126
Robberies of arms	207	530
Firing into dwellings	51	116

eighteen months to the end of 1848, he underestimated the solid support the House of Commons would always give him for strong measures in Ireland, and in England too. In the event, Clarendon had to be satisfied with a compromise; and on 29 November 1847 Grey, the Home Secretary, introduced the Crime and Outrages Bill to the Commons. He noted in his introductory speech that although there had been some reduction in ordinary crimes during the previous year, the increase in the crimes under the heading of outrages had been considerable. Grey quoted the returns for the six months ending October 1847 compared with the same period in the year 1846, and for the whole of Ireland the figures showed a sharp increase. These increases in the number of crimes in the classes shown in Table 3 had begun from about the middle of September 1847 and they were markedly localised. For the single month of October 1847 71 per cent of the total under these headings were committed in three counties: Clare, Limerick and Tipperary. The provisions of the new Bill included permission for the Lord Lieutenant to 'proclaim' a district, to draft any number of extra police into the disaffected areas, the cost to fall entirely upon local resources, and to order all arms to be handed in: the exceptions included magistrates, special constables and gamekeepers. The special reserve force held in Dublin at the disposal of the central authority was to be increased, if it was felt desirable, from 400 to 600. Further:

justices and constables, where any murder has been committed, or where there has been any attempt to commit murder, or where there is reasonable ground for believing that a murder to have been committed, shall have power to call on all male persons within the ages of 16 to 60, residing or being within the district in which that murder has been committed, to assist in the search for and pursuit of the parties charged with the commission of the crime; and thereupon every person refusing to join in such pursuit shall be guilty of a misdemeanour, and shall be liable, upon conviction, to be imprisoned, with or without hard labour, for any term not exceeding two years.[22]

John Bright spoke in the debate in the second reading. He had presented a petition signed by 20,000 Manchester people against the Bill, and he wished to explain why he felt obliged to vote for the Coercion Bill. The ordinary law in Ireland, he began, was 'utterly powerless'. There was no popular support for the observance of the law as there was in England, an argument which he generalised in prophetic words: 'These assassinations are not looked upon as murders, but as executions.' Bright was not, of course, satisfied with the conduct of the government in Ireland:

We maintain a large army in Ireland, and an armed police, which is an army in everything but name, and yet we have in that country a condition of things not to be matched in any other civilised country on the face of the earth, and which is alike disgraceful to Ireland and to us. The great cause of Ireland's calamities is, that Ireland is idle. I believe it would be found, on inquiry, that the population of Ireland, as compared with that of England, do not work more than two days a week. Wherever a people are not industrious and are not employed, there is the greatest danger of crime and outrage. Ireland is idle, and therefore she starves; Ireland starves, and therefore she rebels.[23]

It was a brilliant polemic that had much in it of the substance of the Irish problem; but when he came to solutions, Bright meandered off into a discussion of the evils of entail and progeniture and wholly missed the qualitative differences between the land question in Ireland and the particular legal complexities of aristocratic landholding in England. By the time he reached the end of his speech he had, presumably, 'lost' the House; and he went into the lobby in support of the government.[24]

In the closing months of 1847 the government moved several thousand more troops into Ireland. The Outrages Bill received the Royal Assent on 20 December (11 and 12 Vict. c. 11) and Clarendon immediately 'proclaimed' the counties of Clare, Limerick and Tipperary. To expedite the more speedy trial of offenders – there were now hundreds in jail awaiting trial – he established a Special Commission with two senior judges, the Lord Chief Justice, Francis Blackburne, and Chief Baron Pigot.[25] The procedures of a Special Commission included the summoning of a special jury whose composition was defined by the 1833 Jury Act (3 and 4 Will. IV c. XCI). The special jury in the first Commission to be elected was described by the *Annual Register* of 1848 as 'consisting of some of the principal resident gentry of the county' and it further commented how confidence had been restored by the announcement of vigorous measures under the new Act. There were no abstentions when the special jury roll was called: a most unusual phenomenon in Ireland. The Chief Justice's address to the jury emphasised the great public danger at the present time, and insisted that unless violence was checked 'the very bonds of our social system would be dissolved'. He then proceeded to explain what he meant by such a dissolution: 'The principal object of the combination which exists is the destruction of the rights of landlords, and, if it succeeds, the occupiers of the land will become its proprietors.'[26] It is not wholly clear what the Lord Chief Justice had in mind by the use of the term 'combination'. It was common among the Protestant Ascendancy that what was called 'Ribbonism' was a nation-wide conspiracy, and in 1847 Clarendon himsef was suggesting in his own comments something more than local unrest. Thomas Drummond, in 1839, had been especially concerned to deny the nation-wide or regional character of outrage organisation in his evidence before the House of Lords Select Committee, and Cornewall Lewis had related outrage to local agrarian injustices. There has been much divided opinion among the older tradition of nationalist historians as well as between more modern commentators; but recent research is suggesting that 'Whiteboyism', as the phenomenon of local conditions, must be distinguished from 'Ribbonism' which could have regional networks and was, to a degree, politicised. The evidence is still somewhat shadowy but Clarendon may have glimpsed something of what was happening.[27] The Special Commission completed its work by early February. There was widespread commendation in England for its expeditiousness and efficiency. Russell, who wrote regularly – almost daily – to Clarendon, expressed his satisfaction that 'your Irish juries are excellent'; and Grey, after indicating his own gratification, particularly emphasised that no juror had been excluded.[28] *The Times*, on 7 February, commented on the results:

It is a dreadful contemplation that within a few weeks fifteen human beings, in three counties of Ireland, will have closed their lives under the hands of the public executioner. But such examples must be made. There is a turbulence of spirit amongst the lower classes in that country that can only be kept down by the terrors of the law.

The greater part of the national and provincial press agreed. In most cases there was strong support for what was looked upon as firm and vigorous action by the authorities; and this, for lawless Ireland, was much needed. There were a few dissenting voices: the *Bradford Observer*, for example, argued in an editorial on 27 January 1848 for the commutation of death sentences to transportation and deplored 'so much gratuitous cruelty and barbarism' – very unusual sentiments when applied to British conduct in Ireland. The editorial went on to notice the 'extraordinary facility' with which verdicts were obtained, due, no doubt, to the 'better class' of jurymen compared with those who normally sat at ordinary assizes.

There were two items of news during the period of the Special Commission, almost commonplace in their way, which illuminate some of the problems of contemporary Ireland. Both appeared in *The Times*. The first, from the issue of 27 January, was a report of resolutions passed at a meeting of the Catholic clergy of the diocese of Killala. The second resolution read:

That the result of the Special Commission, now sitting, will prove, as the experience of ages hath already too clearly proved, that the relations between landlord and tenant are the never-failing source of the miseries as well as the murders of Ireland; and that Parliament, if it sincerely wishes to alleviate former and prevent the latter, must devise some means by which the weal of the poor, as well as the rights of the rich, may be secured.

The second item appeared in *The Times* on 2 February without comment, except for the heading which read, in capital letters, 'A distinguished bench of magistrates':

The following gentlemen have, within the last few years, usually attended the sittings of the Cashel bench of magistrates: R. Long – father shot, himself twice fired at; W. Murphy – father shot; Samuel Cooper – brother shot; E. Scully – cousin, Mr. Scully shot; Godfrey Taylor – cousin, Mr Clarke, shot; William Roe – shot; C. Clarke – brother shot, a nephew, Mr Roe, shot.

While the Special Commissioners were performing their duties so efficiently, a considerable debate had opened in *The Times* around a letter addressed to the Prime Minister from the most controversial cleric in the Catholic hierarchy: John McHale, Archbishop of Tuam.[29]

McHale (1791–1881) was archbishop of the poorest province in Ireland with a population that was about 96 per cent Catholic. As a child McHale had seen the French troops marching from Killala to Castlebar, and his own parish priest had been summarily hanged for giving shelter to the officers of the invading army. McHale was the first prelate to be wholly educated in Ireland since the Reformation. He was intensely nationalist, felt deeply the sufferings of the poor, became Daniel O'Connor's most important clerical supporter and was always prepared to take an independent line against his own hierarchy and also with Rome. He was a difficult man, and his Catholic faith stiffened over the years into an unyielding dogma, fed by his nationalism as well as by the aggressive Protestant evangelicalism that directed missionary activity into his own region. His open letter to Lord John Russell was published in the Dublin *Freeman's Journal* on 1 January 1848 and reprinted in *The Times* on the 4th. It took two full columns of *The Times*, and was intelligently argued, humane and rational – until the last paragraph. The English certainly needed to be reminded of the devastation that the famine had caused in Ireland for there was remarkably little discussion in most of the press; and by 1848 Irish misery had mostly passed from the consciousness of the English, if, indeed, except for the radicals and the small groups of charitable Christians such as the Quakers, it had ever been seriously appreciated or recognised. The nub of McHale's argument was that in the hour of need, the Irish peasantry, as members of a large and wealthy Empire, ought to be able to claim a basic sustenance:

when the harvest is not sufficient to pay the usual rent and maintain their families, they are ignorant of any divine or natural law which should oblige them to hand over the entire of the produce to the proprietor of the land, and to consign their families, the companions of their toil in raising it, to utter starvation . . . Brought to this humiliating crisis by a process of laws which made every provision for commutative justice generally answered by coercion, they repeat their loyal and constitutional claims to participate in the hour of their distress, in those common funds of a united people to which they have so amply contributed.

McHale insisted upon the peaceful influence of the Catholic hierarchy and clergy; and the letter, while written in a tart, sharp style, provided a wholly reasonable argument to anyone who was aware of the frightening and frightful consequences of the famine for the people of Ireland. It was not, however, likely to have an appeal to those to whom the principles of political economy were articles of faith; and it was not only C. E. Trevelyan, custodian of the British Treasury during the famine and a prime example of those in history who have created or sustained suffering on a large scale from more or less disinterested motives, who were quite out of sympathy with the McHale argument.[10] The majority of the press and journals on mainland Britain used one version or another of the free-market arguments against all those who proposed subsidised relief in any form whatever. But what destroyed McHale's general case were the sentiments of his final paragraph, in which he fell into a frenetic sectarianism that for a political bishop concerned with arguing the Irish case can only be described as absurd. He began by attacking the British government's position in the Swiss crisis for its anti-Catholicism, and ended thus:

It is a pity that a people of such good natural qualities as the English should be so often put besides themselves in their estimation of Ireland by the rabid teaching of heterodox pastors . . . Instead of again subjugating our faith, we will aid in freeing yours from the tyranny of error, in which for three centuries it has been bound. England, instead of being as it is now, with all its wealth, a melancholy and miserable country, will become once more merry England, and restored to the centre of unity, it will again reflect the splendour of that faith, and the warmth of that charity which was brought to it from Rome, and was illustrated in the lives of a Lanfranc, a Langton, and an Anselm, as well as in the glorious martyrdom and miracles of Thomas of Canterbury.

The Times, on the same day, expressed its 'unfeigned regret' at having to print McHale's letter, and then proceeded, at considerable length, to abuse him:

That a man who displays such qualities of mind and heart should be set up as a chief pastor in the high places of the Roman Catholic church is, perhaps, the worst feature in the present aspect of that unhappy country. The disease that has fallen upon the staple food of the Irish could destroy but their bodies, but here is matter which destroys body, mind and soul.

And so on. McHale and his follies were matters to which *The Times* returned on a number of occasions in the next few weeks.[31]

The central fallacy for almost everyone in England was that which suggested the normal laws of the market must be interfered with because of the special circumstances of Ireland. This, it was widely argued, was wholly impracticable and in the long run could only worsen the situation. Until the Irish overcame their apparently natural improvidence and developed standards of independence and self-help, outside intervention would only encourage all those personal attributes and characteristics which had brought Ireland to the miserable state it was now in. It was frequently agreed that Irish landlords often neglected their duties, but this did not excuse the failure to develop habits of frugality and hard work. The arguments were depressingly similar throughout most of the press as was the lack of comprehension of the structural and economic problems of the Irish economy. The *Manchester Guardian*, a Whig paper that throughout the coming year was to support the government and take the hard line on matters of internal security, explained on 12 January that there were many small farmers in England capable only of sustaining a single family:

But they do not dream of such a thing as dividing into four farms that which is only just sufficient for one. What, then, do they do? They bring up their children in habits of frugality and industry, which qualify them for earning their own living, and then send them forth into the world to look for employment.

Except, of course, that there was no work for young people in Ireland, and to find it they had to emigrate.

The famine had begun in 1845–6, and Peel's relief measures, while on no scale commensurate with the numbers of the hungry, the sick and the dying, were an attempt to stem catastrophe. The Whigs, with Trevelyan in command at the Treasury, cut back on relief expenditures, drastically reduced what public works had been started and by the beginning of 1848 were refusing any further aid which would fall to the account of the Consolidated Fund. In the Cabinet and outside in the country at large, there was an insistence upon the generosity of the English towards Ireland which had gone unrecognised by the recipients, and a firm determination to offer no more financial assistance. The refusal to allocate more monies was summed up by *The Times* on 1 February 1848: 'Vestigia nulla retrorsum – we must decline more loans, even had we the money to make them'. Clarendon on several occasions asked for serious consideration to be given to a public works policy, but he was answered by silence or by an insistence that the British public had reached the limit of their toleration for further expenditure on Ireland.[32]

The number of deaths in the Irish famine approached one million between 1845 and 1851; and another million emigrated. Those who went across the

Atlantic could not always avoid the possibility of being dead on arrival.[33] Measured by the number of dead, the famine was Europe's most horrifying catastrophe in the nineteenth century. This was not how it appeared to the English at the time, nor how it has been discussed in history textbooks in England. Conditions in the Irish rural areas were often described in the English press, and the *Illustrated London News*, for example, often printed graphic commentaries on the horrors and devastation. It was not difficult from what was published in mainland Britain to become well-informed on the Irish question, but it is necessary to underline the more widespread indifference that settled upon the greater part of English public opinion. The average reader of the national and provincial press was more likely to remember the violence and the lawlessness and the degradation of the ordinary people of Ireland than to appraise the deeper causes of the tragedy, and so to feel that Carlyle's savage attack on the immigrant Irish, with their 'wild Milesian features' and their descent from 'decent manhood to squalid apehood', was a reasonable judgement upon an impossible people.[34] By 1848 certainly the famine for most people in Britain might well have taken place in far away Bengal for all the emotional impact the hundreds of thousands dead made upon public life on the mainland. The hordes of starving, filthy, disease-ridden Irish who wandered through the industrial districts of the North and into London in the closing years of the forties only confirmed the massive popular prejudice against these alien people.

Meanwhile, Dublin Castle continued not only to administer the country, but to fulfil its role as the centre of social life for those with access to the hospitable world of the Castle. Lord Bessborough, who was not in good health at the time of his appointment as Viceroy, had complained to Lord John Russell that it was 'the Balls and Drawing rooms' that 'knocked him. up', but Clarendon, according to contemporary witnesses, encouraged the tradition of the social round. Elizabeth Smith, in her revealing journals, wrote under the date 1 February 1848: 'It was a bright day for poor Lord John when he thought of sending Lord Clarendon to Ireland, 1,300 gentlemen at the Levée. Such a Drawing-room as Dublin Castle has not seen for many years'.[35] In January 1848 there was a drawing-room of 1,527 persons and two large dinner parties; in February there were three balls for 1,300, 400 and 450 persons respectively, with five large dinner parties; and in March two balls for above 900 and 550, with four large dinner parties. The average number at the Viceroy's dinner table each night for the first three months of the year were thirteen, sixteen and fifteen; and the cost of running the household – food, wine, wages and stores – was £1,662 in January, £1,842 in February and £2,098 in March. In the first week of January the weekly wine list showed a consumption at the Viceroy's table of sixteen bottles of port, thirty-six bottles of best sherry with six of ordinary sherry, one bottle of Madeira, twenty-one bottles of best claret, nineteen bottles of best champagne, five bottles of best brandy, and a few oddments of hock, ordinary brandy, curaçoa, alaye and cherry brandy. The wine merchants' bills for the whole of 1848 amounted to £1,297, the butchers to £1,868 (in addition to supplies from the home farm), the poulterers to £619, and the fishmongers to £352. The coal merchants were paid £622, and there was a remarkable £562 for the 'Butter Man'. The levées and drawing-rooms seem to have ended in March, but there were several large dinner parties each month until October, when for the last three months of the year none are recorded in the daily accounts.[36]

The working-class movement in Britain at the beginning of 1848 was looking forward to a steady improvement in its political future. An editorial in the *Northern Star* on 1 January noted that

Throughout England, lectures, public meetings, and assemblages of local delegates, attest that the 'dry bones' are once more quickening into life and action. The very numerously attended and enthusiastic meetings recently holden in the metropolis, exhibit a most hopeful sign of the times.

The editorial went on to commend support for the third national petition which was already under way; it noted the Reform banquets in France which it prophesied would be the 'beginning of the end' for the regime; it welcomed the triumph of the Swiss Diet for the impetus it would give to the cause of democracy throughout Europe; and it concluded by congratulating the Fraternal Democrats on their decision to convene a democratic 'Congress of all Nations' in Brussels in the coming autumn. The Land Plan continued to occupy a good deal of space in the columns of the *Northern Star*, and for Feargus O'Connor – partly, of course, because of the parliamentary enquiry into its financial position – it remained the most important single issue of the coming year. 'My dear children' he wrote in the issue of 15 January, 'having nearly completed the cottages at Minster Lovell, and having created a Paradise in the wilderness, I arrived here [Snigs End, near Cheltenham] yesterday'.

The most important political question of the year ahead, although it was not one that was recognised in these early weeks, was the relationship between the Irish Confederates, the most radical of the Irish Repeal movement, and the English Chartists. The *Northern Star* was reporting Confederate meetings throughout January, and there were at least five Confederate clubs in London that were mentioned in its columns. The Irish leadership under Daniel O'Connell had been consistently hostile towards the Chartist movement since the 1830s. There had been an important change in 1837. Down to that year O'Connell had showed himself in broad agreement with most of the radical policies that were being pursued in

England. But in 1837, and especially because of O'Connell's attitude towards the Glasgow Spinners' strike of that year, he made a sharp break with radicalism in England, and henceforth there was open hostility between the leaders of the Repeal movement and those of the Chartist movement. O'Connell was especially critical of the principles of trade unionism and it was this that occasioned the break with such moderates as William Lovett. There were other factors, of course, including O'Connell's agreement with the Whig administration of Melbourne.

There are two important questions for historians. The first is the extent to which the considerable Irish communities in Britain were involved in the day-to-day politics of Chartism; and the second is the extent to which 1848 differed, in this context, from what had happened in the past. The debate on these matters has been summarised in two carefully argued essays by J. H. Treble and Dorothy Thompson.[37] Treble took the view that not until 1848 did the 'vast majority' of the Irish in the industrial counties of the North have any serious contact with the Chartist movement while at the same time he recognised that individual Irishmen were important in the Chartist leadership at different levels of prominence. Dorothy Thompson, by contrast, documented the involvement of Irish workers in local Chartist groups, especially in the industrial towns, and it is reasonable to accept the important qualifications that have to be made to Treble's analysis. However, 1848 was different in a number of respects from anything that had gone before, and here Treble was right in emphasising the differences. In this year there had taken place important shifts in attitudes on the part of the Irish leaders. O'Connell's death in mid-1847, the establishment of the Irish Democratic Federation in London in August–September 1847 to campaign for Repeal, the important influence of Fintan Lalor's ideas upon the minds and policies of Young Ireland from the early months of 1847, Feargus O'Connor's vigorous parliamentary denunciation of the Crime and Outrages Bill in the House of Commons: all these helped towards establishing a new understanding and provided the basis for an informal but firm agreement between the Confederation and the Chartists. When James Leach, the Manchester Chartist, spoke in Dublin on the first anniversary of the Irish Confederation it was a portent of the new relationship that was coming about;[38] and what made it come to active political life was the similar reaction to the revolutionary events in Paris at the end of February. By the time T. F. Meagher spoke at the St Patrick's day meeting in Manchester the fraternal and political connections between the radical movements on both sides of the Irish Channel were being taken for granted.

These developments presented the English government with problems of a kind they had not previously experienced. In 1839, for example, it had been possible, because of the relative quiet of Ireland, to move troops from

Ireland to the more disturbed mainland. To a lesser degree that had also been true of 1842. But now in 1848 the threat of insurgency in Ireland and the consequent build-up of troops might well be hindered by diversionary movements in the Irish-Chartist areas of Britain. Treble quotes a leading article in the *Liverpool Mercury* of 25 July to this effect; but it was also being discussed seriously in other parts of the press and within government departments.[39] What soon became clear in 1848 was that the main centres of Chartist unrest were precisely the towns and regions where the concentration of Irish communities was most evident: London, Bradford and West Yorkshire, Manchester and its surrounding towns, and Liverpool.

There is one other matter in this context that requires consideration, and it is a somewhat grey area for which firm evidence is not always available. And yet it was a problem that was important, and indeed in certain situations could be crucial. This was the attitude of the mainland English towards the Irish in their daily lives; and not only the English for there was a good deal of evidence of the hostility of many people in South Wales and in parts of the lowlands of Scotland towards the Irish immigrants. Distrust and antagonism towards ethnic minorities can be documented by correspondence in the press, by physical assaults or the larger scale riots; but much remains concealed from the historian although the contemporary significance of racial hostility was often important. There were and are times when there is a wide gap in social consciousness between ordinary people and political radicals. For example, the involvement of sections of the Jewish minority in Britain, and especially London, in the radical movements of the 1930s co-existed with quite widespread anti-Jewish feeling, not least in working-class areas such as the East End of London where there were concentrations of first generation Anglo-Jewish groups or more recent immigrants. So it was with the Irish in the 1840s; and exactly what part the anti-Irish feeling played in the formation of working-class public opinion outside the radical movements is difficult to determine. It may be assumed that among middle-class strata the close connection between Chartists and the Irish, given the identification of violence and outrage with the Irish, was an additional influence in the support by middle-class England for the forces of order which is such a remarkable feature of the year. It is also difficult to believe that the varying degrees of anti-Irish feeling among the working people did not play some part in the formation of general political attitudes during this crisis period.[40]

During the 1840s Paris had been encircled with a ring of eighteen fortresses; and on the eve of the February Revolution there was an army of 100,000 in Paris under the command of Marshall Bugeaud.[41] The army in Algeria had been provided with some excellent training in the arts and crafts of killing, and of warfare generally, and Bugeaud was highly thought of. Everyone who wrote of the critical situation that they saw was approaching in France over the Reform banquets controversy seems to have concluded that while trouble could be expected, it was nevertheless unlikely to be beyond the control of the coercive power at the disposal of Louis-Philippe and his ministers. And this continued to be said up to and including 22 February, the first day of the revolution. Normanby, as usual, was a well-informed guide to the events which were unfolding. In his long despatch of 19 February, part of which has been quoted above, Normanby set out his fears and concerns in terms that must have left Palmerston and the Whig ministers in no way surprised at what happened a few days later:

I am not disposed to attribute any fixed design even to the Republicans to engage in any conflict of physical force, but in any speculations as to the probable conduct of such a population as that of Paris one must never forget the powerful influence on the event which at any moment may be excited by the unforeseen chances of such a day, and accidental conflicts at any point provoked by a few hot heads may overturn all previous resolves . . There is no doubt in the present state of public opinion that an imposing and perfectly peaceable demonstration attended by many Peers and Deputies, almost all the mayors of Paris, the Municipal Guard and thousands of National Guards in uniform would be the death blow of the present system of government, and such a consequence is dreadful and by no means certain in its result. The great probability is that with the immense garrison ably directed and all the complicated procedures taken, in the first instance, the triumph of the Government would be complete. But on the other hand the information taken within the last few days shew them that they must count upon the decided hostility of the great majority of the National Guard. The Ministers are aware of the importance in the way of influence upon the Troops of the Line, that they should have the appearance of acting with the National Guard.[42]

Normanby went on to reveal that the government had been trying to select individuals from each legion of the National Guard to form a reliable group but that this attempt had been discovered and publicised in the newspapers, thereby encouraging a further decline in the credentials of the government. Normanby was to return several times and at length to one of the central problems of the revolution: the disaffection among the National Guard whose social composition ought to have aligned it firmly with the government against 'les blouses'; and the comparison with the attitude and conduct of the middle classes in Britain was to be constantly made.[43] In the days before 22 February, however, the public prints were more optimistic than the private communications from the British Embassy in Paris. *The Times*, whose reports were more extensive than any other of the London papers and much more so than any journal in the provinces had a leading article on Monday 21 February which accepted that the govern- ment would have to give way on the Reform banquets issue but quoted extensively from the increased military preparations that were being made.

The second edition of 23 February and the first edition of the 24th reported what happened on 22 February as 'only the routine of an ordinary *émeute*' although it agreed that round the 'terre classique' of insurrection, the Faubourg St Antoine and surrounding areas there might still be some misgivings entertained by the authorities. *The Times* blamed both sides: the government for not agreeing to the proposals for parliamentary reform and for banning the Reform banquets at the same time as these compromises would have strengthened the government's hand in checking the agitation. But it was 'absurd' to compare the present situation with that of 1830, not least because at that time there was no efficient military force at the disposal of the authorities, whereas today:

It will require a most extraordinary and unforeseen combination of circumstances before any Government supported by an army of 100,000 men under the command of Marshall Bugeaud, quartered with great skill on the outskirts of Paris, perfectly prepared for action, and backed by eighteen fortresses, will be compelled to capitulate to a popular insurrection. We suspect, however, that it will turn out that no serious popular insurrection is even probable. The people have been stirrred but not inflamed.

By the second edition of 24 February and the first edition of the 25th, *The Times* had appreciated that the French government had prepared for a riot but had 'succumbed' to a revolution. Even then, however, *The Times* was still arguing that the combination of the National Guard and the people of Paris was unlikely to prove stable: the social groups who made up the National Guard had 'tendencies and wishes' totally different from those of the 'populace'.

By the end of the first week of the Paris upheavals *The Times* and the press in general were recognising the suddenness of the change and the rapidity with which events had escalated. Of all the comments made at the time it was the rapidity with which the bloodshed before the Ministry of Foreign Affairs on the evening of 23 February had encouraged the revolution to sweep through Paris that was given most emphasis.[44] Normanby was saying the same thing to Palmerston through the diplomatic bag. Already on 24 February, and probably early in the day from the context of his general remarks, Normanby wrote of the changes taking place 'with a rapidity unexampled in any former revolution.' He added that when he closed the official bag on the previous evening it seemed as though the situation had stabilised. Count Molé had been asked to form a government, and the dismissal of the Guizot ministry had been received with enthusiasm, evidenced by the dismantling of many barricades. It was the firing in front of the Foreign Affairs ministry that led to all Paris being in uproar; and by morning 'the whole population was in the greatest state of exasperation'.[45] De Tocqueville had a corroborative passage in his *Recollections*:

As I left my bedroom the next day, the 24th February, I met the cook who had been out; the good woman was quite beside herself and poured out a sorrowful rigmarole from which I could understand nothing but that the government was having poor people massacred. I went down at once, and as soon as I had set foot in the street I could for the first time scent revolution in the air: the middle of the street was empty; the shops were not open; there were no carriages, or people walking; one heard none of the usual street vendors' cries; little frightened groups of neighbours talked by the doors in lowered voices; anxiety or anger disfigured every face. I met one of the National Guard hurrying along, rifle in hand, with an air of tragedy. I spoke to him but could learn nothing save that the government were massacring the people (to which he added that the National Guard would know how to put that right). It was always the same refrain which, of course, explained nothing to me. I knew the vices of the July government all too well, and cruelty was not among them. I consider it to have been one of the most corrupt, but least bloodthirsty, that has ever existed, and I repeat that rumour only to show how such rumours help revolutions along.[46]

There was almost unanimous agreement in Britain concerning the character of the regime of Louis-Philippe and the benefit to Europe with its demise. The *Nonconformist* of 1 March quoted with approval the comment of the *Daily News*: 'The fall of Louis-Philippe from the throne of July, and his exit from the Tuileries in a *Brougham*, is an event which, however momentous, will be welcomed with contented laughter by perhaps three-fourths of mankind'; and the *Illustrated London News* wrote in its opening article of 11 March: 'No one who has not studied attentively the history of the last ten years can conceive the utter loathing and contempt which was felt for the system of Louis Philippe, which he had identified with himself: it was corruption calculated in the coldest and most sordid spirit.' The radical *Manchester Examiner* which had at this time a circulation of about five and a half thousand, offered its readers on 26 February an interesting historical analysis, noting that although the July revolution had been accomplished by the middle and working classes coming together in 1830, since then a gap had been opening up between 'the Republican workman and the conservative bourgeois'. It was the policies of Louis-Philippe and Guizot that had brought them together again. And so it should be in England: 'The English middle classes and the working classes united in peaceful agitation against the Whigs and their Budget, which presses intolerably on all classes – what could for a moment resist such a combination as that.' It was common, right through this disturbed year, for British writers and politicians to draw political lessons from the events on the Continent of Europe, or in Ireland, and always to the advantage of Britain. On 26 February also, *The Times* produced a long leading article explaining why Britain was stable when France was in turmoil. It was, *The Times* wrote, because governments have steadily improved the institutions of the country: by extending 'immensely' the basis of parliamentary representation, by municipal reform, by the extension of free trade principles and so on.

Court circles could not be expected to share the general enthusiasm for the downfall of the French monarchy. There were impassioned letters from various European dynasties to Victoria in the early days of the revolution, and both the Queen and Prince Albert inevitably, for family as well as other reasons, had much sympathy for the dispossessed and those who feared a similar fate.[47] The particular constitutional position of the monarchy in Britain, however, allowed them little opportunity to provide any serious help. It was possible for the Queen to object to phrases such as 'most cordial friendship' in a draft despatch to the Provisional government in Paris. It struck the Queen, she wrote, 'as rather too strong'. There are two letters in the published correspondence of Victoria which established the constitutional position precisely. The first was from Lord John Russell to the Queen, dated 29 February 1848:

Lord John Russell presents his humble duty to your Majesty, and has the honour to transmit a short note from Lord Normanby, which is very satisfactory.

Lord John Russell declared last night that your Majesty would not interfere in the internal affairs of France. But in repeating this declaration, in answer to Mr. Cobden, he added that the sacred duties of hospitality would be, as in all times, performed towards persons of all opinions. Both declarations were generally cheered. In extending this hospitality to members of the Royal Family of France, it is only to be observed that no encouragement should be given by your Majesty to any notion that your Majesty would assist them to recover the Crown. In this light it is desirable that no *Prince* of the House of Orleans should inhabit one of your Majesty's palaces in or near London.

The day following, on 1 March, Victoria wrote to her uncle, the King of the Belgians who had married a daughter of Louis-Philippe; and her letter is interesting for the clear perception she had of the diplomatic course that the British government – any British government of this time – would pursue without hesitation. After a few family details, she continued:

We do everything we can for the poor dear Family, who are indeed most dreadfully to be pitied; but you will naturally understand that we cannot *make cause commune* with them, and cannot take a hostile position opposite to the new state of things in France; we leave them alone, but if a Government which has the approbation of the country be formed, we shall feel it necessary to recognise it, in order to pin them down to maintain peace and the existing Treaties, which is of the greatest importance. It will not be pleasant for us to do this, but the public good and the peace of Europe go before one's feelings. God knows what *one feels* towards the French.[48]

The news from France dominated public discussion in Britain; in Ireland enthusiasm was unbounded. All the nationalist papers emphasised the harmony which was reported between the Provisional government and the people of Paris. The *Freeman's Journal*, less fiery than the *Nation*, ended a long editorial on Monday 28 February with the phrases: 'Honour to the Brave Citizenry of Paris. Success to the Cause of the People'; and the next day it continued its exultation of the Paris events and exhorted the Irish to be up and doing. As Russell wrote to Clarendon on the last day of February: 'I feel very anxious for Ireland and for you'.[49] But while it was true that even conservatives among the Repealers began to talk in more lively and positive terms, and there was undoubtedly a great surge of hope at the continuing news from France, the movement in Ireland began from a very low point of disunity and low morale. A Dublin correspondent of *The Times* wrote on 29 February that because of the divisions in the movement there were less grounds for apprehension than there would have been three years earlier.

In Britain the response of the radical working-class movement was naturally also one of elation and enthusiasm.[50] On the first day of the year the *Northern Star*, in an editorial presumably written by Harney, had predicted the continued growth of the Reform banquet movement: 'The truth is, that these Reform banquets are 'the beginning of the end', and that end will be the destruction of Louis Philippe's throne and something more'; and the issue of the 26 February, the first after the revolution had begun, carried four columns of news from Paris with an enthusiastic editorial:

Whatever may be the results of this conflict – forthwith or remote – for France, the immediate effect upon Europe will be immense. Germany will be roused to action, and Italy will at once burst her Austrian bonds.
'For us, too, the tocsin sounds'
If Englishmen are not the most despicable of slaves they will at once set about the work – peacefully and legally – of struggling for their Charter.

In the immediate aftermath of the Paris revolution an address to the people of Paris was adopted by the executive committee of the National Charter Association, the Fraternal Democrats and the Metropolitan Delegates Committee, and wildly acclaimed at a large public meeting in London at which the three delegates elected to take the address to Paris were given a tumultuous send-off. Nearly half a century later, in 1894 George Julian Harney recalled these days in a letter to Engels:

The *old time!* and this is the 23rd February, and tomorrow is the 24th – when seeing the *news* placarded at Charing Cross, I ran like a lunatic and pulled the bell at Schappers like a bedlamite; at some corner, on my way, knocking over an old woman's apple-basket (or it may have been oranges!) I was going too quick to hear her gentle cursing.[51]

It was, no doubt, an old man's memory that allowed him to write 'gentle cursing'; but contemporary accounts from all over the country, reported in the *Northern Star*, testified to the excitement and new-found vigour which the news from France imparted to the radical movement in Britain.

3

MARCH

A France in revolutionary turmoil, with the monarchy no longer in power and a Provisional government already in existence, evoked among the propertied classes in Europe frightening images of the Jacobin past. The left-wing members of the Provisional government – Ledru Rollin especially – had long been critical of Louis-Philippe's pacifism; and the presence in Paris of many thousands of political emigrés consumed with nationalist ambitions – the Poles were only the most prominent of many – all helped to conjure up the fears of a militant and expansionist Jacobinism. The diplomatic activity in Europe in the days following the abdication of the monarchy in France was intense, with Britain at its centre. The central role of Britain was recognised from the outset by Lamartine who had taken the Foreign Affairs portfolio.[1] As interpreted by Palmerston, there were two separate but related problems for Britain; the first was the necessity of restraining France in the general interests of Europe from moving beyond her present boundaries; and this became increasingly important as the revolutionary impulses spread outwards from Paris to Germany, central Europe and Italy. Palmerston was always ready to encourage liberal-type constitutional reforms of the conservative English kind upon foreign autocratic regimes, but the events of 1848, it was very soon clear, were going far beyond the acceptable evolution of political rights. The second and related problem for Whitehall was their perennial security burden: Ireland, and the consequences of the French upheavals upon Irish opinion and Irish actions. There was now a new sense of urgency in the correspondence between Clarendon and Russell. What is notable in 1848 is the care and sympathy shown by Russell in his contacts with Clarendon whom he always appreciated had a heavy responsibility. On 29 February – in the first of two letters on this day – Russell wrote to Clarendon:

I feel very anxious for Ireland and for you. It is therefore with great satisfaction I tell you that Normanby has had a visit from a person in the confidence of the ruling power in France to apprise him that the Government meant peace and would not disturb the territorial arrangements of Europe. He added that even if the Belgians wanted to unite themselves to France, they would not accept the offer . . .

But to Ireland – you alone can judge when it is proper to repress and when to let the rein loose – as an old Athenian said too strong a use of the curb, or leaving the reins on the horse's necks are both faults – and to judge between them is a matter of the nicest and this must exact judgement on the spot. I can only give you general maxims and support you here.[2]

Russell in the days ahead continued in this same vein, encouraging Clarendon and always listening to him with understanding and sympathy. He expressed his own doubts quite freely – it is one of the features of this correspondence – and through March and April always related what was happening in France to events, actual or potential, in Ireland. He also flattered Clarendon – presumably he mostly meant what he wrote – as when he reported to Clarendon that he frequently showed the letters from Dublin Castle to the Queen and Prince Albert: 'as they contain news so just and so well expressed'. In this particular letter of 1 March, Russell expressed the fear that 'some attempt may be made in Dublin to emulate the barricades of Paris . . . The Irish are not the French but they have a great knack of imitation. Blakeney [the Commander in Chief] must keep a good garrison at Dublin.'[3]

Russell was probably serious about the insurrectionary possibilities of Dublin, and elsewhere, but he kept cool and unexcited. The Duke of Wellington was in no doubt. The Duke, in these last years of his life, tended towards a highly coloured view of the risks confronting the realm – as he had done in the imagined French invasion affair – and his colleagues, in their own inner counsels, never took him too seriously, although his immense reputation was of great public support to the Whig government. On 2 March Wellington sent a memorandum to the Commander-in-Chief in Dublin. Wellington's covering letter began:

I was informed yesterday by good authority that the Irish Revolutionary or Repeal leaders had sent over to Paris persons to enquire respecting the mode of constructing the Barricades in the streets which have been used there and have been considered so formidable.[4]

To this letter was attached a detailed memorandum on the problems of troops in a large city confronted with barricades. There was a close account of how they were constructed, often from an overturned carriage, and a warning that on the first intimation of trouble all heavy carriage traffic should be stopped immediately. If barricades were erected they were to be fired on with howitzers, with troops in position in the rear and on the flanks to trap those trying to escape; and above all Wellington emphasised how important it was to keep communications open. In Dublin both sides of the Liffey must be kept under control for the passage of troops; and further all houses and buildings that overlooked approaches or important centres such as the Castle must be at once occupied. Naturally, the memorandum concluded, the final decisions in all these matters must rest with the Viceroy, but military preparations should be put in hand immediately.

Wellington was to repeat all these points in a long letter to the Marquis of Anglesey on 17 June when the situation in Ireland looked especially threatening;[5] and it is clear from the correspondence of senior ministers that his general ideas had been well taken. Sir George Grey wrote to Clarendon on 2 April, in a letter which mainly reported the measures being taken in London to counter the forthcoming Chartist demonstration on Kennington Common, but to which Grey added: 'I hope your artillery is in good order. It is very important to do without the soldiers but if it is necessary to use them the artillery is the most formidable and efficient arm.'[6]

Normanby was greatly helped from the beginning of the establishment of the Provisional government by his excellent personal relations with Lamartine. On his side Lamartine displayed the same friendly approach, and constantly emphasised – sometimes rather pathetically – the crucial need for good relations with Britain. Normanby took much trouble to emphasise to Palmerston and his colleagues how important a force for stability Lamartine represented. In a despatch of 27 February Normanby noted that Lamartine had taken the side of the tri-colour as against the Red flag; that he (Normanby) had been visited by 'many persons of eminence in all the different parties in France' who all agreed to rally round the new government and 'trust to the efforts to moderate the popular feeling and re-establish order and confidence'. Normanby was adamant that there could be no attempt to revive the monarchical principle, and he referred more than once to his despatch of 30 July 1847 which had severly criticised the 'blindness' of the King and his government.[7] At the same time Normanby was consistently hard-headed in his estimate of the new French government, and he was not in favour of offering any concessions without reciprocal treatment. Thus when the American ambassador informed him that his government was going to recognise the Provisional government, Normanby argued very strongly against the proposal but made it clear when reporting to Palmerston that he was certain recognition would be accorded.[8] Inevitably in these early critical days there was close agreement between Palmerston and Normanby. They had constant and regular communication, Normanby on occasion writing three official letters a day. The despatch of 27 February quoted above was sent by special arrangements in order to reach Palmerston before any discussion the next day in the House of Commons. The French government, because railway services were not yet normal, provided a special escort for the British courier.

In the House of Commons on 28 February Russell was asked by Hume what the government's intentions were towards France, and Russell replied briefly:

I can assure the House (indeed I should hardly have thought it necessary to make the declaration) that we have no intention whatever to interfere with the form of government which the French nation may choose to adopt, or in any way to meddle with the internal affairs of that country.[9]

Russell and his colleagues were in agreement with Normanby that there was no question of any return to monarchical rule; and in Paris Normanby was equally emphatic about the necessity of staying in Paris. He made this latter point to the many English visitors to the Embassy. When he received instructions from London to relinquish his functions as ambassador – since he had been accredited to Louis-Philippe and the British government had not recognised the Provisional government – he explained the matter with great sympathy to Lamartine; and reported a frank, off-the-record discussion in a despatch to Palmerston marked 'Private and Confidential'. Lamartine desperately wanted recognition, and when he raised the question again on 2 March Normanby reiterated the British position: that his government would not at this stage offer formal recognition to any government called 'Provisional' but that they would support all efforts to maintain order and that short of recognition the British government wished for the most friendly relations.[10]

The first international question of serious concern was the publication of a major policy statement on foreign affairs by the Provisional government. Almost as soon as he had taken the Foreign Affairs portfolio Lamartine had circulated a short note to the foreign embassies in Paris, emphasising his government's wish to maintain 'harmonious relations' with all countries.[11] There was great pressure upon Lamartine to renounce what the radicals considered the pacific foreign policy of Louis-Philippe and his government, and a long and detailed statement was approved by the Council of the Provisional government on 2 March and published in Le Moniteur on 5 March. The general principles embodied in the document had already been communicated to Normanby and reported by him to London.[12] The most important part of the statement was prefaced by an insistence upon the central importance of peace for the new French Republic and this was followed by a denunciation of the treaties imposed upon France after Napoleon's defeat: 'The treaties of 1815 no longer exist as law in the eyes of the French Republic; nevertheless, the territorial delineations of these treaties are a fact which she does recognise as a basis and as a point of departure in her relations with other nations.' The manifesto went on to dissociate itself from the July monarchy's attitude over the Spanish marriages question; it supported the nationalist aspirations of the Italian peninsula; it referred to Switzerland as 'our faithful ally since the time of Francis I'; and it gave general support to all 'oppressed nationalities in Europe and elsewhere'. The statement was an intelligent and diplomatic outline of a new foreign policy for the Republic, based upon an Anglo-French *entente*, and a hoped-for relationship with emerging liberal states. Inevitably, given the political background of a tumultuous Paris, the statement was drafted with due regard to the susceptibilities of public opinion; and a denunciation of the 1815 treaties was obligatory for any Republican government. Clarendon wrote to Grey that 'years ago Mignet told me that the object nearest to every Frenchman's heart was to *déchirer les Traités de 1815* and to *arrondir le Territoire* and that Europe would see the determination acted on the first opportunity'.[13]

Palmerston understood these matters. On 9 March he wrote a despatch to Clarendon in which he commented that the manifesto on foreign policy would be read in quite different ways by different governments, and that it represented 'a piece of patchwork' put together by the various factions within the Provisional government. He himself was in complete accord with the arguments for general support of Lamartine which Normanby had been sending, and he summed up: 'I should say that if you were to put the whole of it into a crucible, and evaporate the gaseous parts, and scum off the dross, you would find the regulus to be peace and good-fellowship with other governments.'[14] Before this letter was written there had been the curious incident of the letter from Lamartine to the Duke of Wellington. On 3 March Wellington wrote to Russell informing him of the receipt of a letter which underlined Lamartine's respect for Britain and his desire to develop good relations with Britain:

M. de Lamartine considère la constitution de l'Angleterre comme le "ne plus ultra" des républiques liberales, ayant un magistrat souverain héréditaire pour chef. Le Governement Provisoire veut amener la France au même état de liberalisme.

and the Duke, after consultation and agreement with Russell, had replied in diplomatic terms. Russell, in the last letter of this instructive affair in terms of what it revealed about Lamartine, wrote in good Whig style to Palmerston that he saw 'no course open to us but to take M. Lamartine's professions in the most pacific sense without relying too much on his power of making good his meaning'.[15]

The reaction in Paris to the foreign policy statement varied sharply according to the political positions involved. The extreme Right thought it a provocation; the extreme Left much too moderate. The European powers exhibited similar variations but within a conservative spectrum. The representatives of the Austrian government in Paris and London, together with the Chevalier Bunsen in London, were notably hostile; and Victoria, prompted no doubt by family ties as well as by the Prince Consort, was similarly incensed. Indeed, throughout these early critical months of 1848 Victoria was quite often wrong in her understanding of what was happening

in Europe, and markedly obtuse in her lack of appreciation of what
Palmerston was attempting. International peace was the first requisite for
the ultimate restoration of the forces of order, and it was the self-willed
obstinacy of Victoria and Albert that often prevented them from analysing
the situation in terms that were not wholly white and black. Normanby
naturally also came in for their disapprobation and their hostility to him was
continuous. Some of the gossip against Normanby and the Russell
government in general that circulated in court circles came from within his
own family. Lady Normanby liked to chatter in her correspondence, and
Normanby's brother, General Phipps, was equerry to the Prince Consort;
and these two were the sources of much tittle-tattle against Palmerston and
government policy.[16]

Throughout the weeks of March and April up to the elections at the end of
April Normanby continued to exercise a restraining influence upon the
foreign policy of the Provisional government. It was largely a matter of
giving sustained support to Lamartine and the majority of moderates in the
French government in opposition to their own radicals, both inside the
governing circles and especially those outside in the Clubs. Normanby's
support was firm, but by no means automatic; there was much plain speaking
and at times Normanby behaved in arrogant fashion. On his side Lamartine
fully appreciated from the beginning the importance of the British
connection. He knew that no serious coalition against France could succeed
without English assistance and English gold.[17] Three months later, on 25
June, during the days of the uprising when Lamartine was being subjected to
what Normanby described as 'unmerited obloquy', Normanby wrote in a
despatch to the Foreign Office in London:

I cannot but feel that the cause of civilisation will always owe him a debt of gratitude
for the energetic manner in which he then opposed himself to any designs of armed
propagandism . . . it will always be a consolation to me that by promptly and
faithfully interpreting the intentions of H. M. Government I was the first to fix him in
that position . . . Whilst he remained at the Foreign Office, when I saw him almost
every day, I found him always reasonable in conversation, although not always very
punctual in acting up to his professions.[18]

Lamartine appreciated that England was the only nation in Europe with
whom a liberal, republican France could expect to have good working
relations; the problem was whether France, in spite of the efforts of
Lamartine and those who thought like him, would remain liberal. Certainly
the pressures from London, communicated through Normanby, were
emphatically not limited to diplomatic affairs, important though these were.
As early as 3 March, in a letter marked 'Most Confidential' Normanby
conveyed to Palmerston a summary of a long discussion with Lamartine in

which he had expressed the disquiet being felt in England at the possible social consequences of the revolution. The report as a whole is an interesting indication of the Whig understanding of the nature and character of bourgeois society:

He must be aware that in a country like England its complicated interests were all bound together by the security derived from the protection of capital and its free employment, and therefore there were some of the former doctrines of one of his present colleagues, Louis Blanc, which some were afraid appeared likely to be put into practice.

Lamartine replied that he too regretted Louis Blanc but that in the government, Blanc 'was now less injurious than he would be elsewhere'. Lamartine had refused to lend his support to 'nonsense' such as the Organisation du Travail and thought that the Commission sitting at the Luxembourg 'was a useful safety valve to allow the effervescence on this subject to escape.[19]

There were a number of matters on which Normanby took a very strong line. Of those immediately affecting British domestic politics the reactions to the delegations of Chartists and the Irish to the Provisional government were of especial interest. The Provisional government was constantly receiving congratulatory addresses from nationalist and radical groups all over Europe. The Chartist delegation of Harney, Ernest Jones and Philip McGrath were received by Ledru Rollin, Garnier Pagès and Armand Marrast. Garnier Pagès made a somewhat incautious speech which suggested that the English government did not possess the complete confidence of the British people. Normanby made an immediate protest when these words were published, and Lamartine replied with his usual apology for the indiscretions of his colleagues; and there the matter ended: a passing incident.[20] The reception of the Irish was a very different matter. On 17 March – St Patrick's day – an Irish delegation from among those who lived in Paris presented themselves at the Hotel de Ville and were received by Lamartine. In a speech which was reported in *Le Moniteur* the next day he referred to Irelands's 'religious' and 'soon-hoped-for constitutional independence'. The published report further included the information that the Irish delegation had given the Provisional government an Irish flag, to be flown by 'the side of their brothers'. Immediately on reading the report Normanby sought an interview with Lamartine. The latter was at a Council meeting but Normanby insisted that he come out for an interview. Normanby, so he reported to Palmerston, told Lamartine that he was much distressed to have to make 'a serious complaint' in the way that the Irish had been received, and that he was especially concerned with the gift of the Irish flag, which could only be a 'rebel flag'. Lamartine denied that there was any flag but Normanby insisted upon a public contradiction – 'such a statement [about flying the Irish flag] was likely to cause the worst impression on England, and if repeated, I would not answer for its effect upon the relations between the two countries'. Lamartine went back into the Council, drafted a paragraph to which Normanby said he did not wish to make any verbal criticism, although in his letter to Palmerston he added that he thought it could have gone further in its explanation.[21] On 22 March Palmerston replied to Normanby instructing him to make the British government's position quite clear to Lamartine; that the United Kingdom had refrained from interfering with the internal affairs of France, and that 'HMG trusts that, in return, the French government will abstain from interfering or meddling in any manner whatever with the internal affairs of the United Kingdom.'[22]

This political sensitivity towards the Irish was further exhibited at the end of March when a delegation from Ireland, led by Smith O'Brien, arrived in Paris, also to deliver a congratulatory address to the Provisional government. By this time the political situation in both Britain and Ireland was beginning to show menacing features and the spread of the revolution in other parts of Europe all contributed to a situation that daily seemed to be becoming more tense. As soon as the government in London learned of the proposed visit by the Irish, diplomatic initiatives were begun by Normanby. From 23 March Normanby was emphasising in his daily discussions with Lamartine the principle of non-intervention in the affairs of other nations and relating especially to the forthcoming visit of the Irish. The matter of the flag was a particularly sensitive matter. The discussion between Lamartine and Normanby on 31 March was reported in a despatch to Palmerston which Normanby first read over to Lamartine who agreed it faithfully represented his position.[23] Lamartine saw Smith O'Brien privately before the official meeting and made it clear to him that the Irish could expect no help or encouragement from the French government. The *Moniteur* of 4 April gave the full text of the address of the Irish deputation and of Lamartine's reply, which was firmly discouraging. Lamartine made the general point that there could be no interference in the affairs of people with whom there was no blood relationship, and that France was at peace with Great Britain 'as a whole' and not with individual parts of the kingdom.[24] The Irish were distinctly discouraged and it was widely recognised, not least in the British press, that Lamartine had inflicted a serious set-back upon the Irish nationalists. Lamartine was widely abused in the radical clubs of Paris who had given an enthusiastic welcome to members of the Irish delegation, most of whom had already been charged with sedition and were returning to face their trial in Dublin. It was at the interview with Lamartine that Smith O'Brien gave such offence to Normanby with his reference to the Irish contribution to the victory at Fontenoy. But Normanby's anger was

submerged beneath a general satisfaction at Lamartine's vigorous rebuff to
the Irish radicals. Palmerston, after receiving a copy of Lamartine's reply,
wrote to Normanby asking him to convey the British government's thanks
for 'his handsome and friendly conduct about the Irish deputation'.[25]
Lamartine was to find the problems of other national groups not quite so
easy to deal with as those of the Irish. The dampening effect was widely
remarked upon in Ireland as well as in the rest of Britain, and henceforth
there was much less attention paid to France in the speeches of Mitchel and
the other Irish nationalist leaders.[26]

The first manifestation of the French spirit came, however, not from Ireland
but from within Britain. On Monday 6 March, there occurred rioting in
Glasgow and London; and immediately, and not unreasonably, the
connection was made with the revolutionary events in Europe. In London it
all began with a curious late aftermath of the agitation against the income
tax. The proposed increase had been withdrawn at the end of February –
there could be no encouragement to the middle classes to waver in their
support for the established order of things, even though no one suggested
that a rise in income tax was a sufficient cause for recourse to the barricades
– but there was still among many the firm conviction that income tax as
such was an unequal burden upon the commercial and industrial classes;
and a protest meeting in Trafalgar Square had been called by Charles
Cochrane, a middle-class politician with minor pretensions to radical
opinions. The meeting was banned by the Police Commissioners and
cancelled by Cochrane; but although he placarded the area with notices of
the ban 'the notice came too late', reported *The Times* on the next day (7
March) 'and was treated with a good deal of indignation'. By noon on the
Monday eight to ten thousand people were in the Square, and at 1 p.m. G. W.
M. Reynolds – a newcomer to the Chartist movement[27] – took the chair. His
speech said much about the glorious French Republic, the tyrannical Louis-
Philippe and the great Parisian people. Other speakers followed; the crowd
gave three cheers for the brave Parisians and the Peoples Charter. When the
meeting finished Reynolds and some groups in the crowd went along to his
house in Wellington Street where he again spoke; but meanwhile, fighting
had broken out in the Square and it continued intermittently, but on quite a
large scale, until it was dark. The police were withdrawn after 6 p.m. in the
hope that things would quieten down; but crowds remained in the Square
and by 8 p.m. their numbers were increasing rapidly. Just before 9 p.m. a
small group of about 200 rushed off towards the Mall, moved into St James
Park and made for Buckingham Palace. The guard was turned out; some
lamps and shop windows were broken, and a couple of bakers' shops looted.
By midnight the Square was more or less empty and the streets around were
quiet.[28]

It is clear, from later press comments and from correspondence within government departments, that the police were taken by surprise and that their techniques of crowd control proved quite inadequate. There was further rioting on the following night and only on Wednesday did the police achieve full control. It was a lesson they quickly learned, or perhaps relearned would be more accurate, since by 1848 the metropolitan police had considerable experience in controlling riots and unruly groups. The mistakes of this first demonstration in March were quickly appreciated. The urgency was borne upon them not just because of the French events, although they were in everyone's mind, but also because news had reached London by the evening of Monday that there was also serious rioting in Glasgow: more serious, it turned out, than in London. Most of the reports from Glasgow agreed that the greater number of those involved were unemployed. There had been meetings of the unemployed for several previous days, and McDouall, the Chartist leader, had been active in addressing groups.[29] On the Monday the 'grand break-out took place'. Gunsmiths and bakers' shops were looted; the police were ineffective; the rioters armed themselves with torn-up iron railings and other mostly home-made weapons, and a barricade was thrown up at one point. The cavalry, infantry and pensioners were called out, and at 5 p.m. the Riot Act was read. In the shooting which followed there were a number of casualties including one killed and two who died later from wounds. *The Times* reporter on the 8 March wrote that, 'The alarm flew over the city like wildfire, and coupled with the late events in Paris, gave rise to a general dread of some political disturbance.'[30]

By Thursday of that week the press round the country were in reassuring mood. A leading article from *The Times* began: 'We beg to assure our neighbours on the banks of the Seine, that they need not attach overmuch importance to any rumours of an approaching revolution which may happen to reach them from the British metropolis', and the *Scotsman* (which was published twice weekly) approached the matter in ways that were typical of much of the press throughout this year, emphasising the non-participation of the great mass of the working people in both cities and the large number of petty thieves in the crowds. The *Scotsman* continued with an explanation why Britain would be free from revolution, again a constant theme of press commentary:

Britain, besides possessing a franchise ten times wider than that of France, has free and popular municipalities and the most perfect liberty of the press and of public speech to be found in any Kingdom of the world. The liberty of Great Britain contrasts favourably even with that of the United States.[31] The Revolution in France arose out of the people not being even allowed to *ask* for far less than we already possess.[32]

As soon as these troubles in London and Glasgow became known, the Home Office was immediately in correspondence with the metropolitan police, and with local authorities in Scotland. Dragoons and infantry were sent from

Edinburgh (with 250 Enrolled Pensioners taking their place in Edinburgh Castle); a special train left Stirling on Tuesday morning with 300 soldiers for Glasgow; and large numbers of special constables were sworn in. There were about 130 arrests in Glasgow; and of the local disturbances elsewhere Edinburgh was the most serious, with rioting for two nights. There was minor trouble outside a workhouse in Manchester, and the operatives of Oldham were reported to be 'in an excited condition'.

This first week of trouble in Britain, on a minor scale compared with what was occurring on the Continent where rioting in Berlin was to be the prelude to a general escalation of events in central Europe,[33] was nevertheless taken seriously by the British authorities. They felt themselves to be living on the edge of a social volcano. News from France still filled the press and the violent speeches of the Irish, who were responding to developments in France, were being widely reported. There were several policy reactions to the week's upheavals. The first was the way in which the Home Office took control of all the security arrangements for the whole country. This centralisation of power in the political hands of the Home Secretary was of crucial importance in the coming months. It was not, of course, a new departure but a practice which went back decades. What was different in 1848, even compared with 1842, was the efficiency with which the component parts of the system now operated. It was not just that there was now a Home Secretary who was immensely competent and who never faltered under strain – his predecessor Sir James Graham had also been efficient – but that the whole network of arrangements was more effective than ever before. This was true especially of the professional police. The second reaction was the speedy mobilisation of the Enrolled Pensioners and above all of the special constables, the response of the latter being more wholehearted than at any previous time. And the third was the immensely successful campaign by the government and the leading newspapers and journals to justify what was being done in terms of the liberties and freedoms already achieved by the British people; and except in Ireland the arguments were to prove remarkably effective and convincing. Above all they provided the legitimation for all those who took the side of the forces of order.

A week after the Trafalgar Square meeting a further Chartist demonstration was convened by Reynolds on Kennington Common, south of the river. This was on 13 March. Although neither the Metropolitan Delegate Committee nor the Chartist executive were responsible for calling this demonstration, leading Chartists, including Philip McGrath and Ernest Jones, were present. The Home Office had been fully alerted to the proposed meeting and extensive preparations were made that constituted an early rehearsal for the April Kennington Common meeting. S. M. Phillips, Under-Secretary of State, had already written to the Clerk of the Westminster

Paving Commissioners following the Trafalgar Square troubles requesting that 'during the present disturbances' all laying of broken granite should cease; and the reply, on the following day, acceded to the request adding that all loose chippings had been covered. The metropolitan police issued a poster dated 11 March urging 'all well-disposed persons' not to attend the forthcoming meeting, and stating that moving in procession at any 'unseasonable' hour would be prohibited. A private order to the police, published in *The Times* on 13 March, specified what was meant by 'unseasonable'. The meeting, so long as it was peaceful, was not to be interfered with, and there was to be no offensive language by the police. The caution in the public notice against numerous bodies of persons moving about was not to be acted on until after dark.

On the day of the meeting 4,000 police were in attendance, dispersed first in groups of fifty or more at various places round or near the Common. The bridges across the Thames were guarded by several hundred regular police, and according to one edition of *The Times* there were twenty thousand special constables: a total that was certainly much too high. The police courts were open from 9 a.m. with magistrates in attendance for the purpose of swearing in special constables, and other precautions included instructions to gunsmiths to unscrew the barrels of all firearms in their stock; all public offices, including the Bank of England and Buckingham Palace had extra guards; and the military were posted, out of sight, around the approaches to the Common.

At the Kennington Common meeting Ernest Jones announced the decision of the London Chartists to accompany the presentation of the Third Petition with a procession of 200,000. If the rest of the country followed the London example they would soon have the Charter. The meeting was peaceful and dispersed in an orderly fashion, except for a group of about four to five hundred who broke away, and a number of shops were looted: events which received a great deal of publicity throughout the country.[34] There were demonstrations this day in other places: in Liverpool, Manchester and Aberdeen. A Sheffield meeting of some twelve to fifteen thousand congratulated the French, and one at Salford specifically disclaimed Chartist responsibility for window breaking. *The Times* report of this Salford meeting noted 'two important facts . . . that the agitation for the Charter is to be renewed under the stimulus of recent events in France, and that the breach which has so long existed between the English Chartists and Irish Repealers is to be healed'.[35]

There was a long report in *The Times* of 16 March of a large indoor meeting in Birmingham, convened by the Chartists to show their sympathy with the French Republic. The local authorities took what were now becoming standard precautions. The police were in full strength, artillery was stationed at Coleshill, and sixty men were sent from Weedon to augment the infantry in the area. The most interesting speech of the evening came from the middle-class reformer, Joseph Sturge, who had recently returned from Paris. He had gone to represent the Peace Societies of England and had been granted an interview with Lamartine. In a rather striking statement for which it is difficult to find anything comparable later in the year – when liberal attitudes had hardened against working-class 'violence' – Sturge said he thoroughly approved of 'the soldiers who refused to fight against their quiet and peaceable fellow citizens. He hoped the time was coming when soldiers would not fire upon people who demanded their rights.'

At this time, however, it was Ireland which seemed more potentially dangerous. St Patrick's Day (17 March) was approaching and it was known that there would be demonstrations in Dublin, and in the Irish areas in Britain. There was considerable apprehension in Dublin, the garrison was reinforced, and all the main buildings were occupied by troops in the early hours of the morning of the 17th. On the same day, *The Times* published long extracts from the Dublin papers which had given details of the military preparation, and it reprinted a general order of 29 March 1835 concerning the decision to open fire by the military. Hitherto troops had often fired over the heads of rioters and bystanders had sometimes been injured or killed. Henceforth it was to be made clear that if troops were ordered to open fire 'their fire will be effective'.

On the 16th Sir George Grey had written to Clarendon saying that there was good reason to hope that all would pass over quietly. The authorities were on the alert 'but there is a bad spirit abroad, and if it is met with any encouragement it will break out. On the other hand there is a strong loyal feeling which would show itself to a very great extent if any real danger was apprehended.'[36] The day was, however, peaceful everywhere. The forces of order in Dublin were much assisted by wet and stormy weather. In Liverpool between two and three thousand special constables were mustered. Manchester had a particularly quiet day partly because the Catholic priesthood had issued a special proclamation warning against participation in illegal or immoral acts. At the Chartist meeting Feargus O'Connor was joined on the platform by T. F. Meagher and other Confederate leaders, indicating the new unity of purpose between the English and Irish radicals. It was the Paris revolution, Meagher said, which had made him a democrat.

Clarendon's appreciation of the situation had been sound. He had written to Grey on the 16th that he felt the Irish leaders were going to be cautious, among other reasons because they were fully aware of all the preparations which had been made. Clarendon, who was in most respects a hard-liner, added that he himself would have been happy to have a confrontation 'that we might have done with it one way or another', but he was always conscious of the complexities of the situation and that it 'would not be done with' in a single struggle. He further told Grey that on the day not a soldier would be visible and that he had warned Blakeney 'to take care that the usual uproariousness of St Patrick's day is not mistaken for tumult'.[37] Clarendon had problems on both sides of the nationalist and loyalist grouping. The Lord Mayor of Dublin, Clarendon informed Russell, 'is an idiot and a tool in the hands of designing men' and he had been swearing in special constables without regard to their social position or religion, and the radical leaders were calling them a civic guard. 'Here is a new element of mischief.' At the same time 'I have as almost as much trouble in dealing with exuberant loyalty as with rampant disaffection';[38] and on the next day, in a letter to Sir George Grey, he explained what this meant: 'By holding up a finger the whole of the old Orange spirit and Yeomanry might be revived and in action before the end of the month. To check and not offend these hyper-loyal gentlemen requires rather nice steering.'[39] When St Patrick's Day was over Clarendon reported that the towns outside Dublin had been quiet, and also the rural areas, and that the Catholic clergy everywhere had preached peace; and he summed up for Grey: 'Sedition may be kept under – if we quarrel with France nothing can prevent its breaking out into rebellion and active support of an invading army.'[40] It was these considerations that provided the background to the anxieties which Dublin Castle and Whitehall showed over the Irish delegation to Paris at the end of the month. Meanwhile, Clarendon continued his usual social life. The evening before St Patrick's Day, an anxious affair, was also a sober one: only eight to dinner and eight bottles drunk, fewer than what appears to have been a special allocation to the kitchen staff. But on the evening of St Patrick's Day, the traditional Viceroy's ball saw dinner first with eleven at table and fifteen bottles drunk, and nearly one thousand at the ball itself.

Ireland always remained more vividly in the minds of the English as a potential insurrectionary centre than their own country, although the presence of so many Irish, in the Northwest especially, and the political junction of Confederates and Chartists, were increasingly noted. On 13 March Russell had suggested to Clarendon that it would be helpful if he wrote an official memorandum to the Home Secretary on the state of Ireland, and his proposals for the future. 'I suggest this ', Russell continued, 'as I think in such invidious circumstances some statement should be placed on record, and you ought not to be left with individual responsibility'.[41] Clarendon sent the memorandum Russell had asked for to Sir George Grey, as constitutional propriety required.[42] It was dated 27 March and it began with a statement of the endemic character of political agitation in Ireland and the change which had taken place since the death of Daniel O'Connell.

Peaceful campaigning was now less favoured and the Young Ireland party had become much more influential. General distress had encouraged ideas of change, and then there had come the Paris revolution:

Such was the condition of parties – such the temper of the public mind – in a country which for years had been the scene of continued political agitation in favour of an independent legislature and 'nationality' as it was termed – when the grave events of the recent French revolution occurred, and the power of a people was so impressively displayed by its rapid and easy triumph over old constituted authority. These events gave a sudden shock to public feeling in Ireland. At once the wildest dreams of every political agitator appeared to be realised; and that change which had long been promised to the masses of the people, was looked upon by all as on the eve of being accomplished.

Clarendon went on to comment that the Confederation and all classes of Young Ireland felt that the events in France were a vindication of their opinions; that Cork, after Dublin, was the most solid base for Young Ireland; that the rural areas were by no means convinced and that in the most distressed districts of the Southwest the people were naturally of 'a peaceful character'. Only in the Home counties such as Meath did sympathy for extreme radical opinions exist, although there could be no doubt that a war with France, or active sympathy from France, would encourage disturbances. He further noted that all news of rioting and upheavals in Britain were always magnified in the public press and in daily conversation. While Clarendon was happy to report the signs of loyalist support – in the shape of addresses and petitions – he ended by emphasising the critical economic situation and the need for constant vigilance; and he asked first for an increased military presence and then made a strong case for Treasury assistance for Public Works.[43]

This memorandum, and the letters Clarendon also wrote in the closing days of March, were circulated to members of the Cabinet. Russell sent his own comments in a statement dated 30 March. It began: 'The increasing danger of an outbreak in Ireland, and the prospect of the misery it would occasion' made it necessary to review the security measures available or required. The suspension of habeas corpus for a year was a serious possibility, and Russell also included his favourite scheme of subsidising the Irish priesthood.[44] Russell had often expressed his views on this matter. Earlier in 1848 he had written to Clarendon: 'My object has always been to raise the Roman Catholic clergy. Anything that can be devised that will give them rank, power and *responsibility* I should be glad to see.'[45]

The response of other leading members of the Cabinet brought predictable replies. There was agreement about the need for increased military forces; and these the Home Secretary arranged. But Grey himself was not in favour of more drastic constitutional changes at this particular time. In a private letter to Clarendon on 3 April he wrote that he thought it would be very impolitic to suspend habeas corpus. It should only be done with the greatest amount of support from public opinion that can be mobilised, and that would come about 'by letting these gentlemen put themselves completely in the wrong, and giving them no pretext for exciting sympathy with their cause'. He went on to say that he expected the reply to the Irish from the Provisional government in Paris would be discouraging, and that 'if we get quietly over the 10th – of which I have every hope' that, too, would exert a good effect. What Grey was most concerned about was the fear that the suspension of habeas corpus would provoke an insurrectionary outburst in Ireland, and that the British government would inevitably bear much of the opprobrium. But Grey was always positive: he suggested as a first step that with certain qualifications the Act of 36 Geo. I I I c. 7 (made perpetual by 5 7 Geo. I I I c. 6) should be applied to Ireland. The original Act was concerned with treason and its clauses did not apply to Ireland; and Grey informed Clarendon that he had already asked the Attorney-General to consider the legal changes necessary.[46] A new Bill was in fact introduced in the House of Commons on the evening of 10 April. In his introductory speech to what was styled the Crown and Government Security Bill, Grey said that its main purpose was to substitute the offence of felony for that of treason, and that those found guilty under the Act would be punishable by transportation for life or for any period not less than seven years.[47]

Palmerston was also against the suspension of habeas corpus. It had to be passed, Palmerston insisted, by an overwhelming majority of the House of Commons, and Palmerston was probably in agreement with most of the senior Whig ministers when he expressed doubts that such a majority would be forthcoming. In this they were almost certainly wrong, although Grey was correct to argue that the longer the threats of violence and actual violence continued, the greater would be the support by the general public and in the Commons. Palmerston expressed the problem very clearly, and it is of great historical interest; certainly not just for this particular year:

The question is whether we shall lose more by the Progress of sedition while we are waiting for a stronger or more public case, or whether we shall gain more by restraint which even an application to Parliament might impose on the proceedings of the conspirators. According to all appearances days and not weeks will suffice to determine this question.

And then Palmerston, in commenting upon the various remedial measures that Clarendon had suggested in his memorandum, became an Irish landlord. He was emphatically opposed to 'any interference with the right of ejectment' since the rights of property must not in any way be impaired. Indeed, he continued, the extensive changes required in Irish agriculture necessarily involved 'a long and continued and systematic ejectment of smallholders and of squatting cottiers'. He was, however, in favour of the fundamentally conservative nostrum that Russell was always trying to persuade opinion to accept: the payment of the Catholic priesthood.[48]

The most extreme reply from within the Cabinet came, as might be expected, from Trevelyan. He listed the large amount of loans and help that had already been given to Ireland; he was in favour of the suspension of habeas corpus; and he recommended the immediate arrest of all the seditious leaders of nationalist opinion. His analysis of the security problem reflected the growing apprehensions of these days, and summed up very well the general approach of wide sections of the British people, if statements in the press can be taken as a guide to public opinion: 'Above all let us take and keep the lead *while there is yet time.*' He went on to suggest a solemn declaration in Parliament of the freedom and security and property the people enjoyed under the present institutions of the country. As for the forthcoming demonstration of the Chartists on Kennington Common:

The stream of Chartists on Monday should be turned off *at a distance* from the Houses of Parliament and the Public Offices, and the whole of Whitehall and Parliament should be filled with Special Constables. The head of the Chartist column should be met *by a body of Special Constables*, and the Chartists should be made to see that there is a power in the Society itself sufficient to put them down. It should be shown that as the disaffected are bandied and organised, so are the well-affected. The National Guards – the middle classes – can *keep* the upper hand, if proper arrangements are made, but it would be difficult for them to recover their position if once the Chartists got the upper hand, and the end would be attained only through a fearful civil war.[49]

And being Trevelyan he ended this section with the argument for 'A decided declaration of Economy'.

It was not to be expected that the widespread mood of sympathy with the French in their rejection of the July monarchy and the Guizot ministry would last for long. The fear of Jacobinism, never far below the surface in the minds of the propertied classes during the first half of the nineteenth century, quickly reasserted itself and became alive and real as the news came in daily from Paris. While the British press noted the explicit renunciation of the execution of political offenders by the Provisional government,[50] the tumultuous behaviour and subversive ideas of the Parisian crowds soon dominated the news from France. And the spread of revolution and upheaval in other parts of Europe naturally deepened the growing fears that the world was being turned upside down. The *Illustrated London News* is one way to follow the changes in public opinion and the growing impact of riot, mayhem and uncertainty upon British middle-class opinion. It was a liberal journal, attractively produced, which was enjoying a growing success.[51] In its issue of 26 February its critique of Louis-Philippe was hostile as was the double number the following week which was entirely devoted to the events in Paris. But the emphasis in the drawings and engravings was beginning to change; ordinary French citizens and soldiers now looked rougher and more capable of violence; and towards the end of the special number there was a double page of five drawings, with text, and all representing mob rule. The captions were: 'The people in the throne room at the Tuileries' – smashing furniture and holding the Cap of Liberty above the throne: 'Orgies in the Palace wine cellar'; 'Scenes in the courtyard of the Tuileries' – two smaller drawings of ordinary citizens, with their bottles, and looking decidedly villainous; 'Sketched in a salon of the Tuileries' – soldiers in uniform and armed civilians, all again looking very wild. This double-sized issue of 4 March had further drawings from Paris which included 'Scenes of the destruction of the Palais Royal' and 'Burning the royal carriages at the Chateau d'Eu'. The text of an article included a warning that whenever 'the light of popular Government has begun to dawn' calamitous enthusiasm can often be expected: 'It has often been the deplorable destiny of France to furnish more than one such lesson to the world, written in characters of blood, and read by the torchlight of rebellion.'

What the *Illustrated London News* was able to depict so vividly in drawings was set out in long columns in the London and provincial press. The connection between foreign revolutionaries and a breakdown of the social order was not difficult to make, and since the Chartist movement warmly supported these Jacobins in Paris, the lesson for the home front was explicit and obvious. There was, of course, a large *lumpen-proletariat* in the London of the middle decades of the nineteenth century, as there was in Paris; petty criminals and pickpockets always attached themselves in considerable numbers to meetings and demonstrations of any kind. The national and local press in Britain always made the point, and for the shopkeeper contemplating the broken glass of his windows in Glasgow, London and other towns during 1848, the identification of Chartist, rioter and Jacobin was complete.

It was also necessary to emphasise the fantasy, and unreality, of the social ideas of the Parisian workers. 'There is no doubt' wrote the *Illustrated London News* in the issue of 11 March in which it continued its sharp criticism of Louis-Philippe 'a deep under-current of Communism – theories respecting property that may produce a war of classes'; and no theme was more discussed at this time than the subversive nature of French ideas, contrasted always with the good sense of those of the British. *The Times*, whose news columns were often republished in the press outside London, printed one and a half columns from an English resident in Paris, dated 27 February. This letter, which was full of interesting information on the early days of the revolution, argued strongly for a policy of non-intervention: 'I hope to God we shall not repeat the blindness which Mr. Fox would have prevented at the beginning of the first revolution.' But most of the commentary related to attitudes and sentiments:

it is important to recollect that the present revolutionary tendencies are social rather than political – aiming at equality of possessions, or an equal distribution of the national revenue, rather than the mere establishment of democratic institutions. This is the alarming feature in the present condition of France. In England Socialist opinions and feelings have not as yet a definitive shape; they are rather dispositions or tendencies than distinct theories or *formules* . . .

I can assure you that my fears of Socialism, or Communism, are anything but fanciful. The late violent explosion was caused mainly by the severe and extensive distress of the Parisian *ouvriers*; and by the opinion, widely spread amongst them, that the Government and the wealthier classes might and ought to have prevented it.

This correspondent was not a liberal. He went on to warn against the creeping tendency in Britain towards unacceptable policies: the clamour for tenant right which he equated with a partial confiscation of the Irish landlord's property or the attitudes and work of 'ignorant humanitarians' such as Lord Ashley. At the same time his clear-sighted conservatism allowed him to recognise the degeneracy of the French ruling classes compared with the better feelings of the lower orders whom, he was happy to suggest, entertained 'a great deference for all the superior classes'. In a statement which had clear implications for his British peers he wrote:

The melancholy fact is most of the higher classes are morally or intellectually a more complete canaille than the great majority of the lower. Some don't care for the well-being of the people, think them destined to a miserable and servile condition, and would keep them down by force or terror; others, with better dispositions, wont give themselves the trouble to master social questions, diffuse opinions which lead the people to anarchical courses, or would give the people an education confined to sectarian religion which has not the tendency to enlighten them and raise their condition.[52]

There was a populist issue during this first month after the revolution which was made much of by the press and in public speeches and which occasioned much ill-will towards the French – always easy to encourage – and this time mostly against the French workers. Unemployment in France was at serious levels before 22 February, and it rapidly became worse during the chaotic days which followed. There were many thousands of foreign workers in France – and a sizeable number were British – and almost immediately the French workers began to demand the expulsion from France of all foreign workers in employment. The expulsion of British workers began in the early days of March. The issue begins to be noticed in the British press around the end of the first week in March; Normanby himself was engaged in correspondence with London from 6 March enclosing a letter from the British consul in Le Havre who had personal dealings with many expelled British workers. Normanby saw Lamartine several times on the matter and always expressed his great concern at the dangers to the good relations between their two countries. Lamartine expressed his regrets but emphasised that the government was unable to use any coercive power to remedy the situation. All that Lamartine could promise was that compensation would be on a liberal basis. There were later complications, when for a time the British workers were refused withdrawal from savings banks of their deposits. The British press gave the whole episode in its various aspects a great deal of publicity; there were welcoming receptions at the ports of debarkation for the British workers who had been expelled; and Lord Ashley and others appealed in a letter to *The Times* for financial help for the workers and their families. This was on 16 March. The British response to distress funds of this kind is always uninhibited. The Queen and the Prince Consort sent £200, and *Punch*, alongside many other papers, had great play with the principles of *Fraternité* and the expulsions. It was not a happy issue for spokesmen on Chartist platforms.[53]

By the closing days of March the upper and middle classes in Britain were thoroughly aroused to the dangerous possiblities of upheaval and unrest within their own national boundaries. The spread of revolutionary ideas and movements in the weeks that followed 22 February in Paris seemed to have no end. Already at the end of February there had been demonstrations in Mannheim and other parts of Germany; the ten-hour working day was introduced in France on 2 March; there were riots in Berlin on the 5th and a Liberal congress in Heidelberg decided to convene a parliament. Metternich was dismissed on 13 March; two days later revolution broke out in Budapest, and on the same day the Emperor at Vienna promised a Constitution. And so the story had continued throughout the month. France, as ever, was the pivot of all hopes and fears, and France during March looked increasingly unstable to British opinion. The demonstration of 16 March when 30,000 from the more conservative groups within the National Guard went onto the streets of Paris was countered the following day with a hundred thousand of the urban masses. Although the day was a triumph for the Centre rather than the Left, it was not understood as such by many outside observers: 'The people reigns in Paris' wrote *The Times* on 20 March. 'It was not till just now that its success was complete.' Normanby considered the 16 March demonstration by the 'friends of order' to have been a mistake at this time, since there was insufficient power behind their opposition; and on 18 March he wrote a notably gloomy letter to Palmerston, more striking because Normanby was usually so cool and balanced in his appraisal of events. It is an interesting indication of what must have been the general feelings among the propertied classes in Paris:

But there is no denying that within the last two or three days we have been advancing rapidly towards anarchy. In the Convention and in the reign of Terror there was formerly personal insecurity arising from capricious cruelty, but there was at any rate a strong will which made a government, but here there is no confidence in anyone – no credit – no employment – no troops – no physical force anywhere but in the masses. The only chance is that there is still some vestige of moral force in a part of the National Guard and some members of the Government.[54]

Normanby soon recovered his astuteness as a reporter of the revolution and historians are generally agreed that 16 March represented the beginning of active opposition to the government and more particularly to the levelling tendencies of the radical groupings. The counter-demonstration of the masses on 17 March had, as Marx noted in *The Class Struggles in France*, a profoundly equivocal character in terms of what the Left conceived to be their purposes. Marx wrote:

March 17 revealed the ambiguous situation of the proletariat, which permitted no decisive act. Its demonstration originally had the purpose of pushing the Provisional Government back on to the path of the revolution, of effecting the exclusion of its bourgeois members according to circumstances, and of compelling the postponement of the election days for the National Assembly and the National Guard. But on March 16 the bourgeoisie represented in the National Guard made a hostile demonstration against the Provisional Government. With the cry: *à bas Ledru-Rollin* it surged to the Hotel de Ville. And the people were forced, on March 17, to shout: Long live Ledru-Rollin! Long live the Provisional Government! They were forced to take sides *against* the bourgeoisie in support of the bourgeois republic, which seemed to them in danger. They strengthened the Provisional Government, instead of subordinating it to themselves.[55]

The immediate impact and influence of the 16 March and 17 March demonstrations in England were to encourage the conviction that the 'accidents' which so powerfully assisted the course of the revolution in Paris must not be allowed to happen in Britain. The example of France, and its day-to-day history from 22 February on, was always in the minds of the ruling groups in Whitehall. All threats to order were taken seriously and never underestimated; at the same time there was never any doubt that unrest and discontent, in whatever forms they would be expressed, could always be controlled and contained without bloodshed. However, there was never confidence in this matter in respect of Ireland. The month of March in Britain provided a series of dress rehearsals for the forces of order throughout the whole of the kingdom, and it already revealed, in mainland Britain, that the government could rely upon social groups right down to limited sections of the working people. It was this fact which made the political situation in Britain so different from anywhere else, and the breadth of support for 'order' was constantly referred to and emphasised by politicians as well as by the various mouthpieces of public opinion. As early as 14 March Palmerston set down the terms within which the leading ministers were to work in the months ahead. He was writing to Normanby to explain that the rioting which had already taken place in London, Glasgow and elsewhere must not

be exaggerated, and that much more important was the recognition of the
social classes upon whom the government already knew it could rely:

But the general temper of the lower and middle classes in all places where these riots
have taken place has been excellent, and the best disposition has been shown by the
great mass of the inhabitants of those places to assist the magistrates in maintaining
order in London, and Glasgow and Edinburgh. Thousands of persons volunteered
their services as Special Constables on these occasions, and in London, especially the
whole body of coalwhippers offered their assistance in support of the Law. At
Manchester the workpeople declared that they were so thankful to the Government
and Parliament for having passed the Ten Hour Bill that they would all combine to
use every effort to assist the Government in maintaining order.

The Government have also received numerous offers from Edinburgh and
Glasgow for the formation of Volunteer Corps for the Preservation of Peace, but these
offers have with thanks been declined, Her Majesty's government preferring to trust
to the usual means at their disposal for the maintenance of Peace and Order.

Your Excellency will not fail to have observed by what an overwhelming majority
the House of Commons confirmed last night that the Income Tax should be
continued for three years instead of being limited to one year, and you will at once see
in that Vote a fresh example of that high Public Spirit and National Feeling to which
in times of Difficulty or Doubt prompts the people of this country to submit to any
sacrifice to which they may think necessary for upholding the Honour and Dignity of
their Country.[56]

What is interesting about this letter and so much of the correspondence
between the leading politicians is how they constantly exhorted and
comforted each other about the rightness and the righteousness of what
they were doing. They offered sustenance: emotional, political, spiritual;
and the result was a boundless confidence which radiated through all those
who occupied the directing positions in political life. In this letter of
Palmerston's that has just been quoted, Normanby would have especially
appreciated the observations about the solidarity of the middle classes with
the government, and their support for the forces of order. In his analysis of
the causes of the failure of the French government and the alienation of the
middle strata from the policies of Louis-Philippe, Normanby was constantly
urging upon his colleagues in London the lessons that had to be learned. It
was advice they wholly accepted.

4

APRIL

By the beginning of April 1848 the sense of alarm and apprehension was accumulating steadily in the minds of all those who, for various reasons of self-interest, ideology and an awareness of property rights feared for the stability of the established order. Tories, Whigs, Liberals and middle-class radicals were at one in denouncing the verbal attacks upon existing society and the growing indications that physical assault was soon to follow. On 2 April, the London *Weekly Dispatch*, a liberal paper which sympathised with Irish grievances, carried a leading article headed 'Ireland and sedition' in which it discussed the link between Chartism and Irish insurgency. The tone, as well as the substance, were typical of press comment round the country:

We observe that they [the Irish Confederates] are endeavouring to organise the Irish, who are either settled or are vagrant in England, to be prepared to create a diversion in their favour whenever their purposes are ripe for execution. From the centre of Confederation Hall the riots of Edinburgh, Glasgow, Manchester and London were worked, and the English Chartists are lending themselves to the same stupid conspiracy against the peace, order and stability of the empire [the *Dispatch* then continued to indicate its understanding of Irish grievances]. We will not identify the Irish people with the spirit or the acts of the fustian makers . . . But at such a time as this, when peril threatens us from every side, when the very existence, because the integrity, of this great empire is put to hazard, and when internal disorder and financial confusion are aggravating the difficulties of our Government, we know of but one cause, that of our common country, and one way to save it and serve it, by union, fidelity, order and public spirit. Every Englishman who is worthy of such a country will feel that the stability of this majestic fabric is his first care, his chief interest, his primary duty. We want no foreign propaganda to settle our quarrels. We want no revolution of shoplifters and pick pockets. The wise and worthy leaders of the French Republic will send back the coal-hole martyr who has asked them to conquer us for them, with a flea in his ear, as wise, or rather as foolish, as he went. Let him sharpen his pikes, and scour his gun barrels, and drill his Thugs as he may. There are patriots enough in Ireland to put them down. If they cannot, let them be assured they will have John Bull to deal with.

The announcement that the third Chartist petition would be presented on Monday 10 April had been formally made in the *Northern Star* on 18 March;

102

but it was the assembling of the Chartist Convention in London on Tuesday 4 April that enormously heightened public alarm. Everyone, whichever side they favoured, felt the levels of excitement rising throughout the country. The whole of society had been reading for weeks past about the clubs in Paris: their communistic statements, and their importance as the bases for the popular demonstrations that seemed to be taking place daily.[1] The month of March in Britain had seen a series of minor riots and disturbances, and against the background of a Europe in turmoil the tide of fear was already seeping into the consciousness of the better-off classes throughout the kingdom. And now here was the Chartist Convention meeting publicly in the centre of the capital city, bringing together the local and national leaders of a great mass movement which had been stirring the country for the past decade, and which now seemed stronger than ever. The debates and deliberations of the Convention have been somewhat ignored by historians in the build-up to the Kennington Common demonstration, yet it was the daily reports, published in full in the London press and copied by the provincial papers, which steadily influenced, and hardened, public opinion against the general aims of the working-class movement; and which, above all, convinced the propertied classes that physical force was being planned.

The Convention opened on Tuesday 4 April at the Literary Institute, John Street, Fitzroy Square, and Philip McGrath was elected chairman, with Christopher Doyle as secretary. The number of delegates was limited to 49 'in order to escape the penalties of the Convention Act'.[2] The first two days were spent mainly in listening to reports from the delegates of different towns. Ernest Jones representing Halifax, made a somewhat wild speech on the first day in which he said 'that his constituents had urged upon him the desirability, if possible, of conducting the movement on moral force principles; but they warned him not to stoop to one act of unnecessary humility in urging their claims. To a man they were ready to fight (cheers). They were eager to rush down the hills of Yorkshire in aid of their brother patriots in London'; and the delegate from Barnsley reported that he had been instructed to say that 'if the Government let the military loose upon Ireland, something else would be let loose here'. On the second day the most militant speeches were made by Cuffay[3] and the Irish delegate from London, Charles McCarthy. Both favoured the establishment of rifle clubs. There were other speakers, however, on both these and later days, who specifically repudiated violence. A letter on behalf of the Metropolitan Committee from John Arnott had appeared in the London *Times* of 4 April dissenting from the violent language which Vernon had used about the forthcoming Kennington Common meeting; and the chairman of the Convention appealed for less rash talk at the beginning of the session on Thursday morning. It was, inevitably the violent language which impressed the

outside world as well as the constant reiteration of the new unity between
the Irish and the Chartists. On Wednesday 5 April the Convention issued a
placard which was extensively posted throughout London and which made
a special appeal to the Irish in the metropolis:

Irishmen resident in London, on the part of the democrats in England we extend to
you the warm hand of fraternization; your principles are ours, and our principles
shall be yours. Remember the aphorisms, that union is strength, and division is
weakness; centuries of bitter experience prove to you the truth of the latter, let us
now cordially endeavour to test the virtue of the former. Look to your fatherland, the
most degraded in the scale of nations. Behold it bleeding at every pore under the
horrible lashings of class misrule! What an awful spectacle is Ireland, after forty-
seven years of the vaunted Union! Her trade ruined, her agriculture paralysed, her
people scattered over the four quarters of the globe, and her green fields in the twelve
months just past made the dreary grave yards of 1,000,000 of famished human
beings. Irishmen, if you love your country, if you detest these monstrous atrocities,
unite in heart and soul with those who will struggle with you to exterminate the hell-
engendered cause of your country's degradation – beggary and slavery.

In its final paragraph the placard reminded the working people of London
that 'the eyes of EUROPE *are fixed upon you*' and it concluded with a general
exhortation that the great demonstration would strike a great 'moral blow'
for the achievement of 'liberty and happiness to every sect and class in the
British Empire'. The discussion in the Convention during Thursday further
revealed the differences of approach and opinion within the movement, and
the Friday session was dominated by the decision of the metropolitan police
to ban the meeting and the procession. There was again some very violent
language from certain of the delegates, but the Convention agreed in the
morning session to send a deputation to the Home Secretary to emphasise
the peaceful nature of the demonstration on the coming Monday. Reynolds
led a deputation of three and he reported back in the afternoon. Sir George
Grey was not available and the deputation had been received by the Under-
Secretary at the Home Office, Sir Denis Le Marchant, the Attorney-General
and the chief magistrate from Bow Street. It was indicated that Sir Denis Le
Marchant 'exhibited great coldness' and it was made clear that whatever the
deputation said on behalf of the Convention there was no possibility of the
government changing its mind. A letter was left for Sir George Grey which
he read to the House of Commons that evening.

Some of the discussion on this day continued the previous days' threats of
physical force. Charles McCarthy 'would not say what would be the fearful
consequences if a blow were to be struck by the police force or the military.
They were determined, in the name of liberty, if attacked, to resist the blow to
the utmost'. Ernest Jones argued that the government did not seriously
intend to stop the procession, and in a later intervention he moved a

resolution to the effect that they should circulate all towns asking for simultaneous demonstrations on Monday 'in order that in case the lamentable event of a collision with the troops should take place here, the myrmidons of the law would be kept in their respective districts'. And Harney, just before the Convention closed its session for the day, moved for a committee to select alternative delegates 'so that in the event of the present Convention being mowed down in the streets of London or swept into Newgate, there would be others to take their place'.[4]

Reports of this kind in the press were hardly calculated to allay fears, and middle-class hysteria continued to mount. The Saturday session of the Convention heard a long rambling speech from O'Connor and in the afternoon reports from some delegates who had been to see various members of Parliament. All these matters were reported in detail in the London press on Monday morning as was a public meeting in Victoria Park on Sunday, 9 April, at which Ernest Jones was the main speaker. Jones had been among the most violent speakers during the Convention and this speech, as reported in the *Morning Chronicle* on the day of the great demonstration, would have been confirmation again of the militant intentions of at least some of the Chartist leadership. After repeating his argument that he did not think the government were serious in their intention to suppress the procession, Jones continued:

If the Government touch one hair of the head of the delegates – if they place them under arrest, or attempt the least interference with their liberty – every town represented by the delegates, would be in arms in less than 24 hours [tremendous cheers]. If I were to be killed, or wounded, or arrested, the moment the intelligence arrived at Halifax the people would rise and disarm the troops – imprison the authorities – and 100,000 Yorkshiremen would march upon London [enthusiastic cheers]. So help me God I will march in the first rank tomorrow, and if they attempt any violence, they shall not be 24 hours longer in the House of Commons [cheers].

These words of Jones were echoed by the chairman of another Chartist meeting at Blackheath: 'We are determined to conquer tomorrow; nothing shall put us down. We shall not be terrified by bullets or bayonets. They have no terrors for oppressed starving men.'[5]

It is not by any means surprising, as the general level of apprehension rose, that precautions and countermeasures were put in hand. The Queen and her family left London for the Isle of Wight on the morning of 8 April. Waterloo station was cleared and several hundred special constables moved into place. The day before, Palmerston had written to Lord John Russell: 'I conclude that you have made all the necessary arrangements for the security of the Queen at Osborne; but it is a rather unprotected situation, and the Solent Sea is not impassable.'[6] The Royal Family themselves were

concerned at the public reaction to their departure from the city where so
many were fearful of what was likely to happen in the coming days. Prince
Albert instructed his equerry, Colonel C. B. Phipps, to report on the public
sentiment in this matter, and in a letter dated 9 April Phipps noted that he
had found no negative reaction in general, and that he ignored the tittle-
tattle of 'aristocratic Drawing Rooms'. The justification for the Queen's
departure was clearly that of a constitutional monarch accepting the advice
of her prime minister. Phipps ended his letter with a statement of his
impressions of the public temper:

There is every shade of opinion as to what will occur tomorrow. Some say that there
will not be the slightest disturbance of the peace, others that there will be serious riots
– and then again that there will be some partial disturbance, such as breaking
windows – the latter is my opinion – I think that in the present excited state of the
lowest classes, the day can hardly be expected to pass over without some
disturbances but that they will be easily suppressed.[7]

Colonel Phipps travelled from Windsor to London early on the morning of 10
April, and his report to Prince Albert, written at 5.30 p.m. the same
afternoon, gives an interesting statement of what so many were thinking
and discussing in the hours before the expected demonstration:

The morning, which was very beautiful, brought all kinds of sinister reports; even at
Windsor before arriving at London by the train I was informed that immense bodies
of people were collecting, and that all the bridges would be occupied by troops and
Guns pointed, and that an immediate battle was expected. Coming from Paddington
Station to Buckingham Palace the town certainly wore a most warlike appearance –
all the Park Gates were closed and each guarded by a Picquet of the Foot Guards, with
haversacks and Canteens upon their backs, prepared for actual service. At
Buckingham Palace I heard that very large bodies had assembled at Kennington
Common, and that numerous additions were marching towards the meeting in
different directions.[8]

The correspondence of leading politicians and the columns of newspapers all
over the country were full of the expressions of anxieties and fears which had
affected the whole country, and which without question had a very marked
influence upon the Chartist leaders themselves. One piece of evidence of the
latter is the well-known statement which Ernest Jones is reported to have
made on the evening of 9 April concerning the willingness of some at least of
the Chartist leaders to abandon the Kennington Common meeting.[9] The
most pervasive sentiment was undoubtedly that which equated the possible
outcome of 10 April with what had occurred in France. It was revolutionary
Paris, and the rapidity with which the revolution had spread, that was in
most people's perceptions of what might be the possible consequences of a
large gathering in London of those hostile to the existing order. Every paper
in the country, without exception, carried in each issue the news from

France; and along with the rising phobias against the French and French ideas about work and property went the reports of the violent speeches in the Chartist Convention. As *The Times* wrote two days after the Kennington Common meeting, on 12 April,

It cannot be denied that the public mind, stunned and confounded by the events on the Continent, had become, as the ancients would have expressed it, *meteoric*, unsteady, open to strange impressions and diffident of its own most habitual beliefs.

It is necessary to distinguish the attitudes and responses of those concerned in the practical business of maintaining public order from the rest of the propertied classes, whatever the size of their property stake in the country. Government ministers in Whitehall were in no doubt about the gravity of the situation in early April. The revolution in France had shocked them with the rapidity of its escalation, and they were fully alert to the consequences of accidents such as the shootings in front of the Ministry of Foreign Affairs in Paris. Moreover they were equally aware of the possible repercussions in Europe of any demonstration of weakness on the part of the English government in dealing with unrest and disturbance. The reports that had appeared in the French and Irish papers of the quite minor rioting that had occurred in Britain during March had greatly exaggerated the scale of the incidents; and uncertainty and irresolution at this time would only encourage the Jacobin element in all the nations affected by revolutionary movements. British diplomacy in March had achieved its main objective: the neutralisation of France as an active military force in Europe. This, for the Whig ministry, was as important for western and central Europe as it was for Ireland.

There was, however, never any doubt among the leading political groups in England that the coercive forces at the disposal of the British government were wholly capable of dealing adequately and successfully with any confrontation that might occur, either on the mainland or in Ireland. The problem, and really the only problem, was that Britain was not Ireland. The Irish had always been treated as a colonial people, and a scale of deaths acceptable in Ireland could not possibly be admitted in England. A soil stained with English blood would bring forth martyrs. No minister at this time seems to have mentioned Peterloo in his correspondence or in speeches, but the need to avoid bloodshed and implicitly the political consequences of bloodshed were clearly understood and strongly emphasised on a number of occasions.[10] At the same time the Whigs never allowed their liberal principles to obstruct the security requirements of the state. Their own position in society depended on the preservation of the existing order, and they were conscious of how far class hostility from the lower orders should be allowed to express itself given their own capacity for constraining its violent manifestations. Clarendon wrote to Sir George Grey on 7 April during the period of growing anxiety and concern prior to the Chartist meeting on the 10th:

There is so much loyal and good feeling in the Country, such mighty interests are at stake, the circumstances of Europe are so grave, the future is so menacing, that I feel sure you will not appeal in vain to the 'Haves' in England against the 'Have nots'. But this is not the time for stickling about Constitutional forms or party consistency. If we lose Ireland, it will be as much owing to the want of an Arms Bill and to the imprudent policy of the Whigs two years ago as any thing else.[11]

The impression accepted by many historians that the plan for the defence of London was largely the work of the Duke of Wellington is incorrect. The reputation that the Duke enjoyed in the country was an enormous asset to the government of 1848. Greville wrote on 13 July 1847:

the Duke of Wellington was if possible received with even more enthusiasm. It is incredible what popularity environs him in his latter days; he is followed like a show wherever he goes, and the feeling of the people *for him* seems to be the liveliest of all popular sentiments; yet he does nothing to excite, and hardly appears to notice it. He is in wonderful vigour of body, but strangely altered in mind, which is in a fitful uncertain state, and there is no knowing in what mood he may be found; everybody is afraid of him, nobody dares to say anything to him; he is sometimes very amiable and good-humoured, sometimes very irritable and morose.[12]

The much quoted comment of Chevalier Bunsen which suggested that Wellington was in command of the preparations for the Chartist demonstration was no doubt an accurate statement of what passed between them.[13] Wellington was certainly brought into the discussions at a rather late date when the crucial choices had been made, and he was present on the day of the demonstration itself, but all the basic decisions had been taken by Sir George Grey and Lieutenant-General Lord Fitzroy Somerset, the Military Secretary. Wellington had contributed his own memorandum on 5 April which began very curiously:

Having seen in the newspapers statements that 200,000 Chartists are to be assembled in and around London on Monday next the 10th instant; and knowing that Her Majesty's Servants have ordered the movement of certain troops upon the metropolis . . . I have not heard that the Government has adopted any measures to dissuade or to prevent these large bodies from assembling near the Metropolis. I do not know whence they will come, or what is their avowed or their real or their supposed object.

Wellington then proceeded to set out quite reasonable precautions which could be taken. He was especially concerned to place great emphasis upon the need to keep communications open: similar to his insistence on the matter for Dublin in his memorandum of 2 March which has been noted above.[14] His main points, however, had already been well taken.

It was on 3 April that Sir George Grey issued a general circular to all the relevant authorities in the country recommending the swearing-in of special constables, although by this time many thousands had already been enrolled. The Home Office was in continuous correspondence with all parts of the United Kingdom, but until the Kennington Common meeting, except for Ireland, there was an inevitable concentration on the preparations within the London area. The tactics overall were simple and straightforward. The decision of the metropolitan police commissioners to ban the procession on Monday was phrased as 'assemblage or procession' and this was generally taken to refer solely or mainly to the procession back from Kennington Common which would accompany the petition to the House of Commons. In a memorandum to the Lord Mayor of London dated 9 April[15] Sir Denis Le Marchant set down the precautions which had been agreed and which were already for the most part in operation. Le Marchant wrote that the meeting on Kennington Common would be allowed provided that it remained peaceful, but no procession would be permitted under any circumstances. The main force of professional police would be on and around the bridges across the Thames, with a special concentration on Blackfriars Bridge. Cavalry and foot soldiers would be stationed out of sight at various strategic points and especially at the bridges. At Blackfriars, for example, four houses at the north end were taken over, with the consent of their owners, for a large party of infantry. Only in the event of the civil forces being unable to contain the demonstrators would the military intervene; and it was assumed by all who were involved in these decisions that military intervention would come only as a very last resort. There were 7,122 military including cavalry in London for the 10th; 1,231 enrolled pensioners; just over 4,000 police – metropolitan and city – and about 85,000 special constables.[16] The disposition of troops was the responsibility of the London Military District subject to the agreement of the Home Office. The main problem was to find suitable accommodation for the military in order that they would be out of sight but within reach of central London. Several owners of large houses put their stabling at the disposal of the cavalry, and a director of the South West Railway arranged for 500 infantry and 100 cavalry to be accommodated at Nine Elms station on the Sunday and Monday.[17] Many of the infantry were inside government offices and buildings.

Army morale had always been appreciated as a matter for close concern.[18] This was the great objection to billeting. Palmerston's experience at the War Office had taught him that the contact of ordinary soldiers with civilians could be a subversive matter. In Ireland, partly because of the potentially more explosive political situation and partly because of the very poor housing conditions in the country as a whole, there was no choice but to provide accommodation; and almost all the army was quartered in their own barracks. On the mainland, however, even by 1848 there was often not sufficient barrack buildings to house the troops as they were moved rapidly round the country where disaffection was threatened; and tented camps, as in Liverpool in the summer of 1848, often had to be accepted.

Every scrap of information about the political conversation of ordinary soldiers – nearly always supplied by the local police – was carefully scrutinised; but there was very little. In London a constable of the E Division reported a conversation with a sentry on duty at the west entrance of the British Museum in Great Russell Street in which the soldier was alleged to have said: 'You'll find that if we are called out we shall not do much, and he thought that plenty of his people had signed the Charter but did not say if he had signed it'; and in the week before 10 April there were reports of up to a dozen soldiers of the Scots Fusiliers, stationed at Charing Cross barracks, talking in public houses of the Kennington Common meeting:

one of them further stated that he had an aged father and mother in the country, who were reduced in circumstances and who now received for their maintenance from the Parish only three shillings a week – and what use was three shillings a week to an old couple of their age – He, for one, knew others of the same mind, would never fight for any Government or any other system which would behave so to any poor people'.

On another occasion, again with no precise dating but in the week before 10 April, a report of four soldiers of the same regiment stated that a civilian addressing the soldiers said: 'I hope my lads you will not interfere with us next Monday' and one of the soldiers replied: 'There is little fear of that, my boy. Do you do your Duty and we will do ours – And if we are called out and ordered to fire – we shall fire over your heads.' In this episode one name was quoted with identification markings. The only other incident reported in this particular War Office file was a short report dated 5 April when a police constable noted that he saw three privates of the Grenadier Guards stop and sign the Chartist petition on Westminster Bridge.[19]

These were trivial affairs and cannot have caused the military authorities any serious concern. It is worth remarking that there do not appear to be any reports in government papers of the slightest anxiety about the metropolitan police. It was, of course, the Roman Catholic part of the army which the authorities were worried about in 1848, but this was a new problem. In the years preceeding 1848 the Catholic hierarchy in England had always come out strongly against physical force politics, and the influence of O'Connell against the Chartist movement was powerful.[20] In 1848 itself there are a number of reports in the Home Office papers where evidence was given of the steadying influence of the local Catholic priest, evincing disapproval of the link with militant Chartism.[21] The new situation in 1848 was one in which Irish soldiers might come into contact with Irish Repealers united with English Chartists. As events turned out, there was nothing to worry about on the English mainland. Ireland was, as ever, likely to produce disturbance; and on the night before the Kennington Common meeting in London, when there was rising excitement in Dublin as everywhere else, fighting broke out in Dublin between the soldiers of two regiments over the Repeal question. Clarendon, in a letter dated 10 April, described the incident in a letter to Sir George Grey:

There was a disagreeable row here last night between the soldiers of two Regiments about Repeal and they fought in the street. They were soon brought back to Barracks . . . We have heard too that the Repeal soldiers will attempt to break out of their Barracks tonight – the whole spirit of the garrison (or the R.C. part of it) appears to have altered since the 57th came here. We have fortunately got rid of them now by sending them to the North but P[rince] George tells me he inspected the two foot companies before they marched yesterday, and that he never saw such a mutinous and sullen set of fellows – he expected they would knock him down.[22]

In later letters of the next few days Clarendon reported that the military commanders had investigated the incident and were now less troubled. He especially emphasised that the account in the *Nation* was 'entirely false' and that only two regiments had been sent out of Dublin; and it was the 57th alone about which there were still doubts.[23]

The protection of strategic buildings was an important part of the general security precautions. In the early weeks which followed the Paris revolution there had been a number of reports in *The Times* especially from various correspondents in the French capital, which provided much detail as to the logistics of revolution by the masses;[24] and Normanby, in his despatches to the Foreign Office, was also full of information on these matters. It was plain that the occupation of important buildings in the centre of the city, thereby providing permanent bases, was a quite crucial factor in the escalation of the revolution, allowing the possibilities of constant demonstrations, invasion of the Assembly, and a continuous renewal of revolutionary spirit and morale. The matter was well understood in Britain beyond the small groups of ministers and their military advisers. There were constant demands from those in charge of buildings for additional troops and arms in the days leading up to the Kennington common demonstration, among them an interesting letter from the director of the British Museum, Sir Henry Ellis, who asked the Home Office for additional protection, on the grounds that it could now be expected that disturbances would be more serious than had previously been anticipated. He added:

Please to remember if it should by any accident happen that the Building of the Museum fall into the hands of disaffected persons it would prove to them a Fortress capable of holding Ten Thousand Men.[25]

The date of the letter was 9 April. All the main buildings in Whitehall were heavily protected. At Somerset House a portcullis had been built; the roof of the Bank of England was parapeted with sandbags, and guns mounted through the apertures; all the prisons in the central London area were reinforced with additional arms and soldiers or pensioners. Other precautions included the earlier lighting of public lamps in the areas of London most likely to be affected; renewal of the instructions to gunsmiths to make their weapons unusable in the event of looting; and the compulsory taking over by the government of the national Electric Telegraph system for the whole week beginning Sunday 9 April. A month earlier the Home Office had asked for a special line to be constructed between the central office of the Electric Telegraph at Euston and the Home Office.[26]

The distinguishing feature of the measures taken by the British government against its own radical movement, compared with the situation in Paris in the days before 22 February, was the overwhelming support given throughout the country by the middle strata of society. It could be taken for granted that the landed aristocracy and gentry would support the forces of order, but it was the middling groups – from the wealthy bourgeois at the top to those referred to in contemporary literature as the shopkeeping class – who rallied in large numbers and with great determination to oppose the radical disaffected. Already, in the aftermath of the Glasgow riots of 6 March, Archibald Alison, the high Tory deputy sheriff of the County of Lanark, had written to the Home Secretary commenting on the 'most excellent' disposition of the 'whole middle classes';[27] and in London Rowan, the senior commissioner of the metropolitan police, was also taking it for granted that he would be able to rely upon a large inflow into the ranks of special constables.[28] It had not always been so, which is why leading Whigs and Tories were now so ready to congratulate their middle-class allies. Corn Law repeal was, after all, still in everyone's mind; and there had always been hesitation and uncertainty among some groups of the middle ranks of society in times of social crisis: in part ideological, but much more, it may be conjectured, because of doubts about the efficiency as well as the efficacy of government security measures.[29] Even in 1848, when the Whig government acted throughout with competence and expedition, there was hesitation in the early days in some areas; but this was probably the fault of the local authorities rather than of central government.[30] What can be said of this year is that the firm direction of affairs by the Home Office encouraged confidence that demonstrations of support by middle-class groups would be strongly reinforced by government action. Certainly by the middle of March the tide of opinion was running strongly in favour of the government; and in the weeks preceding the Kennington Common meeting an upsurge of confidence and support for the government of a quite extraordinary kind took place. Normanby had been constantly emphasising to Palmerston the failure of the July monarchy and of the Guizot government to maintain the confidence of its own supporters, and Normanby came back again and again to what he regarded as the crucial factor in the revolutionary process: the falling away of middle-class support for Louis-Philippe and all that he stood for.[31] The urban middle classes in Britain were, of course, more numerous and more powerful economically than similar groups in France; but there was at the same time a widespread anti-aristocratic sentiment among many business circles and within middle-class nonconformist chapels. The threats from below to social stability and to the rights of property were, however, of such a kind that there was no doubt on which side the middle classes would stand; and the firm determination of the government overcame doubts and fears that the middle-class support of security measures – in their role as special constables – would receive the full backing of the coercive powers of the state. These considerations were especially important for the shopkeeping classes; and all over the country the middle classes offered their services in overwhelming numbers. Never before had there been such a mobilisation of all who for many different reasons were self-interested in the preservation of the existing structure of society. The mayors of all the large towns in the industrial North reported large numbers of special constables having been sworn in, and there were similar reports from less threatened areas. But it was London, inevitably, upon which national attention was focussed in the days before the Kennington Common meeting; and here the response was solid everywhere in the central parishes of the city and in some it was overwhelming.[32] By 27 March Hackney had 200 special constables each with a staff and white arm-band. Limehouse divided their recruits into sections with different colours in their button-holes: the rank and file wore blue, sub-leaders red and the leader of five or more sections had blue and white. Towards the west of the town the upper classes took over. Marylebone had a printed notice calling for a meeting on the Saturday evening. The officers had already been elected, presumably more or less self-elected. Lieutenant-General Sir James Bathurst, a Peninsular veteran on the retired list but still Governor of Berwick for which he received £568 15 shillings and 10 pence per annum, was Superintendent-in-Chief;[33] his deputy was Lieutenant-Colonel Sir J. J. Hamilton; and among the superintendants of the divisions into which the special constables were grouped were two rear admirals, one knight and one colonel. There was a good deal of self-help. Before the Kennington Common meeting – the exact date is not given – between thirty and forty tradesmen formed themselves into a company ready to be sworn in as special constables. They met at the Bell Inn, Kings Cross.[34]

There were, inevitably, some rather unusual offers of help which the government felt it necessary either to do nothing about or to reject. On 7 April a gentleman farmer from Essex offered his services: 'I am an experienced sportsman and a good steady shot'; the young gentlemen of Rugby school who were seventeen years or over offered to assist the authorities;[35] and two days after the Kennington Common meeting the Keeper of the Queen's prison in London wrote to Sir George Grey enclosing letters from various inmates serving time who were offering their services to help put down any disturbances: the Keeper adding that 'I confidently believe I should have received the most loyal and efficient support from most of the Prisoners had there been any real occasion for their services'.[36] Thomas Allsop, in a letter to Robert Owen, who was in Paris, summed up the prevailing mood in London: 'Very great alarm prevails here, and very grave apprehensions are entertained for the peace of the country generally by grave and reflecting men. The worst feature is the antagonism of classes shown by the readiness of the middle classes to become special constables.'[37]

Allsop's letter was dated 8 April. Two days after the Chartist meeting *The Times* summarised the political lessons: 'London will crush treason at once, and that all classes are at one in this respect. Such is the new strength we have gained by that noble day's work, a strength we could not easily have gained in any other way'; and on the same day the *Nonconformist*, whose anti-aristocratic sentiments have already been quoted and whose political position was liberal-radical and certainly not Whig, insisted that while armed forces cannot kill 'a living sentiment', it nevertheless emphasised the importance of the 'counter-demonstration on the part of the middle classes, not against the principles of the Charter, but against that recklessness of counsel which sought to realise them in social confusion and streams of blood. A physical-force revolution is thus, we hope, become an impossibility, never again to be attempted.'[38]

The most controversial question concerning the special constables of 1848 is the extent to which working people themselves enrolled for 10 April. It was widely stated, and if not stated then assumed, by contemporaries of most political views outside the Chartist movement itself that at least many of the respectable artisans had volunteered in London and elsewhere in the country. What happened in the months which followed has hardly ever been discussed, and it is still a matter unresolved. We can list the working-class groups who wore armbands as special constables in London and other towns and about whom there is no argument. These were those employees who were either in a close master–servant relationship in which it would have been impossible to retain employment without being sworn in. Such were male domestic servants and the country employees of the landed classes. Many aristocratic families sent their women and children out of London and kept back their male servants as well as bringing up from their estates their gamekeepers, on the principle no doubt that good marksmen might be useful – as the Essex farmer noted above had assumed. There were a number of accounts in the contemporary London papers of titled persons enrolling as special constables along with their complete male establishments. Then there were the employees of railway companies and of public utilities such as gas companies. The railway companies ran their organisations for decades with a quasi-military discipline, and it was expected that their employees would volunteer. A letter of 5 April from the London and South Western Company to the Home Office reported that three to four hundred were already sworn in and that the number would increase to 800 on the day following: 'of this number 40 or 50 are *superior* officers and clerks, upon whom I can thoroughly rely.[39] Among the gas companies which provided lists of officers and workmen sworn in during the period preceding the Chartist demonstration were the Commercial Gas Company of Stepney; the Imperial Gas Works, Margaret Street, Shoreditch, and the Independent Gas Company, Haggerston. There was some opposition by workers to this voluntary conscription, but hard evidence is difficult to establish.[40] The magistrates who received the oath also had problems, and there were several letters to the Home Office asking for guidance when large establishments tried to enrol their workers in the mass. The original circular from Grey of 3 April had referred to the enrolment of 'respectable individuals' but as 10 April approached the Home Office indicated its approval of these mass registrations.[41] There was one particular group which received much publicity and which was certainly beyond the pale of working-class respectability. These were the Thames coal-whippers for whom Parliament had legislated in 1844;[42] and their offer of service was widely used to indicate the extent to which the Chartist movement did not represent the whole of the working classes. It was also used, by Gladstone among others, as an example of the returns governments could expect from social reform measures.[43] The coal-whippers were at the lower end of the labourers' group, and although so much publicity was given to their commitment to public order, a report in the *Weekly Dispatch* suggested that many in fact had been more or less compulsorily enrolled by their labour superintendent.[44] After the demonstration of the 10th was over, the coal-whippers demanded payment for their services since they had lost a day's work, or in some cases, part of a day. Their request set up a mild flutter in Whitehall, but they had been so useful in the government's propaganda that there was no question but to pay them. Richard Mayne, the metropolitan police Commissioner wrote to C. E. Trevelyan at the Treasury – whose economic heart must have been much displeased at the prospect of this frittering away of public funds: 'it would be mischievous and impolitic to make them dissatisfied especially after the public notice taken of them'. There was careful calculation of the rates of pay deemed politic.[45]

Many workingmen were either committed Chartists or like Mayhew's costermongers, were for 'us' and against 'them', but there must have been quite large numbers who took no clear attitude or who followed their masters. Any quantitative analysis is obviously not possible, but there is an interesting phenomenon that has not been much commented on, and yet was to be found, in these early days in April at any rate, both in London and in the industrial North; and it may be significant as an indication of changing political attitudes. This was where working operatives refused to be sworn in as ordinary special constables but were prepared to act within their own works to protect their working premises from outside attack and, presumably, in Manchester, against visiting bands – pickets – who in the past had forced a turn-out. Magistrates who accepted workers on these terms were acting illegally in that the terms of a special constable's appointment were such that while it was usual to employ them within their own neighbourhood they were obliged to serve anywhere in their own county; and according to a later ruling from the Home Office, even in another county as well.[46] Service within their own working establishment was much more common than has so far been noted. There is, in the return of special constables made by the metropolitan police to the Home Office an interesting comment against Lambeth (St Mary's parish): 'Mr Maudsley, Engineer, has 1000 for his own premises most of whom are thus secured from taking the wrong side as they are on ill terms with the Police.'[47] There are also scattered pieces of evidence which show opposition to enrolment, one of the most important being a letter of 8 April sent to the Home Office by a London magistrate, a Mr P. Bingham who attended the Geological Museum to swear in the considerable number of workers employed in its building:

I am sorry to have to apprise that the feeling exhibited by them was anything but satisfactory. Some refused to be sworn, and those who consented, insisted on limiting their services to the inside of the Building. I willingly assented to this under the circumstances I have stated, considering they might otherwise be on Kennington Common.

I was then desired to attend at Lord Ellesmeres, where a very large body of workmen is employed. The Foreman informed me that the whole of them, with the exception of three, refused to be sworn, but that they had promised to defend the building in case of attack.

After this, I thought it better to abstain from going further.[48]

Much was made by contemporaries of the business establishments who signed up all their workers and this support has been used by modern historians to buttress their own belief in working-class involvement in the maintenance of public order against the potential or threatened Chartist violence. One of the most striking examples of a large-scale opposition to service as special constables came from the industrial North during the second half of March. The story was told by Sir Thomas Arbuthnot commanding the northern military district who added to his report that he had made particular enquiries on the matters stated and found them to be 'essentially correct'. What happened was that the Lancashire and Yorkshire Railway Company swore in 700 of their workmen as special constables. The day after, a mass meeting of the men was held to protest against their involvement 'at a moment's notice' and the resolution given below was unanimously adopted:

Resolved, first: That we, the workmen of the Lancashire and Yorkshire Railway Company, do disapprove of the abrupt manner in which we were called up to be sworn in as special constables by the authorities, and that we did fully expect to be treated as men capable of comprehending right from wrong – Secondly: That this meeting is of opinion that it is in the interest and duty of all classes to protect life and property, and that we, the workmen of the Lancashire and Yorkshire Railway Company, do pledge ourselves to do so, as far as it in our power lies, providing the middle class do pledge themselves to protect our capital, namely, our labour – Thirdly: That it is the opinion of this meeting that the present distress of the working classes arises from class legislation, and that it is their unanimous opinion that no permanent good can be effected for the community at large, until the working classes are fully and fairly represented in the Commons house of parliament, and that intelligence and virtue are the proper qualifications of a representative. The workmen here present do pledge themselves to offer no resistance to any body of men who may struggle for such a representation.

The resolution just quoted was taken from a press cutting from the *Manchester Examiner* of 18 March which Arbuthnot enclosed in his report to the Home Office. His accompanying letter said that it appeared that a number of the railway workers were well-known Chartists and some were in well-paid positions; that at the meeting there were some good speakers and that cheers were given for the Charter.[49] Without doubt the resolution had been drawn up by someone or group accustomed to political activity.

One example of a group of militant railway workers does not make a case for the total opposition of working people to middle-class appeals for the law and order approach of the Whig government; even when put alongside the evidence already quoted from London. It does, however, encourage scepticism and highlight the need for more serious research into working-class attitudes, both in the run-up to the London demonstration of 10 April, when the hysteria in the country at large was widespread and pervasive, and in the months which followed. Most of the discussion about working-class involvement as special constables has related to the April days, and little to the weeks which followed when in some parts of the country – in particular London and the industrial North – the combined Irish and Chartist movements were growing and violence was coming to be accepted. From the evidence which is available, it would seem that the gap in later months between social classes was widening. This was certainly true of the liberal grouping within the middle classes whose attitudes towards working-class radicals were appreciably hardening; and, as political bitterness developed, it is probable that working-class enrolment in the security forces, whatever its original size and social composition, was lessening or being completely eliminated.

On the morning of 10 April the National Convention met at 9 a.m. in its usual hall in John Street. G. W. M. Reynolds took the chair in the absence of Philip McGrath, and Doyle reported that he and McGrath had waited on the police commissioners on the previous day to inform them that the Convention, as an indication of their desire to lessen tension, had changed the route of the procession as originally planned, and now intended to keep it some distance from the Houses of Parliament. The police, on their side, had replied that there could be no change in the decision to ban the procession. The Convention then heard Feargus O'Connor at his most rambling and, after shorter speeches from the floor, the Convention concluded at 10 a.m., and the leading Chartists then entered the vans outside the hall. These wagons contained the petition and were drawn by horses supplied by the Land Company. This official group then drove slowly down Tottenham Court Road, through Holborn and Farringdon Street over Blackfriars Bridge, and arrived at Kennington Common about 11.30 a.m.

The police had set up a control centre in the Horns Tavern on the edge of Kennington Common early on the Monday morning. Richard Mayne, the junior of the two Police Commissioners, was responsible for its direction. Messages from all parts of London came to this control point where the Chartists were assembling and later marching; and these reports were then sent on to the Home Office. Some examples follow:

9.15 a.m.:
'Report from Clerkenwell Green that 3000 assembled.' (The *Globe* reported in its second edition that on two poles carried by the demonstrators there was a cap of liberty, a tri-coloured flag and an American flag).
Police Station, Stepney, 9 a.m.:
'There are at present about 2000 persons assembled on Stepney Green, who are now being formed in procession five deep, with Music, Flags etc. All seems peaceable, and no appearance of their being armed'
E. Div. 9.50 a.m.:
'The procession is now moving from Russell Square about 10,000.'
11.15 a.m.:
'The procession is now filing onto the Common having arrived by the Walworth Road. There are numerous flags and banners but not the slightest appearance of arms or even bludgeons.'[50]

Soon after O'Connor arrived at Kennington Common he was called for a discussion with the police who informed him that the meeting would be allowed but that the procession would not. Mayne reported the interview at length in a communication to Sir George Grey. O'Connor returned to the demonstration and addressed it from one of the vans, arguing that they had established the right of meeting and to avoid a physical confrontation with the authorities they should accept the presentation of the petition by a few people; and that the meeting should disperse. 'He would again call on them for God's sake not to injure their cause by intemperance or folly', and he ended: 'Let every man among you now take off his hat and bow to the Great God of Heaven – thank him for his goodness, and solemly promise not to break his law.' Ernest Jones was the next speaker and, to quote the *Morning Chronicle* report:

said that he was a physical force Chartist, but in their present unprepared state he deprecated any attempt at collision with the authorities. He had recommended that the procession should not have been brought on this side of the water, and that the bridges should not have been placed between them and the House of Commons. He believed that if they had met on the other side of the water the police would never have attempted to stop the procession. But at present they had been completely caught in a trap. They would, however, meet on the other side of the water, if their petition were not granted, and carry their remonstrance to the foot of the throne. He entreated them to disperse peaceably on the present occasion, and they might depend upon it, if they followed his advice, they would be able to meet in larger numbers upon another occasion, joined by thousands of the middle classes.[51]

There was opposition to the platform from militants such as Cuffay, and this was the beginning of an alternative leadership in London to the hitherto accepted personalities of Chartism. It is possible that Ernest Jones, despite the discredit which this day must have brought upon him in the minds of some Londoners at any rate, might have continued to move to the Left; but he was the first of the major figures of the movement to be arrested in early June, and was not therefore part of the illegal movement that began to grow during the summer months. In the rest of the country the failure of the Kennington Common meeting had remarkably little, if any, effect upon the morale of the Chartist movement; in the industrial North especially, it continued to increase its political activities until the mass arrests of the late summer.

For the government 10 April was of crucial importance. The Chartist demonstration was never intended to be a physical confrontation with the government; and when the Chartist leaders protested their peaceful intentions, they were not dissembling. The Whig government, however, did not overreact, as has often been suggested.[52] A demonstration of their coercive power over their own radicals, in the context of this period, was of central importance, both at home and abroad. As the Chartist Convention correctly noted, Europe was looking anxiously and carefully at what was happening in England; and it was not hysteria but calm resolve that moved the Whig ministers to their elaborate precautions in their own capital city. They had absorbed the lessions of Paris, and to have permitted a mass demonstration to accompany the petition to Westminster might have offered opportunities for disturbance or riot the consequences of which, in the tense atmosphere of these days, were certainly incalculable. Again there would have been no doubt about the outcome; but a bloodless victory – one indeed that could be laughed off, as this one was – offered confidence and relief not only inside Britain but in every European capital that was beleaguered. To contemporaries in 1848 the affair of Kennington Common was certainly not as trivial as it has mostly been portrayed in the history textbooks.[53] It provided evidence, as noted already, of the wholehearted support of all the various groups within the middle strata. The House of Commons could have its fun at the expense of the fictitious names on the Chartist petition as well as at the grossly exaggerated claims of its total signatories, but the government was under no illusion that the radical movement had disappeared or was suffering any serious loss of morale. As Palmerston wrote to Clarendon on the day following the Kennington Common meeting: 'Things passed off beautifully here yesterday, but the snake is scotched, not killed.'[54] The actions of the government were clear proof that while ministers took heart from the success of 10 April, they did not underplay the movement that they knew was continuing to grow in strength and numbers. The Irish were, perhaps, decisive: with the very large Irish communities in Britain, there could be no complacency in Whitehall while Ireland remained in a state of turmoil. Certainly there is none in the interdepartmental correspondence of the coming months.

Sir George Grey was at the centre of the reports coming in from various parts of London during the day of the Kennington Common demonstration; but he was also in close communication with all the major cities of the kingdom. The mayors of Manchester and other large towns had all underlined the importance of news from London on 10 April, and information was awaited with great anxiety. In Leicester the local magistrates were so convinced that what happened in London would directly affect radical politics in their own town that they sent one of the magistrates' clerks to London to telegraph information back; and they requested the Home Office to afford the necessary facilities. In Manchester, when news was received on the 10th of the peaceful character of the Kennington Common demonstration the officers of the corporation had the details printed on large posters which were distributed throughout the town.[55]

Throughout 1848 the areas most affected by disturbance and riot, actual or potential, were the industrial towns of West Yorkshire and Lancashire, and the metropolitan centre of London. Scotland, including Glasgow, was relatively undisturbed during this year, in spite of the numbers of Irish in counties such as Lanarkshire; and the same was true of South Wales where there had been relatively little political agitation of the Chartist kind since the Newport rising. The numbers of Irish in South Wales were fewer than in the industrial North although the hostility of the native Welsh towards the Irish was quite marked. The Catholic Church here, as elsewhere in England, was always a conservative influence. There was a meeting at Merthyr Tydfil on 12 April when about 2,000 were present; and the rumour was that the local Catholic priest was to take the chair. It was denied by the priest who went on to emphasise his complete disapproval of the meeting itself.[56] The Catholic hierarchy everywhere in England had been active in the week preceding St Patrick's Day. In Manchester, for example, a large poster placarded in the town, signed by sixteen local priests, warned against being led astray by those acting against authority:

Our Religion teaches us to obey the law, and to respect the Civil authorities; and it would be sinful for any Person to take part in Proceedings which the law prohibits, or which the Authorities pronounce to be illegal . . .
[And after noting that a meeting was advertised for St Patrick's Day]
We conjure you to be more than usually cautious to do no Act on that day which . . is calculated to dishonour the Festival, or bring scandal upon the Holy Faith.[57]

1848, however, was to be turbulent in most of Lancashire, and troubles centered upon Manchester and Liverpool. Manchester was the more important town although the proportion of Irish in Liverpool was higher: by 1848 nearly one quarter of the population was Irish, native born or immigrant. The military headquarters for the whole of the North were at Manchester, stretching from Newcastle-upon-Tyne to Birmingham and the Midlands. The General Officer Commanding was Sir Thomas Arbuthnot, a Peninsular veteran whose family home was in County Mayo. By 1848 Arbuthnot had been in his command for six years, and he was highly respected in Whitehall for his remarkably informative intelligence reports. His years of office had given him a great deal of experience in dealing with all aspects of the problems of maintaining the public peace, and not least in assessing the reliability of local magistrates in their all too common appeals for the help of the military.[58] March 1848 had brought the first serious intimations of new levels of political unrest and Arbuthnot had close associations in Manchester with the stipendiary magistrate and the Lord Mayor. Elkanah Armitage was mayor of Manchester during this year. He was born in 1794, so was considerably younger than Arbuthnot, and had begun with a small drapers shop from which he graduated to bedding manufacturer with mills at Swinton and Pendleton. In 1834 he was elected councillor for Exchange ward, was Boroughreeve of Salford in 1838, alderman in 1841, and elected mayor on 9 November 1846 and served for two years. At the end of his term of office the Home Secretary recommended him for a knighthood for services rendered.

Armitage was an exemplar of the self-made middle class who came to prominence after the Municipal Corporations Act of 1835. Liberal in politics, well-to-do in business affairs, able and energetic: a reader of the

Whiggish *Manchester Guardian* rather than the *Examiner*, a Cobdenite, that is to say, rather than a follower of John Bright. He was anti-aristocratic in the way these northern businessmen were, but with no anxieties or hesitations when the social order was threatened by democracy. Arbuthnot, a Peninsular veteran of good Irish Protestant family, and Armitage, the self-made millowner: as symbolic a combination of those defending the social order in 1848 as could be wished for.[59]

Manchester as the centre of the cotton industry was strategically more important than Liverpool and it had a richer tradition of radicalism. But in 1848 it was Liverpool that was potentially, and probably actually, more dangerous than Manchester. The Irish presence was much more powerful, and they were concentrated within the inner city, especially in the Scotland and Vauxhall wards. The majority were labourers, particularly to be found in transport undertakings and especially in the docks.[60]

Disease and crime were higher – in most cases much higher – than in any other large city in Britain. Politics took on a different colouring; and the police force was both large and efficient. The new Watch Committee under the 1835 Act controlled 350 men; by 1839 the total was 574, the largest provincial police force in Britain. In 1848 alarm and anxiety among the middle class began to spread immediately after the events in Paris at the end of February. Sir William Warre, GOC Chester District, which included Liverpool, visited the town at the request of the mayor in early March in order to consider what additions were required to the existing military forces. Warre reported to Arbuthnot who passed on the information to the Home Office that great excitement prevailed in the town; that there was much unemployment; that the dock employers had introduced new terms of working which gave preference to their own permanent labour force (most of whom were likely to be Protestant); and that more troops were certainly needed. Arbuthnot requested an additional regiment, the greater part of which would be allocated to Liverpool, and it was agreed that the 52nd should move to Northern Command by 14–15 March.

The immediate concern was St Patrick's Day on 17 March. The mayor, T. B. Horsfall, a Tory (the Tories had a majority on the Council since 1842 and were to retain control for most of the next forty years), made extensive preparations. All the regular police were mustered, and distributed all over the town; the county police were also brought in and stationed at the 'Old Swan'; enrolled pensioners were called out and used to guard the Bridewell and the Borough Gaol; and cavalry and infantry were stationed at points round and in the town. Many special constables were sworn in. Their commander-in-chief was Charles Turner, a merchant who was chairman of the Dock Board. The specials were organised into sections, each with their own captain. On the day, the mayor and magistrates assembled at 7 a.m. at the Sessions House before which the special constables had assembled, and after consultation between their officers and the magistrates the specials were dismissed to return to their own place of work or home, but to hold themselves in readiness if required. Any disturbance or outbreak in the town would be signalled during the hours of darkness by the ringing of church bells. The number of specials was put at between two and three thousand.[61]

It was an effective dress rehearsal for the events of the coming months. In all the large towns of the United Kingdom where there were Irish in large numbers, St Patrick's Day was peaceful, helped in some places by rain. In Liverpool an outside meeting was prohibited and an evening meeting passed off without incident. The towns in the industrial North were quiet during the closing weeks of March. The military commanders were unremitting in their pressure upon magistrates to swear in more special constables. The local commander in Nottingham, for example, complained to Arbuthnot of the dilatoriness of the mayor in this matter; and on 4 April Arbuthnot made this a general point in a letter to Sir Denis le Marchant: saying how important it was for his military officers to impress 'on the minds of magistrates, not only the expediency but the absolute necessity of their causing large numbers of Special Constables to be sworn in on such occasions for the preservation of Property'. Arbuthnot went on to emphasise that what was crucial was the sense of power behind the special constables, 'to inspire them with confidence'. He ended this particular letter with the 'lament' that 'large numbers of the working classes' in Bradford were unemployed.[62]

References to the state of employment were common in the military reports from Northern Command as well as in those from magistrates, and in comments in the press. They were often linked with anxious appraisals of the attitudes of the respectable working class, as compared with the residuum (although this latter term was not yet being used). Armitage for example wrote to the Home Office on 4 April reporting the considerable excitement which prevailed among the unemployed, although there had been no disturbances; and he further noted that 'Operatives do not evince any inclination to join with the disaffected.' This last point he repeated in a letter three days later to the effect that his information was still that 'the employed operatives are still well-disposed and opposed to any disturbance in their employment'.[63]

The patterns of agitation, and the execution of the counter-measures by the security forces, were broadly the same all over the country. Chartist meetings continued to be held without disturbance; the language used was often violent; and the presentation of the petition on the 10th in London was the focal point for most Chartist speakers. The levels of excitement, apprehension and concern, in anticipation of the demonstration in London, mounted steadily. Rumours abounded, especially rumours in the more disaffected districts about arms sales or the movement of arms through the country. Birmingham through Liverpool to Ireland were the towns and routes most talked about. Arbuthnot was sceptical about much of this kind of information, whether it came from magistrates or members of the public, or even from some of his own commanders.[64] Arms rumours fed the demands for more troops which came from magistrates all over the industrial North and Arbuthnot had limited resources of manpower. Moreover, he was well aware that a rising level of unrest in Ireland could mean that his own command might be expected to supply some of the troops required. One of his main domestic problems was that of proper accommodation when troops were sent to towns or districts where no permanent barracks existed; as indeed was the case in most of his command. On 8 April, for example, he wrote to the Home Office about the disposition of troops in the West Midlands. He explained why he had ordered the withdrawal of a cavalry unit and a small detachment of infantry from Dudley: 'as both have been kept in Billets there it having been found impossible to obtain a building fit for temporary barracks at that place and with the existing political feelings amongst the lower orders, it certainly must be considered very desirable to avoid placing troops in Billets'.[65]

While most towns in these days before 10 April were assembling large numbers of special constables to buttress the regular police, enrolled pensioners and the military, there were some exceptions in addition to those whose officials were dilatory. Birmingham was among the most interesting. The local commander reported a meeting with the magistrates who after much discussion refused to swear in special constables on the grounds that 'numbers in the Town are inspired with feelings towards the Chartists and unless there is an active breach of the peace they will not act'. Arbuthnot told the Home Office that he had repeatedly urged the military officers in Birmingham to impress upon the mayor and his colleagues the necessity of a large number of specials and to point out that while every assistance would be given to the civil power to help preserve the peace, if property was destroyed they would bear considerable responsibility for its destruction. In a later letter Arbuthnot offered the Home Office an explanation for the attitudes in Birmingham. He was writing on 19 April a general comment on the mobilisation of the shopkeeping class in the preservation of public order and he added:

this, however, is not the case at Birmingham when in many instances in the handicraft trades there is not much difference between the station in society of the employers and the employed, and unfortunately large numbers of the latter are now out of work in consequence of the low state of trade.[66]

A somewhat different picture of Birmingham emerges from other parts of the Home Office correspondence. A letter from the Lord Mayor on 10 April – no time given – reported that 500 special constables had been sworn in although another letter on the 11th agreed that there had been a large number of refusals. In the 10 April letter the Mayor wrote that 'There appears the greatest willingness on the part of persons called upon to undertake their duty. In the large Carriage Building Establishment of Mr Joseph Wright all his workmen to the number of 300 have expressed their willingness to be sworn in, and they will be so tomorrow.'[67] This may have been the panic reaction of this extraordinary day; or the general tone of the mayor's letters may have been a rather optimistic gloss on his local situation.

There were several common trends in the country as a whole that can be generalised from the Home Office correspondence. There were few reports, for example, before 10 April from police agents or self-appointed informers. It was reported from Birmingham on 13 April that the local police had a police constable who was not known to the Chartists and who attended their meetings; but at this time most reports came from journalists and newspaper accounts. It is noticeable too that the Home Office was reluctant to sanction the arrest of local Chartist leaders for violent speech. For one thing, at this stage, they were not at all anxious to have trials for which the evidence was not overwhelming and they preferred to wait until middle-class opinion was more thoroughly aroused. Premature arrest might inflame radical opinion that was still drinking in the delights of the news from revolutionary Paris. The Home Secretary and his colleagues were quite clear on all these matters, and they preferred to delay until middle-class attitudes had become more solid and unyielding.

Once 10 April was over two things happened in the weeks which followed. One was that the failure of the Kennington Common meeting – and it was a failure – appears to have had no demoralising effect upon the Chartist movement in London or in the industrial North: the two regions where the levels of political activity were greatest during 1848. What happened in London, and almost certainly in parts of the industrial North, is that there developed over the next few months the embryo of an illegal movement, the growth of which was real enough but in its details is still shadowy. On the ground itself the scale of demonstrations and meetings increased until the mass arrests of the summer brought the whole movement throughout the country to an end by September. The second thing that happened was the stiffening of the resolve of the middle ranks of society against the constant disturbances and turbulence from below; and the mobilisation of the middle classes, which had been so impressive around 10 April, continued with unabated momentum.

The failure of the 10 April meeting was received with dismay in Paris and Dublin. In both cities much had been made by the various radical groups of the encouragement to their own cause, and of the general encouragement to Europe as a whole, of a successful demonstration in London. Normanby wrote from Paris on 10 April that 'Much excitement is felt this morning in Paris as to what may at this moment be passing in London';[68] and on the Monday afternoon some of the French press published telegraphic despatches to the effect that there had been fighting in London from early morning, and that the town was in general insurrection. In his journal Normanby wrote that Lamartine had told him that this news was not published officially on his instructions; and Normanby added that he was in no doubt that Ledru Rollin had sent the despatch down to Boulogne, to be relayed back to Paris at the appropriate time.[69]

There is no doubt that the success of the forces of order in England was of considerable importance in the politics of Europe. On 26 March, a speaker at a large meeting at the castle of Heidelberg had contrasted France with England, much to the advantage of the latter: 'Let her be our model; she has long enjoyed free institutions; she alone now remains unshaken by the storm which is howling around, and it is to her we must look as our model and guide.'[70] After the Kennington Common meeting Prince Albert wrote to Baron Stockmar that 'We had our revolution yesterday, and it ended in smoke'; and on the same day, 11 April, he wrote to his equerry (Normanby's brother): 'What a glorious day was yesterday for England: How mightily will this tell all over the world!'[71] And Normanby himself wrote in his journal that he could not exaggerate 'the enormous effect produced here by the gratifying results of the London failure'.[72] Lord John Russell summed up in a letter to Clarendon, in words which had meaning for British diplomacy in Europe as well as for the direction of home affairs: 'The first result of the peaceful issue of Monday's proceedings has been to give increased confidence to all peaceable men and increased stability to our institutions.'[73]

Clarendon, in Dublin, had been kept in touch with events in London by special arrangements made through the mayor of Liverpool, and on the 11 April he sent his congratulations to Sir George Grey: 'As great expectations had been formed here of the Chartist meeting in London and the most villainous intentions were to have been carried into effect or attempted if that meeting had led to outbreak.'[74] Throughout this month of April Clarendon continued to send alarming and alarmist reports to London about the state of Ireland, and he pressed constantly for additional legal powers, particularly to deal with the manufacture and distribution of arms, especially pikes. On this particular matter he was not successful in April. Palmerston wrote to him on the 11th setting forth the Cabinet's view, and in a long letter of the 17th Grey was more explicit on the question of arms manufacture; and somewhat tart:

There is clearly much exaggeration both here and in Ireland as to these matters. You have mentioned two instances of it today in your letter to Lord Lansdowne. Here I had information that a large number of Pikes were being made in Birmingham; but on a careful investigation there was reason to believe that not one had been made there.[75]

The government had already been preparing a new measure which would assist the prosecution of political offenders, especially in Ireland. This was the Crown and Government Security Bill, the first reading of which was taken in the Commons on the evening of 10 April. The Bill was introduced by Sir George Grey who explained that while it applied to the whole of the United Kingdom it was particularly relevant to Ireland where the present law was 'utterly inapplicable' to meet the growing problem of treasonable expression. The offences which at present came within the English law of treason were henceforth to be accounted as felonies, punishable by transportation for life or for a period of not less than seven years. Offences against the sovereign remained high treason and were excluded from the changes defined in the new Act. A few radicals in the Commons, including Hume and W. J. Fox, opposed a new clause which would punish 'open and advised' speaking as a treasonable felony and their amendment for its deletion attracted the largest opposition vote. At the Committee stage Lord John Russell intimated that the government were willing to limit that part of the Bill which related to 'open and advised' speaking to two years. The Bill was introduced into the Lords on 19 April and passed the following evening, receiving the Royal Assent on the 22nd.[76] The second Bill introduced by the government at this time was the Aliens Removal Bill which gave the Home Secretary the power to remove any foreigner from the United Kingdom if their conduct was deemed likely to be injurious to the peace of the realm. There had been an absurd minor panic in the press and in Parliament on this question in the days preceding 10 April.[77]

   Smith O'Brien and T. F. Meagher had been arrested on 22 March and charged with seditious libel, while John Mitchel was charged at the same time for publishing seditious articles in three issues of the *United Irishman*. The trial of Smith O'Brien and Meagher was a minor defeat for Dublin Castle, since the Crown failed to secure a verdict owing to the obduracy of one Catholic juryman in both cases. This was on 15 May and 16 May. The trial of Mitchel was to be held under the new Treason-Felony Act, and considerable efforts were made to ensure a jury that would convict.[78] Mitchel's trial began on 26 May, and for weeks before, from the days of the failure of the Chartist demonstration in London, Clarendon had been expressing his growing fears at what he considered to be the worsening situation in Ireland. He remained much concerned that Russell and his colleagues had refused an arms clause in the Treason-Felony Bill, and he was critical of the army command in Ireland. Blakeney, the commander-in-chief, he wanted to keep because of his experience of Irish affairs, although Blakeney was not particularly well-regarded in London; but of the others Clarendon wrote bluntly to Russell on

I 2 April that 'The Staff officers here are a set of twaddling old women and we should have melancholy proof of the fact if an insurrection should take place.'[79] Throughout April Clarendon continued to express his belief that Ireland was steadily becoming more combustible. He quoted Blakeney to Russell that the military resources were 'quite insufficient' for suppressing any general movement, and wholly inadequate for carrying on a civil war with any prospect of success. In the same letter he wrote that the people were arming themselves 'as fast as they can. In short, we have at present prevented the flame from bursting out but it is smouldering and extending and the slightest accident may produce a conflagration.'[80] On the following day, 19 April, Clarendon wrote to Grey expressing similar pessimistic views and adding an indication of his own personal attitude which explains much of the firm resolve so much approved of in England: 'No man seems to recognise any other duty than that of not committing himself. This applies mainly to the Roman Catholics and I am sorry to say that the experience of the last two months has left upon my mind the worst impression of that creed and nine-tenths of those who profess it.'[81]

By this time Clarendon was using secret agents for some of his information, always a hazardous business without the most careful evaluation. J. D. Balfe, who contacted Clarendon in early April, seems to have been someone Clarendon trusted, and Nowlan suggests that Balfe's reports were 'reasonably accurate'.[82] Certainly, from the correspondence surviving in the Clarendon papers, Balfe's material was sober and not wildly exaggerated. He quoted conversations with Confederate leaders that *a priori* were not improbable. Together with the information from police sources, and from the press generally, Clarendon and his officials were well enough served. By the end of April Clarendon was expressing himself in somewhat less anxious terms; and on 2 May he wrote to Russell that 'The accounts from the country are tolerably good' but with the reminder that in another month the distress from the further failure of the harvest could be expected to create new disturbances. He was to be temporarily heartened by the affray at Limerick which led to the withdrawal of John Mitchel and Devin Reilly from the Confederation on 3 May.[83]

April ended with a temporary improvement in the general situation in Ireland and Europe. The serious rebuff from Lamartine to Smith O'Brien and the Irish delegation had affected the Irish more than they were prepared to admit in public, and it is interesting that one of Balfe's early reports quoted Duffy as highly critical of the decision to go to the Provisional government. In the closing days of the month Grey wrote to Clarendon expressing his satisfaction that things appeared to be 'cooling'.[84] The forces of order were beginning to reassert themselves. It was, however, only the beginning. De Tocqueville returned to Paris at the end of April after conducting his election campaign in the Cherbourg peninsula. He found Paris 'sinister and frightening'. He wrote in his *Recollections*:

I had always thought that there was no hope of gradually and peacefully controlling the impetus of the February Revolution and that it could only be stopped suddenly by a great battle taking place in Paris. I had said that immediately after the 24th February, and what I now saw persuaded me that the battle was not only inevitable but imminent, and that it would be desirable to seize the first opportunity to start it.[85]

5

SUMMER

The politics of France, so important in the early weeks of the revival of the radical movement in England and Ireland, became steadily less influential during April. In the middle of the month Normanby had set out in detail the conflicting problems which faced the Provisional government, but with the elections to the Constituent Assembly at the end of April the propertied classes throughout Europe were beginning to see signs of hope. As Sir George Grey wrote to Clarendon on 28 April, 'I trust what appears to be going on in France will have a good effect in Ireland. The elections seem to be going in favour of the moderate party and the Ledru Rollin section of the Provisional Government after all their arbitrary proceedings are at a discount'.[1] The newly elected Assembly which first met in Paris on 4 May was based upon a no property qualification for its franchise, yet de Tocqueville in his *Recollections* was among a number of commentators who emphasised the conservative character of so many members: it had 'more large landowners and also gentlemen' than any of the previous Chambers elected on a restricted franchise. It also had a more powerful religious group. Altogether, for de Tocqueville, it was an improvement on any previous Assembly he had known, although he added that it 'had been elected to face civil war', the outbreak of which was not to come for nearly two months. Lord Normanby continued to provide London with his usual perspicacious reports on the developing situation; and for the months of May and June his *Journal* is less useful than the despatches and correspondence in the Foreign Office files. The demonstrations of 15 May, which might have turned out so menacing to the forces of order, were in fact a victory for the reactionaries, and it was during the closing days of May that decisions were taken by the government to end enrolment in the National Workshops and to offer harsh alternatives.[2] It was to take another month before these policies began to be put into large-scale effect. When the ultimatum was finally delivered on 21 June it was the signal for what was to be the bloodiest insurrection in Europe during the nineteenth century except for the Paris Commune. As Marx noted, the National Guards 'streamed in from the provinces', and the victory of the forces of order over the Parisian masses was the clearest possible signal to the rest of Europe that the tide of reaction was moving in fast. Normanby wrote to the Foreign Office on 25 June:

I trust that one may now anticipate the defeat of the attempt to establish a Republique Rouge, the success of which in the present feverish state of society would probably have produced dreadful attempts at imitation throughout Europe and the triumph of any authority cannot fail to have an equally different salutary effect but to this unhappy city peace when restored will have been purchased at an awful price of human suffering and misery.[3]

These words of Normanby were also the sentiments of de Tocqueville to whom the June days were 'necessary, fateful': having rescued the nation 'from oppression by the Paris workmen and restored it to control of its own fate'.[4] On 26 June, when the military issue was no longer in doubt, Normanby hastened to offer his congratulations to Cavaignac. He gave his account to Palmerston:

I mentioned to M. Bastide that not being personally acquainted with the General I should be glad if he would present me and allow me to express my congratulations on the result and the thanks of the friends of order in all countries at the triumph his energy had obtained over the late anarchical attempt. The General received me very cordially, and said, he was sure that in London and every where else much satisfaction would be felt at the defeat of a party who aimed at the destruction of all society. I did not of course detain the General more than a few moments knowing how much his time must be engrossed.[5]

On the following day Normanby summed up what he felt to be the lessons for France of the events through which the country had just passed:

the moderate republicans . . . should never again be able to traffic on the illusions of the working classes. Already much has been gained in this direction. The socialist doctrine has been thoroughly exposed. It has been clearly proved that some limit must be placed to liberty – it becomes licence and tyrannises in its turn. The right of public meeting in the streets is taken away and it exists only on the sufferance of authority.
The Clubs, I understand, are to be shut up – and it is admitted that there may be occasion when the liberty of the Press must be completely annihilated.[6]

By the time of the June days France was no longer an inspiration to the Chartist movement in England although middle-class opinion was always ready to use the French events of this year as examples of the follies which Chartist ideas and Chartist action also represented; and for the rest of the year, in the middle-class press, references continued to the depths of misery and suffering brought about by the February Revolution.

With the declining influence of France went the increasing importance of Ireland in English radical politics; and Ireland and Irish crises came to dominate the timing of political activity in Britain. In London Chartists politics were somewhat muted in the immediate aftermath of the

Kennington Common meeting, but political spirits soon recovered, and in the closing days of April and throughout May demonstrations and meetings grew in number and size. Goodway's carefully compiled list of Chartist localities in London[7] shows a remarkable increase in their number during May, compared with April and earlier months: to a peak figure of forty-one groups in May. June had the same number and only in July and August were there the first beginnings of a decline, as yet quite small, while the autumn months showed a clear falling-off in political organisation and agitation. By the summer months of 1848, then, the number of Chartist localities in the metropolis was nearly double the total for the first three months of the year, and there was now an especial concentration of groups in the districts of Marylebone and Tower Hamlets. This growth in the number of organised localities meant a general increase and expansion of the Chartist presence; and by the end of May a number of open spaces – Bishop Bonner's fields, the Nova Scotia Gardens in Bethnal Green, St Pancras Fields, Irongate Wharf, Praed Street – had become the regular meeting places for the larger meetings that were now being organised.[8]

The National Assembly met in London from 1 May.[9] Historians of Chartism have mostly concentrated upon the quarrels and the divisions of political aims and methods that characterised the discussions and the Assembly has tended to be considered in terms of the general decline of the movement. Within a broad context this is acceptable within a long-run analysis. Disagreements there were in plenty and there was much criticism of Feargus O'Connor, but in the radical world outside he still commanded support both for himself and his policies. What the Assembly achieved, because of its failures to arrive at positive decisions, was a notable hardening of views among those who advocated physical confrontation with the forces of law and order.[10] Among the few useful conclusions the Assembly agreed upon was the New Plan of Organisation which established the basic unit of a class of ten men, and ten classes to a ward, and so many wards to a locality. It was a type of organisation not new to the movement, or to other organisations of these years, but it could, if required, well serve the purposes of conspiratorial developments.[11]

What has so often been missed is that the quarrels and disagreements of the Assembly appeared to have had no influence upon the growth of the Chartist and radical movement in those parts of the country where the potential for growth was already established: London and the industrial North. In newspaper reports of meetings and demonstrations, as well as in the departmental papers of the Home Office, the increase in political activity is amply documented. As so often happens a growing political movement requires a catalyst for its further development, and this was provided at the end of May by the trial and conviction of John Mitchel. The three leading

Irish radicals – Mitchel, Smith O'Brien and T. F. Meagher – had been arrested on 22 March and then released on bail. Mitchel was charged with publishing three seditious articles in the *United Irishman* and Smith O'Brien and Meagher were prosecuted for seditious speech.[12] The trial of these latter two was in the middle days of May, but the jury in both cases failed to reach a verdict due to the presence of at least one Catholic in each instance. When Mitchel was brought to court the Irish administration took no chances. He was charged under the new Treason-Felony Act, the jury was packed, all Catholics being excluded, and Mitchel was sentenced to fourteen years' transportation. He was quickly hurried out of the country.[13]

Mitchel's trial already led to widespread demonstrations in the areas in England where there were large numbers of Irish, and the whole Chartist movement acknowledged the political significance of the trial. The verdict was delivered on 27 May and it brought Irish and Chartists in closer union. The movement for joint political action was already growing and, on this central issue of support for Ireland and the denunciation of Irish wrongs, the Chartist movement in England exhibited a unity that overrode its other internal differences. Feargus O'Connor had always been consistent on the Irish question and his denunciation of the Crime and Outrages Bill at the end of 1847 had been favourably received in Ireland and in the Irish communities in England. In April the Greenwich (London) Chartists and Irish Confederates had formed a joint organisation, and the Wolfe Tone club, another joint body, was first mentioned in the *Northern Star* on 20 May. During the days of Mitchel's trial, 25 and 26 May, meetings of support had been held on Clerkenwell Green, and it was for their speeches at this time that Sharpe and Williams were later arrested, and convicted. On Sunday 28 May, the day after the Mitchel verdict, a large, mainly Irish demonstration marched four abreast from the Theobald Wolfe club in Cock Lane to Marylebone High Street where the meeting was joined by several thousand other demonstrators. It was addressed by a number of speakers including Francis Looney, a prominent London Confederate leader who was also later arrested. The most striking demonstration of strength took place on the following evening, Monday 29 May. At a meeting on Clerkenwell Green, the crowd, after listening to Fussell, Williams and Daniel McCarthy, left the Green just before 8 p.m. and marched to Finsbury Square where they were joined by a demonstration from Stepney Green which had been addressed by Ernest Jones, Peter McDouall and Charles McCarthy. This now greatly increased crowd then proceeded to move into the West End via Holborn, Seven Dials and Leicester Square, and then up Dean Street to Oxford Street, down Regent Street and into Trafalgar Square: a roundabout route that took them through the great middle-class shopping centres. The size of the demonstration as it moved along was constantly augmented, and it was estimated at 50,000 to 60,000 by a freelance reporter of *The Times*.[14] The procession then passed through Trafalgar Square at about 10.30 p.m. and returned to the East End by way of the Strand and Fleet Street, and dispersed in Finsbury Square. It was an impressive show of strength, and the marchers, so the press admitted, included many 'respectable people'. The only violence that night was at a meeting outside a coffee house in Redcross Street (a few hundred yards away from Finsbury Square) that was addressed by Williams, Vernon and Charles McCarthy, the most fiery representatives of physical force in the London movement.

On the next day, 30 May, the metropolitan police issued a proclamation banning all meetings and demonstrations, but a meeting was held that evening at Clerkenwell Green and, after the meeting had formally ended at 9.30 p.m. and when most people had left, fighting broke out largely as the result of a sweep across the Green by foot and mounted police. By this time the Home Office and the metropolitan police had begun to take vigorous countermeasures, their determination buttressed by reports of serious threats to order in the West Riding of Yorkshire and Lancashire. In London, on the evening of Wednesday 31 May, when a further big meeting was expected at Clerkenwell Green the metropolitan police issued another version of their ban on demonstrations, and considerable forces were mobilised in support of the police. Special constables were mustered, and three squads of Life Guards were stationed at different points in the area. Magistrates were on hand to read the Riot Act if required. By 9 p.m. the Green was crowded although there were no speeches and it was then swept by police four lines abreast. There was no resistance and the Green was cleared; but adjoining streets to the west were not so easily dispersed and it was not until midnight that fighting ceased, attempted demonstrations at Stepney Green, Finsbury Square and Smithfield being also largely frustrated by the police presence. At Stepney Green a police superintendent was stabbed in the leg, an incident which received wide publicity. On the following night there were again further disturbances at and around the Green, with the police once more ending in control, and this was the last conflict of any importance until the following Sunday, 4 June.

There were the makings of more serious riot and turbulence in the industrial North, as will be discussed later, but the metropolis always received most attention in the national press and in Parliament. This was not true, it must be emphasised, of the Home Office and leading ministers who, from the daily flow of letters and reports from all over the country, were always able to comprehend the total situation, and not least the balance that was required between Ireland and England in the disposition of the security forces. Brougham raised the question of the continuous series of meetings and demonstrations in London in the House of Lords on 2 June, and the Duke of Wellington was among those who urged more decisive action.[15] Charles Greville, a sober commentator, had an illuminating comment in his *Memoirs* under the date of 3 June:

The Government are now getting seriously uneasy about the Chartist manifestations in various parts of the country, especially in London, and at the repeated assemblies and marchings of great bodies of men . . . lately, accounts have been received from well-informed persons, whose occupations lead them to mix with the people, Clergymen – particularly R.C. – and medical men, who report that they find a great change for the worst among them, an increasing spirit of discontent and disaffection, and that many who on the 10th of April went out as special constables declare that they would not do so again if another manifestation required it. The speeches which are made at the different meetings are remarkable for the coarse language and savage spirit they display. It is quite new to hear any Englishman coolly recommend assassination and the other day a Police Superintendent was wounded in the leg by some sharp instrument. These are new and very bad symptoms, and it is impossible not to feel alarm when we consider the vast amount of the population as compared with any repressive power we possess.[16]

The London press was already commenting on the wave of marchings and processions that, so it was alleged, were beginning to frighten the shopkeeping classes, and were certainly affecting the stamina of the metropolitan police. On Friday June 2 *The Times* used the same image as that of Palmerston after the Kennington Common meeting: 'The snake was scotched not killed on 10 April'; and at the beginning of the next week it was suggesting that 'ruffianism' should meet with its appropriate punishment.[17] On Monday 5 June *The Times* named Fussell – the man who was alleged to have recommended private assassination – as a likely candidate for arrest and as one to be sent to join John Mitchel.[18] The next day it generalised its advice, and further included the name of Ernest Jones:

We should be glad to see the experiment tried of the arrest and imprisonment of the leading offenders. It is not easy to imagine that there could be any difficulty in effecting this, and still less in obtaining a verdict, according to the justice of the case, from a jury of London merchants and tradesmen.

The Times went on to comment on Lansdowne's remarks in the House of Lords on the previous evening. The matter of the London demonstrations had been again raised and Lansdowne, while reassuring the Lords that the government was alive to the problems, had half suggested that possibly the law relating to meetings might have to be amended. *The Times* was emphatic that the existing legal safeguards 'were amply sufficient for all necessary purposes'.[19] So too the government must have thought for it was in the evening of 6 June, on the day that these comments in *The Times* were made, that warrants were issued for the arrest of Ernest Jones and several other leaders of London Chartism. What had undoubtedly helped to push the Home Office into decisive action was the police riot of Sunday 4 June.

There had been a few days of relative quiet in the capital but a number of demonstrations were advertised for Sunday the 4th. A report of a very early morning drilling practice on the Sunday sent 500 policemen to Victoria Park; but it came to nothing. A meeting at 10 a.m. in Nova Scotia Gardens was suppressed by the police, followed by three hours jeering and taunting of police and special constables. In the afternoon of the same day at Bishop Bonner's Fields there was first a Confederate meeting at 3 p.m. and then an official Chartist meeting at 5 p.m. addressed by Ernest Jones and Alexander Sharpe. It was for his speech on this occasion that Jones was later charged with seditious behaviour and unlawful assembly. The meeting finished at around 6.30 p.m. and Jones himself left to take the train to the West Riding. Many supporters also left but some among those who remained turned their attention to the church which was in the Fields and in which a large number of policemen had been stationed throughout the day. The windows of the church were stoned, and the police then went on the rampage. There was a very mixed crowd, with Chartists and Irish Confederates only part of the usual heterogeneous groupings that came together in public places on a Sunday afternoon in London; but the police fell upon the political and the unpolitical without discrimination and, so it was widely alleged, with considerable savagery.

There had been indications on previous days that the police were under increasing physical strain. Since early March the metropolitan police, always under the scrutiny of the London public, which was much more influential than elsewhere in the country, had been in constant attendance at meetings and demonstrations. Evidence on such matters as strain is often difficult to find but there was in the early days a relevant comment by Colonel Rowan to General Bowles, Master of the Queen's Household at Buckingham Palace. The letter in which Rowan wrote, 'If the office work here had lasted two days more I fear I should have been obliged to give in, but last night I got some sleep', was dated 11 April[20] and while there was never again the overpowering sense of crisis among the public as there had been before the Kennington Common meeting – to which the police and all other branches of the security forces had to react – the turbulence in London had never died away; and the last days of May and the first two weeks of June must have meant continuous overtime work for most London policemen. There are a few incidents reported in the departmental papers of the Home Office and the files on the metropolitan police, as well as the odd reference in Parliament, which suggest the sense of growing strain,[21] but the evidence for the police riot on Sunday 4 June is well attested. Many of the police who took part had been stationed during the day, or part of the day, in the church which stood within the Fields, and it was alleged by several witnesses that cans of beer had been taken into the church and it was certainly common opinion that at least some of the police were drunk. One of the early letters to the Home Office was from Mrs Higgins whose house overlooked the Fields. She began by denying any sympathy with the Chartists and insisted that she never attended their meetings:

It is my opinion, and sir there is but one opinion of the whole of the inhabitants of this neighbourhood near the Park, that the conduct of the Police was the most brutal and barbarous ever beheld . . . The Chartists have held meetings on Bonners Fields for nine or ten Sundays past but we can all bear testimony that the people have separated quietly and never in one instance has it been otherwise. Indeed there has been open air preaching but never been interrupted in the services.

The letter from Mrs Higgins dated 5 June was signed by seven others and among the other material relating to these events was a petition from another group of householders living near the Fields who again insisted that they had taken no part in the Sunday meetings and that the demonstration on 4 June had ended peacefully. They continued:

some idle boys having thrown a few stones, an indiscriminate, wanton, inhuman and brutal attack was made upon men, women and children by the police not only in the Field where the meeting was held but in all the various localities for near a mile round, breaking into houses, destroying the property and dragging your memorialists into the streets. This we are able and willing to prove, and as loyal subjects of her Majesty, we demand a fair enquiry . . . So much is this the general opinion of the inhabitants of the Locality who were Eye Witnesses of the brutal transactions that men devoted to the country and of undoubted loyalty have given up the Staves, and others have declared their intention of refusing to be again sworn in as special constables.[22]

There are a number of other letters in this Home Office file, saying more or less the same thing, including one from a middle-class house-holder who informed the Home Secretary that a committee had been established in Tower Hamlets to investigate complaints against the police. Much of the indictment against the police will be found in the Public Record Office under the listing MEPO 2/66, while MEPO 2/77 contains the counter petitions and statements of sympathy and support for the police in their duties at this time.

The episode was raised in the House of Commons on 5 June by the member for Tower Hamlets, and Sir George Grey, in a brief answer, smoothly brushed aside any suggestion that the police had acted improperly. The matter was raised again on 8 June when once more the local member announced that he now had the testimony of more than sixty witnesses to the police provocation and brutality. This time the Home Secretary, no doubt because of the extensive press comment, as well as the volume of disbelieving noises on the streets of London, provided a more serious apologia than on the previous occasion. He gave a lengthy account of the circumstances of the day, and went so far as to quote in full the report of the police inspector who had been in charge at Bishop Bonner's Fields. Sir George Grey told no direct lies; but like most, if not all Home Secretaries in his situation, he ignored or failed to communicate almost all the really unpleasant evidence, and made good parliamentary play with conflicting statements. It was a very effective and aggressive defence of the metropolitan police, with no ground being given to critics or to petitioners.[23] Sir George Grey could expect, as was indeed the case, the support of the overwhelming majority of the House of Commons as well as almost all the London and provincial press. Richard Mayne, the junior of the two police commissioners, wrote to some of those who had asked for an enquiry, emphatically denying the alleged assaults by the police, and enclosing a printed leaflet headed 'The Late Chartist Disturbances at Bethnal Green' which was signed by nineteen middle-class residents of the East End, including eight clergy. Most of the latter were Anglican. The text of the leaflet was a straight defence of the police of the area who had been 'subjected to an unusual and harassing amount of duty which has uniformly been exercised with great judgement, firmness and forebearance'.[24] These were sentiments widely subscribed to in the rest of the country.

The week between the police violence of 4 June and Monday 12 June, which was Whit Monday, was filled with increasing rumours and a general apprehension that a serious confrontation was about to take place. The arrest of Ernest Jones and other London Chartists during this week added to the levels of tension. There were a number of reminders from local magistrates and officials that the term of service of many special constables, usually for two months, was about to run out, and the Home Office encouraged their re-enlistment. The call of the executive of the National Charter Association to assemble on Bishop Bonner's Fields on Whit Monday was met by a ban on all assemblies in London, and the security preparations being put in hand were equal to those of April. The general situation for the government, leaving aside the level of hysteria in April, was now more threatening. Ireland was much more disturbed and turbulent following Mitchel's conviction and transportation, and there had been serious troubles in the industrial North of England. There were newspaper reports in this week prior to Whit Monday of physical assaults in Dublin between soldiers of Irish and English regiments, and such news was not calculated to diminish the general fears that were building up.[25] The London police were issued with cutlasses for the first time this year, although they had already been in use in Bradford, and it was later revealed in Parliament that some of the cutlasses now worn by the metropolitan police on the occasion of special meetings and demonstrations had a serrated edge on one side.[26] At the same time military preparations were on what was now the standard scale for London demonstrations, and were described in detail by Sir George Grey in a letter to Lord John Russell on 11 June.[27] Guns and artillerymen were brought from Woolwich; the commercial steamer companies stood by to convey troops; all major public buildings were heavily guarded. On Whit Monday itself police occupied large parts of Bishop Bonner's Fields and when McDouall arrived at about 1 p.m. he was told by an inspector that any assembly would be illegal; and, confronted with the massive police presence and the knowledge, which had been well publicised, of the considerable military forces in central and east London, McDouall gave instructions that the meeting should be cancelled. A drizzle of rain followed by a thunder storm cleared the Fields of most people, and there were no incidents except the usual hooting and groaning at the police.[28]

It was on this day, according to police informers, that plans for insurrection were begun, only to be ended within seventy-two hours by instruction of the executive committee of the National Charter Association.[29] There followed several weeks of relative quiet and then the second attempt at illegal organisation, this time independent of the Chartist executive.[30] This last phase in London and the industrial North was concluded with the arrest during the second half of August of all the leading figures involved.

The events in London between Mitchel's trial and Whitsun week were only part of the security problems of the United Kingdom. The industrial North was also in turmoil and, because of the large proportion of Irish in the total population of some towns, the situation was potentially more dangerous.

Northern Command in 1848 was the largest and by far the most important military district in Britain except for London. It comprised the whole area of northern England, from the Scottish border down to the great Midland towns of Birmingham, Leicester and Nottingham. Headquarters were at Manchester with Lieutenant-General Sir Thomas Arbuthnot as General Commanding Officer. The districts within Northern Command were the Northwest counties (Lancashire, Cheshire, Shropshire, Flintshire, Denbighshire, Isle of Man) with headquarters at Chester and commanded by Major-General Sir William Warre; Northeast counties (Northumberland, Cumberland, Durham, Westmorland, Derbyshire, Nottinghamshire, Leicestershire and Rutland) with headquarters at York and commanded by Major-General N. Thorn; Midland counties (Warwick, Stafford, Northampton and Worcester) with headquarters at Birmingham and Colonel Arbuthnot as the commanding officer. Sir Thomas Arbuthnot, Sir William Warre and Major General Thorn were Peninsular veterans. Warre had become commanding officer of Northern Command in June 1842 but was replaced by Arbuthnot in August of that year after Warre had shown what was considered to be less than sufficient vigour in dealing with a very disturbed situation; and at the time Arbuthnot took over the Midland district was added to Northern Command.[31]

Arbuthnot's subordinate officers normally communicated with the Home

Office or the Horse Guards through him rather than directly, and they would be expected to obtain confirmation of their actions from their General Commanding Officer. In theory Arbuthnot was obliged to refer all decisions to the Home Office, for the army, in its role as support for the civil power, was always subject to civil control and at the highest level to ministerial control. In practice, with a military commander as intelligent and as powerful a personality as Sir Thomas Arbuthnot, the constitutional fictions were observed from his side, but he was clearly expected by Whitehall to follow his own judgement in many day-to-day matters. The movement of troops was always referred to the Home Office, either for decision or for agreement, and the Home Secretary, in important matters such as the movement of troops from England to Ireland, would expect to take the final decision and inform the local commanders accordingly. There would, of course, be consultation with the Military Staff in London.[32]

At the level of the magistracy, it was they, representing the civil power, who were entitled to call out troops when the local situation looked menacing or when rioting had already occurred; and fire could not be ordered until the magistrates had read the Riot Act. The constant problem with the magistracy, especially their rural representatives, was their general unreliability, their tendency to panic and to exaggerate local dangers, and their resort to the military on quite trivial pretexts. Their requests were not, however, always met by local commanders who at times refused them outright or more often referred these requests to higher levels. The military in general, especially the staff officers, often found themselves having to exercise executive functions as well as their more narrowly military roles in situations which were potentially dangerous.

In the summer months of 1848 Manchester and its surrounding cotton towns, Bradford and its region and Liverpool were the three main centres of unrest and disturbance. One of the interesting facts of the year's confrontation was the accord which most military commanders were able to establish with the civilian authorities in the great urban areas. There were exceptions,[33] but at the centre of operations, Manchester, the agreement between Arbuthnot and Elkanah Armitage, the Lord Mayor, already noted above, does seem to have been remarkably amicable and co-operative. On Arbuthnot's side this was at least in part due to his understanding of the importance of employment levels in the generation of discontent, hence his discussions with local manufacturers to which he referred in his letters to the Home Office.[34] Armitage and his fellow magistrates were mainly Liberal Dissenters, anti-aristocratic as middle-class merchants and manufacturers usually were, and often with an anti-militarist tradition. What brought the military and the civil authorities together in close working harmony was their common opposition to the violation of the public peace, the interference with normal commercial life and the harsh verbal attacks upon property and privilege. Under the constant pressure from below of violent language and threatened or actual physical violence, the middle-class Liberals in Manchester, as everywhere else in the country, steadily hardened their political attitudes; and whatever political position they occupied at the beginning of the year, by the end of 1848 they were not to be distinguished from Whig or Tory on all fundamental issues relating to law, order and sanctity of property rights. An analysis of the public posters issued by the Manchester magistracy between March and the summer months of 1848 – interleaved with manuscript correspondence in the Home Office files – provides an illuminating documentary of the journey towards the acceptance of coercion. One of the first of these posters, dated 11 March, a month before the Kennington Common meeting, was an expression of middle-class liberalism of a relatively untroubled kind. The proclamation, which was closely written, thanked everyone for assisting authority and made a special reference to the labouring classes who had been suffering from economic depression for many months:

Although unprincipled agitators have not been wanting to incite them to violence and crime, the great body of the Working Classes of Manchester have continued to be the guardians of Property and the Maintainers of Peace . . . They are aware that the interest of the Employers and the Employed are essentially the same; that Capital and Labour are equally necessary in a Manufacturing community.

The final paragraph insisted that 'The magistrates, friends of Liberty and Order, have never interfered with the right of free discussion and the public avowal of opinion'; but that there must be no incitement to disorder and the 'few Bad and Mischievous men' who had recently sought notoriety could find themselves subject to legal punishment. The general tone was friendly, optimistic and appealing. At the end of three months of meetings, demonstrations, drilling and some physical turbulence, the accent of these public statements had become quite different. No longer was goodwill assumed. By May the magistrates were banning meetings; and in a poster of 9 June there were harsh references to 'evil-disposed and seditious persons' whose intentions were to arm themselves and to encourage others to do likewise. This was at least in part true, of course; more true of the Irish in the radical movement than of other groups in general; and confronted with the threat of insurgency the effect upon the paternalistic Liberals of Manchester was to transform them into archetypal Whigs.[35]

The weeks following the Kennington Common meeting were as quiet in the Manchester area as they were in the South. Numbers attending meetings were reported as in the few hundreds, although the language was often violent. Activity began to increase towards the middle of May, and on the 19th, the Manchester stipendiary magistrate wrote to the Home Office enclosing a selection of police reports, and asking for guidance in the matter of prosecutions for seditious language. The problem, he wrote, was that it was difficult to obtain a verbatim report of what was said: 'No known reporter would be allowed to be present at the indoor meetings where the greatest violence of language takes place.'[36] To this letter, as to almost all requests of this kind up to this date, the Home Office replied that it was not prepared to recommend legal proceedings. Ministers were waiting for public opinion to harden, and to be certain that the social groups from which juries were selected could be relied upon to take a law and order attitude to their duties.

On the same day, 19 May, Arbuthnot sent a general report of the situation in the areas of his command to the Home Office. He enclosed a letter from Major-General Thorn who 'apprehended disturbances at Bradford', and Arbuthnot had authorised the movement of troops into the district.[37] Troops had also been sent to Leicester at the request of the local magistrates; and two days later further troops went to Bradford and Halifax. The last week of May saw violent demonstrations in many places of the northern industrial districts. The trial and conviction of John Mitchel evoked the same reactions as in London. At Bingley on Friday 26 May two arrested Chartists were rescued from police custody by a large group of armed Chartists, and on Monday 29 May there was serious fighting in Bradford.

It was a difficult and dangerous period for those responsible for internal security; and it went parallel with growing tensions in Ireland. Arbuthnot was writing every day to the Home Office giving the geographical distribution of unrest and the disposition of troops. In Manchester a series of meetings culminated in a call from the Irish Confederation for a mass demonstration in Stevenson Square at noon on Wednesday, 31 May. The poster they placarded round the town advertising this meeting was sent by Maude, the stipendiary magistrate, to the Home Office, in whose files it can be found. It was headed: 'Address of the Repeal Delegates in Manchester Assembled. To all Irishmen and Democrats within 20 miles of Manchester', and it continued with the exhortation: 'And give one day's labour to John Mitchel.'[38]

The Stevenson Square meeting was banned by the magistrates; but they prepared for trouble because all the reports from outlying districts suggested a considerable response. Arbuthnot, writing on 31 May, enclosed letters from the chief constable at Pendleton, and from magistrates at Oldham which 'show that it was fully expected that the Chartist meeting at Manchester this day would have been numerously attended'; and in the same letter Arbuthnot gave an account of the day's events. A large procession from Ashton and Oldham walked along the road to Manchester and were stopped at the Turnpike gate on Oldham Road by a strong force of police and military. On their way the demonstrators had turned out some mills. Pikes were carried by a minority of marchers but there was no serious attempt to break through the cordon halting their entry to the city. Arbuthnot himself was on the scene. Elsewhere in Manchester paving stones were being pulled up, but with troops in support the police fairly quickly won control of the streets. The most important news, which Arbuthnot was much gratified to report to the Home Office – and which was featured in many newspapers – was that the mills inside Manchester had continued to work during the whole day. The Lord Mayor wrote in similar terms on the same day, and the Home Office had already been informed by telegraph at 2.30 p.m. that all was quiet. The Mayor enclosed in his letter a copy of the fourth edition of the *Manchester Guardian*, a distinctly Whiggish paper at this time, which provided a detailed account of the day's happenings. When the mills closed at 6 p.m. there were great crowds on the streets and Arbuthnot called out two troops of the 11th Hussars and two companies of the 63rd Regiment 'to support the Police who would have been overwhelmed by numbers had any riots taken place'; but only minor disturbances occurred, a few arrests were made, and by 10 p.m. the streets were quiet.

The speedy removal of John Mitchel after his sentence, and the absence of any attempt to rescue him, in spite of much boastful talk, does not seem to have affected adversely the level of political activity in the industrial North. Reports to the Home Office continued to flow in with accounts of meetings and demonstrations in many places during the early days of June. Ernest Jones spoke at an evening meeting on 6 June, and the police reported more violent language than he had used in London a few days earlier. The culmination of the agitation was to be a further meeting in Manchester's Stevenson Square on Whit Monday 12 June, to coincide with meetings all over the country. Liverpool was now beginning to be mentioned in serious terms in Arbuthnot's reports and on 9 June he provided Sir George Grey with a further regional report. The week ahead was Whit week when many workers would be idle because the mills were closed, and the result would undoubtedly be seen in increased numbers at demonstrations. 'Most unfortunately', Arbuthnot wrote,' the clerks and others like them who had been sworn in as special constables were likely to leave Manchester during Whitsun week to proceed to places in the country to amuse themselves in the usual way. And although every endeavour will be made to retain them here there is cause to fear that this will not be attended with much success.' Two days later Arbuthnot continued his survey with a report that Birmingham had called on two companies of infantry from Weedon, and they would be housed in the buildings of the London and Western Railway Company. Meetings for 12 June had been called at Northampton, Nottingham and Liverpool but disturbances were not anticipated. Bradford was still reporting drilling and the town of Burslem in the Potteries was said to be in an excited state although the number of troops locally was felt to be sufficient. On the day itself there were no serious disturbances although the language used at the large Blackstone Edge meeting was unusually violent in support of Mitchel. In most meetings there appeared to have been a lessening of violent talk probably connected with a general decline of excitement following the beginning of arrests of a number of leading Chartists. There is evidence, too, of a parallel development with London; the increase in the number of private meetings and discussions in which more serious plans for physical confrontation were under consideration.[39]

The most seriously disturbed towns in the industrial North during these days of late May and early June were Bradford and its region and Liverpool. Bradford was one of the towns of greatest population growth in the first half of the nineteenth century: the increase in numbers being more than 50 per cent in each decade of the 1830s and 1840s. The Irish, who were already in the town in considerable numbers by 1830, were mostly textile workers. There developed an urban environment of gross overcrowding and insanitary conditions, with concomitant violence.[40] In 1841 the magistrates – almost all Tories at this time – decided to build a permanent military barracks on the eastern side of Bradford about two miles from the city centre. Urban politics were lively and vigorous, and it was a highly politicised town in which a combination of Tories and working-class Chartists effectively blocked the incorporation of Bradford under the 1835 Act for over a decade. The Charter of incorporation was not granted until April 1847, at which point the middle-class Whigs, Liberals and radicals took political control. Voters were all male householders who had paid their rates, had lived in the town for at least three years, and who had not been in receipt of poor relief for the twelve months preceding the election. Council members under the new municipal regulations had to possess either personal capital of £1,000 or a tenement with a taxable value of not less than £30 per annum.[41] At the first election after incorporation the Mayor and thirteen other aldermen were almost all Liberals of one kind or another, and the new borough magistrates replaced the traditional county family representatives. Aldermen, the majority of liberal councillors and the majority of the new borough magistrates were all connected with trade, mostly worsted, either as merchants or manufacturers.[42]

Bradford was a town which in many ways epitomised the technology as well as the class relations of the second quarter of the nineteenth century, when industrialisation in the textile trades was making rapid progress. Weaving was almost completely mechanised in the worsted trade by 1850, although many firms continued to operate a mixed system of hand and factory work. The mechanisation of woolcombing was more protracted, and the hand woolcombers, who numbered some 10,000 in the Bradford area during the second half of the 1840s, were now the most exploited of all textile workers. Wages were low and irregular, and housing conditions appalling. George White, already well known as a physical force Chartist when he came to work in Bradford as a woolcomber in 1844, characterised the woolcomber's trade in 1846 'as a sort of reservoir of all the poverty of England and Ireland. It was constantly receiving new competitors from those who were poorer than themselves.'[43] White had been secretary of a committee of the Woolcombers Society which produced in 1845 a report of the general housing and domestic conditions of the woolcombers: one more illustration of the social degradation that was so widely described in the reports of these years.[44]

The Short-Time movement had vigorous support in Bradford – it helped to keep the working-class alignment with the Tories for a number of years – but the catalyst for the unrest of 1848 was the continued decline of the hand workers against a background of economic depression. As everywhere in Britain the political movement was lifted to new levels of excitement by the events in Paris. The first demonstration of a mass kind was on 16 March at Peep Green, a well-known place of meeting some four miles from Bradford, and the campaign for the third Chartist petition naturally helped to carry the movement along. The local leadership of George White, David Lightfowler and the blacksmith Isaac Jefferson was vigorous and intelligent, and Bradford became among the best organised districts in England for Chartist activity.

The propertied groups in Bradford, especially the Dissenter class of merchants and manufacturers, had a number of reforming aims and objectives in common with the Chartists. At least that was what was said in the local middle-class press, and national journals such as the *Nonconformist* were always careful to insist upon the identity of purpose which could bring working-class and middle-class radicals together in common political action. At the same time during this second quarter of the century there were a number of crucial issues which kept working-class radicals apart, among them the belief in the betrayal of 1832, the new Poor Law and the Ten Hours movement. In spite of common hostility to the landed aristocracy, the established Church and the historical facts of power and privilege which resided in the upper classes, it was the issues which divided rather than those which united which were the dominating themes of middle- and working-class relationships. The possibilities of union were always, however, being argued by the more radical middle-class journals; the political possibilities of such united action were never wholly absent from working-class debate and discussion; and after the defeat of Chartism in 1848 they were to be increasingly in the forefront of working-class tactics and strategy. In Bradford during the 1840s there appeared to be a substantial section of middle-class opinion which recognised the justice of working-class demands. Titus Salt, for example, was in sympathy with moral force Chartism as were many of his contemporaries who like him belonged to the Horton Lane Congregational chapel. The practical expression of their views was published in the *Bradford Observer* on 13 April in the form of an Open Letter 'To the Non-Electors of Bradford'. The list of signatories was headed by Titus Salt, Henry Forbes, James Ellis, Henry Brown, James Acworth and practically all the leading Liberals in the town. The statement in the letter deprecated 'the policy which dissociates the Middle Classes from the Operatives' and it expressed full sympathy for the general principles of reform as laid down in the Charter. It further hoped for a united effort 'in the peaceful but vigorous advocacy of this cause'. In the same issue the *Bradford Observer* had a remarkable editorial:

The Charter is a symbol which expresses not the political faith only, but the social wants and hopes of the working classes. It is the child of their wants, and the star of their hopes. It was born of their sufferings. It is the strong expression of their sufferings.

The lesson the *Observer* drew from these generalisations was that the middle classes must fraternise with and not resist 'the legions of democracy'.

This open letter from the Bradford Liberals offered an apparently unexceptionable statement of progressive ideas current among the more advanced groups of middle-class England; and it would be reasonable to analyse the letter in those terms. We have, however, and rather unusually, an account by one of its authors which suggests a somewhat different interpretation. W. E. Forster was one of Bradford's most distinguished Liberal sons, an important figure in Gladstone's first government and remembered above all for the Education Act of 1870. In the two volume *Life* of Forster by Wemyss Reid in 1888 there is a long extract from Forster's diary in which the background to the publication of the 1848 open letter was sketched out. The letter was published on 13 April and the diary entry is dated 16 April so that the discussions reported must have been around the time of the Kennington Common meeting. This is what Forster jotted down in his diary, and his use of words is interesting:

Many of our Liberals, thinking that the best mode of quieting the mob was by evidence of sympathy on the part of the middle classes, and an attempt at least at their guidance, we called a meeting of the more active members of Colonel Thompson's committee, at which I was chairman, and at which, after much palaver, we decided on the electors addressing a manifesto to the non-electors, Godwin and self being appointed to draw it up. So we concocted somewhat of a washy performance, promising to aid them in their efforts for the suffrage, if peaceable, but loudly preaching order and abusing violence. This was signed by most of our big guns, T. Salt, Forbes, James Ellis, John Priestman, and between five hundred and six hundred electors – more than a quarter of the whole constituency – and was, I believe, a real anodyne to the mob, but a sad stumbling block and rock of offence to all Conservatives.[45]

It may be presumed that not all the Liberals of Bradford who signed the open letter were as coarse or as cynical in their thinking as Forster revealed himself in this quotation, but we are, it must be recalled, listening to one of the leading Liberals of his generation.

The testing time for Bradford Liberals was soon to come and, in the days of crisis, the fear of the 'mob', the concern for the stability of the social order of which they were among the beneficiaries, and the frightening prospect of an assault upon the existing property relations, all contributed to an unequivocal support of those responsible for the maintenance of law and order. The Mayor of Bradford, Robert Milligan, a leading worsted manufacturer, had begun to call up special constables in the days before the Kennington Common meeting; but the situation in the town did not become menacing until around the middle of May; and then it quickly worsened. The quite rapid exacerbation of the disturbed politics of Bradford can be clearly traced through the reports of Northern Command to the Home Office. The commanding officer in charge of the Bradford district was Major-General Thorn whose headquarters were at York and who reported regularly to Arbuthnot in Manchester. On 19 May Arbuthnot wrote to the Home Office, enclosing a letter from Thorn which 'apprehended disturbances' at Bradford and the news that troops were being sent. On 21 May further troops were posted to Bradford and Halifax, and on the 23rd Arbuthnot informed the Home Secretary that 1,500 special constables had been sworn in at Bradford 'and nearly the same at Halifax'. But, Arbuthnot added, 'it appears doubtful whether a great number of them would act except to defend their own property'. Here Arbuthnot was being ungenerous to the law and order instincts of at least the Bradford special constables, as events were soon to reveal. In the same letter Arbuthnot reiterated a common argument of all who were involved in security arrangements during this year:

I shall not fail to request General Thorn to impress on the magistrates and through them on the respectable part of the community at large, how essentially necessary it is for the special constables acting under the Magistrates to take an active part in support of the police to ensure the laws of the country being carried into effect, it being understood that the Military will be kept prepared ready to turn out at the shortest notice if required by the Magistrates to do so.[46]

Arbuthnot transmitted details of the troops stationed at Bradford from information supplied by Thorn in a letter dated 27 May. There was a troop of the Royal Horse Artillery and one company of the 31st Regiment in barracks, eight infantry companies in temporary barracks, and two troops of

Guards in billets. Arbuthnot noted in his covering letter that he had requested Thorn to remove troops out of billets as soon as possible. The state of the town, according to Thorn's letter of the 27th, was much more disturbed than he had expected. The Chartists were more extensively organised than he anticipated; indeed by the time that Thorn wrote there were some parts of the town the police were not daring to enter and there had been provocative marches through the city. The trial of Mitchel lifted political excitement to new levels and a visit by Peter McDouall was the occasion of a meeting described as the largest ever held in Bradford. The town had been in a state of feverish excitement the whole of the previous week, and McDouall cautioned against a premature outbreak. On 26 May, at Bingley, half way between Shipley and Keighley, two men who had been arrested for drilling and were being taken by police to York Castle were rescued by a crowd of about two hundred. In his letter of 27 May Major-General Thorn wrote of this incident that it was 'the first act of important aggression which has been committed by the Chartists and their followers in this District'.[47] He added that the local magistrates believed that the Irish 'intend to make a diversion should Mitchel be convicted, to prevent Government from sending more troops to Ireland'. This, it should be noted, was the common belief in all the areas where the Irish were in any number.

The Times and other London papers such as the *Morning Chronicle* offer an instructive illustration of the much lower level of interest in provincial affairs, however serious they might be, compared with metropolitan events. There was nothing in London, in spite of the considerable marches and demonstrations on the last days of May and early June, that was as potentially dangerous as the situation in Bradford or Liverpool. There was no news of Bradford in *The Times* from 25 May to 30 May and it was only on 31 May that the story of what had been happening in the West Riding was fully described. The account given below has been put together from the *Bradford Observer*, *The Times* and the Home Office papers.

The rescue of the two Chartists at Bingley greatly increased the tensions in the whole Bradford region. On Sunday 28 May there was a large gathering at Wilsden, about four miles from the centre of Bradford. Two to three thousand men marched in military style 'preceded in many cases by black banners surmounted by pike heads'. It was on the same day that decisions were taken to begin to break the power of organised Chartism. By this time additional troops had already been sent into the town. They included two companies of the 39th Regiment, two troops of the 5th Dragoon Guards and about thirty of the Royal Horse Artillery, these latter from Leeds. Two companies of the 81st were ordered up from Hull. The second West Yorkshire Cavalry were called out and the Yorkshire Hussars also marched to 'the most advantageous points.' About two thousand special constables had been sworn in, and the police were issued with cutlasses.

The plans for the following day, Monday 29 May, were agreed by the Lord Lieutenant of the West Riding, the Earl of Harewood, Major-General Thorn, Robert Milligan and other local military and civil authorities. The first attempt went badly. At about 7 a.m. some hundred special constables led by the police superintendent moved into the Manchester Road area in order to arrest the two leading Chartists, David Lightfowler and Isaac Jefferson, the latter using the sobriquet of Wat Tyler; and there was to be a search for arms. When they arrived at Adelaide Street they were surrounded by a crowd of about one thousand. There was a ferocious fight in which the special constables were badly mauled and extricated themselves with difficulty. On their withdrawal working-class groups began to move into the centre of the city and they were joined by crowds marching in from the outlying villages and townships. Almost all the shops in Bradford closed, and intense discussions were held among those who had set up the operation. Orders were issued that all special constables should be in attendance by 3.30 p.m. and when the time arrived about one thousand had mustered. The Halifax troop of Yeomanry was held in readiness at Bradford; the Bradford troop was sent to Huddersfield; the Huddersfield troop was sent to Halifax; and from Leeds, one troop went to Selby and one to Bingley. At 4 p.m. the whole of the police force, armed with cutlasses, marched from the Court House, followed by the thousand special constables, the Mayor and magistrates, two hundred infantry with fixed bayonets, and bringing up the rear were two troops of Dragoons. Their objective again was to arrest the Chartist leaders and search for arms. They met fierce resistance at the place of fighting in the morning:

The police drew their cutlasses, and the special constables their staves, and they were met by the Chartists with bludgeons and stones. Each side fought desperately for a short time but eventually the police and special constables were driven back, many of them dreadfully injured. The military, being in the rear, could not act at the onset, and the ranks of the civil power were thrown into confusion and disorder before the dragoons could be brought up. They galloped into the corner where the severest fighting had been and the Chartists began to waver.

The Times continued its report with the information that nineteen were arrested, including one woman; that the leaders had escaped; and that the arms search produced very little. The whole force then returned to the Court House. Publicans were told to shut at 6 p.m. that evening, and in order that action could be taken immediately during the night, the Riot Act was formally read 'in order to empower the military to act instanter if required'. A large group of special constables later paraded through the town, and a troop of the 5th Dragoons remained all night under arms at the Court House.[48]

Bradford was a further illustration of the class relationships of this year. As the most recent historian of the town comments: 'There was more than an element of symbolism in the procession which went to the attack' on the Monday afternoon.[49] The Mayor, Robert Milligan, a self-made merchant, liberal-radical in politics and a Dissenter in religion – an exemplar of the bourgeois in early Victorian England – marched alongside Joshua Pollard, the leading West Riding magistrate, one of the largest landowners in the district, coalmine owner, manager of an iron works and a Tory in politics. Here we have the closing of the ranks of the propertied against the threats from below. For the rest of the century, with a consensus on fundamentals that never threatened the existing order, Tory and Liberal could fight their battles with zest and vigour; but in 1848 with the Paris events always in mind there was a clear perception of the grim possibilities that a successful popular movement might lead to political control, however confused and uncertain its present aims might be. The hand of political co-operation that had at least been formally held out to the disenfranchised in the open letter of 13 April was now the fist of coercion. Only when the turbulence was over, and the relations between classes established upon a more proper understanding of the rightful places of masters and men would the paternalistic liberalism of the worsted manufacturers and merchants once again be given full play. It was not to be delayed for long.

It is not clear whether an uprising was planned at Bradford during these last days of May. There were at least two informers in the Bradford area but their reports do not permit any firm evaluation of what was intended. The intervention by McDouall almost certainly was taken seriously, and it is reasonably clear that no other town was quite so well organised at this time as Bradford. A speech by George White at Manchester on 5 June, reported by a police constable and included in the Home Office papers[50] exhorted his audience to follow the Bradford example 'in forming clubs and sections – clubs has a leader over them and this captain drilled and instructed them – anything from headquarters went to the various captains' who then called their various sections together. White advised the meeting to get arms: he himself had both pike and gun, and he described in somewhat optimistic terms what had happened in Bradford on Monday 29 May: 'how they had got the town into their own hands' and if only other towns had been so well prepared!

The point that White was making could have been well taken. One of the problems of these last weeks for conspiratorial Chartism was the different level of preparations in different towns, and the impediments to close communications. Liverpool was an illustration of the problems involved, since there was no town with more violent potential in the whole of England, and yet its organisational links with the movement in the rest of the country and even with the specifically Irish component of the unrest seem to have been weak.

Liverpool had remained in a relatively peaceful state throughout April. There were minor alarms about the shipment of arms to Ireland through Liverpool, but most of the stories, after investigation, were found to be incorrect or exaggerated.[51] During May political activity, measured by the number of references to meetings and demonstrations reported in the local papers, increased steadily, notably among the Irish, who were always much more important than the native English radicals. Politics in Liverpool were sharpened by religious divisions, and by the fact that the Corporation was controlled by the Tories after 1842. T. B. Horsfall, the Mayor in 1848, had given his backing in the general election of 1847 to the unsuccessful, extreme Protestant candidate, and this undoubtedly exacerbated sectarian feeling. Among the wealthy business groups there was hostility between the minority of advanced Liberal merchants and shipping owners – the Rathbones and the Holts among them – and the remainder of their business contemporaries; and there was the inevitable gulf between the middle class and the labouring population.[52] With the trial and conviction of John Mitchel political activity among the very large Irish community began to surge. By early June there were fourteen Clubs in the town and a police report of 7 June, forwarded to the Home Office, stated that the intention was to increase the number to twenty under the general control of one Central Club Council of 100 members. Five members would form a quorum and the Council would be in session day and night – to 'be supplied with all the Newspapers to see how things were going on in other places and to receive information etc.' Each new member was to pay one shilling. One speaker was reported recommending the purchase of pikes rather than rifles. In his covering letter the Mayor commented that there was a strong feeling in the town that there ought to be a permanent barracks.[53]

The social tensions and alarms in Liverpool increased steadily through June. On 8 June the Mayor enclosed a statement to the Home Office signed by all the magistrates which urged a larger permanent military force in the town; and on the same day a report from the Head Constable claimed that at a demonstration in the next few days 'It is stated they will be prepared with carrier pigeons to inform their friends in other parts how they get on'. Statements about carrier pigeons were common during the troubled months of this year in all areas of the country, but whether they were in fact ever used is not known. On the next day, 9 June, the Mayor wrote to the Home Secretary informing him that accommodation had been made available for additional troops and adding that the recruitment of special constables was proceeding slowly because of a general 'apprehension'; and on several occasions in the next few weeks there were urgent requests that special constables should be armed. One such request, on 8 July, was answered by Sir George Grey to the effect that arming the specials was 'perfectly legal' but that such action should only be taken 'in a case of absolute necessity'; and Grey ended his letter by saying that he would be glad to receive a report from the magistrates on the state of the town.

The report was dated 12 July. It had been carefully prepared and was concerned only with the problem of the Irish in Liverpool and the effect of events in Ireland upon them. It began by noting that from the beginning of the year there had been frequent meetings between Irish Repeal leaders and the Irish in Liverpool and Manchester: the names of Meagher, Mitchel and Doheny were mentioned. One of the main ideas discussed at these meetings, according to information received by the magistrates, was the support of any insurrection in Ireland by the prevention of troop reinforcements leaving England via Ireland. Again, it needs to be said that this was a statement often made during this year and undoubtedly widely believed by the English authorities, but there is no evidence of any direct measures being taken at any time; and the movement of troops to Ireland during 1848 was considerable. The report then continued to note that with the passing of the Treason-Felony Act, local organisations had become secret by the development of the Club system, in Manchester as well as Liverpool; although the magistrates went on to inform the Home Office that they still had some access to what went on within the Clubs. The magistrates put the number of Roman Catholics in Liverpool as over 100,000 out of a total population of 375,000; and it was their belief that the Clubs could throw two to four thousand armed men onto the streets 'without any notice to the public'. It was clear that the magistrates firmly believed the Irish could take over the town and, further, that in the event of a future insurrection, the attempt would be made. The magistrates wrote in anguished terms of this possibility: 'The disgrace which would be inflicted on the authorities of the town, the disastrous consequences which would result to individuals and to property, in the opinion of your Committee, cannot be exaggerated.' The existing military forces in Liverpool were one company of Rifles, three companies of infantry, and the enrolled pensioners. The magistrates recommended, as a matter of urgency, one regiment of infantry, a squadron of Dragoons and a detachment of artillery. They also recommended the arming and drilling of special constables and of the police; and they noted again the reluctance by local inhabitants 'to meet armed men with only the staff of the Special Constable'.

The Permanent Under-Secretary, H. Waddington, replied the next day.

He began by saying that provided evidence would be forthcoming prosecutions should be initiated; and that the Home Secretary could not believe that if an insurrection was planned the local authorities would not hear of it. The Home Secretary had already indicated his opinion that it would be inadvisable to arm the special constables, but a certain quantity of arms would be sent to Liverpool for both the police and the special constables 'but before this is done it will be essential to know that they could be placed in security against any sudden attack'. The total military forces in Liverpool were limited by the accommodation available and if that could be increased then the military presence could be 'immediately increased'. The Home Office further suggested that help might be sought from the metropolitan police – a common practice for many years – and asked that a copy of the magistrate's report be sent to Lieutenant-General Arbuthnot at Manchester and that the Mayor should communicate directly with Arbuthnot on the matter of increased troops for the town.

The Head Constable replied to the Mayor on the 15 July regarding the suggestion that the metropolitan police might be called in to assist the local force. It was an offer that had obviously not been met with enthusiasm. The Liverpool police were among the largest in the country outside London, the Watch Committee was active in promoting efficiency, and it was always recognised as highly competent by the Home Office.[54] It needed to be since the crime rate in the city was a good deal higher than in most comparable towns against the background of appalling figures for overcrowding and incidence of disease. In his report to the Mayor, after the receipt of the Home Office letter, the Head Constable explained the particular problems of the Irish Clubs in Liverpool and of the especial difficulty of acquiring 'a perfect knowledge of all that transpires at their meetings'. Many meetings were held in private houses and the Clubs in general excluded all but members:

There are a few men to be relied upon, who will run the risk of giving information, and fewer still upon whom dependence could be placed, those from whom I obtain particulars at present live in a constant state of alarm fearing that the least discovery would consign them to death.

If it were merely required that each person joining these Clubs should enrol himself and so become a member without the ceremony of others introducing and vouching for him there would be not the least difficulty in acquiring information of every word or movement going on, but it is almost necessary that the candidate should be an Irishman, any other would certainly be looked upon with suspicion. Then the part of Ireland he comes from, his Religion, the known political feelings of his Family, would be canvassed, and scrutinized. The movements of a new resident here would be watched, his mode of obtaining a livelyhood[sic] and of living, noticed, and if the least suspicion were excited his escape from extreme violence or death would be scarcely to be calculated upon. The only benefit to be derived from the assistance of the London Police would be that they would probably be unknown . . . but that would make entry to the Clubs more difficult.

The Head Constable continued his report by emphasising that there was no problem about the storage of arms and ended by underlining once again the critical importance:

at the present time of a strong Military Force, and particularly of Dragoons, and Artillery, for it is scarcely reasonable to expect that either an unarmed Force of Police or Special Constables, would with any confidence advance upon, or contend with, an armed mob even partially disciplined.[55]

The correspondence between the Liverpool authorities, the Home Office and the military commanders in the next week leading up to the suspension of habeas corpus in Ireland – introduced in the House of Commons on the 22 July – testify to the growing fears and general apprehension in Liverpool. The Home Office agreed to the drilling of the regular police in arms, which meant cutlass and musket; the Head Constable produced several more letters and reports on the situation from which it is clear that he had considerable sources of information from within the Irish and Chartist groups, and especially the former; and the two leading figures, Terence Bellew McManus and Lawrence Reynolds, both Irishmen, were obviously being closely watched. Reynolds seems to have been the main contact with the Chartist movement.[56] Threats to burn the warehouses along the dock front were taken seriously, and there were detailed reports of drilling and firing practice by a number of the Clubs.

The suspension of habeas corpus in Ireland brought immediate reaction among the Irish communities in England. The Bill, introduced on 22 July, received the Royal Assent three days later. Clarendon had already proclaimed the City and County of Dublin and rumours in England of a coming insurrection in Ireland were widespread. In Liverpool the strength of the police force was to be increased by 500; considerable numbers of additional troops came into the city, with a tented encampment at Everton attracting most attention; and there were gunboats in the Mersey.[57] The most extraordinary exhibition of the panic that had seized the middle classes of Liverpool took place on the day that the Habeas Corpus Suspension Bill was introduced into the Commons. In the evening of the 22 July, a petition was opened at the Liverpool Exchange newsroom, asking for the extension of the Habeas Corpus Bill to be applied to Liverpool. This astonishing request was signed by the Mayor and all the Liverpool magistrates save one and by the time it was presented to the House of Commons on the 25 July it had around one thousand signatures, including some of the most famous names of Liverpool liberalism, Cropper and Rathbone among them. As an index to the pervasive sense of panic in the town there could have been no more dramatic advertisement.

There was a certain amount of ridicule in the London press when the petition was presented; and there was a counter-petition in Liverpool. But most of the middle class, and their press, were in no doubt about the dangers they confronted. The *Liverpool Journal*, normally a moderate Liberal paper, pointed out to the *Morning Chronicle* that on 10 April London had taken elaborate precautions when faced with a situation of insurrectionary potential. The *Journal* went on to suggest that while the trade of the kingdom would not have been affected if the whole centre of London had been destroyed, in Liverpool the warehouses along the docks were full of cotton, and cotton was at the centre of England's manufactures. 'The great danger in Liverpool was from incendiarism; that danger was imminent – fearful . . . Liverpool was to experience the fate of Moscow.'[58] To be 'moscowed' was a common saying of these days.

The same issue of the *Liverpool Journal* (29 July) agreed that the main danger to the city was now probably passed, owing to the vigilance of the Mayor and the Chief Constable. The case for a greatly increased military presence had certainly been successfully argued, but there had been a surprising exchange of letters on the matter of who was to pay for the additional troops. Since there does not appear to be any other example of its kind anywhere else in the country, a brief summary of the correspondence is of interest. As already noted, the Mayor of Liverpool and his colleagues on the City Council had been pressing hard for additional military in the town, and while the Home Office was sympathetic the problem was the lack of accommodation for the troops. It was especially undesirable to billet, and in the end the problem was met by the setting up of a large tented camp at Everton which overlooked the city. But very late in the month of July, with alarm and fears growing daily, the Mayor had gone on record stating that the Corporation could not be expected to contribute financially to the additional costs of the increased strength of the military in the town. This was on 24 July. Major-General Warre, who commanded the Northwestern district from his headquarters at Chester, was incensed, and informed the Mayor that he would bring no more troops into Liverpool without proper accommodation being provided. The Mayor replied in apologetic but firm tones that the Corporation was not legally obliged to finance the military presence; and the matter was referred to the Home Office who made the point, in equable tones, that it was customary for the authorities to take responsibility for the provision of temporary accommodation if additional troops were needed over and above the normal allotment. And there the matter seems to have petered out.[59] It was, of course, by no means unusual for local authorities to take a parsimonious approach towards expenditure on the security forces, and the small numbers of regular police in these years and for some decades after[60] was testimony to the habits of economy. The Liverpool episode, however, given the widespread alarm in the city, was unexpected and somewhat bizarre.

Vigorous action by the Liverpool police rapidly won control of the situation. Joseph Cuddy, a salesman-courier employed by Reynolds, was arrested in the afternoon of 22 July, and was found to be carrying a bag full of pike heads.[61] Bellew McManus, the leading Irish personality in Liverpool, left for Ireland and took part in the abortive Tipperary affair. The Liverpool police raided Confederate Clubs, minute books and papers were taken away, and a large number of arrests followed. Reynolds escaped through Birmingham and Bristol to New York. The Liverpool Irish were left without leadership. When 500 Irish dock labourers, on the evening of the 29th July, refused to be sworn in as special constables, they were dismissed and their places taken by English labourers.[62] Two days later a number of the Irish asked for their jobs back, without conditions. By early August Liverpool was under complete control of the forces of law and order, with the dismal news of the Ballingarry affair completing the demoralisation of the Irish militants. As it had always been in Liverpool, it was the movement of events in Ireland that dictated the level of activity on the mainland.

Political movements always develop their own internal dynamic and, where illegal organisation is being attempted, at least in part, the pace and momentum may be almost entirely generated from the inside. It must nevertheless be emphasised that in the summer of 1848 the Irish situation remained for all the turbulent or potentially disturbed areas of Britain the most important single political regulator. Changes in the Irish situation normally evoked an immediate response among the Chartists as well as among the Confederates. The official leadership of the Chartist organisation – and in particular Feargus O'Connor – had remarkably little influence upon the way events developed during the months of May to August; and both for London and the industrial north, the main centres of unrest, the quality of the regional leadership remains insufficiently analysed.

There was no break in the anxieties of Dublin Castle or Whitehall about the internal situation of Ireland during April or thereafter. The continuing deaths from starvation and disease and the large-scale destitution in the countryside provided the background against which the administrative structures inevitably absorbed a rising level of coercion. On 14 April Lord John Russell was writing to Clarendon about the need to replace Blakeney, the commander-in-chief, with a more vigorous personality; but this suggestion was resisted by Clarendon on the grounds of Blakeney's experience of Irish affairs and his good standing among the supporters of the administration. In this same period Russell was also suggesting the formation of volunteer corps in all the big towns 'composed of two-third Protestants and one third Catholics, and trained once a week, in sight of all the world . . . It would give confidence to the well-effected.'[63] Russell, along with most of the Whig leaders, was highly conscious of the need to build some kind of social grouping that would act as a buffer between the coercive arm of the authority and the mass of the Irish people. It was a very familiar and much discussed question: the numerical weakness of the middle strata in Irish society, and the sectarian divisions which religion created. Throughout this year Russell havered between a Whiggish reluctance to encourage religious bigotry and the stronger Whiggish recognition that in the last resort, the security of the social order demanded acceptance from any and all groups, regardless of their political or religious views. Like all the Whig leaders, in times of threatened crisis, Russell had no difficulty in overcoming his previously expressed scruples. On 3 April, a few days before the Kennington Common meeting, Russell wrote to Clarendon: 'I dislike having recourse to Protestant force as against Catholic as much as anyone but rather than be weaker against a growing strength I would do it.'[64] There were similar statements throughout these months. In the last crisis of the summer, on the eve of the suspension of habeas corpus in Ireland 24 July, Russell wrote to the Viceroy, on the same matter:

A nice point will be determined how far you will avail yourself of the offers of the Orangemen to arm and form Volunteer Corps - the spirit of religious hatred is very bad, but you cannot let your throats be cut to avoid religious animosity. A more serious point is whether a display of Protestant zeal may not drive many Catholics into the rebel ranks. It is for you to decide.[65]

A few days later Russell had further thoughts, somewhat naive thoughts perhaps. 'It occurs to me', he wrote to Clarendon, 'that the arming of the Protestants might disquiet not only English Catholics but the 8000 Catholics in the army in Ireland'.[66]

Clarendon was receptive to Russell's suggestions, although he was careful, as he always pointed out in his private correspondence, not to offer too crude a display of favour towards the Protestant supporters of law and order.[67] During the early months of 1848 he was already making it plain in his private letters and in private conversation that there was no one among the Catholic population who could be trusted or relied upon. Greville, who got his information from Southern, Clarendon's former secretary, wrote on 3 May that 'Clarendon says not a Roman Catholic in Ireland is to be trusted.'[68] On the other side the alienation of the greater part of the Catholic population from the English administration was hardly a new discovery, but the stark hostility was to be strikingly demonstrated during the tense months of this summer. Examples are abundant. Under the heading 'The Progress of Sedition' a correspondent of The Times on 1 June reported a dinner in Dunboyne in honour of the juryman who had refused to vote guilty in one of the May trials. The individual named did not in fact appear at the dinner which was attended by the small farmers and landlords of the district; and the occasion was turned into a demonstration for the convicted John Mitchel. One speaker said that the people of Ireland 'were ground down by an enormous taxation; by a hostile aristocracy; a standing army; packed juries; a venal House of Commons; a crushed public opinion; trampled rights'. The principal speaker of the evening was Michael Doheny, who had just returned from a propagandist tour of the north of England: 'I know this country well, and I know that at the bottom of every man's heart the deepest conviction is that the Government of England is a usurpation which we must get rid of by all means.' Even in the most politically radicalised areas in Britain, and among the most disaffected groups, there was nothing to compare with the deep, abiding and ineradicable hatred of the ordinary people of Ireland against the English connection. The first number of the *Irish Felon* on 24 June contained a long open letter from Devin Reilly to Lord Clarendon, full of abuse and physical force language. The letter was addressed, in capital letters: 'To the Englishman calling himself George William Frederick, Earl of Clarendon, Her Majesty's Chief Legal Murderer and Jury-Packer General of Ireland'; and it ended: 'My Lord Assassin, your enemy to the death - Thomas Devin Reilly'.

As the situation worsened through 1848, much aided by Trevelyan's self-help policies in a starving countryside, the Whigs found their political options narrowing to the single area of coercion. It was Mitchel's conviction that began the last phase of open defiance and insurgency; and the rising levels of turbulence were met by the familiar methods of an increased military presence, the widespread use of spies and informers and a growing number of arrests. [69] There was increasing apprehension about the growth of the Clubs in Dublin and elsewhere, and there was more talk than usual in government circles about the suspension of habeas corpus. It was always referred to as one possibility in discussions throughout the Whig years of office, but from early June Sir George Grey, Russell and Clarendon were seriously considering suspension as the way to curb the Club movement. At the time they decided that Parliament would not easily accommodate itself to such a drastic measure of coercion, and once again they underestimated the support for strong action both in the Commons and throughout the country. [70] As a stage in the curtailment of the freedom the radical movement enjoyed, the government in Dublin arrested Gavan Duffy, the proprietor of the *Nation*, on 8 July, and the owners of two other papers, the *Irish Felon* and the *Tribune*. Meagher, Doheny and McGee were also arrested on charges of making seditious speeches: the first two were released on bail and the grand jury refused to return a true bill against McGee. [71]

These arrests encouraged more intransigent attitudes among the Young Ireland leaders and their language became steadily more violent. Dublin

Castle reacted with growing uneasiness about the internal situation they were confronted with, and some of the reports received were indeed alarmist. Clarendon's pessimism communicated itself to the ministers in Whitehall although Sir George Grey in particular was never pushed into panic decisions. On 22 July Clarendon wrote what he described as an official letter to Grey for use in the House of Commons and relating to the state of Ireland. Clarendon already knew the decision had been taken to suspend habeas corpus; and he was making his report with that in mind. He quoted 'the General', who presumably was Blakeney, as being of the opinion that 'it will put an end to the movement although we must be prepared for an outbreak, and possibly more than one in the country, but he does not consider they will be formidable'. Clarendon then continued to quote a more alarmist statement: 'The General persists in declaring that in Dublin and neighbourhood there are 12000 men armed and ready to turn out at the command of the executive Council but I think this is exaggerated.' Clarendon himself was certainly not beyond the kind of exaggerated statement born of fear and apprehension. He had a postscript to this particular letter which read:

Is there any serious intention on the part of the Americans to attack Bermuda and rescue Mitchel, and is the place properly defended and the Governor cautioned? I wish he was sent away from there, for it would not only be disgraceful to the Government and most mischievous in Ireland if he were rescued but it might constitute a *casus belli* against the United States.

A senior minister capable of repeating street gossip of this level of nonsense was indeed under considerable strain. The Cabinet had taken the decision to suspend habeas corpus on 21 July, it was introduced in the Commons on 22 July and received the Royal Assent on the 25th. The suspension of habeas corpus was a response to a situation that was obviously becoming more difficult, but there was also a clear-sighted appreciation among political groups in England of the effects that suspension would have upon the radical leadership in Ireland. It was generally assumed that it would be confronted with a stark choice: a humiliating surrender or a premature rising. In retrospect it is by no means certain that the choice was as straightforward as contemporaries believed. There is no doubt, however, about the pressures on the radical leaders. Clarendon had proclaimed the county and city of Dublin under the terms of the 1847 Coercion Act, on 21 July. When the habeas corpus suspension became law Clarendon issued a proclamation which made membership of a political Club sufficient grounds for arrest. This was on 26 July. Two days later Clarendon wrote to Grey:

Things are getting better . . . We made a fine haul at the *Nation* this afternoon as they were just packing off the whole edition of the paper – the Police found there also the letter book of the secretary of the Executive Council with a summary of all the clubs in

Ireland, the population of every county, of every town capable of sustaining a Club. Minutes of proceedings, names of correspondents etc etc . . . [Must now begin] to arrange all this information and if we find it amounts to high treason and we catch the traitors I shall propose to have a Special Commission to try them. The Pensioners are called out.[72]

The emergency which the Irish movement was now in was met by the establishment of a Directory of Five in Dublin, and the scatter of many Young Ireland leaders into the rural districts, especially in the southeast. Although the Dublin administration was still being given wild and wholly unsubstantiated rumours about the strength of the rebel forces ('Smith O'Brien is now in command of 20,00 men and that there is not the least doubt but that there are French and American officers with him'[73]) the attempt at rebellion was quickly brought under control.[74] *The Times* of August made great play with the fact that the 'rebels' were put down by the Irish police, with the military not involved. 'It is a victory of Irishmen over Irishmen, Papists over Papists'; and all over Britain the ineptitude and incompetence of the conspiracy were widely publicised and ridiculed. *The Times*, as ever, was not slow in generalising some of the lessons. In a leading article of 3 August the failure of the 'insurrection' was underlined, and the continued presence of all the evils in Ireland was emphasised: 'The potato still rots. The population still increases. There will still be found in England bankrupt factions, or political adventurers, only too ready to raise a little capital by pandering to Irish disaffection. In fact, the greater part of the work still remains to be done.' The leader continued by insisting that there should be no weakening of resolve on the part of the authorities. It referred to growing evidence 'of a widespread conspiracy'; and it looked forward in prescient terms to what it hoped would be the exemplary punishment of those who were being arrested for their complicity in the conspiracy:

Surely where there is a certainty of guilt, it will be a ridiculous fastidiousness, and an abuse of legality, to risk the punishment and detention of these criminals on the doubtful courage of a jury. We will not speak of rebels being tried by rebels. That of course is impossible. But the trial of a rebel by a jury in fear of their lives is almost equally absurd. Should any of the traitors now waiting their trial be acquitted under evident terror, we trust that the Irish government will take care to give them the benefit of the Suppression Act . . . there is the utmost propriety in maintaining for the present a *quasi* state of siege. As guardians of the constitution we are bound to protect it against the invasions of conspiracy and outrage . . . After a few months it will become a question how far Ireland can again be trusted with perfect constitutional freedom.

As so often in this year, *The Times* was offering a blueprint for ministerial opinion and practice; there was never the possibility of fairly selected jury panels for the trials that were about to be heard in Ireland during the next few months. This time the snake had to be more than scotched.

The radical movement in England was also working its way to its own climax. The government had a number of problems related to the disposition of the security forces over the kingdom as a whole. There had been a considerable movement of the military into Ireland during the last two weeks of July and by the beginning of August there were 35,000 troops, with naval and marine support off the southern coast. Matters were much helped by the return of troops from abroad, but there remained the relative levels of disturbance between London and the industrial North on which judgement had to be made. Rumours were widespread. On the morning of 27 July a report transmitted by the Electric Telegraph said that a rising had begun in Ireland, of quite important dimensions, so it was assumed. 'We have had a terrible day of it here', Sir George Grey wrote to Clarendon, 'owing to the Report brought by Telegraph from Liverpool to which the newspapers gave the widest circulation and which we had no means of contradicting though we believed it to be exaggerated'.[75] During June and especially July and into August the number of political arrests had been steadily increasing in all the disaffected areas of Britain. Ernest Jones and five prominent members of the London Chartist and Confederate movement had been tried and convicted in the second week of July. At the end of the month, with excitement rising in London, especially following the report of the Irish rising on the 27th, for several days large detachments of the metropolitan police, armed with cutlasses, converged on the Cripplegate and Tottenham Road areas where overflow meetings of Chartists and Confederates were being held. A number of leading London personalities were arrested at this time; and at the beginning of August the trials of dozens of West Riding Chartists were being held at the York Assizes. Peter McDouall, the most important national figure along with Ernest Jones, had been arrested on 16 July; and in the issue of the *Northern Star* on 5 August Samuel Kydd issued a statement on behalf of the executive committee:

Fellow Countrymen – The reign of terror progresses, and grows searching and more dreadful. Justice – that hallowed word, which we have long been taught to revere as the ideal of God himself. . . has we fear but a small share in the heart-affections of the rulers of this land . . .

So close has our political atmosphere become, that men are almost suffocated. So crowded are rumours, following in quick uncertainty; so fearful the thrilling doubts and stifled fears of every man we meet, that it requires courage even to think steadily, and boldness and nerve to direct order from this motley chaos.

The main problem for the historians of Chartism at this time is the extent to which an illegal conspiracy was being organised in London and the industrial towns of the North, and the degree of contact between the different areas. From the side of government it was assumed that a conspiracy was in train, for, apart from the considerable movement of masses of men in all the big cities, there were the many reports from spies and informers. The most detailed evaluation for London has been put together by Dr Goodway,[76] while the evidence for the North is still not fully assessed; but enough information was available to Whitehall to indicate that there were some links between Manchester and London, and possibly Bradford, and those responsible for internal security acted accordingly. The middle days of August saw the culmination of the security operations, although whether these were in fact the days of the threatened uprisings is not wholly certain. There was a strong rumour of an expected rising in Manchester on Monday night, 14 August, when increased numbers were observed at the Clubs; and throughout the night of the 14th, so the *Bradford Observer* reported, hundreds of men in the town waited with their pikes for the signal to begin. The most important leaders, however, George White and George Webber, were in Manchester – to be arrested on the 15th – and no message went to Bradford. The event that probably decided the authorities on immediate action was the shooting, and killing, of a policeman in Ashton. The first report from the officer in charge of troops at Ashton said the policeman was first shot and then piked. In Manchester the arrests began in the evening of Tuesday 15 August, and continued for the next week. The police and military backing to these arrests in Manchester was impressive: 300 armed police, two companies of the 30th Foot, and two troops of the Royal Irish Dragoons.[77] In London in the early evening of 16 August eleven men were arrested at the Orange Tree, Red Lion Square; and later that same night an armed group of thirteen was arrested in Southwark. Arrests continued for the next four days.[78] By the end of August several hundred Chartists and Irish Confederates had been arrested and some already convicted; the movement in the country was broken.

What requires emphasis is the physical destruction by imprisonment of the Chartist leadership in these summer months of 1848. The National Assembly in May had elected an executive committee of five: two leading activists were Ernest Jones and Peter McDouall, both of whom were to be imprisoned for two years. The other members of the executive were Feargus O'Connor, who was almost completely dominated at this time by the official enquiry into the Land Plan, and in any case was quite out of sympathy with the militant trends of the movement; and the other two members of the executive, Samuel Kydd and John McCrae were lacking in national stature. More significant for the crucial second-line leadership throughout the country, of the twenty commissioners elected at the National Assembly, at least fourteen can be identified as being arrested and convicted between May and September; and in addition there were a considerable number of local leaders – all the Bradford people for example – who were not national commissioners but whose imprisonment often meant the complete elimination of the local leadership. Arrest and imprisonment; increased fears about spies and informers, as evidence was given at the trials from late August on; the failure of the Irish rising; and the continued pressures of the local police forces on Chartist and Irish activity[79] all contributed to a rapid decline in morale and spirit in the closing weeks of August and throughout September, by which time the major state trials were taking place in England. Local Chartist groups began to dissociate themselves publicly from any connection with physical force action;[80] Feargus O'Connor, who had always remained at a distance from the militants during the summer months, now began to state clearly his opposition to the more radical versions of the Charter ('I am neither a Socialist nor a Communist. The principle is at variance with the ruling instinct of man which is selfishness, self-interest, self-reliance, and individuality . . . The government of that instinct may be varied, one man may be selfish and sordid, another man may be selfish and generous'[81]); and the growing number of those serving prison sentences, including transportation, inevitably discouraged even the most elementary organisation. On 11 November, the same Philip McGrath who had gone to Paris with Ernest Jones and Harney to deliver a message of congratulations to the Provisional government, compared their present state of affairs with the heady optimism and buoyant hopes of the early spring:

Since then all had been one waste blank, one huge monument of misfortune . . . Violent measures were not suited to the general constitution of the British mind . . . Their object should be by lectures, public meetings, and a proper direction of their moral power and by falling back on a legal system of organisation to recover that position which they had lost by want of prudence and common sense.[82]

The government had overwhelmed the radicals by physical force, and they had triumphed in ideas. There was much talk at the time, confirmed by some historians since, of the irresoluteness of the Russell administration, and in certain domestic matters there is no denying the accuracy of the criticism. But in the year 1848 Palmerston's foreign policy effectively neutralised the potentially radical thrust in Europe which France could have exercised in the early months of the revolution, and the measures at home directed by Sir George Grey against the English and Irish radical movements were remarkably efficient. All other issues, however large they appeared to contemporaries, were never as central as these to the political state and the stature of Britain in European affairs. The English press, in their summing up of the events of this year, illustrated the main components of the intellectual and political ideology of middle-class England in the decades which followed. There were three central themes implanted deeply within British political consciousness that had been confirmed by the events of this year. One was the identification of members of the extreme radical movement in Britain with foreign ideas and movements, with Chartist as synonym for rioter, leveller, Jacobin;[83] a second was the folly and stupidities of the ideas and objectives of what became known during the year as the red republicanism of the French, above all, the ideas of equality and of the right to work, all contrary to the fundamental principles of political economy; and the third, the most important and the most pervasive, the belief, which amounted to an article of faith, that in England the liberty of the subject had been assured by the centuries of growth and development and that nowhere else in Europe were the practices of free speech and the possibilities of political change so self-evident as in Britain. The *Economist*, not a journal given to sentimentalising the processes of government, provided a survey of 'the most eventful year in the history of modern Europe' in the issue of Saturday 30 December; and in a leading article of some eight columns and after a lengthy summary of the progress and decline of political turbulence in most countries of Europe, turned to the two areas which had remained more or less immune from the contagion of revolt and sudden change:

Two countries have remained unshaken amid the general convulsions – the two countries whose political systems present the completest contrast – England and Russia. Russia has been peaceful under the most despotic rule, because her population is not yet civilised enough to feel those yearnings after freedom and self-government which have agitated Europe; England has been peaceful because, through the long, plodding, patient industry of centuries, she had already gained all which other nations thought to arrive at *per saltum* in a year. Yet we have had our disturbances, trivial and partial as they were; but they only served to show, in even clearer relief, how thoroughly sound at core is the heart of our people, – how unlimited is our personal liberty, – and how unshaken and lofty our credit, even after so crushing a commercial crisis, and so tremendous a political convulsion.

This well written and intelligent account of the events of 1848, which discussed Lombardy, Tuscany, Rome, Naples, the German states, the small as well as the big issues, the large as well as the less important countries, and which considered at length the internal economic and social history of France after the February days, had not one word on Ireland, or the Irish question. It was not that the *Economist* failed to publish material and comment on Ireland quite regularly, but that in this quite substantial survey of the problems and difficulties of 1848, and of those that remained, Ireland, with nearly one million dead, and with a massive emigration still continuing, was not considered part of the 'momentous happenings' of this momentous year: an interesting insight into the mentality of the view from England.[84] The view from Ireland was different. On 23 August 1848, when the Smith O'Brien 'uprising' was still in everyone's mind, *The Times* published a long two-column report from its Dublin correspondent. It made exceedingly depressing, if all too familiar, reading:

the serious deficiency which it is ascertained will exist in the food for the people. That fact is now well-known here, and exercises an influence which it is impossible to exaggerate. All feel that there is no prospect of assistance from England. Men of property are in despair at the certainty of enormous poor-rates. Those who have no means feel that they must starve. You will understand how these thoughts tell upon a people already reconciled to ideas of spoliation and plunder. You will understand also how it appals the hearts of the gentry, already sufficiently beset. On the one hand, I find a turbulent, rebellious, demoralised population about to be famine-stricken, yet clinging with a death gripe to the possession of the soil on which they inflict their own poverty, and for which they are ready to perpetuate the most frightful crimes. On the other hand I find a landed aristocracy, entirely separated from the sympathies of the people, impoverished by their own extravagance, daunted by the dangers to life and property, from which they are never free, and sinking at the present moment under apprehensions of the working of an Irish Poor Law during a season of scarcity. Between these warring extremes of society, there interposes in the south of Ireland no middle class.

6

DAYS OF JUDGEMENT

When Halévy published his survey of British society in 1815 he was puzzled by the relationship between Bar and Bench.[1] As it had worked out in England, both were open to all and it was always possible for talent, whatever its social provenance, to rise to the highest positions in the legal profession. No doubt there were serious difficulties in the way of those of lower social status, but theoretically and actually barristers could move not only to judicial positions but also within the political world; and the interchange between judicial and political posts was continuous. Thus a barrister, having been elected a member of Parliament and having spoken regularly in his party's interest, could hope for a judgeship in due course in one of the four higher courts: the three Common Law Courts of King's Bench, Common Pleas and Exchequer, or the Court of Equity, presided over by the Lord Chancellor assisted by the Master of the Rolls. The highest judicial position was that of Lord Chancellor, a political appointment which always carried with it a seat in the Cabinet.[2]

Judges were appointed by the Crown on the recommendation of the Lord Chancellor. It was not invariably the case that nominations for judgeships in the first half of the nineteenth century were made on party grounds, since what may be described as qualified custom did permit a choice of judges on the basis of legal ability; but political factors were always strong and mostly present. It was generally understood that faithfulness to party could be expected to be rewarded, and certainly in the case of the law officers of the Crown – the Solicitor-General and the Attorney-General – it was normal that office would lead to a senior position in the judiciary. In a well known essay,[3] H. J. Laski analysed some 139 appointments to the High Courts and the Appeal Court between 1832 and 1906, and found that of this total 80 had been members of Parliament with 63 being appointed by the political party they supported. The most notorious promoter of the party cause in modern times was Lord Halsbury, Lord Chancellor 1886–1892 and again between 1895–1905, of whom it was said that he 'almost invariably put service to the Conservative Party above judicial qualities'.[4]

This constant movement between politics and the legal profession made it difficult for Halévy to characterise with precision the position of the judiciary in the constitutional system of England at the beginning of the century, in part because he was too influenced by the ideas of Montesquieu regarding the theory of the separation of powers; but he settled his own questions on this matter by recognising that powers encroached upon each other, and that the individual parts of the constititution were not in fact clearly distinguished: a historical development, he went on to argue, that had operated against the political influence of the Crown during the reign of George III.[5] In general Halévy paid little attention to constitutional matters and for the nineteenth century it was Dicey's *Law of the Constitution* that effectively answered many of the questions that were increasingly being posed by constitutional historians. Dicey has, of course, been seriously criticised by twentieth-century scholars,[6] but in the context of the present considerations, two sections of Dicey's *Law of the Constitution* are especially relevant: the right to freedom of speech and the right to public meeting. Dicey began his analysis of the first of these freedoms by emphasising that 'At no time has there been in England any proclamation of the right to liberty of thought or freedom of speech'[7] and after quoting a number of authorities to support his argument he summarised in his own words the well-known statement of *The King* v. *Cuthell* of 1799:

Freedom of discussion is, then, in England little else than the right to write or say anything which a jury, consisting of twelve shopkeepers, think it expedient should be said or written. Such 'liberty' may vary at different times and seasons, from unrestricted license to very severe restraint, and the experience of English history during the last two centuries shows that under the law of libel the amount of latitude conceded to the expression of opinion has, in fact, differed greatly according to the conditions of popular sentiment.[8]

No year illustrated more strikingly the difference in interpretation of the liberty of expression than 1848 in England. It was precisely the 'expression of opinion' and the 'popular sentiment' among the jury-serving classes which made the convictions at the trials of English chartists both compelling and inevitable. Juries in London and the provinces accepted what Holdsworth described as their 'usual attitude of deference to the advice of the judges who were able and impartial – an attitude on the part of the jury and qualities in the judges which are the conditions precedent to the successful working of the jury system'.[9] Deference, in 1848, was buttressed by unshakeable convictions among the social groups who provided jurymen that Chartism must be put down and by the wholly partisan directions proffered to the juries by the judges on the Bench. Ireland, as always, had its own quirks and differences.

The right of public meeting was similarly not recognised as a specific or basic right of the citizen. The law did not forbid meetings unless the circumstances of the meetings in some way infringed a prohibition or a provision that the common law had come to recognise. Most of the positions accepted in the common law were restated, often expanded, during the decades of political turbulence that began in the later eighteenth century and went through the French revolutionary years into the post-war period; and the definition of the right of public meeting became inextricably intertwined with the interpretation of what constituted an unlawful assembly. The tests of unlawfulness that were increasingly used were the consequence, or the likely consequences, of persons meeting together. The original purpose for which the meeting was convened could involve neither violence not any other illegality; but reasonable grounds for supposing that some breach of the peace might be committed, or that alarm and fear might be created among those in the neighbourhood, would be sufficient for declaring a meeting unlawful, and allowing magistrates to order its dispersal. 'You must look not only to the purposes for which they meet, but also to the manner in which they come, and to the means which they are using.' So said Mr Justice Bayley at the trial of Orator Hunt in 1820 in a much quoted statement.[10]

The opinion most commonly quoted in the Chartist years by constitutional authorities on lawful assemblies was the charge delivered by Baron Alderson at Vincent's trial at Monmouth in 1839:

You will investigate the circumstances under which the assembly took place . . . whether they have met at unseasonable hours of the night, – if they have met under circumstances of violence and danger – if they have been armed with offensive weapons, or used violent language, – if they have proposed to set the different classes of society at variance the one with the other, and to put to death any part of Her Majesty's subjects. If any, all or most of these things should appear before you, there will, I think, be little difficulty in saying that an assembly of such persons, under such circumstances, for such purposes, and using such language, is a dangerous one, which cannot be tolerated in a country governed by laws; and it is but doing to others as you would that they should do unto you to repress meetings of that description; because what right have any persons to do that which produces terror, inconvenience, and dismay among their fellow-subjects?[11]

This emphasis upon political argument and social discussion was underlined by a further opinion during the early Chartist years. This was in 1842 in an address to the Grand Jury at the Special Commission at Stafford by Lord Chief Justice Tindal, where he noted that those who were 'wickedly intending to bring the religion, laws and government of the country into contempt, and to teach the hearers to despise all those institutions which it is their duty to hold in respect and veneration' must be clearly distinguished from those who provided their hearers with 'an honest declaration' of opinion: one that did not include 'sneers and sarcasm'.[12]

It is not difficult to appreciate that in times of political stress even moderate critics of the existing order were likely to be designated as 'wicked', and subject, therefore, to the penalties of the law. Sir George Grey, three days before the Kennington Common meeting of 10 April, restated the common law on what was lawful and what was unlawful as the government were interpreting it. He was answering a question from John Bright, and he distinguished between the intended procession and the meeting itself on the Common. Whether it was legal or illegal, said Grey, would entirely depend upon the circumstances 'under which the meeting would be held':

Any meeting that may be held, be the purpose of it whatsoever it may, which is accompanied by the circumstances to which I have just alluded – circumstances calculated to inspire just terror and alarm into the minds of Her Majesty's loyal and peaceable subjects – would, I apprehend, be against the common law of England. If, on the other hand, a meeting be held for the purpose of forming or organising a procession, and that procession is contrary to statute law, being for the purpose of presenting a petition to either House of Parliament, accompanied by excessive numbers of people, then I apprehend that that meeting would be identified with and form part of the procession, and therefore come within the provisions of the law applicable to such a procession.[13]

Grey then proceeded to quote Lord Mansfield on the right of Parliamentary petitioning, to the effect that 'the attending a petition to the House of Commons by more than ten persons is criminal and illegal'. Mansfield, in the quotation used by Grey, had referred to an Act of Charles II and this would almost certainly be 13 Car. II, S. 1 c. 5. Grey further drew the attention of the House to the trial of the seven bishops in 1688, where the distinction between petitoning merely and petitioning accompanied by 'tumultuous assemblies' makes the former legal and the latter illegal.

As the spring of 1848 moved into summer, and the disturbances in London and the northern industrial districts grew in number and excitability, the law relating to unlawful assemblies began to be interpreted with increasing strictness. On 2 June, in a charge to a Grand Jury that restated the Alderson and Tindall dicta, Mr Justice Patterson emphasised those parts of the law that laid stress upon the communication of alarm and apprehension to all those who lived or worked in the neighbourhood of meetings and processions. Patterson's statement was widely reprinted in the national and provincial press, and much commented on.[14] Police reports in London, quoted in The Times, henceforth now always included a phrase to the effect that the meeting being reported 'excited terror and alarm among the inhabitants of the neighbourhood'; and when a reporter of The Times was giving evidence at the preliminary hearing of Joseph Fussell, the phrase occurred again: 'The procession caused the utmost alarm to the inhabitants and shopkeepers in every direction, and some of them hurried out and closed their shutters.'[15]

Mr Justice Patterson had referred in his statement to the Grand Jury to 'particular statutes' which gave powers to magistrates and the police in the control of meetings; and there was indeed a long list of enactments which reinforced the common law and offered the authorities very wide powers. These included the Act of 1662 already noted (13 Car. II, S. 1 c. 5) which dealt with tumultuous petitions to the King in Parliament; the Riot Act of 1715; and a considerable body of legislation passed during the years of unrest between 1790 and 1830. Among the latter there was the Incitement to Mutiny Act of 1797 and the Unlawful Drilling Act of 1819, but the most important – at the time and later – was the Seditious Meetings Act of 1817 (57 Geo. III c. 19). This Act followed reports from secret committees of both Houses, and it imposed severe restrictions on the right of public meetings. Assemblies of fifty or more persons were illegal unless due notice had been given as specified in the Act, and any meeting without such notice whose purpose was the presentation of a petition to the Crown or Parliament, or the discussion of legislative changes, was an unlawful assembly. Such a meeting, having been declared illegal, must disperse within the hour, or those persons implicated could be charged with felony without benefit of clergy. There were special regulations with regard to political meetings of fifty or more persons within a mile of Westminster.[16]

These Acts, passed in response to the events of the 1790s and their aftermath, were still in force during the 1830s and 1840s, and in addition there was some new legislation in the twenty years before 1850. The Highways Act of 1835 made it an offence to obstruct the passage of any footpath or highway, and this could be used against public meetings;[17] and the Metropolitan Police Act of 1839 allowed the police to make regulations as to the route processions should take, and section 54 permitted a summary penalty for behaviour likely to cause a breach of the peace. The Town Clauses Act of 1847 empowered the police to prevent disturbances during processions, and allowed a power of arrest without warrant for any person found committing an offence under the Act. The most important legislation of the later Chartist period was the Crown and Security Act of April 1848 (11 and 12 Vict. c. 12) commonly known as the Treason-Felony Act.

Permission to bring in the new Bill was introduced by a long speech of Sir George Grey on 7 April. The first eight columns of his speech as reported in *Hansard* were taken up with the situation in Ireland, since it was the rising tide of unrest and disaffection in Ireland that was the occasion for the new proposals. The offence of high treason which was founded on the old statute of 25 Edward II, c. 2 applied to the whole kingdom, including Ireland, but there was doubt on this score concerning subsequent legislation. The law of treason had been codified and extended in 1795 by the 36 Geo. III c. 7 and it had been made perpetual, after the Union with Ireland, by 57 Geo. III c. 6.

The doubt was whether these later Acts did in fact apply to Ireland and the preponderance of legal opinion, so Grey said in his speech, was that the last Statue could not be used in Ireland, which left Ireland only with the Statute of Edward that was clearly enforceable. Under the new Act being proposed, the old penalties for direct offences against the sovereign would remain, but for the rest, treasons were made felonies, no longer punishable by death but by transportation for life or for a term of not less than seven years, or by imprisonment for two years, with or without hard labour. There was one addition to previous clauses: the introduction of a clause which would make 'open and advised speaking' among the categories under which prosecution could be made. In practice this would be a matter that would depend upon the reports of shorthand writers or police reports; and it was the clause that occasioned the only serious opposition in the passage of the Bill through the Commons. While the Bill as a whole received a negative vote only of between twenty-five and forty during its various stages in the lower House, an amendment deleting the clause which made treasonable speaking a felony received seventy-nine negative votes. The government, of course, had a very large majority, as it did in the House of Lords, and the Bill received the Royal Assent in the third week of April.

The Home Office, from March until the end of May, had followed a more or less consistent policy of refusing requests for the arrests of leading Chartists and Repealers. Such requests had often been made by local magistrates, but the cautiousness of ministers and their senior officials was born of the recognition that prosecutions which failed to obtain a conviction could be damaging to their cause of law and order. Juries were often influenced by previous judgements, and any refusal to pass guilty verdicts would give considerable encouragement to the disaffected and the ill-disposed. This was their reasoning, and it was wholly understandable. Moreover, they were Whigs and some among them, Lord John Russell in particular, had a liberal reputation to uphold, but even the very conservatively minded such as Palmerston, wanted to be certain that public opinion, by which they meant the middle classes in general, was firmly and unequivocally for determined action.[18] What began to alter Whitehall's appreciation of the national situation was the continuing growth of the radical movement throughout the month of May in parts of England as well as Ireland. It was above all Mitchel's trial and conviction that unloosed a mass protest movement among the Irish communities on both sides of the Irish Channel. The police, in all the disaffected districts, were under continuous physical strain; Clarendon's reports from Ireland were always gloomy and sometimes alarmist; requests for troops were steadily growing from both Ireland and England; and not least, since it was the metropolis, respectable citizens in

London were becoming increasingly disturbed by the succession of demonstrations and meetings in the streets of London. This was also happening in the industrial cities of the North, but as always what happened in London made much the greatest impact upon those directing security operations in the kingdom as a whole. It is possible that the serious police riot of Sunday 4 June in London was taken as a danger signal by the Whig ministers,[19] but in any case the general and growing apprehension, strongly reflected in the London newspapers before Whit Monday (12 June) would have been sufficient to propel the authorities into action. During these early days of June, *The Times* offered an excellent illustration of Dicey's recognition that the right to meeting, and the right of public discussion, depended upon the current state of public opinion; and also why the Home Office was now changing its mind about the expediency of arrests. A leading article on Tuesday 6 June began:

It is perhaps as well that the conduct of the rioters in the various remote districts of London should at length have reached such a point that any measures adopted for maintaining the tranquillity of the town – provided they be sufficiently energetic – will receive the sanction of public opinion. The law, in its present state, is amply sufficient for the purpose . . . We have the example of Paris, of Berlin, and of Vienna before our eyes, and, come what will, the citizens of London will take ample care that they are not brought to the same point of social disorganisation, bankruptcy, and wretchedness by the manoeuvres of a set of contemptible demagoges.

The Times then continued with a discussion of the law relating to unlawful meetings; it quoted the judges' statements of 1820 and 1822 about meetings calculated to cause alarm;[20] and then proceeded to bring the legal position up to date by reference to what was briefly noted above: a charge to a Grand Jury by Mr Justice Patterson of the Queen's Bench. On the previous Friday, 2 June, Justice Patterson had taken it upon himself to elaborate the law on meetings in terms of the current London demonstrations:

It is impossible to foresee what consequences may arise from such assemblages, even when the object in the first instance for calling them together may have been just and lawful, since an assemblage of crowds of persons may lead to acts not at all contemplated originally – may lead to outrages which were never thought of by the persons calling them together, but which bring those persons within the operation of the law. This is true of all assemblages, held even in the daytime [and inevitably much more at night] . . . I have no hesitation in saying that such tumultuous meetings at night can hardly, under any circumstances whatever, be otherwise than criminal.

The Times, after this lengthy statement, then quoted Ernest Jones' speech at Bishop Bonner's Field, emphasising the violent parts and concluding with the general advice: 'We speak advisedly when we say it is the general feeling of the inhabitants of the metropolis that matters should be speedily brought to an issue between the peaceable portion of the community and the rioters.' *The Times* ended this editorial by commenting on Lansdowne's remarks in the House of Lords in which he had suggested new powers might be required to deal with the present disturbances; and *The Times* tartly reminded him that the existing law was 'amply sufficient' for all necessary purposes.[21]

On the same day as this editorial, warrants were issued for the arrest of Ernest Jones and several of the other leading Chartists in the London area; and thus the political trials in England got under way. There were eight judges belonging to one or other of the three common law courts who this year sat on most political cases either at the Central Criminal Court in London, or at the Assizes in the provinces. These were the Lord Chief Justice, Sir Thomas Wilde, who presided over the Court of Common Pleas; Cresswell, Maule and Williams, also of Common Pleas; Alderson, Parke and Platt of Exchequer; and Erle of Queen's Bench. The majority of the senior judges in the nineteenth century as a whole came not from the aristocracy or gentry, but from the middle to upper middle classes; and so it was with this group of eight. Four had fathers who had been practising lawyers or solicitors; one was a merchant; one a clergyman; one a medical practitioner, and one from the lower gentry.[22] Their schools were Charterhouse, Westminster, Winchester, Harrow, St Paul's and, somewhat on its own, Macclesfield Grammar. All, except Sir Thomas Wilde, who was at St Paul's, went to university. The Macclesfield Grammar schoolboy was Parke, whose father was a merchant, and who went on to Trinity College, Cambridge. Six of the seven went to Cambridge (four to Trinity College) and one to New College, Oxford (from Winchester). This was Erle. Five of the eight had been in the Commons but only Sir Thomas Wilde was an active politician. He was first Solicitor-General and then Attorney-General in the Whig administration of Melbourne, and was immediately appointed Attorney-General when Russell took office in the summer of 1846; but the sudden death of Conyngham Tindal in July 1846 provided a vacancy in the office of Lord Chief Justice to which Wilde was appointed. In 1850 he accepted the seal of Lord Chancellor in place of Lord Cottenham and was created Baron Truro of Bowes, Middlesex. All the other seven were knighted during their legal careers; and they all left considerable estates at death.[23]

There were differences in the range and depth of their learning, and in their general abilities,[24] but it is hardly remarkable that this group of judges exhibited a sameness of attitude and approach to the political and social events of their time. What is perhaps surprising is that there was not one dissenting opinion among them. A sample of eight senior judges could perhaps have been expected to produce one honest eccentric, but in the political trials of this year they all spoke and responded in the same way.

Differences between Whig and Tory were not to be discerned; the strong prejudices of their upper middle-class contemporaries were their prejudices. Along with many thousands of the propertied classes, large and small, they had glimpsed the red dawn on the horizons of Europe; and within their own kingdom they looked across the Irish Sea at the hordes of starving masses, ready, so it was widely believed and feared, to maim and kill whenever opportunities would occur. With the English middle classes they had contemplated the abyss opening up before them, and they were afraid. Their fears were never far from panic, and the judicial representatives of this year, magistrates and senior judges alike, reflecting these apprehensions and trepidations, jettisoned any element of judicial impartiality. The social beast of Chartism must be put down, a decision made more determined by the relationship with the simian Irish. Not one of the judges who presided at the trial of Chartists and Repealers in England exhibited any appreciation of the political and social issues that provoked men to desperate action, or to thoughts of desperate action. The language they used to the prisoners in the dock, superior no doubt in syntax and larded, naturally, with legal references, was on the level of comprehension and understanding of the Victorian stereotype of the comfortable self-made grocer; respectable, smug, with a mind closed to all but the dogmas of the market-place, and imbued with an implacable hostility to those believed to be a threat to their stability and their social order. The charges and statements of these English judges, at every stage in the trial procedures, were a mixture of the political economy of J. R. McCulloch and the simplistic generalisations of self-help that were later to be expounded in the writings of Samuel Smiles. They were concerned, above all else, in providing the ideological justification for conviction and punishment. The assessment of evidence in order to allow the juries to weigh and adjudicate the facts of the case was never seriously elaborated in any of the English political trials of this year. Large parts of the judges' charges to the juries, or their summing up before the juries retired to consider their verdicts, were concerned with instruction on the virtues of English liberty, or the superiority in general of the English system over its European neighbours, or the wickedness, absurdity or illogicality of the political and social doctrines held by the prisoners in the dock. The English political trials of 1848 were exercises in the miscarriage of justice; the obliteration of reason by prejudice and the subversion of legal principles by partisanship of a virulent order.

By a curious twist of history, there were two political trials in Scotland during November 1848 that exhibited an extraordinary contrast with those in contemporary England: the presence of a high-minded and humane judiciary in sharp relief from the rancorous judges and prosecuting counsel of England. The trials – these were the only political trials of this year – were discussed in detail in Lord Cockburn's *An Examination of the Trials for Sedition in Scotland*,[25] and the absence of a comparable volume for England, and for Ireland, is much to be deplored. Cockburn very properly contrasted the legal humanity and adherence to principle of 1848 with the terrible record of the Scottish judges in the 1790s. In 1848 the charges against John Grant, Henry Ranken and Robert Hamilton – the defendants in the first trial – were libel for conspiracy and sedition at common law under the new Treason-Felony Act: similar, therefore, to many of the indictments in the English trials. The whole spirit of this first trial was, however, quite different. James Craufurd[26] addressed the jury on behalf of the prosecution in the absence of the Lord Advocate, making what Cockburn described as:

the best address that was ever delivered for the Crown, to a jury, in a Scotch trial of sedition. It was able, fair, and temperate; strong for a conviction, but liberally constitutional in public principles; and, above all, it was superior to the paltriness of inflaming, instead of allaying, any prejudice that the jury might be supposed to be under the influence of.[27]

During his speech Craufurd insisted that the Chartists were fully entitled to hold their opinions and that 'This is not a prosecution for opinions.' It was a speech finely tuned to constitutional proprieties, as was that of the main defending counsel, James Moncrieff, who uttered words and phrases that would have had no meaning in the hysterical atmosphere in which the trials were being conducted south of the border:

It is not beyond the recollection of the present generation that there have been times when juries as high-minded as any jury can be have been carried away by the whirlwind of similar excitement. There have been times when verdicts have been returned under circumstances of public prejudice, in which the voice, not of law merely, but reason and sense, was drowned in one overpowering terror; verdicts which filled some, at least, who pronounced them with undying regret; and have stamped an indelible stigma on the times they characterise. I am under no apprehension of that kind today.[28]

This first trial ended with only a partial verdict being returned by the jury; and the prisoners were sentenced to four months' imprisonment. 'It was a trial', wrote Cockburn. 'The convict ship did not darken its close'.[29]

Cockburn's discussion of the Scottish trials of the 1790s provides a useful introduction to the English practices and procedures of 1848. Cockburn emphasised that apart from Braxfield, who was a man of extreme coarseness and illiberality, the Scottish judges of the 1790s were not guilty of turpitude other than that which is implied in 'judicial partiality'. There was no improper interference with witnesses:

But political reasoning, and confident assumption of the truth of the charge, were always conspicuous. A headlong adoption on the bench, of all the judge's feelings in society, was the chief source of their errors. It prevented their ever rising above the instincts of party men, dealing for party purposes with party adversaries . . . Hence, instead of thinking of maturing the law, what they were thinking of was, the conviction of the person accused. The principles, and the forms, of general justice were lost sight of in an exclusive and passionate eagerness about the existing crisis, and the victim at the bar.[30]

It was precisely the political reasoning of the English judges in 1848 that coloured and defined all their statements from the bench. Thus, to give an example, Baron Alderson's charge to the Grand Jury at the Chester Assizes in early December was a lengthy, highly political speech, delivered with the purpose of convincing the juries that their political instincts condemning the accused radicals were properly founded in history and contemporary fact.[31] After adverting to the convulsions in Europe during the past year from which the United Kingdom had been largely spared – 'Our people lived under free institutions, and they knew it' – Alderson then proceeded to consider the argument that there was a need for an entire change in the social order by the acquisition of political rights, which in turn would bring about a material improvement in the well-being of the ordinary people. To refute this suggestion, Alderson then referred to 'certain documents which had been published in Paris', the origins of which he did not specify, but which showed how the physical comforts enjoyed by the poor in France before 1789 greatly exceeded any of later years. Among other indices of comfort Alderson quoted meat consumption in various years. It was an interesting example of an early version of the standard of living controversy[32] except in this case there could be no opposition view to that of the learned judge. Having disposed of the mistaken idea that political rights automatically bring an improvement in the levels of comfort and prosperity, Alderson then asked how could we in England provide for the remedy of existing evils, which he did not deny. His answer was by education in the broadest sense of the term; as a result of which:

the people would readily be brought to understand that the accumulation of capital in the manufacturing districts was a blessing to the workmen . . . Then also would the poor more readily learn that the possession of large estates, not used merely for the purpose of luxury and private gratification, was a blessing to the poor, in promoting the establishment of Schools, churches and other institutions calculated to ameliorate our social condition.

Alderson ended his charge to this Grand Jury by reminding them again of the distress prevailing in the country, and he exhorted his hearers to remember at all times their obligations:

He need not, therefore, urge upon them the importance of sympathising with the poor, and embracing every opportunity of mitigating their privation. For affording an opportunity of exercising virtue in this manner might be one reason why Providence permitted so much suffering; but, by availing themselves of such means for doing good, we might realise the truth of the poet's sentiment:
    The bud may have a bitter taste
    But sweet will be the flower

It is not surprising that Alderson should have seen fit to draw attention to the beneficial effects of the great landed estates, for this was part of the received wisdom of his day; just as his reference to the consequences of the subdivision of land in France as 'one of the greatest sources of misery that could possibly exist' was the accepted corollary; and it was important that all classes in Britain understood what dire results would follow the break-up of the existing structure of land ownership. Orthodox political economy had long insisted upon the economic inefficiency of the small farm, and the tendency of subdivision to encourage a Malthusian rate of population increase. J. R. McCulloch had provided the *locus classicus* of the argument in his famous essay on the 'Cottage System' in the sixth edition of the *Encyclopedia Britannica* in 1819 (and reprinted with only minor alterations in the seventh edition (1842) and the eighth (1854)).[33] Ireland was the most commonly cited example of the impoverishment consequent upon the proliferation of small holdings, and after Ireland it was France that offered the example of the wretchedness associated with the small farm system. Although there was a growing body of opinion by the 1840s which denied that Continental Europe provided evidence for these kind of assertions – and this opinion was voiced by the most eminent economist of the mid-Victorian period who published the first edition of his *Principles of Political Economy* in April 1848 – the benefits of the large farm and the great estate continued to be accepted by the greater part of the middle class throughout the Victorian decades, long after Baron Alderson's references to his Grand Jury at Chester.[34]

The beneficient workings of Providence, which Alderson had accepted as part of the natural order of things in England, were invoked also by some of his fellow judges. Mr Justice Maule, for example, at the York Assizes, addressing a group of prisoners accused of riotous behaviour, reminded them of the possibilities open to those who took full advantage of their opportunities through the upward social mobility which the system encouraged.

They appeared to be hardworking men, and if they wished to raise themselves in the world, the best course they could take in this was to be careful, to work hard, spend as little money as they could, and improve their knowledge whenever they had the opportunity. Some people in Yorkshire had acquired a very large property indeed, who had begun life simply as working men; but he never heard of any one who had raised his condition by going out drilling and joining a Chartist society.[35]

Maule had been senior wrangler in the Cambridge mathematical tripos in 1810, and he became a Fellow of Trinity College before he was called to the bar, where he enjoyed considerable financial success. The *Dictionary of National Biography* wrote that he 'was distinguished for his ironical humour', but it was not irony that he was using upon these Bradford working men. Maule, who was knighted in 1839 and died unmarried, was

obviously hard working and no doubt thrifty, and managed to leave about
£35,00 at his death in 1858.[36]

Sir Thomas Wilde, the key figure in these political trials, also expatiated on
the virtues of a social system which allowed hard work and talent to make
their way in the world:

You have examples enough before you of what a frugal upright workman may do.
There is in this country no limit to the height he may rise to. A man becomes a
tradesman, but there are instances of his entering the House of Peers. No rank in this
country precludes a man from having the results of the fair exercise of his talent. You
have had our profession pointed out. Men who start without patrons, men who
depend only on themselves, rise to the highest branch of the profession. I am myself
an instance; there are many others. Therefore nothing can be more delusive, nothing
more unjust, than to be telling the poor man that the rich are robbing him. The fine
horses, the fine parks, and the splendid equipages, have been the result of labour of
days and nights and of frugality.

This statement of Wilde came in his summing up at the end of the trial of
Ernest Jones. Earlier, in the same speech, he had discoursed on a phrase used
by Jones that had especially irked him: one about bringing the rich man's
nose to the grindstone. Wilde called it 'an extraordinary passage' and he
then instructed the jury into the political economy of wealth and of the ways
in which the expenditure of the rich constantly and continuously favoured
the poor. 'Would the poor be more benefited if the rich did not keep carriages,
which leads to the consumption of iron and wood, and glass, and cloth, and
silk and leather, and of articles of every variety . . . employing hundreds of
workmen? What is to be done if you bring the rich man's nose to the
grindstone, if by that is meant to put down his carriage'.[37] And so on. When
Wilde had completed his summing up, the effect of which was a firm
invitation to find the prisoner guilty, the jury obliged, by retiring at a quarter
to six, and returning at two minutes to six, with a verdict of guilty. The juries
in these political trials in England were notably expeditious in their
deliberations. Time was not wasted. Fussell was disposed of by the jury in
fifteen minutes; and it was rare in any of the trials for sedition and unlawful
assembly for juries to be out for more than half an hour.

The trial of Joseph Fussell, the earliest of the major state trials in England
in 1848, illustrates many of the characteristics and attitudes of the legal
process. It was, first of all, an example of a general problem that does not
appear to have been much commented on but which is a serious difficulty for
the historian: the problem of what constitutes a complete and faithful record
of all that was said at any particular trial.[38] The official *Reports of State Trials*
list the different sources used for the supposedly definitive version of each
trial: sometimes it was a combination of shorthand notes preserved in the
Treasury papers and Cox's Criminal Cases; at other times it was just the
shorthand notes; and at other times it was copied from the Sessions Papers of

the Central Criminal Court, at times amended by the notes of the official shorthand writers. There were a number of sedition trials in this year that were not regarded as justifying a full report, and only the summing up of the presiding judge would be given. Comparison with contemporary newspaper reports, especially those in *The Times*, reveals omissions and discrepancies, and on occasion these can be illuminating. In the trial of William Cuffay, for instance, Sgt Ballantine, for the defence, challenged one of the jurors by asking him whether he had acted as a special constable. The Attorney-General objected to the question as being 'totally irrelevant', and Baron Platt agreed and was reported in the *State Trials* as saying: 'It is a question which has nothing whatever to do with the issue, and I cannot allow it to be put.' *The Times* report of the proceedings and that also of the *Morning Chronicle* have a different answer from the judge: 'Mr Baron Platt concurred that the question was irrelevant. It was like asking whether the party was a loyal man'.[39] As a statement of the political attitudes of the learned judge there could have been no sharper reminder in the courtroom of the Central Criminal Court on 25 September 1848.

The record of the Fussell case was different from most of the other sedition trials since the greater part of the evidence was based upon newspaper reports. He was indicted for a seditious speech at a Chartist meeting on Clerkenwell Green on the evening of Monday 29 May, and for unlawful assembly and riot. The charges were on eight counts, six of which related to seditious words, the seventh to unlawful assembly and the eighth to riot. This last was dropped half-way through the trial. After a legal argument regarding which of the charges should be proceeded with, the Attorney-General opened for the Crown. Sir John Jervis was a political barrister. He spent most of the 1830s in the Commons and took Wilde's place as Attorney-General in the summer of 1846, and he later also followed Wilde as Lord Chief Justice of Common Pleas. His address to the court in the Fussell case was typical of the man; it was firmly argued but with nothing of the sense of constitutional liberties or of the humanity that informed the speech of the prosecuting counsel in the Scottish case against Ranken and others. His explanation of the meaning of sedition relied upon long quotations from the sixth Report (1841) of the Commission on Criminal Law, Tindal's definition in 1842 and Alderson at the Monmouth Assize of 1839. The Attorney-General then proceeded to insist that actual presence at a meeting presumed, declared or likely to become unlawful was sufficient for notice to be taken of their presence regardless of the original motive given for attendance: which could be curiosity, and for which they must take the consequences of their presence. But, he insisted, if persons meet by agreement 'then the act of one is admissible in evidence to prove the guilt of all'.[40]

The indictment was for seditious language uttered at the Clerkenwell Green meeting, and for the procession which formed out of the meeting and proceeded four abreast through the City into the West End and which created 'the greatest terror and alarm in the breasts of the peaceable inhabitants'. The procession was without violent incident of any kind; the only fighting came from a breakaway after the procession had returned to the East End, and that occurred because the police moved in to prevent a further, and much smaller, meeting being held.

What, however, made the Fussell trial sensational was the speech that Fussell was alleged to have made at Clerkenwell Green. The only full record of the speech were the reports published the next morning in *The Times* and the *Morning Chronicle*. The Attorney-General explained to the court that the meeting was held without any previous announcement and that neither the government nor the police had reporters or shorthand writers present and the only evidence was therefore from the public press. The two reporters who took down his speech were in court and were cross-examined separately. One quoted what had been sent to *The Times*, and the other to the *Morning Chronicle*. It should be emphasised that there were quite significant differences between the two reports read out in court, especially in the placing of certain key phrases. Here is what *The Times* reporter read from his notes:

The Government is not worthy the support of any honest man, it is too contemptible to be recognised, and you must use your best endeavours to overthrow it. And now I wish to impress upon you that there is one safe way of getting rid of bad rulers who forget their duty to their country: I openly avow that I mean private assassination. What made the Emperor of Austria fly from his country? Why, the fear of assassination; and it is by these means that other bad rulers will soon fly. I have five sons and I now declare that I would disown any one who would refuse to assassinate any person who may be instrumental in banishing me from my country for such an offence as John Mitchel was convicted of.[41]

It was to be expected that the publication of Fussell's alleged words on private assassination would be widely commented on throughout the country. The Queen wrote to Lord Russell on 31 May asking what action was contemplated;[42] the speech was reprinted throughout the national and provincial press, and Greville noted the furore in a diary entry for 3 June.[43] *Punch* produced a 'Song of the Seditionist', two verses of which ran:

Come, all lovers of Sedition for its own delightful sake;
Come, all disaffected rascals, a disturbance let us make;
Come, at midnight let us meet, ye revolutionary crew,
With no purpose in particular but rioting in view.

Let us shout 'Assassination!' whilst our FUSSELL recommends
Our approval of the sentiment – and take the hint, my friends;
Let us shriek aloud for pikes, and with the Patriot sympathise,
Who suggested flinging vitriol into British soldiers' eyes.[44]

All this was long before the trial, and it would have been difficult to discover a potential juryman in London who had not heard something about Fussell and what he was purported to have recommended.

The reporters who took down the speeches at this Clerkenwell meeting were penny-a-liners: if their reports were printed they would be paid at the rate of a penny a line. T. F. Fowler, whose report was published in *The Times*, proved under cross-examination at the trial to be a dubious character; but much more important than his somewhat shady past was the working arrangement he disclosed with the other reporter at the meeting, H. J. Potter. They lived at the same address, and they often shared meetings between each other – as they had done at Clerkenwell Green – and they divided what profits there were from publication. This was Potter's testimony about the Clerkenwell meeting:

I retired with Fowler from the meeting. We did not compare our notes. He did not read to me what he should send to the *Times*. I wrote out one portion of the meeting while he wrote the other, so that we had no occasion to compare notes. I do not recollect which portion of the meeting Fowler wrote. Sometimes one writes the beginning, and the other the speeches. I recollect writing some of the description of the procession, but whether I wrote it all I do not know. The procession was quite enough. I have an impression that I wrote Fussell's speech, but I am not positively certain. There was a great noise at intervals. While Fussell was speaking I was in the van, immediately behind him. He spoke for about ten minutes, as near as I can recollect: they all took about the same time. There was a noise, unless there was anything sprightly said. There was nothing very sprightly said, to my mind, but that is a matter of taste; when I say I only took the salient points, I mean the points that I thought most likely to be of use in a newspaper report.[45]

Potter denied for a second time that he and Fowler compared copy: 'We could not compare it, because they were different parts. I wrote a portion and he wrote a portion, there could be no comparison; one was grafted on the other.'

The remarkable thing about the cross-examination of these two reporters, who were of course Crown witnesses and whose testimony was crucial to the Crown's case, was the failure of the defending counsel to question these reporting procedures.[46] It was certainly not that Court practice at this period restrained counsel from critical and severe cross-examination of witnesses who could be deemed to be hostile. In both Ireland and England certain informers at sedition trials were totally discredited by persistent questioning,[47] but in the Fussell case almost nothing was brought forward. Fowler, for example, took down his reports not in the usual shorthand but in what he described as 'abbreviated longhand'. Both reporters had their notebooks in court, and it was not uncommon for witnesses of this kind to exhibit their books to the Court or to read exactly what they had written down. This was not done, except in the one instance quoted above, and there were some very obvious additional questions that could have been asked. How was their division of labour arranged, for example? Was it decided upon before they arrived at any meeting – that one would take the speeches or the main speeches, and the other the incidental information? If it was not arranged beforehand, what signal did they convey to each other at the meeting itself in order that there should be no overlap? Potter was not at all sure that he took down Fussell's speech, but no one pressed him on this very important question; nor was Fowler asked what his recollection was of the matter. It must be concluded that this stage of the trial was handled most incompetently by the defence counsel, and the contrast with the liveliness and verve of the Irish defending lawyers in the same months is most striking.

The Crown witnesses included two policemen who had to rely on their memories, and two shopkeepers; and after the Crown completed its case, the leading defending counsel, Sgt Allen, then made his main statement to the jury. It was broadly on the lines that were followed in most of the English trials of this year. Allen made most of the difficulty of making any precise definition of sedition, and commented on the Attorney-General's statement to the effect that 'sedition seems to be any address or words which shall arouse a feeling of contempt against the government, or excite any attack against the constituted authorities'; and he went on to make the obvious point that such a definition would include most politicians at some stage of their career. It was common in these trials for defence counsel to refer, directly or indirectly, to the Whigs during the agitation around the Reform Bill of 1832, and at times to the words and action of Daniel O'Connell in Ireland; and it was on these grounds that Allen made his case in defence of Fussell. The liberties of Englishmen depended on their right to criticise and demonstrate against their authorities in government. What Allen did not attempt, apart from a very proper indictment of Fowlers's character, was an analysis of the ways in which the crucial phrases in Fussell's speech were put together by the two reporters. It was not quite the speech of a latter-day Erskine.[48]

When Allen had finished – and his speech reads very cold in print – it was then the turn for witnesses for the defence; and three respectable artisans – a journeyman carpenter, an optical instrument maker and a bookbinder – all testified that they were close to Fussell when he was making his speech and that the words alleged about private assassination were not made. Fussell's employer, a jeweller, for whom Fussell had worked for the previous six or seven years, bore witness to his sober character. And that was all for the defence, with the prosecution asking quite perfunctory questions.

Under the Court procedures of the period, the prisoner's counsel had no right to sum up in cases of felony and misdemeanours; and it was only later, with the passing of Denman's Act (28 and 29 Vict. c. 18 s. 2) that this right was introduced. In Fussell's case therefore, after the examination of the defence witnesses was concluded, the Attorney-General made his second speech to the jury. He had opened the trial with a speech which concentrated upon the terror and alarm that the Clerkenwell meeting had caused. It reads as a somewhat unimpressive performance, simplistic in its legal statements, but well calculated to appeal to his particular kind of jury; and his summing up, much shorter in length, more or less repeated the points he had already made. The whole of Europe, Sir John Jervis said, 'was in a state of violent excitement and tumult. There was raging in a sister-country [Ireland] a system of circumstances where the ill-judging people thought the property of the people was the right of the people', – an argument which coming before the threatened Irish rising must have made a considerable impact. The Attorney-General, to bring the matter back to London, summed up by quoting at length Mr Justice Patterson's charge to the Grand Jury with its emphasis upon the definition of unlawful assemblies in terms of the fears they created in those around them.

The barristers had now had their day, and Sir Thomas Wilde began his direction to the jury. It was a long statement, taking up about a quarter of the whole account in the *State Trials* series. It is possible that some readers of his speech might consider it unfair to describe what he said as a blatant incitement to convict; for it is always possible to pull out sentences and phrases which insist on the right of free discussion; and besides the prosecuting counsel and the presiding judges, in all the English trials, nodded towards the principles of liberty of opinion. In this speech of the Lord Chief Justice there really could be no doubt in the minds of the jury as to the course their presiding judge expected them to take. It is, of course, wholly reasonable to believe that if the jury had all slept through Sir Thomas Wilde's summing up they would still have exercised their prejudices for a conviction.[49] Wilde naturally discussed the evidence for Fussell's alleged advocacy of private assassination. He made no reference to Fowler's somewhat shady career which had been made much of by the defence counsel, but insisted first on the fact that both reporters agreed on what had been said regarding assassination and second that Fowler's use of longhand was probably more reliable than if he had used shorthand.[50] There was no encouragement at all to the jury to consider some of the questions that might be asked of two reporters who operated according to the agreement between Fowler and Potter; and, Wilde emphasised, if the jury did believe the reports to be accurate, there was no doubt that the words used fell 'within any definition whatever which can be given of sedition'. Since Wilde raised no serious questions for the jury to consider, he slid easily back and forth between minor points of criticism, and a much firmer general assumption that what was alleged to be said was in fact said. He ended with a renewed emphasis upon the theme of the terror and alarm that the meeting and procession had created; and his closing words should be read within that context:

It is beyond doubt a most important case, and much depends on you holding even scales, and exercising a cautious but firm judgement on the part of the Government and between the public and the defendant, taking care to preserve the public right of free, open, vigorous discussion, if people think fit, of public grievances, on the one hand, and that you do not allow it to be abused by the creating of public terror and public mischief on the other. You will consider your verdict, and I dare say you will come to a satisfactory conclusion.

The *Report of State Trials* continues, 'The jury retired, and after an absence of fifteen minutes, returned a verdict of "*Guilty*".'

This trial of Fussell was important in that it set the tone and the approach to be followed by the subsequent trials. Sir Thomas Wilde presided over all those arrested at the same time as Fussell, and all were found guilty and awarded the same sentence: two years imprisonment and large sums for recognizances and sureties for keeping the peace after their release: large sums, that is, for working men, as most of them were. Williams, for example who was tried with Vernon on the day following the Fussell trial was awarded two years imprisonment with recognizances of his own of £100 and two sureties of £50, each for three years after the expiry of his term in prison. On this sentence being pronounced, Williams said: 'Then I am under the necessity of passing imprisonment for five years and one week through my poverty and distress'; to which Sir Thomas Wilde answered that the remission of punishment lay in the decision of the Crown. Here is an aspect of the workings of the judicial system that has been largely ignored by those concerned with legal history, yet it clearly could be of quite a serious nature. In the arrests of fifty-eight persons in the Bradford area at the end of May and early June – cases which were held at the end of July and the beginning of August – only nine could meet the bail requirements which had been fixed too high for the resources of working people, and the remainder then spent the two months prior to their trial in prison; and as far as can be discovered from the reports of the trials and the sentences imposed, no allowance was made at this time for any imprisonment for preventive detention.

The trials of Williams, Vernon, Sharpe and Looney were all held with the same jury which convicted Fussell. The only way that this fact can be discovered was the request by the counsel for the last defendant, Ernest Jones, for a jury which had not disposed of any of the previous cases; and this was reported in *The Times* for 11 July but not in the report in the *State Trials* series: another instance of the partial character of the official record. In his case the Attorney-General said that the request for a new jury could not be taken 'as a matter of right' but that he would offer no objection; and a new jury was sworn in. In his opening speech, the Attorney-General used the opportunity for a nice touch of unction, explaining to the jury that the arrest of Ernest Jones was 'a practical refutation to the charge which has been brought against me and my predecessors that there is one law for the rich and one for the poor, and that the object of the prosecution is to add injury to the sufferings of the working man by selecting its victims from among the poorer classes'. It was in this trial that the Lord Chief Justice expounded his version of the political economy of the rich which was quoted above:[51] an exposition described by the historian of the Victorian Lord Chancellors as one 'for which his habits of mind and study had indifferently qualified him'.[52] The same historian wrote of Sgt Wilkins, the leading counsel for Ernest Jones, that he 'defended with more vigour than discretion'.[53]

When the trial of Jones was concluded, all the other five accused were brought back into court to hear their sentences; and in all cases they exercised their right to address the court. It should be noted that this was the first time the accused had the opportunity to address the court and to present their own case, since none had been cross-examined for the jury's benefit. Fussell once again strenuously denied ever recommending private assassination, and Williams gave up his time to a further statement on Fussell's behalf. Ernest Jones made quite a long statement but was prevented by Sir Thomas Wilde from making a reasoned answer to the economic arguments the judge had used. All the sentences were the same – two years imprisonment, with a few weeks added in some cases – and all were bound over for two or three years, except Fussell, who was given five years after his prison sentence expired. It was this clause on the prisoners of 1848 which goes some way in explaining why so many of the activists and militants of that year were not heard of in the attempted revival of Chartism after 1850.

The later trials of 1848 followed broadly the patterns established by those of Fussell and Jones and their fellow accused. The *Northern Star* of 15 July not unreasonably summed up this first group of trials as the result of: 'A rancorous Whig Attorney-General, a partisan Judge, and a middle-class jury, steeped in hatred towards everything savouring of Chartism . . .' and the same combination assured the conviction of almost all those who followed. The main difference in the later trials, both in London and the North, was that much of the evidence was based upon the testimony of informers and spies. The case against the London Chartists and Repealers arrested during August, for example, was founded almost entirely upon informers. The movement in London had been penetrated for many weeks, and the reliability of the evidence has been considered and analysed in detail by Goodway.[54] It still leaves many questions only partly answered. William Cuffay, for example, made a long and detailed refutation of the evidence relating to himself that had been supplied by Powell and Davis, the two main informers, and Cuffay underlined the important point that Davis must have read Powell's evidence before he himself came into the court on the following day.[55] What is undeniable is that in spite of the many doubts that were raised during the cross-examination of police informers, Powell in

London and Ball in Liverpool for example,[56] the testimony of these and other informers, was broadly accepted by the judges in their directions to the juries. In the London trials it meant that armed conspiracy could be proved and the sentence of transportation imposed.

Baron Alderson, who was on the Bench at Chester and Liverpool for the Chartist trials at those places, provided a footnote to the events of 1848 in a letter to his cousin, Mrs Opie. Writing from Liverpool on 10 December, he said:

You will be glad to hear that both here and at Manchester trade is steadily improving, and all are in good hope and spirits, and say that the crisis is past, if Europe remains tolerably quiet. This will put an end to Chartism more effectively than any trials. Both together will for some time annihilate it – the leaders all in gaol – the people at work again.[57]

The senior judges in Ireland had quite different problems from their brethren in England. The main difficulty was a straightforward matter of the composition of the jury. If those eligible to be included on a jury panel in Ireland were selected at random for jury service, there could not fail to be a Catholic majority or at the least, a substantial Catholic minority. Roman Catholic jurors, however, had a propensity to sympathise with Catholic accused in political cases, or they were afraid of intimidation after the trial if they voted against their fellow religionists: it always was known, so it appeared, who voted on which side. There was certainly a great deal of intimidation, in both urban and rural districts. The jury system, in sum, did not and could not work in a society seven-eighths of whose population was alien in religion from the dominating power and largely hostile to the fact of domination. It is a common enough phenomenon in the colonialist experience. The British also found the same problem in India, especially with the development of nationalist politics in the twentieth century. What was probably the most celebrated political trial in India during the years between the two world wars – the Meerut trial of 1929–33 – was removed from the Presidency towns and transferred to the small town of Meerut in order to avoid the unpleasant consequences of trial by jury.[58] In Ireland politics during the closing months of 1848 became increasingly centered upon the practices of jury-packing, and the trial of Smith O'Brien provided the catalyst for what became a national debate. The earlier trials during May had resulted in acquittals because of the presence of at least one recalcitrant Catholic on each jury.[59] The Crown had, therefore, to take special precautions to ensure that there were no Catholics on the jury which tried the third of the prisoners at this time. As John Clapham wrote in an article of 1934: 'A more judiciously constituted jury sent Mitchel to penal servitude for treason-felony.'[60] The Mitchel case provided an immediate and forceful shock to large parts of public opinion; and not only to Catholics. The 1843 trial of Daniel O'Connell had not been forgotten, when O'Connell was confronted by a wholly Protestant jury and sentenced by judges who were also Protestant. It was also remembered that the Whigs, who were in opposition in these years, had protested vigorously against the malpractices involved. Lord John Russell's remarks at this time are worth noting. He was speaking in the Commons on a state of the nation debate, on 9 August 1844; and in the part to be quoted he was commenting on the arrest and trial of Daniel O'Connell:

> Mr O'Connell and other popular leaders were allowed to go on for seven or eight months without interruption. Their language was unchecked, their meetings uninterrupted . . . But having determined to bring this case to trial, it was so contrived, that there being eleven Roman Catholics among the persons who might have been upon the Jury, those eleven Roman Catholics were struck off by the Crown, and there remained a Jury of twelve Protestants, several of whom were known to be violent partisans in a line of politics opposite to that which Mr O'Connell had embraced. How, I ask, could the internal peace of Ireland be secured by these means? . . . and I hope that before the next Session, the Government will fully consider the question – that they will look to the hopes which have been held out, and to the promises which were made at the time of the Union that Ireland should be placed upon an equality with England; that she should be governed upon the same principles, and should enjoy the same rights and privileges. Let Government determine, in the light of those declarations, to go through those laws which now exist, to go through those maxims of administration which they themselves have followed, and produce a plan which will not countenance Repeal of the Union; but which will, on the contrary, give a death-blow to that agitation by granting to the people of Ireland fully, fairly, and entirely, the privileges which they themselves have solemnly promised to give them.[61]

In Ireland among the eminent Catholics who protested against the packing of the O'Connell jury were J. H. Monahan and T. R. Redington, both of whom were to be in the Whig government of 1848: Monahan was Attorney-General and Redington was Under-Secretary of State.

The most important trial in 1848 after that of John Mitchel was the indictment for high treason of Smith O'Brien following the abortive attempt at a rising in late July and early August; and the course of its proceedings dominated politics in Ireland in the closing months of the year. The precise charge, as given in the *State Trials* report was 'levying war against the Queen in Tipperary between July 17th and 30th 1848 . . . and by compassing to raise insurrection, and subvert the government, and put the Queen to death'. The presiding judge at the trial was Francis Blackburne (1782–1867), Lord Chief Justice of the Queen's Bench who had first been Attorney-General in Peel's administration of 1841 and then Master of the Rolls in 1842. Blackburne was markedly conservative in politics, and regarded with great hostility by O'Connell and the Repealers.[62] Blackburne was assisted by Mr Justice Richard Moore (1783–1857), a Whig in politics who had been Attorney-General in 1846 and then moved to the Queen's Bench in 1847.

The third judge was Chief Justice Doherty whose main career was over and who was to die in 1850.[63]

All three judges were Protestant in religion. The prosecution for the Crown was led by J. H. Monahan (1803–78), a Roman Catholic and a Whig, who, as noted above, had been among the many Catholics who had protested at the jury-packing in the 1843 O'Connell trial. Smith O'Brien was defended by James Whiteside and Francis Fitzgerald. Whiteside (1804–76) was one of the outstanding personalities of the Irish bar in the nineteenth century. He was an erudite lawyer and his eloquence recalled to contemporaries the language of Curran and Burke. His speech in defence of Daniel O'Connell became one of the classics of the Irish bar. In religion he was a Protestant and in politics a conservative. He was appointed Solicitor-General and then Attorney-General in the 1850s, and Lord Chief Justice of the Queen's Bench in 1866. His colleague Fitzgerald (1806–97) was a Protestant in religion, and appointed a Baron of the Exchequer in 1859. Also present on the defence side was Sir Colman O'Loghlen, the eldest son of the man who had played such a prominent part in the Whig administration in Ireland during Melbourne's government.[64] It was a formidable defence team, and their legal ingenuity, energy and command of the law were in striking contrast with the performance of the defence counsel in the English political trials.

The trial of Smith O'Brien for high treason was held at a Special Commission at Clonmel in Tipperary. It opened on 21 September amid elaborate security precautions. The proceedings began with a lengthy charge to the Grand Jury, and after the Grand Jury had returned a true Bill against Smith O'Brien and four others, the trial opened on Thursday 28 September.[65] There was an immediate application by Whiteside to postpone the trial for non-delivery of the copy of the indictment and lists of witnesses and jurors ten days before the trial. This was denied on the grounds that the English statutes quoted by Whiteside did not apply to Ireland. Whiteside then applied for a stay on a further technical matter, and then for a copy of the jury panel 'for a few hours before the trial'. In England, Whiteside said, 'a prisoner would be entitled to a copy of the panel ten days before the trial'. What Whiteside was attempting, with these applications, was to establish that English practice could or would be followed; and in these matters he was unsuccessful. He then made a substantive challenge to the array, that is, to the ways in which the list of jurors, from which individual juries were picked, had been drawn up. Whiteside handed in a long statement in which it was alleged that there was not a jurors' book in existence for the county of Tipperary for the year 1848, and that the accepted procedure for determining the jury panel had not therefore been followed; that previous panels had contained not less than one-third Roman Catholics, but that the jury panel on this occasion had only about one-eighteenth of the number who were Catholics. The law officers of the Crown retired to consult and after two hours returned to Court denying the allegations and affirming that 'the array of the said panel was well, equally, and impartially made'. The defence objected, and two 'triers' were then sworn in, their duty being to examine the allegations made by the defence and to determine their accuracy or otherwise. The triers were picked from the jury panel. Whiteside then argued the case to the triers on two grounds. The first concerned the making up of the jurors' book, and after an intervention from the Lord Chief Justice who advised the triers that there was no case for the defence, the triers found accordingly in favour of the Crown. The second ground for challenge was the matter of the composition of the panel: whether it had been fairly and impartially chosen. Whiteside again quoted the two-thirds Protestant and one-third Catholic as the proportions that had previously obtained with jury panels in Tipperary, and that the present panel contained a very much smaller number of Catholics. There were eighteen or nineteen Catholics out of a total panel of 288; and Whiteside reminded the Court of the denunciation by Lord John Russell of the setting aside of Catholic jurors in the Daniel O'Connell trial. Whiteside made this part of his argument:

I believe out of every twenty or twenty-five names there is one Catholic gentleman. Our right of challenge is thus made a mere farce; and it comes ultimately to this, if this system be continued, while I admit the Sheriff ought to strike off all men who are Confederation men, and the like, yet, if on the score merely of their religion they are omitted, it would be better frankly and boldly at once to re-enact the penal laws.[66]

Whiteside then proceeded to introduce a number of Catholic jurors who had served regularly in the past but whose names were missing from the current list. On several occasions Blackburne intervened with hostile comments. The Sheriff of the county was then cross-examined and it appeared that the panel was in fact drawn up by the Sub-Sheriff, but before he left the witness stand the Sheriff, who admitted he had only heard of the small number of Catholics from the evidence given in Court, agreed that he was surprised at the few Catholics represented. The Sub-Sheriff on examination proved to be a somewhat shifty character who nevertheless maintained on his oath that he had not left off any person from the panel because he was a Catholic. Fitzgerald summed up for the defence, and then the Lord Chief Justice spoke at length, explaining to the triers that there had obviously been no corruption, that the Sheriff and Sub-Sheriff were clearly to be believed, and that there had been no communication between the Sheriff and the Attorney-General. Whiteside protested that he had never used the term 'corruption' and that he had never suggested collusion between the Crown and the local officials. The Bench came back again to the issue of corruption and ignored the simple issues which Whiteside had raised, namely that to discover for this important trial a much lower proportion of Catholics than usual was a matter that ought to be seriously looked into. To no avail, and the triers found in favour of the Crown.

That settled the question, and the jury panel was called over, with a fine of £10 for those who did not answer. About two hundred presented themselves and, as this was a smaller number than had answered the previous day, Whiteside requested that the panel should be called over again, with higher fines for non-attendance. The latter was not agreed and a further call-over produced only six additional jurors. Whiteside then made an ingenious request. He was aware, as everyone was, that if the normal procedure were followed, the Catholic jurors would be told to stand aside until a full Protestant jury had been selected. He therefore applied that the jury for Smith O'Brien should be drawn by ballot and quoted the trial of John Frost as precedent where the request was agreed, the panel being arranged in alphabetical order and a jury drawn by ballot. The report of the *State Trial* in the case of Frost and others after the Newport Rising was held in a more judicial and judicious temper than the present case in 1848[67] and when Blackburne referred the request to the Attorney-General, whose consent was required, the latter insisted that as the triers had found the panel fairly and impartially constituted, there was no case for 'a departure from what has been the settled practice of the courts in both countries' and he denied the application; and this was accepted by the Lord Chief Justice.

The panel was then called and Smith O'Brien told by the Clerk of the Crown that he was allowed twenty peremptory challenges – for which, that is, he did not have to show cause – and as many others as he could show cause for. Whiteside argued that in cases of high treason the prisoner was entitled to thirty-five peremptory challenges, and he proceeded to quote both common and statute law to the effect that this was the practice in England and that the right was not taken away from Ireland. The Attorney-General argued that high treason and petit treason – the latter, it was agreed, was an instance where only twenty jurors could be challenged peremptorily – were one and the same thing in the matter of challenge, and the Lord Chief Justice once again agreed: one of the many dubious decisions in matters of law in this important case.[68]

The jury was then sworn in and the trial proper began. It was a long trial, and it is not intended to discuss its details except in certain matters. The Lord Chief Justice, Francis Blackburne, remained throughout as he had begun: unyielding, unpleasant,[69] with a mind closed to any legal arguments except those which favoured a conviction. Blackburne was certainly more crude than Sir Thomas Wilde, his English counterpart, but it must be recognised that his attitudes derived from a much more difficult situation than any which Wilde had to confront. The nature and character of Irish society encouraged a sense of the beleaguered on the part of those whose interests were intimately involved with its preservation; a harshness of spirit that would be absent in a more socially united country; and a firm and unyielding conviction that order, at whatever cost, was the greatest good that could be offered to a people so sorely in travail.

Whiteside's main speech for the defence was an extraordinary performance, and it would be interesting to have a contemporary account of its effects upon the various groups of his listeners. Whiteside opened with depreciatory remarks about himself, and then proceeded to inform the jury that the defence wanted at the outset the postponement of the trial because they believed the accused had been prejudged. 'I have myself' Whiteside went on 'read a charge composed for the Lord Chief Justice in the confident anticipation of the guilt of the prisoner, and a vehement appeal to the jury to convict'. But, naturally, Whiteside continued, there could be no thought that the judges in this case would ever allow themselves to be influenced by such a statement:

the ermine which has been worn by Mansfield, Holt, and Hale will not be sullied by the distinguished magistrates who preside on this solemn occasion: one of whom has a brilliant reputation in the Senate – all at the bar; and I am as satisfied as of my own existence that they will each and all rejoice if I can convince them of the innocence of my client.

Whiteside proceeded to make even more outrageous statements, for none at least of the lawyers present could have been in any doubt that Whiteside was playing a highly sophisticated game, and that he was fully conscious of the political importance of this trial, and the conviction of the prisoner, to the Irish administration. He then addressed the jury in a rather personal way, apologising for the delay in the choice of the jury, and adverting in high-flown language to the probity and integrity of the jury and the judges, which the defence wholly accepted:

I do most unfeignedly rejoice, from the emphatic charge of my Lord Chief Justice and the verdict of the triers, to find that the jury panel was framed in a manner not only legal, but laudable. I am content with the tribunal: my client is perfectly satisfied with his jury; and I avow openly and publicly that, whatever may be the result, neither this maligned gentleman nor the humble counsel who addresses you will ever breathe a word of objection to your decision.[70]

Whiteside then dropped this legal version of clowning – 'the jury panel was framed in a manner not only legal, but laudable' – and proceeded with the serious business of defending the accused:

Gentlemen, when I say I have no complaint to make of the jury, I have a complaint to make of the law. Had Mr. Smith O'Brien been so fortunate as to have been an Englishman, and tried under the law of England, he would have known, ten days before his trial, the name of every juror on the panel; he would have known the names of all the witnesses who were to be examined against him, with their titles, professions and residences. In this country it has been decided that the like law does not prevail; and a more melancholy example of that unfortunate result never presented itself than in the case you witness before your eyes. A man appeared on that table to swear away directly the life of my client, with respect to whom no human being could give me a suggestion as to who he was, what he was, where he came from, or what was his past life and conduct. Had this trial taken place in England, we should have been enabled to come before you with evidence, if evidence of that nature did exist, to affect the character or the veracity of that witness. But by the law of this country, an informer may appear on the table, though he has never been even seen by the accused, or by any human being who can advise or assist him; he may deliver evidence which he will take care nobody can contradict, and destroy innocence instead of establishing guilt.[71]

Smith O'Brien was indicted for high treason and Whiteside's central purpose in his long speech for the defence was to destroy the grounds for the offence of high treason. His arguments occupied fifty-six columns in the small print of the *Reports of State Trials* (pp. 203–58) and some parts of his speech were only summarised. He quoted at length from past cases of treason, including that of John Frost, heard before Lord Chief Justice Tindal,[72] and he was severe on the witnesses for the Crown. The evidence of the informer, Dobbyn, especially was the subject of a devastating analysis. In summing up his case Whiteside underlined what he described as 'the great question involved in this solemn trial – namely the guilty intent of the prisoner' and he concluded with a long, powerful peroration which appealed for compassion and justice in mercy. As so often in the cases of this year, the words and actions of Lord John Russell had been quoted in support of the defence argument: in this instance it was a letter from Russell to Thomas Attwood of Birmingham, a communication, said Whiteside:

addressed by the present first minister of the Crown, showing by his assent an acknowledgement of the right in the people to insist, by physical combination, on having a free constitution. It is not for the purpose of scoffing at a gentleman of high station and great rank, and the first minister of the Crown, that I read it.[73] I declare, honestly, that I use it because he has written on the constitution of England, and said that the verdicts of juries have moulded that constitution.[74]

The summing up of the Lord Chief Justice was surprisingly inept. He was interrupted both by Whiteside and several jurors who were obviously by no means clear as to certain sequence of events. Blackburne made a great deal of Dobbyn's evidence 'who is', he said, 'unquestionably an important witness'. Unfortunately for Blackburne, his summing up was interrupted by the arrival of a new witness from Dublin – a Protestant in religion – who provided detailed circumstantial evidence which wholly contradicted the statements made by the informer, Dobbyn. It was an extraordinary episode, made possible by the agreement of the Attorney-General.[75] When the examination of the new witness was concluded Blackburne resumed his summing up, making a not very good best of a now exceedingly shaky part of the case against Smith O'Brien. Blackburne was not, however, a man to allow the lies of a key prosecution witness to deflect him from his pursuit of a conviction; and he proceeded at further considerable length to attempt to persuade the jury that their duty should be clear. To the end Blackburne was interrupted by jurors asking for clarification, with Whiteside intervening on matters of law where the Lord Chief Justice had not stated the law accurately or precisely. Even when Blackburne had completed his summing up and the jury had retired, Whiteside suggested to the Lord Chief Justice that he had failed to clarify an important matter relating to the way the jury had to make up their collective mind; and the jury accordingly returned to court. Blackburne made a short statement to which Whiteside added: 'Yes, my lord, that will do.'[76] The verdict was guilty with a strong recommendation for mercy in respect of the sentence of death. That was on the Saturday evening and the court adjourned until Monday, 9 October. When the court resumed, the ingenuity of the defence was once again demonstrated with Whiteside moving an arrest of judgement on two objections. As with many of the legal arguments that had been rehearsed on both sides, much of the substance of the objections related to interpretations of which statutes applied only to Ireland. The Lord Chief Justice repeated his contrary opinions, and the motion was denied. Blackburne then proceeded to sentence according to the usual formula for high treason.[77]

The defence counsel for Smith O'Brien entered a Writ of Error and the appeal was heard in the Court of Queen's Bench, Dublin on 21 November 1848 before the Lord Chief Justice and Justices Crampton, Perrin and Moore. The Writ of Error was an elaborate statement, beginning with a denial of the constitutional position of the Special Commission which tried Smith O'Brien and others, taking each of the five counts of the indictment as incorrectly determined, and itemising matters such as the selection of jurors and a disallowed challenge to a particular juror. The arguments were highly technical, and debated at length. There was no possibility of the Writ of Error being accepted but it was clear from the statements of at least two of the judges – but not the Lord Chief Justice – that there were matters on which doubt could be legitimately expressed. After Blackburne had stated his firm objections to the appeal, each of the other three judges intervened. Mr Justice Moore spoke last and towards the end of his interlocution he summed up what the fundamental argument had been about:

I have brought my mind clearly to the conclusion . . . and I think an uniform, clear, consistent construction to all the Acts may be given, namely, that there are now in Ireland the same treasons as in England, but that those accused of treason in England will be dealt with according to the privileges conferred on persons there, and those accused of treason in Ireland will be dealt with according to the law as it now stands in this country. In my opinion, there never was an intention, or at least I cannot find anything to warrant me in saying that it was the intention of the Legislature, by all or any of these Acts, to remove the differences that before existed, to equalise the laws, or to introduce for the first time in an indirect way, what, if there had been such an intention, would probably have been introduced by direct and positive legislation on the subject.[78]

Mr Justice Moore fairly defined the assumptions upon which the Writ of Error had been dismissed. Much of the argument turned upon the interpretation of the Crown and Security Bill – 11 and 12 Vict. c. 12 – which Sir George Grey had introduced in its first reading on 7 April.

He had explained the law of treason in a straightforward fashion.[79] In England the law was founded upon 25 Edw. III c. 2 and was extended to Ireland in the reign of Henry VII. During the revolutionary troubles of the 1790s, important alterations were made to the law of treason in 1795, by 36 Geo. III c. 7 but this was to last only for the life of the King and for one further session after. By 57 Geo. III c. 6 the first section of the 1795 Act, relating to treason, was made perpetual, but although it was passed after the union with Ireland there were doubts whether the Act applied to Ireland, so that in Ireland, up to the time Grey spoke in the Commons in April 1848, the only law of treason clearly in force in Ireland was the Statute of Edward III. The purpose of the Crown and Security Bill was to extend, without shadow of legal or political doubt, the existing legislation to Ireland, with certain amendments. Previous legislation relating to the compassing of the death of the sovereign, or the personal restraint or imprisonment of the sovereign, would remain. Other offences defined in the Act of 36 Geo. III which did not relate directly to the person of the sovereign but which also related to treason were to be repealed and re-enacted as offences subject to the same penalties throughout the United Kingdom. The commission of these offences should be felony, subjecting those found guilty to transportation for specified terms, or to imprisonment. The new clause introduced was 'the open and advised speaking' discussed above.[80] It was made plain in Sir George Grey's opening remarks and throughout the debates in both Houses that the central purpose of what became known as the Treason-Felony Bill was to limit the offence of treason, and introduce the new concept of treason-felony which did not carry the death sentence, and which would make it easier for the authorities to prosecute. The point must also be made again that the main reason for the introduction of the new Act was the political situation in Ireland.

It is clear why the defence in the Smith O'Brien case were concerned first, to be allowed all the privileges that obtained to those accused of treason in England and second, to try to prove that the indictment of Smith O'Brien for high treason was misconceived; and it is equally clear why the judicial authorities, at all stages of the case and its two appeals, were adamant that neither should be accepted. If the appeals had succeeded, a major defeat for Dublin Castle would have been registered; and everyone was aware of the fact. The judges, therefore, at each stage of the case, moved with the spirit of the times – a Whig spirit in what were felt to be desperate times – and those involved engaged in legal casuistry of a high order of erudition.

The second appeal may briefly be noted. After the Writ of Error had been dimissed by the Court of Queen's Bench, Dublin, a Writ of Error was brought in Parliament to reverse the judgement. The hearing in the House of Lords was on 10 and 11 May 1849. Present were the Lord Chancellor and other Law Lords and the judges in attendance were Chief Justice Wilde and a number of his senior colleagues including some – Erle, Williams, Cresswell, Parke and Platt – who had been on the Bench during the political trials in England. Sir Thomas Wilde delivered the opinions of the judges, and the Law Lords concurred. The appeal of Smith O'Brien was heard at the same time as that for Bellew McManus, it being held that the principles involved were the same. The errors assigned excluded the challenge to the jury and Wilde said that 'it was very properly abandoned, as the question is not open to any doubt'. Wilde's statement was quite short, a more detailed opinion not being required given the satisfactory discussion of the errors by the judges of the Queen's Bench.[81] Among the Law Lords who commended the Irish judges was Brougham who said that he had 'never, in the course of my experience, read a more able and satisfactory argument in every respect than that of Chief Justice Blackburne'. There were three other state prisoners with Smith O'Brien, and they collectively argued that the state could only respite the judgement of death for treason by a free pardon. There was never any possibility that Smith O'Brien or others convicted of treason would hang; that was understood before the trial began and a considerable body of opinion had built up after the sentences on both sides of the Irish Channel.[82] A Transportation for Treason (Ireland) Bill was hurried through Westminster, and under this Act – 12 and 13 Vict. c. 27 – Smith O'Brien and his fellow prisoners were transported to Tasmania. In February 1854 he received a pardon on condition that he did not return to the United Kingdom, and two years later an unconditional pardon.[83]

It may be noted in passing that Francis Blackburne, the Lord Chief Justice, was actually reprimanded in the columns of the *Dublin University Magazine* for his direction of the jury in the trial of T. F. Meagher, whose case followed that of Smith O'Brien. Meagher was tried on the same indictment as O'Brien and in his own speech at the end of the trial Meagher himself referred in measured terms to the vindictiveness of the Lord Chief Justice in his summing up to the jury.[84] The *Dublin University Magazine* was a thoroughly reactionary and unpleasant journal, but it was not unintelligently edited. It was pathologically anti-Catholic, and in the late autumn it attacked the Attorney-General for not prosecuting the Catholic priesthood. In its comments on the treason trials the *Magazine* praised the 'incomparable advocacy' of Whiteside and Isaac Butt[85] and, while – at least in March 1848 – it thought Blackburne 'a cool, clear-handed, sagacious public functionary', it had strong criticism of his charge to the jury in Meagher's trial. It was, it insisted, 'peculiarly objectionable – it is emphatically the speech of a crown counsel', and further: 'it is impossible to read that speech through, without feeling convinced that it was framed with the most consummate skill, so as to put the case in the most damaging point of view against the prisoner; that the learned judge, with that self-reliance for which he is so remarkable, being himself entirely convinced of the prisoner's guilt, was determined to enforce the same conviction on the jury'.[86] The *Magazine*, having said this, went on to underline their full support for the verdict of guilty.[87]

It was in the days after the conclusion of the Smith O'Brien trial that the Irish press began to develop a wide-ranging campaign against the exclusion of Catholics as jurors. The *Freeman's Journal*, for example, published long extracts from the speeches of English politicians – Russell, George Grey, Peel, Macaulay – condemning the practice; and the same paper said on 13 November 1848, 'This is a subject which we have been compelled to discuss and re-discuss, even to the point of public impatience, since the Whigs commenced *their* series of state trials – the exclusion of Irish Catholics from Irish juries', and on 5 December, 'There never has been a subject which so agitated the Catholic mind of Ireland as this jury packing. It involved a principle of the deepest importance to the Catholic world.' The facts of jury rigging were constantly rehearsed. It was emphasised how the Sheriff could leave off any name that he thought undesirable, that he could so arrange the juror's list that Catholic names were low down and often unlikely therefore to be reached, and that any Catholic who got through could be told to 'stand by': a command that was regarded as an insult by Catholic opinion. On 6 December a deputation of Catholic prelates and laymen waited on the Viceroy to urge that Gavan Duffy, whose trial was about to begin, should have a fairly chosen jury, and in their statement there was once again quoted the facts of Mitchel's conviction when on the jurors' book the ratio of Catholics to Protestants was nearly two to one while the Sheriff's panel showed Protestants as four to one. Moreover, eight Catholics only were placed among the first eighty names, and in the event there was a wholly Protestant jury.[88] During early December 1848 a memorial was being circulated protesting against jury-packing. It was signed by 'Nine Irish Prelates, Four Hundred Irish clergymen, and more than 41,000 laymen, including peers, MPs, and the Mayors and Corporations of Dublin and principal cities and towns.'[89] The Viceroy's reply to the memorialists, published in the *Freeman's Journal* of 13 December, flatly denied any improper practices and warmly commended the Attorney-General for his public attitudes on these matters. It was an uncompromising statement, supported by *The Times* and other leading English papers.[90]

In the last issue of 1848 the *Freeman's Journal* published a long letter from a priest in Ballinrode, County Mayo. It was answered by *The Times* in the early days of 1849 and the exchange illuminates certain of the relationships between the imperial power and an Ireland that remained in a subservient condition. The letter from Ballinrode opened with a harrowing account of the deaths in the parish and of the sick and the dying:

Can it be wondered at now, when such scenes are so frequently occurring at the very headquarters of the local establishment, and when its operation should be most regularly carried on, that the roads and ditches in the country part of this much neglected Union should be crowded with the starving poor. No wonder that the priest's heart should be broken seeing creatures made after God's likeness crawling through the fields picking up filthy weeds, striving with them to satisfy the cravings of nature . . .

Such is the present system of poor laws; but not alone are the bodies of the poor abused and their physical wants unattended to, but their very souls are imperilled in the workhouse, whose atmosphere is contagious of vice; where the conscientious scruples of the Catholics are, it would appear, subjects of derision and scorn because they are Papists. A glance at the administration of the Ballinrode workhouse will be of use to Catholic Ireland, and the Catholic ratepayers, in particular of Mayo. There are at present, in this house built to contain eight hundred souls, over two thousand three hundred Catholics. I cannot find that there is one Protestant pauper. Surely your readers will suppose that all the officers are Catholics; but no! not only do the Whigs exclude Catholics from the jury box, but also from the situations of the workhouse, and should they succeed in their schemes of the Godless colleges the same will be told of them.

Our Inspecting Officer is a Protestant
Our First vice guardian is a Protestant
Our Second vice guardian is a Protestant
Our Master is a Protestant
Our Matron is a Protestant
Our Clerk is a Protestant
Our Assistant Clerk is a Protestant
Our Porter is a Protestant
Our Surgeon is a Protestant
Our Assistant Surgeon is a Protestant
Our Poor-Rate Collector is a Protestant
Our Assistant Collector is a Protestant

The pious parson is, of course, a Protestant, besides a well-selected staff of extras of the same persuasion.

I complain of this state of things, not through any bigoted feeling, but as a minister of an oppressed and enslaved people, fully sensible of the responsibility which my sacred profession imposes, and alive to the scruples which would attend my neglect of so manifest a duty.[91]

The Times on 1 January 1849 quoted long extracts from this letter which was written by the Rev. Conway, one of McHale's clergy, a fact which would immediately prejudice many English readers against him. *The Times'* quotations mostly related to the figures of dead in the parish which in an editorial of the next day were strongly disputed. This editorial of 2 January was an extraordinary piece of writing. The facts of the Irish situation with nearly a million dead by this time, were hardly unknown. On 27 December 1848 Clarendon wrote to Trevelyan: 'How are the next six months to be got through in the South and West? I am at my wits' end to imagine. The reports of our own officers are bad enough, heaven knows, but the statements I have received from (credible) eyewitnesses exceed all I have ever heard of horrible misery, except perhaps that of shipwrecked mariners on a yacht or desert island.'[92] The Rev. Conway was certainly not exaggerating. Woodham-Smith comments that the first few months of 1849 saw as much suffering as at any time since the famine began.[93] *The Times* on 2 January 1849 began its first leader thus:

It is one great misfortune of the Irish that their spokesmen are not credible persons. They allow nobody to speak for them but their clergy and some professional agitators – both classes absolutely bankrupt of credit. No rational man in this island believes a statement on the unsupported authority of an Irish Roman Catholic priest. No one attaches any weight to it as a probable approximation to the facts of the case. We know, by long experience, that it is only the language of passion. This, of course, is a deplorable disadvantage for the bulk of the nation to lie under. It is a fundamental maxim of law that a man is best represented by his own proctors and witnesses, but when the proctors and witnesses are men of blasted characters, and absolutely incapable of veracity, it must go hard with the party that employs them. The British public feel not merely curiosity, but a craving solicitude for more thorough information as to Irish affairs. If we could catch a priest who spoke truth, and who would answer any question put to him without subterfuge or gross exaggeration, we could make him one of the sights of this metropolis.

The article then continued with a denial of the figures that the Rev. Conway had published but without offering any contrary data on deaths or the death rate, and it ended:

The only regeneration for Ireland is to take a new start and learn to tell truth. Let her priests no longer count hundreds for tens, and no longer charge upon Governments the visitation of GOD. Let her Bishops no longer put their cross to impudent and extravagant falsehoods. Let the people no longer subscribe their name to any jumble of malice and wickedness their priests may palm upon them. Let them learn that English good sense cannot be so easily deceived; and that we immediately set down these villainous and blasphemous manifestoes at their proper value. When they have made this step, there is some chance for Ireland.

The wilful blindness, and prejudiced ignorance, of *The Times*, as with so much of English public opinion, was summed up in a leading article on 11 January 1849. It was an argument for the strict application of the principles of the English Poor Law to be applied to Ireland:

The basis of the Irish, as of the English Poor Law, is the workhouse test. If there be able-bodied men who will not work, and yet will cry for relief, send them into the house. If they will not go, treat them with stringent poverty . . . The intelligence and the sympathies of England are with the firm and vigorous administration of the law.

The Times was never wholly consistent in its attitudes towards Ireland, although its basic hostility to Ireland and Irish problems was never shaken, and it appears to have been consistently racist. The weight of its opinion throughout the famine years had been against financial help for Ireland, but on 8 February 1848 it announced 'with great reluctance' an acceptance of some 'exceptional' relief for Ireland because of the continuing reports of catastrophic distress from all over the South and the West. In its general attitude of ideological indifference towards the problems of Ireland, especially on economic matters, *The Times* was in accord with majority opinion in England. 'I have always felt a certain horror of political economists,' said Benjamin Jowett, 'since I heard one of them [Nassau Senior] say that he feared the famine of 1848 in Ireland would not kill more than a million people, and that would scarcely be enough to do much good'.[94]

7

A COMMENTARY BY WAY OF CONCLUSION

'I am convinced', wrote the Marquis of Normanby in 1857, that 'ninety-nine out of a hundred of my countrymen could more accurately describe each incident of the peaceful and justly styled Glorious Revolution of 1688 . . . than they could answer the commonest question as to that of 1848'.[1] The same could certainly be said of the Chartist movement of 1848. The myths generated by that year quickly became commonplace:

The agitation which derived its impulse from the convulsions of the Continent prevailed only so far as to disturb for a moment the serenity of her political atmosphere. Awed by the overwhelming strength and imposing attitude of the friends of order, the mischief subsided almost as soon as it appeared, and the cause of rational freedom was materially strengthened by the futile efforts made to undermine it. When a knot of obscure and ill-disposed malcontents would fain have played off in our metropolis the scenes which had been enacted with such sanguinary effects in Paris and Vienna, their insignificance was demonstrated, and their menaces rendered impotent by the firm and imposing attitude of the loyal and well-affected inhabitants arrayed in defence of peace, property, and order.[2]

Thus it was that the *Annual Register* for 1848 established the pattern of historical writing on the events of this year in England. Two years later there was published one of the key books of the Victorian era that was to exercise a powerful influence upon public attitudes. This was the novel *Alton Locke* by Charles Kingsley.

Alton Locke must be read in the context of its historical setting. Kingsley, along with his fellow Christian Socialists, had sympathy of a kind with working-class poverty and suffering, and genuinely sought improvement through the remedy of producers' association.[3] But while many contemporary reviewers of *Alton Locke* emphasised Kingsley's apparent identification with working-class aspirations, and some were hostile because of this,[4] the main lesson of his novel was to exhibit the futility of political action of the Chartist kind, the stupidity of Chartist tactics and the impossibility of a large-scale remedial solution without a full acceptance of Christian belief and faith.[5] In the novel Kingsley used a good deal of contemporary material that would be familiar to his readers; and in the chapter headed 'The Tenth of

April' Kingsley summed up the meaning of the day in words that were to form the historical record for many decades to come:

I have promised to say little about the tenth of April, for indeed I have no heart to do so. Every one of Mackaye's predictions came true. We had arrayed against us, by our own folly, the very physical force to which we had appealed. The dread of general plunder and outrage by the savages of London, the national hatred of that French and Irish interference of which we had boasted, armed against us thousands of special constables who had in the abstract little or no objection to our political opinions. The practical commonsense of England, whatever discontent it might feel with the existing system, refused to let it be hurled rudely down, on the mere chance of building up on its ruins something as yet untried, and even undefined. Above all, the people would not rise. Whatever sympathy they had with us, they did not care to show it. And then futility after futility exposed itself. The meeting which was to have been counted by hundreds of thousands, numbered hardly its tens of thousands; and of them a frightful proportion were of those very rascal classes, against whom we ourselves had offered to be sworn in as special constables. O'Connor's courage failed him after all. He contrived to be called away, at the critical moment, by some problematical superintendent of police. Poor Cuffay, the honestest, if not the wisest, speaker there, leapt off the wagon, exclaiming that we were all 'humbugged and betrayed'; and the meeting broke up pitiably piecemeal, drenched and cowed, body and soul, by pouring rain on its way home – for the very heavens mercifully helped to quench our folly – while the monster-petition crawled ludicrously away in a hack cab, to be dragged to the floor of the House of Commons amid roars of laughter – 'inextinguishable laughter', as of Tennyson's Epicurean Gods.[6]

It was thus that Kingsley helped to confirm the myths of 10 April, and they have remained in many history text books to our own day. Having exhibited the stupidities of Chartism, Kingsley then drove home the lesson by pointing the real way forward. Social regeneration could only follow a spiritual transformation of those involved in organising change, and the leadership for such a change would come from a truly enlightened aristocracy. Towards the end of a discussion with Lady Eleanor, Alton Locke was asked by her if he was 'a Chartist still?' And he replied:

If by a Chartist you mean one who fancied that a change in mere political circumstances will bring about a millennium, I am no longer one. That dream is gone – with others. But if to be a Chartist is to love my brothers with every faculty of my soul – to wish to live and die struggling for their rights, endeavouring to make them, not electors merely, but fit to be electors, senators, kings and priests to God and to His Christ – if that be the Chartism of the future, then I am sevenfold a Chartist, and ready to confess it before men, though I were thrust forth from every door in England.[7]

This was to be a common enough note in the history of the aftermath of radical political movements, and there was no doubt of the sympathetic response to this kind of windy sermonising in the years which followed 1848. There were many who added some hard additions to the preaching of Kingsley; who offered in place of the absurdities and wickedness of Chartism the solid, positive world of Thomas Gradgrind and Samuel Smiles; a world in which working men could look forward to achieving a decent competence, on whatever level they were adjusted to, by taking what society had to offer, on terms which would be realised only by the practice of the virtues of self-help: hard work, thrift and sobriety. Chartism was finally broken by the physical force of the state, and having once been broken it was submerged, in the national consciousness, beneath layers of false understanding and denigration. A radical movement draws essential sustenance from the inspiration of its past struggles and its past heroes; but who was to honour poor half-mad O'Connor on Kennington Common, leading his gullible followers to ridicule and execration? What was quite forgotten was the strength that continued in Chartism in the months that followed the events of 10 April, and even the memory of the mass arrests and jailings were wiped from public memory. The contemporary agencies of the media were extraordinarily effective in traducing this greatest of all mass movements of the nineteenth century; but when all is said the almost complete obliteration of Chartism from public consciousness in the middle decades of the century remains a remarkable phenomenon. There were, of course, intruding events from the early 1850s which much assisted the processes of indifference and forgetfulness. The Great Exhibition of 1851 itself was a symbol of a rapidly expanding economy, and the Crimean War, the Indian Mutiny, the Volunteer movement of 1859, Garibaldi and the Italian Question, the American Civil War, the Reform agitation of the 1860s, all contributed towards the neglect of the mass upsurge which had so shaken the country in the 1840s. In the same year, 1854, that Gammage began publishing his *History of the Chartist Movement*,[8] the eighth edition of the *Encyclopedia Britannica* had three short references only to the Chartist movement. Its account of 1848 read as follows:

While the nation was thus suffering from deficient harvest, mercantile depression, and a defective revenue, the magnanimity with which these evils were endured, and the energy with which they were surmounted bore full evidence to the deep-rooted strength and stability of the British constitution. This was the more remarkable as contrasted with the rest of Europe, where almost every throne at this period was tottering, and royalty itself all but annihilated. An attempt, indeed, was made on the part of Chartism to avail itself of the universal commotion, but all that it could effect was a few monster meetings that evaporated in speeches, or paltry riots that were easily suppressed by the police.[9]

The second reference came in the same volume with a short summary of Chartism in 1839, in fourteen lines, and the third was two sentences also in the same volume, under the heading 'Chartist': 'the name of a party of political agitators in Great Britain, who sprung up about the year 1838, and whose views are developed in a document called the 'People's Charter'; and the second sentence listed the Six Points, and that was all, except a cross-reference to the passage quoted above.

The History of the Chartist Movement from its Commencement Down to the

Present Time by R. G. Gammage was published first in seven parts, beginning in late 1854 and continuing through 1855 when a bound volume was also published. Gammage was a young man of about thirty-four years old when he wrote his *History* and he had himself been active in the movement in its closing years and much involved in its quarrels and disputes. Gammage projected his own version of the internal conflicts into the *History* and he provided a highly partisan evaluation of the leading personalities. His judgements of Harney, Jones and above all of Feargus O'Connor were consistently hostile and unflattering, while Lovett, Vincent and Bronterre O'Brien emerged as the sensible, rational men of the movement. When the book was published it was hardly noticed by the middle-class reviews and newspapers and, apart from *Reynolds Newspaper* and the *People's Paper* which belonged to Ernest Jones, there was a lack of interest which was part of the general indifference towards Chartism. Where it was noticed it confirmed existing prejudices,[10] and its interpretation underlined what was already becoming established as the stereotype for the rest of the century. Sir William Molesworth's three-volume *History of England from the Year 1830 to 1874* contained a long section on Chartism in volume two, large parts of which were straight summaries from Gammage. Molesworth's interpretation of the movement had now become traditional: Chartism in its last years was increasingly overshadowed by the Anti-Corn Law League, and 1848 saw the movement become 'an object of contempt'.[11] Justin McCarthy's four-volume *History of Our Time*, published in 1880, gave less space to Chartism than Molesworth and was even more slighting of its record. Perhaps the most revealing examples of mid-Victorian attitudes are to found in the history books written for schools and students. There was in all the texts which have been analysed a notable aloofness in the treatment of Chartism as though it belonged to the more distant past and was therefore of no direct relevance to Victorian England. In some histories Chartism meant only 1839 and the Newport Rising, and all wrote of the movement as having died away after the Kennington Common meeting. H. W. Dulcken, *A Picture History of England . . . Written for the Use of the Young* (1866) said of the Newport Rising: 'It was quickly suppressed, and the Chartist leaders, who, in other times, would undoubtedly have been hanged, were transported beyond the seas.'[12] And that was all. The novelist G. A. Henty, who produced in 1887 *The Sovereign Reader: Scenes from the Life and Reign of Queen Victoria*, limited himself to the events of 1848. He stressed the thoroughness of the Duke of Wellington's preparations, emphasised the failure of the 10 April meeting and noted the 'ridicule' which followed the examination of the petition from which Chartism never recovered.

The more substantial histories of the nineteenth century which appeared before 1914 told the same story and all wrote in slighting or patronising terms of Chartism, and especially of its leaders. Thus J. Holland Rose, *The Rise of Democracy* (1897) which provided a liberal view of political development, was sympathetic to the moral-force Chartists, hostile to O'Connor and actually used *Alton Locke* to describe the events of 10 April 1848. Herbert Paul's large scale liberal *History of Modern England*, in five volumes (1904), dismissed the events of 1848: 'In the hands of a man like Feargus O'Connor, who was even then more than half-insane, any movement was bound to fail.'[13] M. D. Traill, in *Social England*, first published in six volumes in 1897 and later illustrated in 1904, described O'Connor as 'an empty braggart' and concluded a brief summary of 1848 with: 'Feargus O'Connor's nerves failed him at the pinch, and when the signatories of the huge petition presented to Parliament were discovered to be largely in the nature of practical jokes, Chartism underwent total eclipse.'[14]

Memories of the Chartist movement always remained in some parts of working-class Britain, and not only in the political parts. W. E. Adams tells the story of 'a deaf old lady in Gateshead who was alarmed by the great explosion of that year (1854), and she hurried away to her friends in Sunderland. Asked what was the matter, she replied: 'Aa's afeared the Chartist bodies hev brokken lowse!'[15] Ernest Jones did not give up the attempt to maintain an independent Chartist presence until the end of the 1850s; there were towns such as Sheffield and Halifax where survival of political movements related to the earlier Chartism has been well documented; and there were many individuals such as W. P. Roberts whose political life spanned the middle decades and whose influence on the next generation of radicals was important, for example in Roberts' case upon Annie Besant.[16] But when all is said – and there is much still to be brought together – the loss of general direction and the disintegration of a national movement were the outstanding characteristics of the years that followed the release of Ernest Jones from prison in 1850.

The almost complete obliteration of the awareness of Chartism as a great mass movement and of Feargus O'Connor as a great mass leader was strikingly illustrated in an interesting correspondence in the *Newcastle Weekly Chronicle* in the spring of 1883. A reader asked for details of the *Northern Star* – 'a journal which played an important part in the Chartist agitation' and the request had to be reprinted a second time before it brought any replies. There were some nine letters published, including one from G. J. Harney in the United States, and the quotation given below, from a reader in Heckmondwike, in the West Riding of Yorkshire, reflected the incertitudes in many radical minds concerning events of just over thirty years earlier:

I can very well remember reading aloud, week by week, when a boy, to groups of woolcombers in the neighbourhood of Bradford, the fiery articles of Feargus O'Connor, G. J. Harney, Ernest Jones, Bronterre O'Brien, and others, which appeared in the *Star* when published at Leeds, and also at London. A short time ago I sought in many quarters for books etc which would throw light on the history of the Chartist movement, but to my astonishment could glean very little information – in fact, a history of that remarkable political uprising does not seem to exist, so far as I can learn. If any of your readers can give me the titles and publishers of any books, pamphlets etc, either local or general, I shall esteem it a favour. There must be many persons living who could contribute much information on the subject. If Mr. Harney, or any other of the old leaders would given us a book on the subject it would be sure of a large sale.[17]

This appeal was answered the following week by Alexander Patterson, of Barnsley, a frequent contributor to the correspondence columns of the *Newcastle Weekly Chronicle*. He referred to the volume by Gammage in somewhat unflattering terms which brought a reply from Gammage himself who was then still living at Sunderland.[18] Other letters printed also mentioned the autobiographies of Lovett and Cooper which had been published in the previous decade. But no one noticed Frost's *Recollections* or Linton's *Memoir* of James Watson, both of which had appeared in 1880; and it was only with the revival of socialism and the new interest in the history of the labour movement in the last twenty years of the nineteenth century that material on the Chartist movement began to be published in more detail.[19]

The literature on Chartism in the twentieth century, especially after the Second World War, has been more sophisticated and much more diverse in its geographical setting, than the earlier writings. What has remained unsatisfactory in analysis and explanation has been the historical gap between the end of Chartism as a national movement of any size, usually located in the years immediately following 1848, and the new period of the 1850s, symbolised by the Great Exhibition of 1851. The contrast between the mass demonstrations of the 1840s and the socially much quieter 1850s has always involved awkward interpretations or silences; and some have fallen back upon what is no more than a simplistic economic analysis to explain the shift in social consciousness from class militancy to respectability and relative quiescence – or that is how it has often been phrased. The character of the reformism of the third quarter of the century has been extensively discussed and described, but the nature and character of the transition from Chartism to the radical–liberal politics of the fifties and sixties is less confidently delineated.[20]

The partial obliteration, in some places disappearance, of the memory of Chartism after 1850 must not be understood as a prime cause of the emergence of a style of working-class politics that increasingly attached itself to the Liberal Party, but rather as a consequence which in its turn contributed to the new direction of working-class aspirations. We must begin with material reasons which, while not being a sufficient explanation, are the inescapable foundations upon which an analysis must rest. It has always been recognised that the growth of the economy during the 1850s helped to shape the political attitudes of working people in that decade. What needs emphasis in this context is that the growth patterns of the fifties were related more closely than is often appreciated with those of the previous decade. The depression of the years to 1842 was exceptionally severe, but it was succeeded by a high level of domestic investment which together with the reforms in banking and the changes in commercial policy all contributed to a vigorous upward movement of the economy. The secular expansion of the British economy reached its highest levels between the 1840s and the 1870s, and the difference in growth rates between the decades was not considerable. Indeed, if the low Irish rate for the 1840s is removed from the British data, the decennial differences are further reduced.[21] The economy rode through the commercial crisis of 1847, against the background of Irish famine, with remarkable strength and resilience. It was a contemporary, Thomas Tooke who emphasised the 'solidity and vastness of amelioration in the state of Great Britain' between 1840 and 1856.[22] There was unemployment on quite a large scale in the last quarter of 1847 and for the first half of 1848, but had it not been for the European revolutions the return to increased economic activity would not have had to wait until the last six months of 1848.

This view of 'the hungry forties' as a period of economic expansion and growth after 1842 can be sustained from any sample of economic statistics of this decade.[23] What must not be assumed is a concomitant rise in living standards, except to note that greater regularity of employment always provided a short-term improvement to living conditions. But for the present let it be emphasised that the 'hungry forties' – a phrase made popular in the years immediately prior to the general election of 1906[24] – were still very hungry for very many. What the 1840s represented once the depression at the beginning of the decade was overcome, was a more stable growth in which the railway was to exercise an important steadying as well as expansive influence, in spite of the overheating of the system in 1846–7. The processes of change must not, however, be made to appear as uniformly smooth and even. Different sectors experienced different price trends, and patterns of profitability and investment often diverged widely. Structural changes affected many occupations and trades in ways that were irregular and notably diverse: the London trades of the forties described in detail by Goodway; the woolcombers of Bradford; and the many thousands of domestic lace-workers of the southeast Midlands all had different chronologies in their transition to new patterns of industrial organisation. It was a diversity that encompassed the whole of Britain and its working people[25] and the transitions involved were unpleasant and painful.

It was the cotton industry, the leader in modernising structures in early industrialisation, that exemplified the surge forward into the expansive years after 1850. In 1830 the numbers employed in the factory sector of cotton were 185,000; in 1840 the total was 262,000; in 1850, 331,000; and in 1860, 427,000. Alongside this increase in the factory proletariat went the decline in the numbers of handloom weavers who in 1830 had a larger total than those inside the factories. In 1840 their numbers were still 123,000 and then there occurred a dramatic decline: to 43,000 in 1850. The elimination of handloom weaving was a long drawn-out agony that contributed to the militancy of the radical movements of the second quarter of the nineteenth century, although the degree of that contribution is a matter of argument between historians.[26] The virtual extinction of the cotton handloom from Lancashire by the early fifties meant that there were in existence settled communities around the now typical mills, with established and for the most part regular and stable patterns of work and social life; subject to less violent fluctuations of employment than in the previous quarter of the century. It was this factory economy that weathered the crisis years of the American Civil War with remarkably little turbulence; and it was out of this society of the mill, the co-op, the church and chapel, business unionism and employers' paternalism that Joyce has developed his analysis of the ebbing of class conflict and the emergence of a deferential proletariat.[27]

While the cotton industry dominated the British export trade and employed over half a million workers, males and females, another half a million were in the other textile trades, but their combined total was still lower in 1851 than that of agricultural labourers. Elsewhere, the economy exhibited the unevenness of technical change and the variety of industrial organisation that has been briefly touched upon above. Everywhere there was a continuous thickening of industry within the still fast growing towns, and outside the urban centres the coalfields were expanding rapidly. England was becoming, as Ruskin said, 'the man in the iron mask'. The image was apt, but not perhaps wholly precise, since it has been the diversity of experience, structure and organisation with which historians have been most impressed. This marked variety of industrial patterns meant a similar diversity in the social composition of the working population,[28] the significance of which has not always been appreciated. There are a number of problems here. One is that industrial structures which are broadly similar do not necessarily have the same industrial or political history. Birmingham and Sheffield are obvious examples: both centres of small workshops until the sixties with important differences in their industrial relations, although both developed their own varieties of political liberalism.[29] The second is that Chartism, while representing the largest mobilisation of people in the nineteenth century, must not be conflated with the whole of the working people. It is not uncommon for radical historians to confuse party, or movement, with class, yet in our period there were quite wide stretches of British society untouched by political agitation or mass activity. A related problem is the timing of political agitation and the ebb and flow of political movements within the same town or region, in economic and social circumstances that do not substantially change: a question of consequence for Chartism as for other historical periods.

In a famous essay, 'The Peculiarities of the English', Edward Thompson discussed the consequences of political defeat by 1850. 'For the workers' he wrote 'having failed to overthrow capitalist society proceed to warren it from end to end'.[30] By the 'warrening' process Thompson meant the development of the 'characteristic class institutions' of trade unions and co-operative societies and the rest, by which working people created self-help movements of mutual support to counter the insecurities, the harshness and the exploitation of the capital order they inhabited. As an historical process it went back much earlier than the final defeat of Chartism. When J. H. Clapham considered the 'self-made social institutions of British wage-earners' (Thompson's 'class institutions') in the two decades before 1850 he began with the friendly societies, by far the most important grouping of working people. An Act of 1829 had appointed a barrister to inspect the rules of societies which sought registration, and in 1846 the Registrar of Friendly Societies – the famous John Tidd Pratt – came into office (by 9 and 10 Vict. c. 27). Statistics of membership for the 1830s were not wholly satisfactory, while the return of 1847 was more reliable although still not complete. In England and Wales 10,433 societies were recorded as registered between 1828 and 1847, with a total membership of 781,722. The remarkable rise and expansion of the Affiliated Orders (societies with a national or regional coverage) from the middle thirties to the middle forties took the Friendly Society movement into areas and regions well beyond the artisan communities of the West Riding and Lancashire. There was certainly a marked concentration of membership in Lancashire, but as an example of the spread of self-help the late thirties and early forties witnessed a remarkable growth in numbers in the East Riding of Yorkshire: a wholly agricultural region save for the port of Hull and the fishing villages along the coast.[31] It followed, and was closely connected with, the imposition of the new Poor Law in the area; and there was also an interesting correlation between Primitive Methodist chapel building and the expansion of Friendly Societies.[32] The most significant new emphasis in the recent study by Neave concerns the social composition of the membership of Friendly Societies. Hitherto it has been assumed that membership was beyond the financial capabilities of the unskilled and labouring classes, or that the irregularity of their work and the social habits they developed made sober provision difficult if not out of the question; but in the East Riding, from the earliest days of the first great expansion of 1837 to 1843, agricultural labourers were commonly members, and remained so throughout the nineteenth century. Now the labourer in the East Riding was not the labourer in Dorset, but from scattered evidence, which does not yet allow a firm national generalisation, it would appear that it is likely membership ranged more widely in social composition than has previously been supposed.[33] In the context of the present discussion, Clapham's estimate of the membership of Friendly Societies at the end of the 1840s must be quoted: that it 'cannot well have been much less than 1,500,000 at a time when the total male population of twenty years old and upwards was well below 5,500,000'.[34]

Friendly Societies were the quintessential self-help bodies, with trade unions as the most aggressive of all the defensive organisations. It is to the industrial moderation of the unions after 1850 and their reluctance, often refusal, to engage in political activity that attention is often directed when the reformism of these years is being considered. The unions had long roots in the past. Combined action by working men had been widespread during the eighteenth century, although by no means was it all channelled through formal organisation. Collective bargaining by riot is a well-documented phenomenon. Of the (incomplete) list of industrial disputes recorded for the eighteenth century, just under one-third occurred in London, the centre of the artisan trades; and the next most important were the textile districts, mostly in the woollen trades.[35] The ending of the legal prohibition of combinations in 1824–5 came at a time when the industrial structure of the economy was changing fast, with the emergence of the factory in the cotton areas, the rise of the engineer as a key worker in industrialisation and the rapid growth of coal-mining and iron-working. Trades unions in the second quarter of the century, once the events connected with the Grand National Consolidated Trades Union were over, were developing the characteristics associated with the years after 1850. As was said of certain of the national unions in the third quarter of the century, many aspects of the new model were the old model writ large.[36] The unions included the self-help aspects of the Friendly Societies, but their central concerns were with wages and working conditions – of crucial importance to the levels of surplus value and profit – and trade unions were always regarded by middle-class opinion, and especially by businessmen and politicians, as quite different from the uncomplicated benefit societies. The hostility towards trade unions was endemic.

Edward Thompson's 'warrening' process expanded greatly after 1850. Independent politics for most working people no longer appeared practicable, and their energies went into a wide variety of socially useful, and/or emotionally satisfying, organisations. The chapel as a central part of working-class culture was not to be found everywhere, and in some areas and towns – London is the obvious example – the 'unconscious secularism' noted by the 1851 Census[37] was more prevalent among working people than religious belief or religious practices; but where the chapel was important, as in South Wales or some other mining areas, it imparted a distinctive tone and content to the social consciousness of its members and often to the community in which they resided. One of the new developments of the third quarter was the co-operative movement in its Rochdale form. Most of those involved in the co-operative movement in the 1840s had already made the transition from community building to shopkeeping,[38] and the Rochdale Pioneers illustrated the expansive possibilities of the movement in a dynamic economy. After the initial difficulties of the first few years from the beginning in 1844, the first leap forward in turnover and profits was in the years 1848–9, and thereafter the annual increases were regular and substantial. By 1857 sales were nearly £80,000 as against just under £2,000 ten years earlier.[39] Savings banks deposits showed the same trends,[40] and building societies, which drew their membership from the upper stratum of the working class and the lower middle class, firmly established themselves in the West Riding of Yorkshire in the 1840s, with the years 1845 to 1849 as the period of their consolidation.[41] The case of South Wales is instructive in this context. After the failure of the Newport uprising, and the arrest and conviction of Frost and his fellow Chartists, South Wales never again achieved the levels of militancy of 1839; and in 1848 there was no movement of any significance. From the middle of the 1840s we begin to discern the trends in social development associated with the more respectable years of the following two decades. It was, as everywhere, a slow, uneven process of change, much assisted in South Wales by the export-led boom in coal output after 1850; and by the sixties, as the most recent historian of the Newport insurrection has written, 'the coalfield was covered with day schools, Sunday schools, libraries, institutes, and benefit and temperance societies, and mining families were at last having a little more time and money to enjoy these provisions'.[42]

Over the country as a whole, the extent of involvement was wide-ranging, and as working people improved their position by more effective organisation, so their common interests related more and more to the day-to-day practice of the possible in the here and now. The wider horizons which an independent politics could have provided were either not available or were seen as impracticable, while the returns from the pursuit of economic and social self-interest were obvious and specific.

The network of social and industrial organisations which had been building up in the decades before 1850 and which greatly expanded thereafter helps to explain, in some part, the apparent smoothness of the transition from the turbulent 1840s to the less disturbed fifties. The falling away of a mass political movement still remains, however, to be made intelligible. There was no *a priori* reason why independent working-class politics could not exist at the same time as working people were extending their union organisation or expanding their self-help institutions. Unions and politics do not have to be antithetical or in conflict, and a growing co-operative movement could lend strength to a national political movement. More recent history has made these things plain. An independent political movement can draw sustenance from a groundwork of mutually supporting bodies and institutions which working-class communities develop. Why then was there this historical fracture at the end of the Chartist period? And why, it could be further asked, did it last so long?

We must enquire into the nature of the political process in this period, and it must be noted at the outset that the political sociology of the Chartist movement is still largely unexplored. In general terms, it can be argued that to convert a political programme or a political strategy into a mass political movement has never been easy for working people. Their access to the means by which their views may be disseminated is usually strictly limited, and lack of money is only one of their problems. Moreover a radical movement is rarely if ever united in its aims and objectives. There are many 'interests' involved within the broad class grouping, and sectionalism is normally a seriously hindering factor. During the Chartist years a number of mass agitations, which had their separate origins, came together beneath the central banner of the Six Points of the Charter, and they helped to provide rallying areas for a mass support of the Chartist leadership. The Ten Hours movement[43] and the anti-Poor Law agitation were among the more spectacular examples. At the same time, the economic segmentation and the social heterogeneity of working people were also very marked. As Feargus O'Connor expressed it early in 1848,

we have been most frustrated by those who have measured labour's right by the comparative, instead of the positive scale – by those aristocratic tradesmen who, receiving thirty shillings and two pound a week themselves, scoffed at my battalion of fustian jackets, blistered hands, and unshorn chins, who had but the alternative of entering the comparative labour market, or the Poor Law bastille.[44]

There is much evidence across the whole social spectrum. The particularities of Birmingham have been extensively described;[45] and two textile towns, Paisley and Oldham, offered interesting illustration of the differences in political attitudes from within milieux which were not wholly dissimilar in economic and social structure. Paisley's industries were on a smaller scale than those of Oldham, but both had a growing factory population, and quite large, but diminishing numbers of handloom weavers. Foster has presented

Oldham[46] as experiencing a shift from a labour consciousness to a class consciousness, and that this found practical expression in a remarkable intervention in local politics whereby the town was more or less under the political control of the working people for a number of years. It was only in the later years of the forties that the change towards liberalisation began to take effect. It is not necessary to underwrite the whole of Foster's analysis[47] to accept that there were quite crucial differences between the politics of Oldham in the thirties and early forties, and those of Paisley where majority opinion favoured collaboration with quite moderate middle-class radicals, and where support for a moral force Chartism and the Complete Suffage movement was reasonably sustained.[48] In the country as a whole there was similar variety of opinion and, it must again be emphasised, a chronology of change that was often local or regional in its inspiration. And yet there had always been, for many years, movements and events which pulled large sections of the ordinary people together in a national movement. The distinctiveness of Chartism over the decade of its history was that it had a national leadership, with a national journal, to bind the parts of the movement together. The *Northern Star* was much more the journal of a movement than any previous working-class paper had been: at least on the scale that it achieved, for it was truly national in its news coverage, and national in that it reached out to the whole country.[49] But the *Star* reflected the activities of a mass movement that had a visible and powerful leadership, and within that leadership Feargus O'Connor was outstanding.

No one matched O'Connor in the qualities demanded of a national leader, for above all others he succeeded in articulating the politics of confrontation in terms that won a response from the many different groups who came together behind his leadership. He was a superb platform speaker with a splendid presence, wonderfully racy and vivid in his language, and he could be wildly funny, both on the platform and in his writings in the *Norther Star*. 'Read the article of O'Connor's in the last number of the *Star* against the six radical papers', Engels wrote to Marx on 10 November 1847. 'It is a masterpiece of the genial art of making insults. It is even often better than Cobbett, and recalls Shakespeare.' Many historians have seen only his braggadocio, the bombastic expression of prophecies and claims that could never be fulfilled, the megalomania in his habit of calling himself 'Feargus Rex' and addressing his readers or hearers as 'My Children' or 'My People'. But much more important was the confidence that O'Connor generated among the poor and down-trodden. His extravagant language was a necessary part of the *rapport* between himself and the Chartist masses. O'Connor possessed, in full measure for most of his career, the quality of unbounded self-confidence that has been so strikingly absent in most leaders of the British working class in the past century and a half; and it was just this crucial belief in the righteousness of the cause that he served, and his ability to communicate it in unqualified terms, that allowed O'Connor to tower above his fellow Chartists, whatever their qualities. To the stockingers of the Midlands, the miners of the Northeast, the oppressed and exploited everywhere, this man radiated hope and offered the vision, however incompletely defined, of a better order. Skilled craftsmen like William Lovett, with more than a touch of the eighteenth-century rationalist about them, he often repelled; but among the unshorn chins and fustian jackets, among those who were working twelve, fourteen, and at times sixteen hours a day, housed in crowded tenements or insanitary cottages, living their lives in permanent unsecurity, the voice of O'Connor was the voice of the prophet bringing the tablets down from the mountain. Families named their children after him,[50] and they sang 'The Lion of Freedom' with passionate warmth and feeling. Feargus O'Connor was against what Cobbett called THE THING, and the multitudes who listened to O'Connor in the Bull Ring or on Blackstone Edge laughed at his mockery of their 'betters', and took courage from his blistering denunciation of their exploiters. We know from contemporary evidence that hearing O'Connor speak, or listening to what he had written in his weekly article in the *Northern Star*, was an exhilarating experience for many thousands, and there is no doubt of the affection and love and respect he won from the masses during his lifetime.[51]

To say all this is not to conclude the analysis of O'Connor as a political leader, for leadership does not reside only in the evocation of loyalty and affection from your own people, crucial though that is. O'Connor offered dramatic guidance to the Chartists of a kind no one else was capable of; and in the early years of the movement, for which we have a detailed assessment, his political leadership was shrewd and intelligent. Above all, it was his insistence upon the national character of the movement that provided the cohesion of the Chartist body in the early years of the 1840s. It was after the great strikes of the summer of 1842, the high point in the physical confrontation with the forces of authority, that the movement began to show signs of separating into somewhat fragmented parts; and neither O'Connor nor the Chartist leadership in general was able to devise new strategies or new initiatives. The Land Plan was the exception; it caught the imagination of many, but it was hardly a programme for an industrialising society, although it was understood to be aimed at alleviating the problem of surplus labour.[52] Without doubt, the widespread support for the Land Plan kept the movement together in many parts of the country. At this point it must be emphasised that O'Connor's policies, and the more radical versions elaborated under the slogan 'The Charter and Something More', all assumed that the necessary changes in class legislation would follow working-class representation at Westminster. The acceptance of parliamentarianism was unquestioned. It was Parliament which had passed the Reform Bill of 1832, thereby betraying the hopes of working people; it was Parliament which had passed the hated Poor Law Amendment Act; and it was Parliament which was being pressed to accept the Ten Hour reform. The institutions of the state, so it was believed, could and would respond to the people's representatives: a conclusion that has remained firmly within the beliefs of the mainstream movements of labour in Britain to the present day.[53] At the same time, the Chartist movement took it for granted, without being at all precise in elaboration, that the achievement of the Six Points – the democratisation of the political structure – would be the first major step towards a new kind of social order. Engels expressed the matter very clearly:

Since the working men do not respect the law, but simply submit to its power when they cannot change it, it is most natural that they should at least propose alterations in it, that they should wish to put a proletarian law in the place of the legal fabric of the bourgeoisie. This proposed law is the People's Charter, which in form is purely political, and demands a democratic basis for the House of Commons. Chartism is the compact form of their opposition to the bourgeoisie. In the Unions and turnouts opposition always remains isolated: it was single working-men or sections who fought a single bourgeois. If the fight became general, this was scarcely by the intention of the working-men; or, when it did happen intentionally, Chartism was at the bottom of it. But in Chartism it is the whole working class which arises against the bourgeoisie, and attacks, first of all, the political power, the legislative rampart with which the bourgeoisie has surrounded itself . . . These six points, which are all limited to the reconstitution of the House of Commons, harmless as they seem, are sufficient to overthrow the whole English Constitution, Queen and Lords included.[54]

Leadership and politics are closely interwoven. A radical movement which is not rooted in the political and social needs of its constituents and which fails to evoke a continuing response, cannot expect to maintain its momentum. The radicalism of the first half of the century in Britain evolved a broad ideology of opposition which served effectively the many social strands within the movement, and which adapted to the dynamics of an expanding capitalism. The anti-capitalist political economy of the 'Smithian socialists' of the 1820s,[55] as well as the critique of bourgeois society which came out of Owenism, had been diffused through the columns of the *Poor Man's Guardian*, the *Pioneer* and other journals of the first half of the 1830s and reached a wide popular audience. There came about a more general understanding of the nature and character of capitalism which moved beyond the categories of 'Old Corruption' to a consciousness, no doubt for many a highly simplified consciousness, of the meaning of exploitation and of the reasons for the poverty and insecurity within which their lives were lived. Classical political economy began to be recognised as an apologia for the existing distribution of property, and of the ways in which the capitalist economy organised itself. The *Working Man's Friend* in April 1833 characterised middle-class political economy as the law of buying cheap and selling dear: 'The selfish may call that a science, but if it is a science, it is only the science of trickery.'[56] The vigour and strength of this working-class political economy was countered by a growing stream of articles, pamphlets and popular books from bourgeois publicists and propagandists who included the well-known names of Jane Marcet, Harriet Martineau, Charles Knight and Henry Brougham;[57] and no doubt they had some influence, even in the very short run. But what needs to be emphasised is the pervasiveness of the anti-capitalist tradition which had been so brilliantly established during the 1820s. The language of criticism that now began to be used differed from that derived from 'Old Corruption'; and instead of the attacks upon the sinecurists and placemen, the phraseology was of the millocracy, the shopocrats or capitalists. By the time the *Northern Star* was founded this was the language of denunciation, and it continued throughout the years of Chartism. At the trial of O'Connor and fifty-eight other Chartists at Lancaster in 1843 there were many examples in the speeches of the defendants of their opposition to the manufacturing system. In the verbatim record published by the radical press Thomas Storah, of Ashton, said that he was 'a severe opponent of the manufacturers, or, in other words, of the Anti-Corn Law League, and I believe, that is the sole reason why I am indicted here for conspiracy'. The most vigorous denunciation of the industrial system came from Richard Pilling. It was his personal experience that he used as evidence: first as a handloom weaver until 1840 and then, 'sooner than become a pauper on the parish' he entered the factory where he saw 'the evil workings of the accursed system'. Pilling became a fervent supporter of the Ten Hour Bill; he led opposition to wage reductions; denounced the 'conspiracy' of the masters in their concerted efforts to worsen working conditions; and insisted upon the industrial agitation as the centre of their struggle, 'Whatever it may have been with others it has been a wage question with me. And I do say that if Mr O'Connor has made it a chartist question, he has done wonders to make it extend through England, Ireland, and Scotland. But it was always a wage question, and ten hours bill with me.' Feargus O'Connor, who was never a socialist and who specifically emphasised the fact, nevertheless referred in 1848 to the capitalist employers as 'the traffickers in human blood and in infant gristle';[58] and it was during the last years of the forties that the developing ideas of 'The Charter and Something More' can be discerned in the speeches and writings of the left-wing of the Chartist leadership. The high peak of socialist influence in the Chartist movement was the programme of the March 1851 Convention, which was much more specific than ever before concerning the use of political power to begin to transform the economic foundations of society in the interests of those without property.[59] While Marx and Engels can be credited with some influence upon the ideas of Ernest Jones, who drafted the 1851 programme, its intellectual lineage can be clearly traced in the speeches and writings of the earlier years.

There is, however, a largely unexplored and unexplained area of the radical history of these years. While it is necessary to insist upon the presence among the committed Chartists of a general and generalised anti-capitalist ideology, and of a more diffused 'them against us' sentiment among wider sections of the working people, it remains a remarkable phenomenon that the ideas of Hodgskin, Thompson and others of the 1820s were not developed by younger and later writers. As Noel Thompson phrased it, there was 'no second generation of anti-capitalist and socialist political economists'. Discussion of the application to contemporary society of this working-class political economy appears to come to an end, in the published journals at any rate, around the middle of the 1830s; and the lukewarm response given to J. F. Bray's *Labour's Wrongs and Labour's Remedy*, first published in 1839, is one indication of the failure to develop the insights and analysis which the Smithian socialists had provided.[60] The same phenomenon may be observed with regard to Owenism. There was no sustained discussion or development of Robert Owen's ideas by his radical contemporaries; no attempt to separate out the millennial elements from the realistic analysis of social questions; no attempt, indeed, to argue what was millennial and what was realistic.[61] One of the most hopeful developments, the evolving working partnership between James 'Shepherd' Smith and James Morrison, came to an end about the time that the *Pioneer* closed down on 5 July 1834, and Smith began to shrug off his militant socialism without any apparent emotional or intellectual difficulty.[62] The Owenism that had so stirred his imagination sharply narrowed its concerns in the 1840s and only to a limited degree permeated the thinking of the mainstream of the Chartist constituency. Chartism continued with its radical terminology, 'purely a working-man's cause freed from all bourgeois elements', as Engels described the movement in 1844. In the long run, the intellectual weaknesses of the Smithian socialists, who were unable to provide an explanation for periods of relative prosperity, and whose theories of exploitation were inadequate, would no doubt require to be remedied if they were to serve as an essential underpinning to a root and branch critique of capitalist society; but it can hardly be argued that these theoretical shortcomings had any serious effect upon the course of events in 1848 and the years that immediately followed. In the longer run there is certainly no doubt that the absence of anything approaching a theory of capitalist exploitation – even something equivalent to the fuzzy analysis that has served the greater part of the labour movement in Britain during the twentieth century – seriously limited the scope of working-class radicalism after the 1850s, and thereby encouraged the emphasis upon the defensive organisations of the working people that has been discussed above.

The historical fracture that occurred between the period of mass discontents in the 1840s, and the quieter years of the decade which followed, was consequent upon the events of 1848; and it is here that an analysis of the relationship between the British state and the radical movement must begin. It has recently been argued, in a major revision of Chartist history, that the changing nature and character of the British state in the 1840s, compared with the 1830s, must account in considerable part for the political disintegration to which Chartism became subject.[63] Stedman Jones, whose argument this is, followed, and expanded for his own analytical purposes, an earlier article by Richards which suggested that between the 1830s and 1840s there was a shift away from the 'aggressive liberalism' of the 1830s towards a reappraisal of attitudes and policies in the decade which followed.[64] Richards uses the word 'abandonment' to describe what happened, which is much too strong, but a more limited version of the argument is acceptable. There are two parts to his thesis. The first is that there were measures to stimulate the growth of the economy, and that these included the Bank Charter Act of 1844 and the commercial changes introduced by Gladstone at the Board of Trade which culminated in the abolition of the Corn Laws in 1846. All the economic changes carried through in this decade were in the direct interests of a more efficient economy in which the horizons for profit-making were being steadily enlarged. Contemporary middle-class opinion would not have been wholly in agreement with these generalisations, especially with regard to the reimposition of the income tax, or the restriction of factory hours, but those whose economic interests appear immediately involved do not always read the future accurately; for the changes which were introduced helped to even out the jerkiness of previous economic growth and to stimulate what was already a high level of activity in both domestic and international sectors. The second aspect of the argument relates to social and political attitudes. It is Richards' case that the widespread popular discontents of the 1830s, among them the violence associated with the attempts to impose the new Poor Law upon the industrial North in 1837, as well as the Chartist movement itself, forced a revision of social and political policies which moderated the harshness of existing legislation and which drew attention to a range of social problems subsumed under the general heading of 'The Condition of England question'. And certainly this is an argument which can be accepted in general terms, although the processes of change were more complex than has been suggested. The Whig policy towards the Irish famine, as carried out by Trevelyan, can hardly be accounted as an abandonment of 'aggressive liberalism', and with the exception of the prohibition of woman and children underground in coal mines and the Factory Acts, there was notably little change in the workings of social policy. There was great disquiet over the vigorous reactions of working-class communities to the new Poor Law in the West Riding and Lancashire; Dickens was publishing the instalments of *Oliver Twist* in 1837; a national uproar erupted in the mid-forties over the Andover scandal[65] – but it cannot be argued that anything changed in the ways in which the Poor Law was being operated. The political agitation over the Poor Law declined sharply after 1842, but this was because employment conditions in the industrial areas improved substantially, and access to public relief was no longer required by most of the able-bodied. The actual workings of the Poor Law remained harsh and unpleasant, but its subjects were now mainly those who have never been able to make their problems articulate: the sick, the aged, one-parent families, orphan children and those with physical or mental disabilities. Similarly, although there was massive documentation of the appalling conditions of the industrial towns in the 1840s, the implementation of Chadwick's 'Sanitary Idea' – the public cleansing of streets and courts, the proper disposal of night soil, and the provision of adequate supplies of clean water – was to take several decades before elementary standards were achieved on a national scale.[66] Liberal-minded contemporaries were aware of the importance of providing a reasonably clean physical environment for working people. If it was not as central as spiritual well-being, the connection was appreciated by the more intelligent of the philanthropists and reformers. As R. A. Slaney wrote to Brougham in August 1840, the problem of the health of towns was:

closely connected with the moral as much as the physical state of large masses of the working classes in our populous districts. The Report and Evidence show how little probability there is of any effectual prospect of Education amid these multitudes unless some strenuous efforts are made to improve the state of their dwellings in decency and comfort.[67]

It is interesting that throughout 1848, during the months of tumults and disturbances, there were constant references in Parliament and in the press to the social legislation relating to the coal-whippers and to the Ten Hour Act of the previous year, as examples of the state's benevolence which in turn was now being repaid by the coal-whippers' support as special constables on 10 April and by the factory operatives of Manchester who on a number of occasions refused to join the Chartists on the streets, and continued working in the mills. The most dramatic illustration of the awareness of the potential working-class responses to government action was probably the constant emphasis, before the great demonstration on Kennington Common, that it must be contained without bloodshed;

although this attitude, it should be noted, went back at least as far as the aftermath of Peterloo. With such a large proletarian constituency, martyrdom was not to be encouraged; and even though such considerations were of much less consequence in Ireland, those found guilty of high treason in 1848 were transported, not executed.

These arguments relating to the changing character of ruling class attitudes in the 1840s have been put to specific use in the Chartist study by Stedman Jones mentioned above; and the general argument has been stretched a good deal beyond that put forward by Richards. Stedman Jones has two related parts to his analysis: the first is that Chartist rhetoric and the ideology of the movement remained within the framework of 'Old Corruption', and that as a result there was an inability to come to terms with those legislative measures, such as the repeal of the Corn Laws or the Factory Acts, which were not promulgated for 'obviously malign class purposes'.[68] Chartists, working within the ideology of 'Old Corruption', must assume that all legislation was wholly class biased and carried through by a thoroughly selfish Parliament. Any legislation which was not blatantly class oriented could not be understood or accommodated within the Chartist order of things; and the 'conviction and self-certainty of the language of Chartism' would thereby be undermined, deflated and weakened. And the other part of analysis is that the legislation of the 1840s was precisely of this kind. From the end of the 1830s 'the State was already beginning to withdraw' from the policies of straightforward repression; and legislation 'was now beginning to be nuanced by moves of a less sinister character' than that of the early and mid-thirties, 'towards state-provided education, for instance, and the discussion of measures to improve the health of towns'.[69] And further, when we look at the 1840s, it is necessary to appreciate 'the high moral tone of the proceedings of the government and the effective raising of the state above the dictates of particular economic interests – whether landlords, financiers or manufacturers'.

The proposition that Chartist ideology remained within the terms understood by 'Old Corruption' has been denied in the previous discussion,[70] but in any case it is the argument about the state that is at the centre of Stedman Jones' analysis. We need not spend much time debating the 'high moral tone of the proceedings of government' since this is what most governments in a bourgeois democracy endeavour to inject into their statements, however reactionary the outcome of their actions; and in any case Victorian England provided many examples of the general belief of most English politicians in the modern era that it has been the Lord who was directing their activities. What is missing from Stedman Jones' general thesis is the recognition that coercion is the other side of the government coin marked conciliation. If consent can be obtained without violence, so much the better; and the history of British domestic politics after 1850 is eloquent testimony to the success of hegemony in the sense used by Gramsci.[71] But the 1840s came at the end of half a century of popular discontent and radical agitation. The decade opened with the most serious crisis of the century; and although the growing numbers and prosperity of the middle classes in the second quarter of the century were steadily adding stability to the social structure of the country, it was not until 1848 itself that there was demonstrated, beyond question and doubt, the complete and solid support of the middling strata to the defence of existing institutions. From the 1790s the coercive powers of the state had been tested and slowly improved in confrontation with a succession of radical and democratic movements; and by the 1840s, the last decade of mass agitations, there was now a much more experienced and more efficient administrative apparatus than ever before. 1848 showed a notable improvement in security matters than the earlier years of the forties, mainly because of the large-scale mobilisation of the special constables, itself predicated upon the more effective handling of the police and military forces. Stedman Jones has considered only the beginnings of the political and social changes in attitudes during the 1840s, and has omitted the more immediate actions of the state in the effective exercise of its coercive powers. Moreover, it must be remembered that 1848 was not the first but the third occasion in this decade when the various arms of the state used their repressive mechanisms. The turbulent events of 1839–40, 1842 and 1848 each evoked similar reactions: cool, ruthless calculation with not much evidence of high moral tone. South Wales never recovered after 1840, nor did the Potteries after 1842; and neither Scotland nor the Midlands was prominent in 1848. What happened in these three main periods of repression was that while some national leaders moved away – Thomas Cooper is an obvious example – more important was the elimination of sections of the middle-range leadership; and most of those who suffered prison sentences did not return to the movement.[72] The convictions of the summer and autumn of 1848 effectively neutralised a large part of the local and regional leaderships in London and the industrial North, and the general situation of the early 1850s was not conducive to their revival, or to the generation of new cadres of militants. Ernest Jones, now the only personality of national stature, was a fluent and effective speaker, and he was not lacking in strategic sense, but he did not match all the qualities of a mass leader that Feargus O'Connor exhibited at the height of his career. It was not, however, charisma that defeated Jones, but rather the cumulative effects of the physical repression of the 1840s within a discouraging combination of factors that became more aggravated as the years moved away from 1850. It is not to be doubted that for all its tensions and appalling social problems British society in 1848 was too solidly based to have been seriously shaken by any action that the existing grouping of forces against it could have developed. In spite of the anxieties and fears expressed before the Kennington Common meeting and all though the summer months about the Irish situation, the coercive powers at the disposal of the British state never lost control. They were aided by the tactical and strategic irresolution of the radical groupings. The Chartist leadership had no coherent political strategy. What was to be done if and when the National Petition was rejected was never considered except in wild and sensational terms, and indeed it is unlikely that any of the leaders in 1848 had clear ideas on the question. The absence of a strategy pushed the militants into at least considering physical force action, although again it is by no means certain that anyone looked beyond the possibility of taking over a particular town. A tradition of insurrection had not been established on the British mainland, and how much of the activity in 1848 was in fact generated by the Irish has not yet been clearly defined. Without a detailed 'crowd' analysis it is not possible to say what was the Irish component of the English demonstrations of 1848, but it was certainly considerable, since almost all the areas of militant activity were also areas of Irish settlement. If there had been a coherent leadership, whether open or undergound, it is likely that the Irish would have followed, since Repeal was an avowed aim of the Chartist movement. But there was no planned programme, and neither on the mainland nor in Ireland did the preparations for a physical outbreak offer evidence of likely vigour in execution, or a sense of confidence in the future. The contrast with the executive abilities of the Whig government was striking, and while 1848 exhibited the solidity and strength of the bourgeois state, it also revealed the inadequacies of a divided leadership in the popular movement. And this cannot be judged surprising. With the full weight of the police and the military deployed against the Chartists, with the judiciary acting as a dependent and thoroughly dependable arm of the state and with the media in continuous and very effective denunciation of Chartism and all its works, it is not remarkable that counsels were often divided and that radical opinions were often at variance one with another. Large-scale arrests are not helpful in encouraging the confidence of those left free, and by the early autumn of 1848 there was widespread demoralisation among all levels of the Chartist movement. George White, one of the most active of the second rank of leaders, went on tour in the Midland counties in November 1848, just before his own trial and conviction; and his account will serve as an epitaph for the Chartist movement in this year:

During the last few weeks I have been through Nottingham, Arnold, Loughborough, Leicester, Birmingham, Coventry, Wednesday, Bedworth and Nuneaton. I have found that the Chartist feeling is predominant amongst the intelligent portion of the working men, but they are sadly disorganised, and, in some places, split up into parties, partly through the bickerings of local leaders and partly through the suicidal cant of moral versus physical force, and also through the doggedness with which a few professing Chartists assert the necessity of a junction with the middle classes. This, added to the later arrests of some of our most active men, has thrown a damp upon the people which is taken advantage of by the Whigs and 'go betweens' and has brought Chartist meetings to a standstill. But the spirit of the people is still good, and they look forward with hope in resuscitation . . . As this is possibly my last letter for some time to come, I once more desire to urge on our friends the necessity of a friendly union among themselves. And remain Mr Editor

            Yours in the Good Old Cause
            George White[73]

In his discussion of Marx's attitude towards the Paris Commune, Lenin noted that England was omitted from Marx's insistence that to achieve a revolutionary transformation the existing state machine would have to be completely broken up and destroyed. Marx had written to Dr Kugelmann on 12 April 1871:

If you look at the last chapter of my *Eighteenth Brumaire* you will find that I say that the next attempt of the French revolution will be no longer, as before, to transfer the bureaucratic-military machine from one hand to another, but to *smash* it, and this is essential for every real people's revolution on the Continent.[74]

Lenin's gloss on this passage in his *State and Revolution* read:

It is interesting to note two particular points in the passages of Marx quoted. First, he confines his conclusions to the Continent. This was natural in 1871, when England was still the model of a purely capitalist country, but without a military machine and, in large measure, without a bureaucracy. Hence Marx excluded England, where a revolution, even a people's revolution, could be imagined, and was then possible, *without* the preliminary condition of destroying the 'ready-made state machinery'.[75]

It is not at all certain that Marx would have agreed with Lenin's interpretation of his words, but in any case Lenin was wrong, as the analysis of 1848 in this present volume has shown. By this year the state apparatus in Britain, while comprising a very small bureaucracy by any standards, was able speedily and efficiently to mobilise adequate coercive power to subdue and control any scale of unrest likely to be achieved in Ireland or on the mainland of Britain. As it happened, the physical force content of what unrest and turbulence there was remained manageable and it was contained without much difficulty by the combined strength of the regular police and the special constables, with only a relatively limited intervention by the military. The directing authority in the United Kingdom was not more than about a dozen men, and these took all the major decisions, for Ireland as well as for the rest of Britain. Lenin's reference to the absence of a 'military machine' was also misleading. The military in Britain had long been used for purposes of internal security, and they were accustomed to being used by the civil authorities in the maintenance of public order. Barrington Moore, in his perceptive analysis of British society in the nineteenth century, also emphasised the policy of 'well-timed concessions': one made necessary by 'the absence of any strong apparatus of repression'.[76] No one denies the policy of concessions, but most reforms came after years of repression when the forces of radicalism were effectively curbed and contained. Barrington Moore's formulation is a version of Stedman Jones' 'high moral tone', which itself is an echo of a famous statement by Gladstone in the 1860s and just as erroneous. Gladstone had been warned by his brother-in-law Lord Lyttelton that his new liberal approach to a number of political issues, especially the matter of the extension of the suffrage, was causing alarm as well as opposition; and Gladstone replied (April 1865):

After all, you are a peer, and Peel used to say, speaking of his peer colleagues, that they were beings of a different order. Please to recollect that we have got to govern millions of hard hands; that it must be done by force, fraud or goodwill; that the latter has been tried and is answering; that none have profited more by this change of system since the corn law and the Six Acts, than those who complain of it.[77]

The 'millions of hard hands' had remained a turbulent and difficult problem throughout the first half of the nineteenth century, and it was the remarkable political success of the second half of the century that violence from below became localised; in political terms it was marginalised. The greater part of the violence after 1850, in what remained a violent society, was within the working-class communities, and some of its most unpleasant exhibitions were against the strangers in their midst: in particular the Irish. There had often been tensions in the past, and Daniel O'Connell's attitude to the Chartist movement had exacerbated the bitterness within these communities where the Irish existed in significant numbers. A footnote in the published record of the trial of Feargus O'Connor and other Chartists in 1843 referred to an Anti-Corn Law meeting in 1841 'where the Irish bludgeon-men of the Anti-Corn Law League, and the Irish police, in the presence of Corn-Law repealing magistrates, assailed the Chartists in a most brutal and ferocious manner, for daring to express their opinions on the resolutions submitted to the meeting'.[78] It was the working compact between the Irish nationalists and the English radicals that made 1848 such a promising year; but the repression on both sides of the Irish Channel destroyed the possibilities of continued co-operation between the radicals of the two peoples. Irish nationalism for nearly twenty years then took relatively quietist forms with an increasing colouration of Catholicism in much of its sentiment; and there also ended the attempt by the radicals of Young Ireland to develop an alliance between middle-class Protestants and Catholics. In England the disintegration of a mass movement on a national scale promoted single-issue reforms and organisations, and encouraged the spaces within which occurred the anti-Irish riots that punctuated the years of the third quarter of the century.[79]

It was Marx's position in his early writings that proletarian revolutionary consciousness would develop more or less in a straightforward way from the relationships within the capitalist mode of production. In *The Holy Family* and particularly in the more mature *German Ideology* the emphasis was upon the inevitable development of a revolutionary consciousness as a result of man's alienation: 'It is not a question of what this or that proletarian, or even the whole proletariat, at the moment *regards* as its aim. It is a question of what the proletariat is, or what, in accordance with this *being*, it will historically be compelled to do.'[80] Marx's analysis of the failure of Chartism was a combination of increased prosperity and the weakness of political leadership. Communist consciousness, he believed, would come from within; and he therefore gave no emphasis to the influence, or possible influence, of bourgeois ideas upon the working classes.[81] There was no room in this analysis for a connection between Marx's themes of mystification and the fetishised nature of social relations and of a tendency towards acquiescence or a passive acceptance of the capitalist order on the part of working people. The question is not that capitalist society failed to generate attitudes, feelings, sentiments of class hostility – the most obvious as well as the most general of the conclusions that run through the whole corpus of Marx's writings. The problem is that of agency: how class attitudes become translated into class consciousness, and this has very properly occupied a central, if not the central, position in Marxist analysis in the twentieth century. At the same time, it would be wholly erroneous, as some historians and sociologists have suggested, to argue that during the nineteenth century there was a growth of conformity within the working-class communities in Britain that came close to, or was identical with, incorporation within bourgeois society. If, for instance, we take respectability as a significant indication of conformity, it is a respectability, as has been argued in a number of studies,[82] that comes from within working-class culture, and is indigenous to the ways of life of particular communities. As a social attitude related to a system of values, respectability within working-class society has a different provenance from the concerns of the lives of the middle classes. Central to the argument must be the work situation: the conditions of work, its regularity or uncertainty, the levels of pay, the housing and the environment traditionally associated with the particular type of employment. When we refer to working-class cultures, it is the work situation that in the last resort determines the mix of ideas and values that shapes and moulds working people in their daily lives. Work is not the whole of life, but it is at the centre of the proletarian world; and in the nineteenth century workers inhabited a hostile world. It may not have been a world that was always unpleasant, but what is deemed pleasant or unpleasant is conditioned by tradition and culture; and in the Victorian period the horizons of acceptance were mostly very narrow. For all working people in these years, except a small minority, life was hard and employment was often uncertain. Conflict at the point of production was always near to the surface of working life in the mill or the pit. Kirk noted that in Lancashire and Cheshire in the two decades after 1850 industrial relations 'were rarely placid or harmonious'.[83] The Lord Mayor of Manchester during 1848, Elkanah Armitage, who earned himself a knighthood for his services, was vigorously anti-union, and his factory at Salford was involved in a bitter seven months' strike in 1850–1.[84] Outside the factories, workshops and mines, the Master and Servants Acts remained on the statute book until the 1870s; and the judiciary, at all levels, could be expected to hand down hostile judgements against strikers or their trade unions. It is the contradictions between employers' anti-unionism and their paternalism, between working-class respectability and working-class industrial militancy that make it so difficult to offer any generalisations that do not require some degree of qualification about the decades after 1850. There was a trend towards business unions in some areas and some occupations – some of the Lancashire unions for instance – but on the central issues of unionisation, such as working with 'knobsticks', or blacklegs, there could be no compromise.[85] Historians have often gone astray in emphasising one aspect – usually the 'respectable' aspect – of a social reality that was much more complicated. In 1948 J. B. Jefferys published a book of documents which included a poem by a Hull boilermaker that seemed to epitomise the class collaboration thesis of these middle decades of Victorian England. The Hull boilermakers had obtained a pay rise in September 1872, and at a dinner provided by the union, they invited the chairman of the main shipbuilding firm in the district, as their guest of honour. This was E. J. Reed and it was at this dinner that a boilermaker called Bostock read his poem. The first verse set the scene:

> Capital and Labour seem
> By our Maker joined;
> Are they not like giant twins
> In the world of mind?
> What can Labour do alone?
> Grind its nose against the stone,
> Turn a gristless mill!
> What can Capital indeed
> By itself? but hoard its seed,
> Eat a golden pill.

Within twelve months the story had begun to develop certain complications. Reed was a Liberal and when the local Liberal MP died he was chosen to contest the by-election. This was in 1873. Unfortunately for Reed this had become a time of conflict within the firm. There was plenty of work, but there were technical problems and Reed brought in skilled men from London. The local boilermakers were incensed and a leaflet signed 'A Boilermaker' urged workmen to vote for the Tory candidate who did in fact just win the seat. A few months later, in the general election of 1874, a Liberal was again returned, but it was not Reed; he stood successfully for Pembroke which was some distance from Hull and its particular industrial problems.[86]

It has been suggested in this Commentary that the institutional and sociological foundations of reformism were established before the final years of Chartism. But reformism is not a single, simple concept or practice, and as a political or industrial activity it can and does change over time, or operate differently in different environments. With the quite rapid decline of a national political movement which offered working people some kind of alternative vision of their contemporary society, historians have inevitably been concerned with the impact and influence of middle-class ideas upon the subordinate class. It would be historically unreasonable to postulate a direct indoctrination during the late forties or the early fifties; but there is no doubt of the growing importance of what Bottomore calls the weaker version of the dominant ideology thesis: the capacity of a dominant ideology 'to inhibit and confuse the development of the counter-ideology of a subordinate class'.[87] The decline of anti-capitalist ideas as an ideology in the 1850s meant that by the 1870s it was an attack upon the landed aristocracy and not upon the millocracy that would win applause at a working-class meeting or demonstration.[88] But in the list of questions prepared by the Parliamentary Committee of the Trades Union Congress in late 1873 all the seven items concerned trade union and labour matters: to the law relating to trade unions (three questions), for a Workmen's Compensation Bill, factory legislation, the Plimsoll demands and the abolition of truck.[89] The Labourist philosophy that was taking shape at this time had many deficiencies as a working ideology for the politically articulate among trade unionists, not least their liberal understanding of parliamentarianism, but it was concerned centrally with Labour questions, and it could never therefore be completely absorbed within a non-proletarian tradition.

The ability of the dominant ideology to inhibit and confuse can, however, never be doubted. Throughout 1848 there was the constant reiteration of the moral rightness of the existing order of society, and this provided sustenance for the spiritual and political needs of the middle ranks of society. In the longer term it was the political values associated with the Whig view of history – the evolution in England of civil and religious liberty, representative government and equality before the law – that provided the central component of the political commonsense universally accepted by the middling and upper strata of society, and which was not without some influence upon sections of working-class opinion.[90]

It was the longer term with which Macaulay in his *History of England* was mainly concerned, and the vision that he offered to his own, and subsequent, generations of the blessings of the political settlement which followed the Revolution of 1688 has remained acceptable to our own day among most educated opinion. But when Macaulay retired from politics in April 1848 – after the Kennington Common demonstration which he hailed as a great victory for the forces of order – his immediate aim was to underline the lesson of 10th April. He changed the design of the second volume by the introduction of the famous third chapter in which he expressly contrasted the material benefits for ordinary people in his own day compared with the levels of wages and the general living conditions at the end of the seventeenth century. It was these contrasts that especially appealed to his contemporaries, and their immediate political implications were well understood: 'It has come at a moment when the lessons it inculcates ought to produce great practical effects', Halifax wrote to Macaulay early in 1849.[91]

It is instructive not only for 1848 but for the decades which followed that there was no serious intellectual criticism of the Whig government for their repressive actions, and no support for the cause of Chartism outside its own ranks. John Stuart Mill provided a reasoned evaluation of the 'desultory invective' poured out by Brougham in his *Letter to the Marquess of Lansdowne* against the revolution in Paris,[92] but this was in April, and there were only snippets in Mill's correspondence for the remainder of the year. George Eliot had a perceptive comment in early March that showed considerable insight into the political sociology of contemporary England, but apart from one later and brief remark about Louis Blanc, there was a blank in her correspondence of this year.[93] There were scattered comments and gestures from a handful of romantics – Holman Hunt and Millais were said on one occasion to have joined a Chartist march – but Ireland seems to have passed almost everyone by, and the Chartist trials were apparently taken at their face value as legitimate punishment for wrongdoing. The initiative that caught most attention, and has been given undue emphasis by historians, was the movement that became known as Christian Socialism. But it was very small scale in its impact, and it has attracted attention – apart from the theology of F. D. Maurice – largely because there was so little else.

The outstanding feature of 1848 was the mass response to the call for special constables to assist the professional forces of state security. This was the significance of 1848: the closing of ranks among all those with a property stake in the country, however small that stake was. It must not be thought, however, that the middle classes would respond automatically to the call of law and order. They answered positively when it was a matter of their self-interest, as they conceived that to be. But when Englishmen were physically assaulting Irishmen and their families, as in the Stockport riots of

1852 or the Birkenhead Garibaldi riots of 1862 the special constables who were mobilised were either decidedly lethargic in their duties (or, occasionally, actually took part in the rioting) or they were not used operationally because of their prejudice against the Irish.[94] In 1848 there were some who stood aside, either from fear or political disagreement, but their numbers were far fewer than in earlier years. Although it has been the mobilisation in London on 10 April that has caught the historical imagination, middle-class support was more important in the provinces. With the exception of great cities like Manchester and Liverpool, the local police forces, even in quite large towns, were not as numerous in relation to population, or as experienced as the situation often demanded, and the special constables in their hundreds, and sometimes thousands, were an important steadying factor. Politicians, military commanders and newspaper editors constantly emphasised the importance of civilian aid as a necessary auxiliary to the police and the military; and always the lessons of Paris were underlined. Lord Normanby from the French Embassy had constantly reiterated the neglect by Louis-Philippe of 'the armed aristocracy of the Bourgeoisie' organised in the National Guard; and this was the theme of many newspaper editorials. As *The Times* wrote on 2 June 1848 after the large-scale demonstrations of the previous days: the Chartists forgot 'that they had to fight it out with a middle class differently composed from the Garde Nationale'. What was different, of course, was first and above all, the competence and the confidence that government ministers displayed; and then the firm conviction of the English middle classes concerning the superiority of the British constitution, and the benefits which flowed therefrom. There was always, at bottom, a foundation belief in the inviolability of private property, but what parsons preached from their pulpits, and judges elaborated from the Bench, and what newspaper editors wrote about, were the positive, overwhelming virtues of social peace in a society which encouraged hard work and thrift, and which offered rewards for what they defined as good citizenship. *The Times* was the great rostrum of the larger part of the newspaper public, and the ideas *The Times* developed in its long leaders were repeated in newspapers and journals throughout the country. Much of the argument in 1848 arose out of the refutation of the French 'madness', universally ridiculed in Britain by all the middle-class press, whether radical, Whig or Tory. Newspapers such as the *Nonconformist* or the *Manchester Examiner*, and there were similar radical/liberal journals in most towns of size, would not accept many of the sentiments expressed in Whig or Tory papers, but the basic arguments – in particular that reform was practicable and must come about in constitutional ways – were not in question. In a remarkable catalogue – remarkable not least for its complacent exaggeration – of the blessings bestowed upon the British people since 1830, the year when Louis-Philippe took the throne of France, *The Times* provided a history of the day that most middle-class readers could accept without serious question. It was published on 26 February, a few days after the revolution had begun in Paris and it could have been reprinted on 1 January 1849, with appropriate comments as to why the stability of British society had been maintained in the year which had just passed.

During this remarkable period [since 1830] the Sovereigns and Governments of England have been steadily improving and popularising all the institutions of the country. They have immensely expanded the basis of representation. They have evidently and deliberately increased the power of the Commons. They have opened the municipalities. They have qualified or destroyed the monopolies of companies or of classes. They have liberated manufactures and commerce. But why need we linger on details? In a word, they have thrown themselves into the arms of the people. They have cut the very ground from under democracy by satisfying, one by one all its just desires. Let any one, who has not even yet attained to the midday of life, compare the popular agitations of the present kind and that preceding the last French revolution. England was then incessantly disturbed by clamour for organic change. Revolution was on the lips of the factions, and in the terrors of the peaceful. The peerage, the church, the rights of property, law, monarchy, and order itself, were to disappear. Mark the change which has come upon that turbulent scene. Popular agitation in these days is of a purely rational, and, so to speak, legislative character. Thousands and tens of thousands meet to impress upon representatives their opinion – and generally their wise opinion – on a pending question, not concerning the fundamentals of society or the reconstruction of the state, but some minor and debateable point. The discussion is lawful in its subject, and regular in its tone, because the people feel that under the existing state of things they have a voice in the government of the country, and can utter that voice with effect.

Notes

Prolegomena

1 Peel's ministry was defeated on the second reading of an Irish coercion bill, a matter which the Whigs were later to be reminded of many times during their own period of power. There is a good introduction to the new Whig administration in H. Paul, *A History of Modern England*, vol. 1 (1904) ch. 1, and see also N. Gash, *Sir Robert Peel. The Life of Sir Robert Peel after 1830* (1972), ch. 17. Richard Cobden had urged Peel, in a letter written three days before the Commons' defeat, to consider seriously a dissolution of Parliament which Cobden predicted would result in a parliamentary majority. The letter, and Peel's reply is in ch. XVII of John Morley's *Life of Richard Cobden* (various editions). For Russell, see Spencer Walpole, *The Life of Lord John Russell*, 2 vols. (1889); and for the background to the decision to bring down the Peel government, J. Prest, *Lord John Russell* (1972) p. 213 ff. Palmerston alone objected to the offer being made to the Peelites: *ibid*, p. 223. The Cabinet list is always given each year in the *Annual Register*; for 1848 see Appendix to Chronicle, p. 173.

2 Prest, *Lord John Russell*, p. 263.

3 Clarendon (1800–70) was greatly liked by the Queen and Albert. Through Henry Reeve he had close relations with *The Times*. The standard biography is Sir William Maxwell, *The Life and Letters of George William Frederick, Fourth Earl of Clarendon*, 2 vols. (1913). See also G. J. T. H. Villiers, *A Vanished Victorian* (1938). For Normanby's period as Viceroy, see below, pp. 42, 51. The Lord-Lieutenant of Ireland was often referred to as the Viceroy, but the term had no official recognition.

4 The matter arose in a curious way. There was a debate on the attendance of members in the House of Lords on the occasion of the opening or proroguing of Parliament, and there was back-bench opposition to Cabinet ministers being given precedence; they argued the constitutional position that 'Cabinet Ministers had no real status in this country: the Cabinet Council was an unconstitutional body which originated in the reign of Charles the Second': *Hansard*, 3rd ser. CXVIII, col 1943, 7 August 1851. Cf. also W. I. Jennings, *Cabinet Government* (Cambridge, 1947) ch. 1; G. H. L. le May, *The Victorian Constitution. Conventions, Usages and Ceremonies* (1979), ch. 4.

5 Apparently he needed the salary; as did Palmerston. See the interesting account of Russell's finances in Prest, *Lord John Russell*, p. 220 ff.

6 There are many editions of *The English Constitution*. It was first published in 1867 with a second edition in 1872 which has an important new introduction.

The standard edition of Bagehot's writings is edited by N. St John-Stevas, *The English Constitution* in vol. 5 (1974).

7   J. Ridley, *Lord Palmerston* (1970) pp. 587–8. See also H. C. F. Bell, *Lord Palmerston*, vol. 2 (1936), pp. 424–9.

8   Palmerston's finances do not seem to have been comprehensively studied. Ridley, *Lord Palmerston*, has details scattered through his biography. Palmerston's father died heavily in debt (*ibid*. p. 89) and Palmerston himself worked hard to improve his financial position but for most of his life seems to have needed his ministerial salary.

9   The Lansdowne estates, at the time of the *Return of Owners of Land* in the mid-1870s (popularly known as the New Domesday Book) comprised 122,000 acres in Ireland (rental £32,000 p.a.); 11,000 acres in England (rental about £21,000 p.a.); and 10,000 acres in Scotland (rental about £9,000): *Complete Peerage*, revised . . . Vicary Gibbs, vol. VII (1929). The *DNB* has quite a full entry, but fails to mention that he was an Irish landlord.

10 Dugald Stewart (1753–1828) was Professor of Moral Philosophy at the University of Edinburgh. He was originally a supporter of 1789 but recanted although he remained a Whig all his life. His course on political economy, in which he mostly followed Adam Smith, exercised considerable power over the young men who were to establish the *Edinburgh Review*: Sydney Smith, Jeffery, Brougham and Francis Horner – the last named probably his most fervent admirer; and it was with this group that Palmerston and especially Henry Petty (Lansdowne) were quite close. For Stewart *see DNB*, XVII; J. Clive, *Scotch Reviewers. The Edinburgh Review 1802–1815* (1957), esp. pp. 24–5, 108; Sir A. Grant, *The Story of Edinburgh University*, vol. 2 (1884), pp. 340–2.

11 R. Blake, *Disraeli* (1969 edition) p. 279.

12 F. C. Mather, *Public Order in the Age of the Chartists* (Manchester, 1959), p. 33.

13 Cf. R. Blake, *Disraeli*, p. 280: 'We have already discussed the fear of revolution as a cause of the repeal of the Corn Laws. This element in early Victorian politics is often forgotten, but it was very important. The great Whig noblemen with their cosmopolitan London outlook were more aware of the danger than the provincial gentry. They knew Europe and saw what was happening there. To them the Reform Bill and free trade were necessary concessions made in order to avoid a revolutionary alliance between Manchester and the mob.' Elie Halévy provided a well-known statement of the problem in *A History of the English People in 1815* (1924), book III, pp. 339–514. Halévy's emphasis upon religion as a conservative force in English society has been discussed by E. J. Hobsbawm, 'Methodism and the Threat of Revolution in Britain', *Labouring Men* (1964), pp. 23–33. The literature on the subject is now considerable.

14 His actual words were: 'For, admitting that some of our squires and landlords are vultures with iron bowels, and that their hardness and severity is a great discouragement to the tenant . . .' *A Word to the Wise or an Exhortation to the Roman Catholic Clergy of Ireland* (1749) in *The Works of George Berkeley*, vol. 6 (edited by T. E. Jessop, 1953). p. 243.

15 M. W. Cahill, 'Peerage Creations and the Changing Character of the British nobility 1750–1850', *Engl. H. Rev.*, XCVI, no. 379 (April 1981), pp. 259–84; and see also A. S. Turberville, *The House of Lords in the Age of Reform, 1784–1837* (1958), *passim*.

16 See the Table on p. 368 in D. Large, 'The House of Lords and Ireland in the Age of Peel, 1832–1850', *Irish H. Studies*, IX, no. 36 (September 1955), pp. 367–99.

17 By Dr Large for instance, in the article cited above, note 16 at p. 379. This is not to suggest a greater weight in Tory policy than the Orange faction actually had in the thirties and forties, but it is to insist upon the general impact of a continuous criticism on more moderate attitudes in helping to effect a steady attrition of principle.

18 'The House of Lords and Ireland', p. 368.

19 *History of the English People in 1815* (1924), book I, p. 174. On the same page Halévy repeats John Wilkes' prediction that the multiplication of peerages would make the House of Lords the 'deadweight' of the Constitution.

20 Bagehot, *The English Constitution*, ch. 4 'The House of Lords'.

21 *Hansard*, 3rd ser. xcv, col. 988 (13 December 1847).

22 'The British Constitution' in K. Marx, *Surveys from Exile. Political Writings*, vol. 2 (edited by D. Fernbach, 1973), pp. 281–2. In the German original Marx made the distinction between the '*herrschenden* (ruling) Bourgeoisie' and the '*offiziell regierenden* (governing) Grundaristokratie'. (Marx-Engels, *Werke*, XI, p. 95). I owe this reference to Mr Monty Johnstone.

   The Succession Duty was introduced by Gladstone when Chancellor of the Exchequer in the Budget of 1853. Hitherto legacy duty had been confined to personal property and was not paid on real property, a matter that was a constant complaint of the well-to-do middle-class community. The 1853 proposal was that in future the legacy duty should apply to both real and personal property. 'It was', wrote Morley, 'the first rudimentary breach in the ramparts of the territorial system . . .' and it aroused a storm of protest from the landowning groups in both Houses: J. Morley, *The Life of William Ewart Gladstone*, vol. 1 (1903), book IV, ch. 2.

23 Marx, 'The British Constitution', in *Surveys from Exile*, p. 282.

24 The business interests of the landed aristocracy have been well documented. See, for general surveys, F. M. L. Thompson, *English Landed Society in the Nineteenth Century* (1963), and J. T. Ward and R. G. Wilson (eds.), *Land and Industry* (1971). For examples of more detailed regional studies: J. T. Ward, 'West Riding Landowners and the Corn Laws', *Engl. H. Rev.*, 81 (April 1966), pp. 256–72; B. A. Holderness, 'Landlords Capital Formation in East Anglia, 1750–1870' *Econ. H. Rev.* 2nd ser. xxv, no. 3 (1972), pp. 434–47; E. Richards, *Leviathan of Wealth: the Sutherland Fortune in the Industrial Revolution* (1973).

25 This is now a commonplace of historical writing. See the review article by Sheldon Rothblatt, 'Some Recent Writings in British Political History, 1832–1914', *J. Mod. History*, vol. 55, no. 3 (September 1983), pp. 484–99. Analysis of the 1832 Reform Act has revealed quite different assumptions from those accepted by Whig or Whiggish historians. Cf. D. C. Moore's comments on 1832: 'If the Act is considered as a whole, and if its various provisions are related to actual happenings on the contemporary political scene, it becomes obvious that the members of the Grey Ministry were not trying to transfer political power from the aristocracy and gentry to the 'new middle class'. Nor were they trying to create an individualistic electorate. Rather, they were trying to arrest the loss of political power of the landed interest. And they were also trying to arrest the collapse of those traditional communities, urban as well as rural, through which social discipline had been channelled: 'Political Morality in Mid-Nineteenth Century England: Concepts, Norms, Violations', *Victorian Studies*, XIII, no. 1 (September 1969), pp. 5–36, p. 18. Later in the same article (p. 19) Moore reprinted the statement, by now much quoted, that Lord John Russell

made in the House of Commons, 21 November 1837 (col. 107): 'at the time the Reform Bill passed, I stated my belief that it must necessarily give a preponderance to the landed interest; and, although it may be deemed that such a preponderance has been somewhat unduly given, I still think that a preponderance in favour of that interest tends to the stability of the general institutions of the country'. See also D. C. Moore, 'Concession or Cure: the Sociological Premises of the First Reform Act', *Hist. J.* IX, no. 1 (1966), pp. 39–59.

26 A point made also by Prest, *Lord John Russell*, quoting G. B. A. Finlayson, 'The Politics of Municipal Reform, 1835', *Engl. H. Rev.*, LXXXI, no. 321 (1966), pp. 673–92.

27 H. W. Carless Davis, *The Age of Grey and Peel* (Oxford, 1929), p. 249. Josef Redlich, a European scholar untroubled by English inhibitions, saw very clearly how the 1835 municipal reform was diluted by the opposition of the landed interest: 'A comparison of the Bill with the Act, coupled with a perusal of the debate in both Houses of Parliament will afford the politician and the sociologist a most interesting study in the art of legislation as practised in England. Certainly the Act is a very favourable specimen of political compromises'. *Local Government in England*, vol. 1 (1903), pp. 127–8. D. N. Chester, *The English Administrative System 1780–1870* (Oxford, 1981) p. 328 ff. gives a clear account of the provisions of the Municipal Corporations Act but fails to indicate how more elitist the Act was compared with the original Bill.

28 D. Fraser, *Urban Politics in Victorian England* (1979), Table 3, p. 124.

29 See the interesting analysis of 351 Lancashire textile employers in A. Howe, *The Cotton Masters 1830–1860* (Oxford, 1984).

30 This is a much debated matter. For a critical survey of some of the literature, see, J. Hart, 'Nineteenth-Century Social Reform: a Tory Interpretation of History' *Past and Present*, 31 (1965), pp. 39–61; reprinted in *Essays in Social History* (edited by M. W. Flinn and T. C. Smout, Oxford, 1974); and for some later views, the essays in G. Sutherland (ed.), *Studies in the Growth of Nineteenth-Century Government* (1972).

31 The pages of the weekly *Economist* are as good a guide as there is to be found for the policy requirements of the business classes from the mid-1840s on. See also J. E. Thorold Rogers, *Cobden and Modern Political Opinion* (1873), which offers an excellent statement of moderate radical views in the middle decades of the century.

32 The two books by W. Strange mentioned in the text have not so far been located in any British library. They were summarised in some detail in the *Northern Star*, 8 July and 29 July 1848. There is an important pioneering article by W. D. Rubinstein, 'The End of "Old Corruption" in Britain, 1780–1860', *Past and Present*, 101 (November 1983), pp. 55–86. The decline of patronage is discussed in ch. 1 of H. Parris, *Constitutional Bureaucracy* (1969).

33 J. E. Thorold Rogers, *Cobden and Modern Political Opinion*, ch. 3; J. Morley, *The Life of Richard Cobden* (1906), ch. XXXVII. The quotation in Rogers omits the words in the middle of the passage – 'I would take Adam Smith in hand – I would not go beyond him, I would have no politics in it . . .' For a general discussion of the politics of the land question, F. M. L. Thompson, 'Land and Politics in England in the Nineteenth Century', *Trans. Roy. H. Soc.*, 5th ser. XV (1965), pp. 23–44; B. English and J. Saville, *Strict Settlement: A Guide for Historians* (Hull, 1983), pp. 105–15.

34 P. Richards, 'The State and Early Industrial Capitalism: the Case of the Handloom Weavers', *Past and Present*, no. 83 (May 1979), pp. 91–115.

35 M. Bowley, *Nassau Senior and Classical Economics* (1937). Edited extracts from this volume are in A. W. Coats (ed.), *The Classical Economists and Economic Policy* (1971), ch. 2 and esp. pp. 68–77. Senior was on the 1832 Commission of Enquiry into the Poor Laws and was particularly opposed to relief partly for the able-bodied. He later changed his mind, for which see his article, 'Poor Law Reform', *Edin. Rev.*, CXLIV (October 1841), pp. 1–44. See also the introduction by J. Saville to *Working Conditions in the Victorian Age: Debates on the Issue from Nineteenth-Century Critical Journals* (1973), pp. 1–19.

36 The first quotation is from G. Woodbridge, *The Reform Bill of 1832* (New York, 1970), p. 79 and the second, N. Gash, *Aristocracy and People* (1979), p. 166.

37 M. Blaug, 'The Myth of the Old Poor Law and the Making of the New', *J. Econ. H.*, XXIII, no. 2 (1963), pp. 151–84; *idem*, 'The Poor Law Report Re-examined', *J. Econ. H.*, XXIV, no. 2 (1964), pp. 229–45. For an inadequate critique of Blaug, not accepted by the present author, J. S. Taylor, 'The Mythology of the Old Poor Law', *J. Econ. H.*, XXIX, no. 2 (1969), pp. 292–7; and see also the introduction by S. G. and E. O. A. Checkland (eds.), *The Poor Law Report of 1834* (1974).

38 Quoted in the introduction by S. G. and E. O. A. Checkland (eds.), *The Poor Law Report of 1834*, p. 42.

39 The standard history is C. L. Mowat, *The Charity Organisation Society 1869–1913* (1961). The Fabians were the most incisive of the critics of the C. O. S: see Mrs Charlotte Townshend, *The Case Against the Charity Organisation Society* (1911).

40 One of the earliest academic discussions of the problem of labour adaptation which drew for many of its ideas upon the final section of Marx's *Capital*, vol. 1 was W. Sombart, *Der Moderne Kapitalismus*, First vol./second half (1924) pp.785–835. There has not been an English translation. Weber had a number of comments, scattered through his writings, and Sombart's views were largely translated in F. L. Nussbaum's *History of Economic Institutions in Modern Europe: an Introduction to Der Moderne Kapitalismus of Werner Sombart* (New York, 1935). E. Furniss, *The Position of the Labourer in a System of Nationalism* (New York, 1920) was an interesting pioneering analysis; and for the considerable writings on the subject see the bibliographies to A. W. Coats, 'Changing Attitudes to Labour in the Mid-Eighteenth Century', *Econ. H. Rev*, 2nd ser. 1 (1958), pp. 35–51 and E. P. Thompson, 'Time, Work-Discipline, and Industrial Capitalism', *Past and Present*, no. 38 (December 1967), pp. 56–97; both articles are reprinted in M. W. Flinn and T. C. Smout, *Essays in Social History* (1974).

41 For the legal background, R. Y. Hedges and A. Winterbottom, *A Legal History of Trade Unionism* (1930), and K. W. Wedderburn, *Cases and Materials on Labour Law* (Cambridge, 1967); and for an excellent account of a major strike around the mid-century, H. I. Dutton and J. E. King, *Ten Per Cent and No Surrender. The Preston Strike 1853–1854* (Cambridge, 1981).

42 This much neglected subject was admirably discussed by Daphne Simon many years ago, in 'Master and Servant', *Democracy and the Labour Movement* (edited by J. Saville, 1954), pp. 160–200; but it deserves a more extended treatment. There is some material in C. R. Dobson, *Masters and Journeymen* (1980).

43 This formulation excludes factory discipline on which the literature is considerable. The classic introduction is J. L. and B. Hammond, *The Town Labourer. 1760–1832. The New Civilisation* (1917), esp. ch. 2. For a more

recent, and more analytical account, S. Pollard, *The Genesis of British Management. A Study of the Industrial Revolution in Great Britain* (1965). For a case study in great detail, the articles by N. McKendrick: 'Josiah Wedgwood and Factory Displine', *Hist. J.*, IV, no. 1 (1961) pp. 30–55; 'Josiah Wedgwood and Thomas Bentley: An Inventor – Entrepreneur Partnership in the Industrial Revolution', *Trans. Roy. H. Soc.*, 5th ser. V (1964), pp. 1–33; 'Josiah Wedgwood and Cost Accounting in the Industrial Revolution' *Econ. H. Rev.* 2nd ser, XXIII, no. 1 (April 1970), pp. 45–67.

44 The most vivid account of the movement for factory reform, which gives proper place to the involvement of working people, is C. Driver, *Tory Radical. The Life of Richard Oastler* (N.Y. 1946); and the best contemporary account was by 'Alfred' [Samuel Kydd] *The History of the Factory Movement*, 2 vols. (1857; reprinted in one volume, New York, 1966). On the economic consequences of the factory legislation, M. Blaug, 'The Productivity of Capital in the Lancashire Cotton Industry during the Nineteenth Century', *Econ. H. Rev.*, 2nd ser. XIII, no. 3 (April 1961), pp. 358–81 who noted that 'once the agitation over the Ten Hours' Bill had died down, child labour once again grew faster than adult labour and this trend continued until 1874' (p. 368). Blaug further commented that labour costs per unit fell steadily down to 1860, and this in spite of a twenty per cent reduction in hours worked.

45 *Hansard*, 3rd ser. CLXI, col. 1511 (6 March 1861).

46 Morley, *Gladstone*, vol. 1, pp. 297–8.

47 As his biographer wrote: 'Lord John had never been businesslike, and when he became prime minister, he escaped from the discipline of a department. Wherever he went, papers were mislaid, letters became separated from the enclosures to which they referred, and laboriously compiled statistics were lost and had to be copied again . . . Official boxes were left lying around for days on end when Lord John forgot to give them to the messenger, and papers which ought to have been in one box turned up in another.' Prest, *Lord John Russell*, pp. 345, 347.

48 *ibid.*, p. 348.

49 For a detailed account of the relations between the Sovereign and the Cabinet, W. I. Jennings, *Cabinet Government* (1947), ch. XI ss. 3 and 4; le May, *Victorian Constitution*, p. 73 ff. In addition to foreign affairs, Queen Victoria also considered the Army and the Church as among her special prerogatives.

50 Quoted in le May, *Victorian Constitution*, p. 70. From June 1848 Prince Albert kept a dossier of Palmerston's misdoings: B. Connell, *Regina v. Palmerston* (1962), pp. 78–80. D. Southgate, *The Most English Minister* (1966), p. 243, suggests that Palmerston might not have survived at the Foreign Office after 1848 had the Palace tried less hard to get him out. See also J. P. Mackintosh, *The British Cabinet* (3rd edition, 1977), pp. 126–7.

51 Palmerston's dismissal came as a result of his verbal approval of Louis Napoleon's *coup d'etat*, in a conversation with the French ambassador. The constitutional position of his dismissal is set out in Jennings, *Cabinet Government*, p. 157 ff. See also Ashley, *Palmerston*, I, pp. 289–299; and for the general background Prest, *Lord John Russell*, p. 331 ff.

52 All British prime ministers of the nineteenth century, given the perennial unrest and potential insurgency of the Irish situation, were inevitably involved more or less continually in Irish matters. See the interesting discussion of the first eighteen months of Peel's government, 1841–2, in Gash, *Sir Robert Peel*, p.

394 ff. The Russell papers in the PRO are in 30/20/7A, B and C; his letters in the Clarendon Collection, Bodleian Library, for July 1847 to December 1848 are in Box 43, Clarendon's replies in the Out Letter books.

53 L. Radzinowicz, 'New Departures in Maintaining Public Order in the Face of Chartist Disturbances', *Cambridge Law J.* (1960), pp. 51–80. Most of his examples refer to the early years of Chartism, and in particular to 1839–40. Much of the material in this article was incorporated in *History of the English Criminal Law, and its Administration*, vol. 4 (1968). There is now a growing literature on the organisation and methods of the internal security forces in Britain before 1850: C. Emsley, *Policing and its Context, 1750–1850* (1983); and the references below, p. 19 ff.

54 Sir George Grey (1799–1882) was educated privately and at Oriel College, Oxford. He was called to the bar in 1826 and two years later succeeded to the baronetcy on the death of his father. His uncle was the first Earl Grey of the 1832 Reform Bill. Sir George Grey held various positions in the Melbourne ministries, and he became Home Secretary in 1846. He was to hold this position as Secretary of State with only a few interruptions for nearly twenty years. His parliamentary career ended in 1874. He had succeeded to a family estate at Falloden, Northumberland, on the death of an uncle in 1846, and it was here that he spent his last years. In 1884 Mandell Creighton published a *Memoir*, privately circulated; it was reprinted in 1901. Creighton also wrote the *DNB* entry.

Sir James Graham's life and work is in C. S. Parker, *Life and Letters of Sir James Graham, 1792–1861*, 2 vols. (1907).

55 Sir James Fitzjames Stephen, *A History of the Criminal Law of England*, vol. 1 (1883), p. 185.

56 There is a general survey in Sir E. Troup, *The Home Office* (1925); and a detailed study of the second half of the nineteenth century, with a useful account of the position in 1848, in J. Pellew, *The Home Office 1848–1914* (1982). Most of the relevant statements in the text are taken from this volume.

57 The standard work on Irish administration in the nineteenth century is R. B. McDowell, *The Irish Administration 1801–1914* (1964). See also the same author's *Public Opinion and Government Policy, 1801–1846* (1952) and V. T. H. Delany, *The Administration of Justice in Ireland* (4th ed. rev. C. Lysaght, Dublin, 1975); O. Macdonagh, *Early Victorian Government 1830–1870* (1977), ch. 10.

58 *Hansard*, 3rd Ser. LXXIV col. 857 (9 May 1844).

59 Pellew, *Home Office*, p. 3, is incorrect to suggest that the Parliamentary Under-Secretary always sat in the House of Commons, although this was usually the case. But there were exceptions. Sir Denis le Marchant, who lost his seat in the general election of 1847, was Parliamentary Under-Secretary until he resigned in May 1848: *DNB*, XI.

60 *SC on Miscellaneous Expenditures*, 1847–8, XVIII, part 1. Q. 4164 (19 May 1848). The last part of Grey's examination, relating to the clerks' experience, confirms the point made by A. J. Donajgrodzki, 'New Roles for Old: the Northcote-Trevelyan Report and the Clerks of the Home Office, 1822–48', in G. Sutherland (ed.) *Studies in the Growth of Nineteenth Century Government* (1972), namely, that the work of the H. O. clerks could not wholly be fitted into the intellectual/mechanical model of the 1854 Report.

61 *SC on Official Salaries*, 1850, XV. Q. 2880.

62 The details of official positions, with dates of appointment, together with a short

but useful introduction, are in J. Sainty, *Office Holders in Modern Britain. v. Home Office Officials 1782–1871* (1975).

63 Le Marchant (1795–1874) was the second son of a Peninsular war veteran. Educated at Eton and Trinity College, Cambridge, and called to the bar in 1823. In 1850 he became Clerk to the House of Commons, and retired in 1871: *DNB*, XI. George Cornewall Lewis (1806–63) was a most interesting man, with a considerable knowledge of Ireland. Educated at Christ Church, Oxford, and later called to the bar, he edited the *Edinburgh Review* 1853–5. He became Chancellor of the Exchequer in Palmerston's first administration 1855–8: *DNB*, XI; *The Times*, 4 November 1874.

64 For the Law Officers in England and Scotland, Mather, *Public Order*, pp. 46–8; Chester, *English Administrative System*, pp. 274–5.

65 Mather, *Public Order*, pp. 49–52.

66 Grey to Clarendon, 19 July 1848: HO 79/9.

67 Archibald Alison (1792–1867) was a son of the manse who accepted the office of Sheriff Deputy of Lanarkshire in 1834 at a salary of £1,400 a year. He had strong Tory prejudices. He became nationally known for his vigour and efficiency during the Chartist years. He was a prolific writer and published in ten volumes a *History of Europe from the Commencement of the French Revolution* (various editions from 1833); and a two-volume *Principles of Population and their Connection with Human Happiness* (1840), which is still of some interest to historians of ideas. His wife edited an autobiography in 1883: *DNB*, I.

68 S. and B. Webb, *English Local Government from the Revolution to the Municipal Corporations Act: Parish and County* (1906), estimated (p. 384, n. 2) that one quarter of the magistrates in England and Wales were Anglican clergymen. Eight English counties had a majority of clerical JPs. This was for the early 1830s. Warwickshire had 40 per cent in 1830 and 7 per cent in 1868: R. Quinault, 'The Warwickshire County Magistracy and Public Order, c. 1830–1870', in *Popular Protest and Public Order* (edited by R. Quinault and J. Stevenson, 1974), p. 189. The major fall in clerical representation was after 1850.

69 Bagehot, *English Constitution* ch. 4. Dr Philips has argued that the Home Office was always concerned with the social and political consequences of a too repressive policy towards disorderly groups or movements; and that the police were early recognised as a more flexible organisation for riot or crowd control than the Yeomanry or the military: the former being much more disliked by ordinary people than the latter. D. Philips, 'Riots and Public Order in the Black Country, 1835–1860', in *Popular Protest and Public Order* (edited by R. Quinault and J. Stevenson), p. 151.

70 J. Hart, 'Reform of the Borough Police, 1835–1856', *Engl. H. Rev.*, LXX no. 276 (July 1955), p. 243. On the matter of aid by the metropolitan police to local authorities, Ms Hart corrects C. Reith, *British Police and the Democratic Ideal* (Oxford, 1943), for the years before 1838 when she writes 'one must be careful not to exaggerate the number of men who were lent or transferred to municipal corporations' (p. 421). High charges were made for assistance, and there was a dislike of the Londoners for what was considered to be their arrogant attitudes. The attitude of Liverpool's Chief Constable in July 1848 was probably not untypical: for which see below, p. 153

71 Dr Quinault in his article, 'The Warwickshire County Magistracy . . .', suggests that the role of the Home Office in combating disorder, with the major exception

of London and a few provincial outbreaks, 'was a largely passive one' (p. 182). This is a generalisation not in any way supported by the Home Office files of 1848, and it may be doubted whether it can wholeheartedly be applied to earlier years. Cf. the testimony of Sir Denis le Marchant, Parliamentary Under-Secretary to the Home Office, who from the context was not limiting his remarks to May 1848: 'For instance, you have great correspondence with Ireland? – Very considerable correspondence with Ireland, but also still more correspondence with different parts of England. Every magistrate who feels alarmed at the state of his district, immediately applies to the Secretary of State for instruction.' *SC on Miscellaneous Expenditures*, 1847–8, XVIII, part I, Q. 2847.

72 For the bibliography of the law relating to unlawful assemblies and the powers of the magistracy, see below, p. 167 ff. The arming of special constables – outside Ireland – was never completely rejected, and there were occasions when deposits of arms were made in certain towns at times of crisis; but so far as the evidence goes, there was never an occasion when the special constables were armed: not even in the very serious situation of Liverpool in the summer of 1848. There were, however, decisions in 1839 which could have led to the arming of the special constables although whether it actually happened is not clear: *Copy of Lord John Russell's Letter to Magistrates in Sessions, to Mayors of Boroughs in Certain Counties Directing them how to Proceed for the Preservation of the Peace in Disturbed Districts.* 1839, XXXVIII, and see Mather, *Public Order*, pp. 81–2. After 10 April 1848, Col. Rowan, the senior metropolitan police commissioner, produced a memorandum which suggested putting the special constables on a more permanent basis: MEPO 2/65 (18 April 1848). The Duke of Wellington, who was always alarmist in these years, also suggested arming a section of the special constables. Neither suggestion was acted on.

73 The best introduction to the relations between the military and civil authorities is Mather, *Public Order*, ch. 5. The details in the text of the organisation of military districts in Britain are taken from Captain H. G. Hart, *The New Army List for 1848* (1848), pp. 319–21. General histories also contain relevant detail: C. M. Clode, *The Military Forces of the Crown*, 2 vols. (1869); J. S. Ormond, *Parliament and the Army 1642–1904* (Cambridge, 1933); S. E. Finer, *The Man on Horseback: the Role of the Military in Politics* (1962).

74 Sir William Warre was Commander in Chief of the Northern District until mid-August when he was demoted for what was felt to be his lack of firmness in dealing with the very disturbed situation of the summer and early autumn. Arbuthnot was appointed in his place, and the Northern District was extended to include the Midlands. For Arbuthnot, see *DNB*, I.

75 A. H. Graham, 'The Litchfield House Compact', *Irish H. Stud.*, XII (1960–1); see also R. B. McDowell, *Public Opinion and Government Policy in Ireland, 1801–1846* (1952), ch. 7; and the general conclusions in A. D. Kriegel, 'The Whig Government and Ireland 1830–1835' (Ph. D. Duke University, 1964; facsimile Ann Arbor, 1975).

76 'Had the Irish in England taken any part with the Chartists? They had grievances – they had sufferings – they had many causes of complaint. Did they join the Chartists? No; even the tradesmen of Dublin, whose combinations he opposed at the peril of his life, even they rejected Chartism. Ireland had become tranquil; no more calumnies would be uttered against her upon that score. Her military force was diminshed, and why? Because the troops, which were necessary to struggle against rebellion, sedition, and treason in England, were

not required to maintain the good order which prevailed in Ireland'. *Hansard*, 3rd ser. LI (31 January 1840), col. 1014; reprinted, *The Speeches and Public Letters of the Liberator* (edited by M. F. Cusack, Dublin 1875), vol. 2, p. 21. There is a revealing comment in Napier's journal, 29 July 1839: 'If Lord John send for troops from Ireland, which I earnestly hope he will do, it is desirable that regiments which yet have the greatest number of Irishmen should be selected: the difference of religion and country offers additional guards for the soldier's fidelity': *Life and Opinions of General Sir Charles James Napier* (edited by Lieutenant-General Sir W. Napier, 1857), vol. 2, pp. 60–1.

77 *SC on Railways, Fifth Report* . . ., 1844, XI, Q. 1955.

78 There is a good deal of literature on the Yeomanry, of varying degrees of usefulness, Fox Maule (Secretary at War) had some informative comment on the Yeomanry in his evidence before the *SC on Army and Ordnance Expenditure*, 1850, X: 'The establishment of the Yeomanry does not belong to my department, it belongs to the Home Office entirely' Q. 1627. 'If the Yeomanry are wanted in aid of the Civil Power, the Secretary of State is the sole judge by whom they should be called out' Q. 1629. And when Fox Maule was asked whether it would be correct to describe the Yeomanry as an armed police force, he replied: 'It is no more a police force than the pensioners under the Home Office are a military force. I look upon it as a volunteer military body; I should not degrade it by calling it a police force' Q. 1641. The Yeomanry, when called out on service, operated under martial law. For background, see G. C. Ricardo, 'The Evolution of the Yeomanry' *Cavalry Journal*, II (1907), pp. 21–8; O. Teichman, 'The Yeomanry as an Aid to Civil Power, 1795–1867', *J. Soc. Army H. Research*, XIX (1940), pp. 75–91. Among the more useful local studies: Major G. Tylden, 'Yeomary in Berkshire' *ibid*, XXVIII (1950), pp. 96–101; L. E. Buckell, 'The Surrey Yeomanry Cavalry', *ibid*, XXVIII (1950), pp. 171–2. Mather, *Public Order* pp. 141–50, is as reliable as always.

79 The Napier quotation is in *The Life and Opinions of General Sir Charles James Napier*, vol. 2, p. 73. The full sentence reads: 'If the Chartists want a fight, they can be indulged without yeoman, who are over-zealous for cutting and slashing.' Russell was speaking in the House of Commons, *Hansard*, 3rd ser. XLII, col. 651 (27 April 1838).

80 HO 45/2410 part 1 (n.d. April–June 1848?). The total numbers of Enrolled Pensioners were given in *Accounts and Papers. Army Commissariat*, 1849, XXXII, p. 107: Great Britain, 1847–8: 8, 720; 1848–9: 9,394, and in Ireland for the same years the figures were 4,600 and 5,446.

81 *SC on Army and Ordnance Expenditure*, 1850, X, Q. 2165. For the administrative position Fox Maule occupied, see Olive Anderson, 'The Constitutional Position of the Secretary at War, 1642–1855', *J. Soc. Army H. Research*, XXXVI (1958), pp. 165–9.

82 The Duke of Alva (1508–83) arrived in the Netherlands in 1567, and his whole period as Captain-General was characterised by pillage and massacres. The savage atrocities in the towns of Mechelen, Zutphen and Naarden in 1572, and Haarlem in 1573 were especially horrific: G. Parker, *The Dutch Revolt* (1979), esp. chs. 2 and 3.

83 Most general histories provide surveys before 1700. The standard work of a few decades ago was E. Curtis, *History of Ireland* (6th edition, 1951). R. Bagwell, *Ireland under the Stuarts*, 3 vols. (1909–16), is a straightforward political history of the seventeenth century. There is an interesting essay by Owen Dudley

Edwards in *Celtic Nationalism* (edited by O. D. Edwards *et al.* 1968). J. O'Beirne Ranelagh, *A Short History of Ireland* (Cambridge, 1983), is now probably the most useful summary introduction, while E. Strauss, *Irish Nationalism and British Democracy* (1951), is still the most stimulating.

84 Ranelagh, *Short History*, p. 69. An estimated 120,000 left Ireland between 1690 and 1730.

85 The Irish House of Commons passed, without opposition, an elaborate bill against all Catholics, one clause of which was that all unregistered priests, when discovered, should be branded on the cheek with a red-hot iron. The Irish Privy Council changed the punishment to castration, and forwarded the bill to England for ratification. This was in 1719. The English ministers restored the penalty of branding: Lecky, *History of Ireland*, vol. 1, pp. 162–3. There is a short study by M. Wall, *The Penal Laws* (1961). Apparently there was a castration law against Jesuits in contemporary Sweden.

86 For the economic development of Ireland in the eighteenth century: G. O'Brien, *Economic History of Ireland in the Eighteenth Century* (Dublin, 1918); Conrad Gill, *The Rise of the Irish Linen Industry* (Oxford, 1925); J. C. Beckett, *The Making of Modern Ireland, 1603–1923* (1966), ch. 9; E. M. Johnston, *Ireland in the Eighteenth Century* (1974); and the essays and bibliographies in *Ireland and Scotland* (edited by T. M. Devine and D. Dickson, Edinburgh, 1983).

87 Lecky, *History of Ireland*, vol. 1, p. 282. For a general discussion of the corruption and misuse of Irish revenues by the English, *ibid*, p. 197 ff.

88 See T. M. Devine, 'The English Connection and Irish and Scottish Development in the Eighteenth Century', *Ireland and Scotland 1600–1850* (edited by T. M. Devine and D. Dickson) pp. 12–29.

89 The address is reprinted in full in Marquis of Normanby, *A Year of Revolution. From a Journal Kept in Paris in 1848*, vol. 1 (1857), pp. 287–90. For the political context of the Irish address, see below, Ch. 3.

90 The battle of Fontenoy was for long a *locus classicus* for military theorists. In the context of the present discussion the interesting question is the way the Irish contribution to the French victory has been described in English histories. Lecky, *History of England in the Eighteenth Century*, vol. 1 (1879), p. 420, wrote of the last effort of Saxe against the British which included the household troops of the French King and the Irish Brigade 'who were burning to avenge themselves on their oppressors. Their fiery charge was successful. The British column was arrested, shattered, and dissolved, and a great French victory was the result.' J. W. Fortescue, *History of the British Army*, vol. XI (1910), commented that the Irish Brigade 'which consisted of six battalions, was made up not of Irish only but of Scots and English also, desperate characters who went into action with a rope around their necks, and would fight like devils' (p. 118). The eleventh edition of the *Encyclopedia Britannica*, usually regarded as the most scholarly of all the twentieth-century editions, had only a passing reference to the Irish Brigade at Fontenoy, in spite of the fact that the account was long and detailed. Both editions of 1934 and 1957 of the *Cambridge Modern History* have only passing references to Fontenoy and nothing about the Irish Brigade; and the new revised edition of *Chambers Encyclopedia* (1973) has half a column on the battle with the comment: 'A legend arose that the "Irish Brigade" saved the situation for France. This is incorrect; the credit is due to the Régiment Normandie and the French General Löwendahl.' Normanby, *A Year of Revolution*, referred to the Irish at Fontenoy as 'mercenaries' and this would be

the general attitude of the English upper classes in the nineteenth century. A modern Irish historian, author of *A Short History of Ireland* (J. O'Beirne Ranelagh), found space to note that at the battle of Fontenoy the Irish Brigade 'led by Lord Clare, routed the Coldstream Guards and turned the battle into a French victory' (p. 73). This was written in 1983, and the 'legend' is apparently still alive.

91 The literature on the Union is considerable. Lecky, *History of Ireland*, devoted most of his five volumes to the decades immediately preceeding 1800. The constitutional history is discussed in E. M. Johnston, *Great Britain and Ireland 1760-1800* (Edinburgh, 1963). Useful earlier histories are W. O'Connor Morris (a self-described Irish liberal who was against Home Rule), *Ireland from 1798 to 1898* (1898); J. R. Fisher, *The End of the Irish Parliament* (1911); H. M. Hyde, *The Rise of Castlereagh* (1933); P. S. O'Hegarty, *A History of Ireland Under the Union, 1801-1922* (1852). Irish financial history is in general much neglected, although see J. Kiernan, *The Financial Administration of Ireland, 1782-1817* (Dublin, 1925); R. B. McDowell, *Public Opinion and Government Policy in Ireland, 1801-1846* (1953).

92 The literature on Ireland is still limited. E. Stokes, *The English Utilitarians and India* (Oxford, 1959), had some interesting suggestions, and there was a pioneering article from R. D. Collinson Black, 'Economic Policy in Ireland and India at the time of J. S. Mill', *Econ. H. Rev.* 2nd ser. xxi, no. 2 (August 1968), pp. 321-36. India is much better served: A. K. Bagchi, 'De-industrialisation in India in the Nineteenth Century: some Theoretical Implications', *J. Devl. Studies*, xii, no. 2 (1976), pp. 135-64; M. Vicziany,' The De-industrialisation of India in the Nineteenth Century: a Methodological Critique of A. K. Bagchi', *Indian Economic and Social History Review* xiv no. 2 (1979), pp. 105-46; A. K. Bagchi, 'A Reply', *ibid*, pp. 147-61. For a general survey, R. Chandavarkar, 'Industrialisation in India before 1947', *Modern Asian Studies*, 19, no. 3 (1985), pp. 623-68.

93 The administrative structures of Ireland after the Union are set out in detail in R. B. MacDowell, *The Irish Administration, 1801-1914* (1964). For the Viceroy's household accounts, see below, pp. 71-2. In May 1844 Joseph Hume introduced a motion for the abolition of the office of Lord Lieutenant of Ireland, and the debate is useful for its discussion of administration and organisation in Ireland. For the domination of the English – as against the Irish – in the holding of office, see the speech by Captain R. Bernal, col. 841 ff. The whole debate is in *Hansard*, 3rd ser. lxxiv (9 May 1844), col. 834 ff.

94 Strauss, *Irish Nationalism*, ch. 8.

95 There is a description of the offices of the Chief Secretary and the Under-Secretary in *Reports of Committees of Enquiry into Public Offices* . . . 1854, xxvii, p. 67 ff.

96 De Beaumont, *L'Irlande*, vol. 1 (1839), p. 198; A. de Tocqueville, *Journeys to England and Ireland*, p. 137. For a commentary, see S. Drescher, *Tocqueville and England* (Cambridge, Mass., 1964), esp. ch. 6, 'Ireland 1835: the Alienation of Aristocracies'.

97 The quotation in the text is from evidence before the *SC on Jury System (Ireland)* 1874, ix, Q. 1294; and for a more extended discussion of the jury system, see chapter 6.

98 C. S. Parker, *Sir Robert Peel, From his Private Papers*, vol. 1 (1891), p. 282.

99 Cf. the comment by O. MacDonagh, *Early Victorian Government 1830-1870*

(1977), p. 181: 'By 1850 the local authorities [in Ireland] had been shorn of very many of even their surviving functions and replaced by national and centralised organisations. Whereas the first stage in administrative reform in English local government represented an attempt to broaden electorates and break Anglican and squirearchical monopolies, the equivalent phase in Ireland was marked by the passage of the old and almost all the new functions of government from local to central control.'

100 See the discussion in J. J. Tobias, *Crime and Industrial Society in the Nineteenth Century* (1972), part 1; and the more detailed analysis and commentary in V. A. C. Gatrell and T. B. Hadden, 'Criminal Statistics and their Interpretation', E. A. Wrigley (ed.), *Nineteenth Century Society. Essays on the Use of Quantitative Methods for the Study of Social Data* (Cambridge, 1972), pp. 336–441.

101 See above, n. 13; and for an introduction to some of the historical problems, M. I. Thomis and P. Holt, *Threats of Revolution in Britain 1789–1848* (1977).

102 *Return of Persons Killed or Wounded in Affrays with the Constabulary Force in Ireland*, 1830–1, VIII, p. 403 quoted in C. Broeker, *Rural Disorder and Police Reform in Ireland, 1812–36* (1970), p. 115. For a vivid, and sober, contemporary account of the problem, including the matter of faction-fighting, see H. D. Inglis, *Ireland in 1835. A Journey throughout Ireland . . .* 2 vols. (3rd ed. 1835), vol. 1, ch. XI.

103 Smith O'Brien requested the return on 13 March 1846; the figures were published in *Accounts and Papers. Return of Numbers of Persons who Have Lost their Lives in Affrays with, or Otherwise by, the Constabulary in Ireland*, 1846, XXXV, p. 237.

104 *Accounts and Papers. Crime; Police*, 1849, XLIV, p. 3.

105 C. Townshend, *Political Violence in Ireland. Government and Resistance since 1848* (Oxford, 1983), p. 21.

106 pp. 312–3. Cornewall Lewis included a footnote, indicated in the quotation in the text by (x), which referred to the impossibility of the labourer living by wages alone, and which thereby accounted for the immoderate rents they were prepared to pay for very small plots of land. He denied (p. 335) that Irish peasants were more ignorant or illiterate than peasants elsewhere; there was a common deficiency of education among peasants of all kinds. His own answer to the Irish problem (p. 336) was that 'the true cause of the want of employment is the subdivision of the land, and the absence of a class of capitalist cultivators'.

107 L. A. Clarkson, 'The Writing of Irish Economic and Social History since 1968', *Econ. H. Rev.*, Second ser. XXXIII, no. 1 (February 1980), p. 103.

108 W. A. Maguire, *The Downshire Estates in Ireland 1801–1845* (Oxford, 1872), p. 78. The figures for income from rent, quoted in the text, are from ch. 2.

109 There were a number of variations upon this theme. It was commonly argued that the Presbyterianism of the North and its accompanying social attitudes contrasted very favourably with the attitudes encouraged by Catholicism. Froude, later in the century, was firm in his belief that the Irish (save the Presbyterians in the North) 'were innately incapable of self-government': A. Wyatt, 'Froude, Lecky and 'the humblest Irishman', *Irish H. Stud.*, 19, no. 75 (March 1975), p. 263. Inglis, *Ireland in 1834*, denied the argument that linked poverty with Catholicism: 'I have some experience of Catholic countries; and I have found nothing to warrant the belief, that misery is always the accompaniment of Popery; or that, in order to be provident, and industrious, and happy, one must be a Protestant', vol. 1, p. 218. Much more common were

the ideas of a disillusioned liberal, writing in 1838: 'If then, in addition to these differences, quite irreconcilable in their *nature*, we consider their present state of semi-barbarism (our politicians appear *not* to consider, or do not know, that the Irish are, as a people, centuries behind England in their civilisation) it is quite clear that the claim, on their account, of our laws is absurd, and if granted, would be mischievous': Mancuniensis, *Desultory Remarks on Ireland in 1838, containing reasons why an English Reformer has changed his Opinions of the Irish Community and of Irish Politics* (1838), p. 26.

110 L. Perry Curtis Jnr, *Apes and Angels. The Irishman in Victorian Caricature* (1971), p. 37. The quotation in the text occurs in ch. 4 'Simianizing the Irish Celt'. A review by R. B. McDowell of P. O'Farrell's *Ireland's English Question: Anglo-Irish Relations, 1534–1930* (1972) suggested that a too monolithic approach was being suggested and that 'if harsh stereotypes of Irishmen were current in nineteenth-century England, ugly stereotypes of some English groups, could easily be assembled from *Punch*', *Irish H. Stud.*, XVIII, no. 72 (September 1973), p. 628. By other groups Dr McDowell could only mean the Jewish people or more likely those whom the Victorian propertied classes referred to as 'the great unwashed' or 'the Residuum'. It can be agreed that class prejudice in the nineteenth century was as virulent among most upper-class and middle-class Englishmen as was their racist prejudice against the Irish, but the one important difference was that the Irish were always more difficult to handle, and more threatening to the social order, and therefore more to the front in the public mind.

111 Peel to Leveson Gower, 14 August 1829 (Peel Papers, BM Add MSS. 40337), quoted Broeker, *Rural Disorder and Police Reform*, p. 188.

112 For Peel's reforms, Broeker, ch. 4; Gash, *Mr. Secretary Peel* (1961), p. 167 ff.

113 *Hansard*, 3rd ser. XXX, col. 1003 (26 August 1835).

114 Evidence of Major-General Sir Duncan MacGregor to *SC of House of Lords . . . the Consequences of Extending the Functions of the Constabulary in Ireland to the Suppression or Prevention of Illicit Distillation . . .* 1854, X, Qs. 1495 ff. App. p. 285, gives the numerical data on the Irish Constabulary and stipendiary magistrates from 1840.

115 Engels to Marx, 23 May 1856: Marx-Engels, *Ireland and the Irish Question*, p. 93.

116 A. Somerville, *The Whistler at the Plough . . . with Letters from Ireland*, vol. I. (Manchester, 1852), p. 437.

117 There was a constant stream of verbal and written criticism of the Mulgrave administration throughout its years of office. For an example, see [H. H. Joy] *Letter to the Right Hon. Lord Lyndhurst on the Appointment of Sheriffs in Ireland under the Earl of Mulgrave. By a Barrister* (1838), 94p. The issue the pamphlet centred upon was the appointment of Catholic Sheriffs against the advice of the Lord Chancellor and a specified number of judges. The most extended attack on Mulgrave was in a Select Committee of the House of Lords which the Orange peers were able to persuade the House of Lords to set up to enquire into matters of crime in Ireland. The voting to establish the committee was close, and came about because a number of Conservative peers, who normally would not support the Orangemen, were themselves becoming concerned about the liberal tendencies of the Mulgrave administration. On the committee the Orange peers were in considerable strength, and their questioning was so hostile and unpleasant that a considerable scandal was created; and the Select Committee, after accumulating two large volumes of evidence, never produced

a report. For an example of the bitterness the whole episode encouraged, see the exchanges in the Lords, *Hansard*, 3rd ser. XLVII, (18 April 1839) col. 217 ff.

118 *SC of House of Lords Appointed to Enquire into the State of Ireland in Respect of Crime* ... 1839, XI and XII. See the evidence of W. Fausset, Provost of Sligo, Qs 2268 ff., and especially Q 2611 ff. which discussed the Viceroy's visit to Sligo.

119 *Hansard*, 3rd ser. XCV (9 December 1847), col. 870.

120 Quoted in Broeker, *Rural Disorder and Police Reform*, p. 222. Colonel Duncan MacGregor, who had been seven months in office in the Irish Constabulary, confirmed before the *SC of the House of Lords* of 1839 that the only secret society members of the police were allowed to join was 'the Society of Freemasons', Q. 1436, 29 April 1839.

121 Most of the material in the text has been taken from the article 'Freemasonry', *New Catholic Encyclopedia* (Washington D.C., 1967), vol. VI.

122 *Reports from Commissioners. Constabulary (Ireland)*, 1866, XXXIV, p. 13.

123 *ibid.* p. 14. In 1886 there was published a revealing account of service in the Royal Irish Constabulary by an ex-Sergeant-Major who had clearly enjoyed his years in the police force. Writing of the officer class he emphasised that service was usually the way in to county society, and that for the sons of the Anglican clergy and for the middle-class landed gentry the employment opportunities were of considerable importance: M. Brophy, *Sketches of the Royal Irish Constabulary*, (1886).

124 T. Gray, *The Orange Order* (1972), p. 132.

125 This is generally accepted. Thomas Drummond, who was cross-examined several times by the House of Lords SC on Crime in June 1839 made this one of his important points throughout his evidence. See his statements on the general decrease in crime 1836-8 in spite of his belief that the condition of the peasantry had deteriorated (Q. 13135).

126 There do not appear to have been any serious problems of army morale during the 1840s, but E. H. Spiers, *The Army and Society 1815-1914* (1980), p. 768, quotes the significant incident involving the 87th Foot, an overwhelmingly Catholic regiment which traditionally marched to the RC chapel on Sundays with its band playing Irish airs. When the regiment was stationed in Ulster in 1830 the playing of music was forbidden on the grounds that it was provocative. There developed much bad feeling on both sides, and on 4 October there was a brawl between members of the regiment and local Orangemen. On 10 October six companies at Newry refused to march to chapel without their music. Discipline was restored, but the incident remained in the memory of army command. On 23 May 1843 Sir H. Hardinge wrote to the Home Secretary citing the insubordination of the 87th and warning against the deployment of soldiers within earshot of the demagogues and priests at political meetings in Ireland (p. 79). The background to this comment was the rapidly developing Repeal agitation, for which see K. B. Nowlan, *The Politics of Repeal* (1965), ch. 2.

127 The details of the military establishment in Dublin are in McDowell, *Irish Administration*, p. 15. The figures of the distribution of the General Staff are taken from *Accounts and Papers, Army Estimates ... from 1 April 1848 to 31 March, 1849*, 1847-8, XL, pp. 46-52.

128 *Second Report from SC on Army and Ordnance Expenditure*, 1849, IX, Q. 6610 (1 June 1849). The details of barracks in each county are given on p. 850 ff.

129 W. E. H. Lecky, *Leaders of Public Opinion in Ireland*, vol. 2 (1903), pp. 99-100. When Lecky discussed municipal reform in the 1830s he pointed out that 'not a

single Catholic had sat on the corporation of Dublin, though it had been open to them for forty years, and it was now a centre of ultra-Tory and ultra-Protestant politics', p. 159–60.

130 McDowell, *Irish Administration*, ch. IX.

131 Peel Papers, BM Add. MSS 40211, quoted Broeker, *Rural Disorder and Police Reform*, p. 43. The details of the 1815 enquiry into the magistracy are given on p. 42.

132 Legal history is not very advanced in Irish historical writing and there is needed a social history of the magistracy, and much beside. Broeker has a good deal of interesting material scattered through his *Rural Disorder and Police Reform*, and there is a mass of information to be excavated from parliamentary papers; for which see the references in note 134 below and Chapter 6.

133 Redlich and Hirst, *Local Government in England*, vol. I, p. 204.

134 It was evidently always difficult to ascertain precisely the property qualifications of those who came, or those who could be expected to come, within the terms of the jury legislation. All subsequent enquiries in the second half of the nineteenth century made this point, among their many other criticisms. See the evidence to the *SC on Jury System (Ireland)* 1874, IX, and especially that of John Leahy, chairman of the County of Limerick, Q. 1275 ff. The most useful compendium on the qualifications, duties etc. of juries, and the standard work at the time of its publication, is W. Forsyth, *History of Trial by Jury* (1852). The Irish jury system in the nineteenth century was always under discussion, both at parliamentary enquiry and in the press. For examples of the latter, 'Trial by Jury', *Law Journal*, 12 April 1872, pp. 238–9; 'Irish Jury Laws', *Irish Law Times*, 24 September 1881, pp. 500–1.

135 *SC on Jury System*, 1873, XV, Q. 1 ff.: evidence of C. H. Hemphill, QC; 1874, IX, Q. 1275 ff.

136 The foregoing paragraph is based mainly on *Accounts and Papers. Tables Showing the Number of Criminal Offenders committed for Trial or Bailed for Appearance at the Assizes and Sessions in each County in the Year 1848*, 1849, XLIV. The quotation in the text is on p. 5. See also *Accounts and Papers, Criminal Offences (Ireland)* 1852–3, LXXXI, esp. p. 97.

137 *SC on Jury System*, 1874, IX, Q. 1291.

138 ibid., 1873, XV, Q. Q. 58.

139 ibid., 1874, IX, Q. 1294.

140 ibid., Q. 1350.

141 *SC of House of Lords appointed to enquire into the State of Ireland in respect of Crime* . . . QS. 13572–13918 (21 June 1839). Michael O'Loghlen (1789–1842) matriculated at Dublin University 1805, entered the Middle Temple 1809, and was called to the Irish Bar in 1811. He was seventeen years on the circuit, and was one of the first Catholics to be appointed KC. In the Whig administrations he was first Solicitor-General and then Attorney-General. He was appointed Baron of the Exchequer in 1836, the first Catholic to be called to the Bench since Emancipation. He became Master of the Rolls in 1837.

142 ibid., Q. 13626 ff. O'Loghlen's letter of 24 January 1836, issued when he was Attorney-General, was reprinted in *Accounts and Papers. A Copy of the Instructions given to Crown Solicitors . . . respecting the challenging of Jurors in Crown Cases . . . 1842*, XXXVII.

143 *SC of House of Lords . . . Crime*, 1839, Q. 13581.

144 H. Paul, *History of Modern England*, vol. I (1904), p. 65. Clarendon's

correspondence during 1848 fully bears out Paul's generalisations.

145 *SC on Official Salaries*, 1850, XV, Qs. 410, 432.

146 'Palmerston subordinated every moral and ethical consideration to the task of upholding England's greatness. His policy towards France was determined by the economic and political rivalry between the English and French middle classes. With the full support of the English middle classes, Palmerston did all he could to hinder France's expansion': F. Fetjö, 'Europe on the Eve of the Revolution', *The Opening of an Era: 1848* (edited by F. Fetjö, 1948), p. 4.

147 A. B. Cunningham, 'Peel, Aberdeen and the *Entente Cordiale*', *Bull. Inst. H. Res.* XXX, no. 82 (November 1957), pp. 189–206, p. 191.

148 *ibid.*, p. 205; see also D. Johnson, *Guizot* (1963), p. 275 ff. For a brief general account W. L. Langer, *Political and Social Upheavals 1832–1852* (1969), ch. 9 section 5.

149 *The Paris Sketch Book. The Works of William Makepeace Thackeray*, XVI (1897), pp. 115–6; cf. an English historian's comment: 'Le *Paris Sketch Book* de Thackeray est une oeuvre vulgaire écrite en un style John Bull pour plaire John Bull, et, pour cette raison, il constitue un excellent exemple de la façon dont l'opinion publique considérait la France': E. L. Woodward, 'Les Caractères généraux des relations Franco-Anglaises entre 1815–1870', *Revue d'Histoire Moderne*, XIII (1938), pp. 110–25, p. 121. See also Sylvane Marandon, *L'Image de la France dans L'Angleterre victorienne 1848–1900* (Paris, 1967), pp. 44–7; E. Halévy, 'English Public Opinion and the French Revolutions of the Nineteenth Century', *Studies in Anglo-French History* (edited by A. Colville and A. Temperley, 1935), pp. 51–60.

150 D. Johnson, *Guizot*, p. 286 ff.

151 J. R. Baldwin, 'England and the French Seizure of the Society Islands', *J. Mod. History*, X, no. 2 (June 1938), pp. 212–31; N. Gash, *Sir Robert Peel. The Life of Sir Robert Peel after 1830* (1972), pp. 507–12.

152 quoted in E. Hodder, *The Life and Work of the Seventh Earl of Shaftesbury* (1882), pp. 289–90. For a general discussion of some aspects of workaday protestantism in the middle decades of the century, G. Best, 'Popular Protestantism in Victorian England', *Ideas and Institutions of Victorian Britain* (edited by R. Robson, 1967), pp. 115–42.

153 Joinville joined the Admiralty Board in 1843 and persuaded the Ministry of Marine to appoint a special commission to enquire into the application of steam power to naval vessels. For the detailed background to the Joinville affair see C. J. Bartlett, *Great Britain and Sea Power 1815–1853* (Oxford, 1963), p. 158 ff; *Annual Register, 1848*. Bartlett, p. 158, note 1, says the most useful of the various English translations of Joinville's pamphlet is that by W. Peake (4th edition, 1844). There is no reference to the pamphlet, or to the excitement it produced, in Joinville's *Memoirs* published in English in 1895.

154 Richard Cobden's pamphlet *The Three Panics* (1862) which went through six editions provided some of the background to the extraordinary fixation of the British public on the threat of a French invasion; and for a more specific study, E. Daniels, 'Die Engländer und die Gefahr einer französichen Landung zur zeit Louis Philipps und Napoleons III', *Delbrück = festschrift* (Berlin, 1908), pp. 257–91.

155 The Swiss crisis was an important harbinger of the revolutionary events of 1848. It dominated the European headlines in the closing months of 1847. See J. Halperin, 'The Transformation of Switzerland', in *The Opening of an Era* (edited

by F. Fetjö) pp. 50–66; and for general surveys of these years, W. L. Langer, *Political and Social Upheavals*, chs. 8 and 9; J. Droz, *Europe Between Revolutions 1815–1848* (1967), pp. 236–44.

156 The Marquis of Normanby began his *Journal* published in 1857; 'During the course of the month of July 1847, many circumstances had occurred, which had seemed to strengthen my unwilling conviction that we were upon the eve of a great convulsion in France' (p. 3); and Normanby had been sending despatches to London in the six months before the February revolution which underlined his 'unwilling conviction'. See below, for the months of January and February.

157 The most useful introduction to mid-Victorian radicalism in terms of its aims and objectives is J. E. Thorold Rogers, *Cobden and Modern Political Opinion* (1873); N. McCord, 'Cobden and Bright in Politics 1846–1857', *Ideas and Institutions of Victorian England* (edited by R. Robson, 1967), pp. 87–114.

158 *Poor Man's Guardian*, 6 August 1831.

159 The quotation comes from the introduction O'Brien wrote to the English translation he made of Buonarroti which was originally published by Henry Hetherington in twenty parts, at twopence each. The English title was *Buonarroti's History of Babeuf's Conspiracy for Equality*: A. Plummer, *Bronterre. A Political Biography of Bronterre O'Brien 1804–1864* (1971), ch. 4. There is debate among scholars as to whether Buonarroti gave a faithful account of 'Babouvisme' in the years 1706–7, but there is no doubt of the book's influence after its publication in Brussels in 1828. One of the most useful introductions is still A. G. Garrone, *Buonarroti e Babeuf* (Turin, 1948), and see also: S. Berstein, *Buonarroti* (Paris, 1948); A. Müller Lehning, 'Buonarroti and his International Secret Societies', *Int. Rev. Soc. H.*, I, vol. I (1956) pp. 112–40; E. L. Eisenstein, *The First Professional Revolutionalist: Filippo Michele Buonarroti 1761–1837* (Cambridge, Mass., 1959). Among others, the first Polish Socialist group, Lud Polski (the Polish People) considered themselves the disciples of Buonarroti: Peter Brock, 'The Socialists of the Polish "Great Emigration"', *Essays in Labour History* (edited by A. Briggs and J. Saville, 1960) pp. 140–73; M. Dommanget, *Sur Babeuf et la conjuration des égaux* (Paris, 1970).

160 The standard biography is A. R. Schoyen, *The Chartist Challenge: a portait of George Julian Harney* (1958) and see *The Harney Papers* (edited by F. G. Black and R. M. Black, Assen, 1969). Harney appears in almost all Chartist histories. J. P. Marat (1743–93) whose pen-name Harney used, changed the title of his paper from *Le Publiciste Parisien* to *L'Ami du Peuple* on 16 September 1789.

161 J. Saville, 'Friedrich Engels et le Chartisme', *La Nouvelle Critique*, no. 72 (1956), pp. 73–90; Schoyen, *Chartist Challenge*, ch. 7.

162 D. McLellan, *Karl Marx, His Life and Thought* (1973) quotes Bruno Hildebrand's account of an evening at the German Workers Educational Union in April 1846, pp. 168–70. This was in the Red Lion public house near Piccadilly. There is a description of the room in which an annual banquet of the Union was held in the White Hart Tavern, Drury Lane, in J. Saville, *Ernest Jones* (1952), p. 92.

163 The membership of the Commmunist League in the summer-of 1848 was 84, according to B. Nicolaevsky, 'Towards a History of the "The Communist League" 1847–1852', *Int. Rev. Soc. H.*, I, part 2 (1956), pp. 234–52, while the Workers Education Union was 187. There is a history of the Communist League by Engels, reprinted in a number of places, including D. Ryazanoff, *The Communist Manifesto of Karl Marx and Freidrich Engels* (1930), pp. 1–14.

164 There was some suspicion within Chartist ranks about the Fraternal Democrats, and Harney took especial trouble to allay fears: Schoyen, *Chartist
Challenge*, p. 135 ff.
165 *ibid.*, pp. 149–52. There is an account of the election speeches in F. J. Snell,
Palmerston's Borough (1894), pp. 77–88: *The Times*, 29, 30 and 31 July, 2 and 4
August 1847.
166 Schoyen, *Chartist Challenge*, ch. 7; McLellan, *Karl Marx*, p. 173 ff.

January–February

1 A. H. Imlah, *Economic Elements in the Pax Britannica: Studies in British Foreign
Trade in the Nineteenth Century* (Cambridge, Mass., 1958), provided estimates of
the balance of payments; these were reprinted in B. R. Mitchell and P. Deane,
Abstract of British Historical Statistics (Cambridge, 1962), p. 333. The balance on
current account (in millions of pounds sterling) was:

1840	1841	1842	1843	1844	1845	1846	1847	1848	1849	1850	1851	1852
−2.3	+1.1	−0.6	+9.3	+10.4	+9.3	+8.0	−1.1	+2.1	+3.9	+10.6	+9.2	+7.7

2 The standard work for many years has been C. N. Ward-Perkins, 'The
Commercial Crisis of 1847', *Oxford Econ. Papers*, II (1950), reprinted in E. M.
Carus-Wilson (ed.), *Essays in Economic History*, III (1962), pp. 263–79. The most
recent study, which modifies a number of previously accepted conclusions, is H.
M. Boot, *The Commercial Crisis of 1847* (Hull, 1984), and the doctoral thesis of
1978 upon which the published monograph was based. Dr Boot's analysis is in
line with Phyllis Deane's 'New Estimates of Gross National Product for the United
Kingdom 1830–1914', *Rev. Income and Wealth*, series 14, no. 2 (1968). Among
contemporaries Tooke and Newmarch, *History of Prices*, vol. V (1857), p. 448,
emphasised the considerable economic growth between 1840 and 1856; and it
is now generally accepted that the rates of growth of the British economy after
1842 were not substantially different from those of the 1850s and 1860s. For a
succinct general discussion, with an extensive bibliography, see R. A. Church,
The Great Victorian Boom 1850–1873 (1975).
3 J. H. Clapham, *An Economic History of Modern Britain*, I (3rd ed. Cambridge,
1939), p. 145.
4 A statement which can be illustrated from every sector of the British economy.
Clapham, vol. I, esp. ch. V, provides an excellent introduction to the variety of
industrial organisation in the first half of the century; and see also R. Samuel,
'The Workshop of the World: Steam Power and Hand Technology in mid-
Victorian Britain' *History Workshop*, no. 3 (Spring 1977). D. Goodway's *London
Chartism 1838–1848* (Cambridge, 1982), part 4, has a detailed discussion of the
London trades during the 1840s.
5 The letter was widely publicised in the national and provincial press. The most
accessible text is probably the *Annual Register, 1848*, Chronicle, pp. 5–7.
6 E. Longford, *Wellington*, vol. 2 (1972), pp. 376–7. Wellington apologised to Lord
John Russell in a letter dated 7 January 1848: PRO 30/22/7A.
7 C. J. Bartlett, *Great Britain and Sea Power 1815–1853*, pp. 155–74 and 183–95.
8 Letter to Russell, 11 January 1848: PRO 30/22/7A.
9 *The Times*, 6 January 1848. It was headed 'London taken from the French' and
purported to be a bulletin from General Bugeaud who was in command of the
invasion.

10 *Nonconformist*, 26 January 1848. For the historical background to the anti-Norman attitude reproduced in this quotation see J. E. C. Hill, 'The Norman Yoke', *Puritanism and Revolution. Studies in the Interpretation of the English Revolution of the Seventeenth Century* (1962), pp. 50–122.

11 This is not to ignore the considerable hostility to Britain at many levels of French opinion. *The Times*, 3 February 1848, published a three-quarter column letter from a correspondent in Paris who wrote, quoting examples, that the French press was full of 'malignant calumnies' against England.

12 *Annual Register, 1848*, History, p. 43.

13 Especially his letter of 30 July 1847, FO 27/781, almost all of which Normanby published in his *Year of Revolution. From a Journal Kept in Paris in 1848*. vol. 1, (1857), pp. 5–19. In his introduction to the journal Normanby carefully explained that he had been scrupulous in omitting matters directly affecting governments and individuals with whom he had had confidential discussions; but he published a great deal and the text follows fairly closely his despatches from Paris to the Foreign Office in London. Yet the journal lacks the sparkle of the original correspondence which may account for its comparative neglect by historians. G. Duveau, *1848: The Making of a Revolution* (1967), says that 'Lord Normanby's account is one long diatribe against Louis Blanc and socialism in general' (p. 121): a statement that is a total misreading of the text; and L. Blanc, *1848. Historical Revelations: inscribed to Lord Normanby* (1858), makes an equally incorrect appraisal when he writes that Normanby's book was 'a one-sided register of idle rumours and unsifted reports' (ix). Normanby's commentaries from Paris during 1848 were those of a highly intelligent member of the British aristocracy deeply imbued with the Whig version of British interests and naturally hostile to the radicalism and socialism of the Paris clubs. In these terms he provided intelligence reports from Paris of a serious quality.

14 All the January correspondence from Normanby to the Foreign Office is in FO 146/341.

15 An example is the long letter of 19 February, FO 146/341, in which Normanby, after emphasising the immense coercive power at the disposal of the French government: 'But on the other hand the information within the last few days shew them that they must count upon the decided hostility of the great majority of the National Guard. The ministers are aware of the importance in the way of influence upon the Troops of the Line, that they should have the appearance of acting with the National Guard. . . Should the collison unhappily be provoked in a manner to place the National Guard on the side of the People, it is still more doubtful whether they would continue to act against them.'

16 A. de Tocqueville, *Recollections* (edited by J. P. Mayer and A. P. Kerr, New York, 1971), pp. 18–19.

17 *ibid.* pp. 21–2.

18 T. Garvin, 'Defenders, Ribbonmen and Others: Underground Political Networks in Pre-Famine Ireland', *Past and Present*, no. 96 (August 1982), pp. 135–55, describes Cornewall Lewis' work, *On Local Disturbances in Ireland, and on the Irish Church Question* (1836), as 'a still unrivalled example' of the thesis that rural outrages were essentially apolitical and closely related to local agrarian problems.

19 See Clarendon's letters to Russell in October 1847 in Clarendon Papers, Letter Book 1, Bodleian Library; and the Russell papers, PRO 30/22/6. The landlord-tenant bill, very conservative in its proposals, was referred in April 1848 to a

Select Committee: *Hansard*, xcviii, cols. 60–9; and for a brief discussion, K. B. Nowlan, *The Politics of Repeal* (1965), pp. 162–5.

20 Orange support was always conditional, on both sides. Clarendon's dismissal of the Earl of Roden, Lord Lieutenant of County Down, and one of the outstanding personalities of the Orange Order, from his position as a magistrate in the summer of 1849, caused a tremendous uproar: see Maxwell, *Life and Letters*, vol. 1, p. 292 ff.

21 Quoted in *ibid.*, p. 285.

22 *Hansard*, 3rd ser. xcv (29 November 1847) col. 311. The table of crimes for 1846 and 1847 was given in col. 276.

23 *ibid.*, 13 December 1847, cols. 983, 984–5.

24 The attack on the land laws was a staple item for middle-class radicals in the middle decades: Thorold Rogers, *Cobden and Modern Political Opinion*, ch. 3; W. L. Burn, 'Free Trade in Land: an Aspect of the Irish Question', *Trans. Roy. H. Soc.* 4th ser, xxxi (1949), pp. 61–74.

25 Francis Blackburne (1782–1867) was the principal judge in the political trials of 1848, for which see Chapter 6. David Richard Pigot (1797–1873) became Chief Baron of the Exchequer in 1846 and remained in office until his death. He was a Roman Catholic in religion and a liberal in politics: *DNB*; F. E. Ball, *The Judges in Ireland*, vol. 2 (1927), p. 357.

26 *Annual Register*, *1848*, law cases, p. 332. The detailed accounts of the sittings of the Special Commission are in several places. The most convenient is the *Annual Register*; and see *Freeman's Journal* (Dublin) and the London *Times*, both from 4 January 1848. There is an important letter describing the work of the Commission from Clarendon to Brougham: 5 February 1848, Clarendon Papers, Box 79.

27 Garvin, 'Defenders, Ribbonmen and Others': M. R. Beames, 'The Ribbon Societies: Lower-Class Nationalism in Pre-Famine Ireland', *Past and Present*, no. 97 (November 1982), pp. 128–43.

28 Russell to Clarendon, 16 January 1848, Clarendon Papers, Box 43; Grey to Clarendon, 10 February 1848, HO 122/20.

29 The standard biography of McHale is B. O'Reilly, *John McHale, Archbishop of Tuam: His Life, Times and Correspondence*, 2 vols. (New York, 1890). For a modern assessment, see D. A. Kerr, *Peel, Priests and Politics. Sir Robert Peel's Administration and the Roman Catholic Church in Ireland, 1841–1846* (Oxford, 1982), p. 21 ff.

30 The literature on the now almost universally damned Trevelyan in respect of his policies towards the Irish famine is extensive. See C. Woodham Smith, *The Great Hunger. Ireland 1845–9* (1962), for a detailed criticism. The orthodox political economy of the period is analysed at length in R. D. Collison Black, *Economic Thought and the Irish Question 1817–1870* (Cambridge, 1960). Policies in respect of the famine are discussed passim, but see especially pp. 112–31.

31 See, for example, the hostile comment on McHale's long letter to the Earl of Shrewsbury on Saturday 22 January 1848. The letter, which took up five columns of *The Times*, was reprinted on Monday 24 January.

32 Clarendon on a number of occasions tacked on to his letters to Lord John Russell and his colleagues, the idea of public works as a means of relief. It became almost a ritual, done so mechanically and so feebly that the reader may doubt whether Clarendon really believed what he was advocating. Examples are the letters to Grey, 6 May 1848, Clarendon Papers, Letter Book 2; and the interesting account he wrote to Russell about the condition of the peasantry in Guernsey, and the

operations of the Prussian Land Bank. He continued: 'I am of course prepared for Sir C. Wood's opposition to a scheme so unprecedented and so divergent from the straight and narrow path of political economy, but the spirit of association exists not here. The people may in time become fitter for local and self government; but in the meantime while they may starve and become rebellious and we may have to fight them or lose them, so I want instead to dry nurse them and that the government should do what they would do for themselves if they were Saxons and not Celts': 6 May 1848, Clarendon Papers, Letter Book 2. Clarendon was rarely as forceful as in this letter, but he never pushed these sort of arguments for serious decision, or perhaps more accurately, he always seems to have accepted Whitehall's point of view. He was much more persistent in matters of internal security.

33 For the horrors of the emigrant ships, Woodham Smith, *The Great Hunger*, ch. xi.

34 T. Carlyle, *Chartism* (1839), p. 18.

35 D. Thomson with M. McGusty (eds.) *The Irish Journals of Elizabeth Smith, 1840–50* (Oxford, 1980), p. 169.

36 Clarendon Papers, iii A, Account Books, vol. ii, Household, July 1847–March 1851: from which all details in the text have been taken.

37 J. H. Treble, 'O'Connor, O'Connell and the Attitudes of Irish Immigrants towards Chartism in the North of England, 1838–1848', *The Victorians and Social Protest: a Symposium* (edited by J. Butt and I. F. Clarke, Newton Abbot, 1973), pp. 33–70; D. Thompson, 'Ireland and the Irish in English Radicalism before 1850', *The Chartist Experience* (edited by J. Epstein and D. Thompson, 1982), pp. 120–51. The literature on the Irish in England has been growing steadily, and among material relevant to the present discussion are: R. O'Higgins, 'The Irish Influence in the Chartist Movement', *Past and Present*, no. 20 (1961), pp. 83–96; C. Richardson, 'Irish Settlement in Mid-Nineteenth Bradford', *Yorks. Bull. Econ. Soc. Res.* (May 1968), pp. 40–57; W. J. Lowe, 'The Irish in Lancashire 1846–71: a Social History' (Ph.D. University of Dublin, 1974); D. Goodway, *London Chartism 1838–1848* (Cambridge, 1982), passim. but esp. pp. 61–7; R. Swift and S. Gilley, (eds.) *The Irish in the Victorian City*, (1985).

38 Treble, 'Attitudes of Irish Immigrants' p. 64 ff.

39 It was, indeed, a very common argument in government circles and among the military; referred to on several occasions by Lieutenant-General Sir Thomas Arbuthnot, commander-in-chief of the Northern District. It was especially emphasised in the weeks following John Mitchel's conviction at the end of May: HO, 45/2410 pt. 4.

40 The social attitudes of the English towards the Irish are on the whole less well documented for the years before 1850 than for the following decades. The localised fighting between English and Irish navvies is well known, and regional and area studies are beginning to uncover a great deal of hostility which after 1850 expressed itself in the racial riots which are now being more seriously studied. From the growing literature see: J. Foster, *Class Struggle and the Industrial Revolution* (1974), pp. 243–6; N. Kirk, 'Class and Fragmentation: Some Aspects of Working-Class Life in North-East Cheshire and South-East Lancashire 1850–1870' (Univ. of Pittsburgh, Ph.D. 1974), which provides a great deal of documentation on the Irish riots of the 1860s and particularly on the years of hysteria in the late sixties; *idem, The Growth of Working Class Reformism in Mid-Victorian England* (1985), ch. 7; and W. L. Arnstein, 'The Murphy Riots: A Victorian Dilemma', *Victorian Studies*, xix (1975), pp. 51–71.

41 Bugeaud (Thomas-Robert) Marquis de la Piconnerie, Duc d'Isly (1784–1849) was well-known for his ruthless behaviour, both in France ('the Butcher of the Rue Transnomain') and in Algeria. When he was summoned to take command in Paris on the morning of 24 February 1848, at a time when the revolution was spreading fast, he alarmed Thiers by repeating more than once: 'After all I shall have the pleasure of killing a good many of these swine', T. E. B. Howarth, *Citizen-King* (1961), pp. 321–2. There is a somewhat bland entry on Bugeaud in *Dictionnaire de Biographie Française*, vol. 7 (1956), pp. 632–4.

42 FO 146/341.

43 During the months of March and April Normanby reverted on several occasions to his analysis of the causes of the revolutionary upheaval in Paris. He very properly believed that there were important lessons to be learned by the propertied classes everywhere: seè, for an example of his approach, a letter to Palmerston dated 19 March 1848, FO 146/342.

44 The most convenient summary of the events in revolutionary Paris is probably G. Duveau, *1848: The Making of a Revolution* (1967). An older text, but more analytical, is F. Fetjö (ed.), *The Opening of an Era* (1948), and the list that follows is only a small collection of the items found most useful for present purposes, beginning with the two essays by Marx: *The Class Struggles in France* and *The Eighteenth Brumaire of Louis Bonaparte*; D. C. McKay, *The National Workshops* (Cambridge, Mass., 1933); P. Robertson, *Revolutions in 1848. A Social History* (Princeton, 1952); L. Girard, *Le IIe République* (Paris, 1968); A. Lefevre, 'La Reconnaissance de la Seconde République par L'Angleterre', *Revue d'histoire diplomatique*, LXXXII (1968), pp. 213–31; R. Price, *The French Second Republic: A Social History* (1972); M. Agulhon, *1848 ou l'Apprentissage de la République* (Paris, 1973); C. Tilly and L. Lees, 'Le peuple de juin 1848', *Annales*, 29 (Sept.–Oct. 1974), pp. 1061–91; G. Fasel, 'The Wrong Revolution: French Republicanism in 1848', *French H. Stud.* VIII, no. 4 (1974), pp. 654–77; M. Agulhon, *Les Quarante-huitards* (Paris, 1975); R. Price, *Revolution and Reaction: 1848 and the Second French Republic* (1975); W. H. Sewell, *Work and Revolution in France* (Cambridge, 1980).

45 FO 146/341 dated 24 February. Normanby's account in his *Journal*, p. 88 ff. follows closely what he wrote in this despatch to Palmerston.

46 A. de Tocqueville, *Recollections*, pp. 46–7.

47 For the diplomatic history in the early days of the revolution, see L. C. Jennings, *France and Europe in 1848* (1973), ch. 1: the most useful text for European affairs in this year.

48 *The Letters of Queen Victoria* (edited by A. C. Benson and Viscount Esher, 1907), vol. 2, pp. 182–4. Lord John Russell's statement on non-interference was welcomed round the country, the Whigs and Liberals being especially gratified. Cf. the *Scotsman*, 1 March: 'This will relieve much anxiety in the country, a fear having got abroad that an attempt might be made to repeat the abominable and unfortunate policy of 1793'. This was a common enough sentiment, but it had no basis in fact. The Cabinet was united in its firm adherence to a policy of non-intervention.

49 Clarendon Papers, Box 43, 29 February 1848. This was the first of two letters from Russell on this day.

50 Feargus O'Connor had a characteristic reaction that was wholly consistent with his general attitudes. In the *Northern Star* for 26 February he wrote: 'When the struggle between pure Democracy and Despotism shall take place in France,

then we will not be slow to communicate our sympathy for the struggles; but I tell you that as long as I live, the Charter and the Land shall never be lost sight of, not placed in abeyance by any foreign excitement or movement, however we may use events for the futherance of those great objects.'

51 *The Harney Papers* (edited by F. G. Black and R. M. Black, Assen 1969), p. 355.

March

1 The most useful account of the diplomatic history of the early days after the revolution is L. C. Jennings, *France and Europe*, chs. 1–4; and apart from the general works cited above, p. 252, n. 44 see also P. Henry, 'Le gouvernement provisoire et la question polonaise en 1848', *Revue historique*, CLXXVIII (Sept.–Oct. 1936), pp. 198–240; G. Wright, 'A Poet in Politics: Lamartine and the Revolution of 1848'. *History Today*, VIII (Sept. 1958), pp. 616–27; A. Lefevre, 'La Reconnaissance de la Seconde République par l'Angleterre', *Revue D'Histoire Diplomatique*, LXXXII (1968), pp. 213–31.

2 Clarendon Papers, Box 43, 29 February 1848.

3 *ibid.*, 1 March.

4 HO 45/2368 (File: Irish Disaffection, 1848).

5 The Marquess of Anglesey (One-Leg), Peninsular and Waterloo veteran (1768–1854), became Master of the Ordnance in 1846. A close personal friend of Wellington. See Marquess of Anglesey, *One Leg. The Life and Letters of Henry William Paget, First Marquess of Anglesey (1961)*. The letter of 17 June is in WO 30/111.

6 Clarendon Papers, Box 12, 2 April 1848.

7 FO 146/341, no. 98, 27 February 1848.

8 FO 146/341, 27 February 1848.

9 *Hansard*, XCVI, col. 1389 (28 February 1848).

10 Jennings, *France and Europe*, ch. 1, for the background; and see the correspondence between Paris and London in late February and early March: FO 146/341.

11 Jennings, *France and Europe*, p. 10 ff.

12 Normanby to Palmerston, 3 March, FO 146/341, no. 118.

13 Clarendon Papers, Letter Book II, 29 February 1848.

14 E. Ashley, *The Life and Correspondence of Henry John Temple, Lord Palmerston, 1846–1865*. 2 vols. (1879), vol. II, p. 76. There is a note in Ashley to the effect that 'regulus' is the pure metal left after melting.

15 The notes, letters and internal correspondence are given in Spencer Walpole, *The Life of Lord John Russell*, vol. II (1889), pp. 31–9.

16 The published letters of Queen Victoria during 1848–9 illustrate the Queen's disapproval of Palmerston and those who worked with him in matters of foreign policy: *The Letters of Queen Victoria* (edited by A. C. Benson and Viscount Esher, 1907), vol. II, 1844–53. H. C. F. Bell discusses the Court's antagonism to Palmerston at length in *Lord Palmerston*, vol. I (1936) pp. 419 ff. and 434 ff. Bell noted (p. 434) the influence of the Continental exiles – Louis-Philippe, Guizot and 'the vindictive Princess Lieven' as well as Metternich in encouraging the Queen's antipathy towards the Foreign Office. From June 1848 Prince Albert kept a dossier of Palmerston's misdoings: B. Connell, *Regina v. Palmerston* (1962), pp. 78–80.

17 A. de Lamartine, *Oeuvres complètes* (Paris 1860–6), vol. XXXIX: *Mémoires*

politiques, p. 148, quoted in Jennings, *France and Europe*, p. 6
18 FO 146/343, no. 414.
19 3 March 1848, FO 146/341, no. 120.
20 15 March, FO 146/342, no. 162. The account of the report back from the Chartist delegates is in *Northern Star*, 18 March 1848.
21 18 March, FO 146/342.
22 Palmerston to Normanby, 22 March, FO 146/329, no. 117.
23 Normanby to Palmerston, 1 April, FO 146/342.
24 The background to the delegation's visit is given in Nowlan, *Politics of Repeal*, pp. 186–92 and Normandy, *Journal*, vol. 2, pp. 276–7, although Normanby's despatches in the FO papers are more enlightening.
25 It was a general matter of congratulation between all the leading members of the Whig Government; and in the country at large. The *Morning Chronicle* (London) had an editorial on 6 April noting with great satisfaction the rebuff to the Irish leaders; the *Stockport Advertiser* for the same date wrote that 'Lamartine has well repulsed the Irish deputation'; and the *Weekly Dispatch* which had sympathy with Irish grievances had none for the radical leaders who went to Paris.
26 'Lamartine's excellent answer has been a blow to Young Ireland though Mr. Mitchel announced last night that it was a mere State paper and like all such unmeaning.' Clarendon to Sir George Grey, 6 April 1848, Clarendon Papers, Letter Book II.
27 G. W. M. Reynolds (1814–79) was already known as a radical novelist and journalist before he entered the Chartist movement. He was anti-aristocratic, anti-clerical and republican, and his most lasting contribution to the radical movement was the establishment of *Reynolds Weekly Newspaper* in 1850. It became the leading radical paper of the third quarter of the century: *Dictionary of Labour Biography* (edited by J. M. Bellamy and J. Saville), vol. 3 (1976), pp. 146–51.
28 There are detailed accounts in all the London newspapers, especially *The Times* and *Morning Chronicle*, 7–9 March; and see Goodway, 'Turbulent London', *London Chartism*, p. 68 ff. There is a little material in HO 45/2410 part 1.
29 P. M. McDouall was imprisoned 1839–40 and again in 1848. There is a great deal of scattered information about his life and career which has not yet been brought together; for which see M. Jenkins, *The General Strike of 1842* (1980); J. Epstein and D. Thompson (eds.), *The Chartist Experience* (1982); C. Godfrey, 'The Chartist Prisoners 1839–41', *Int. Rev. Soc. H.*, vol. XXIV (1979), pp. 189–136. McDouall, according to Gammage, emigrated to Australia in 1853, where he died.
30 The Scottish newspapers consulted were the *Glasgow Chronicle*, *Glasgow Examiner* and the *Scotsman*. See also A. Wilson, 'Chartism in Glasgow', *Chartist Studies* (edited by A. Briggs, 1959), pp. 249–287; *idem*, *The Chartist Movement in Scotland* (Manchester, 1970), ch. 16. There is internal correspondence within Scottish departments and correspondence with the Home Office in the Scottish Record Office, AD 58/74–9. There is more detail in the reports from the Acting Chief Magistrate and Archibald Alison Sheriff of Lanarkshire, in HO 45/2410 part 5 (Glasgow file). Fifty-four shops were entered and damaged and the reports to the HO made an estimate of the damage in financial terms. Alison wrote to the HO on 8 March: 'The disposition of the whole middle classes throughout these occurrences has been most excellent, and I rejoice these feelings are shared in by a large and by far the most respectable of the working people. Above 2000 special

constables were on duty last night . . . The disturbances have undoubtedly been owing to Chartist oratory working on the passions of the unemployed. But generally speaking there do not appear to have been the least disaffection to Government, or a desire for organic change except in the very lowest and most depraved class in which it is synonymous with the wish for Plunder.'

31 The United States was often held up by English radicals as being much nearer their ideal of a 'democracy'; with 'democracy' having more radical connotations than the parliamentary democracy of the second half of the nineteenth century. See G. D. Lillibridge, *Beacon of Freedom* (Univ. of Pennslyvania, 1955).

32 *Scotsman*, 11 March 1848. The *Scotsman* would rank as a liberal paper in respect of internal politics in Britain. It was violently anti-Irish during this year, a not uncommon combination.

33 *1848: The Opening of an Era* (edited by F. Fetjö) has a useful chronological list of events in 1848.

34 *The Times* and *Morning Chronicle*, 13, 14, 15 March; *Spectator* 18 March; HO 45/2410, part 1, various letters between 9 and 13 March; Goodway, *London Chartism*, pp. 71–2.

35 *The Times*, 14 March 1848.

37 Clarendon to Grey, 16 March 1848, Clarendon Papers, Letter Book 2.

38 *ibid.*, Clarendon to Russell, 15 March 1848.

39 *ibid.*, Clarendon to Grey, 16 March 1848.

40 *ibid.*, Clarendon to Grey, 18 March.

41 Clarendon Papers, Box 43.

42 The copy of the Clarendon memorandum summarised in the text is in a separate file, HO 45/OS 2520A dated 27 March.

43 Clarendon again emphasised the peaceful role of the Catholic clergy; and he once more argued the case against the idea of a National Guard, on the grounds presumably that such a formation would encourage sectarian bitterness.

44 Russell Papers, PRO 30/22/7B, 30 March 1848. In his memorandum Russell set out a series of five propositions which included a bill to control 'ejectments . . . in the principles I have already stated to the Cabinet'. Most of the replies from other Cabinet ministers are included in this PRO file.

45 Russell to Clarendon, 17 February 1848 Clarendon Papers, Box 43.

46 Grey to Clarendon, 3 April 1848, HO 79/9. This was a private communication, not the official reply to Clarendon's memorandum which was also dated 3 April: Clarendon Papers, Box 12.

47 *Hansard*, 3rd ser. xcviii, col. 73 ff. (10 April 1848). The Crown and Security Bill is discussed in detail below, Chapter 6.

48 Palmerston to Russell, 31 March 1848, Russell Papers, PRO 30/22/7B.

49 Trevelyan to Russell, 4 April 1848, Russell Papers, PRO 30/22/7B.

50 Normanby, writing in the early days of the revolution noted the respect for religion 'shown upon several occasions by the great mass of the people' in striking contrast with the 'profanations of the first Revolution, as the Abolition of death for Political offences is a pledge that the passion for blood no longer exists except among a desperate minority': FO 146/341, 1 March 1848, no. 107.

51 Celina Fox, 'The Development of Social Reportage in English Periodical Illustration during the 1840s and early 1850s', *Past and Present*, no. 74 (February 1977), pp. 90–111.

52 *The Times*, 1 March 1848. The correspondent included a complimentary reference to the work of the British ambassador.

53 Normanby's main reports on the expulsion of the English workmen are in FO 146/341 dated 6, 15, 25 and 26 March; and there are references in the national and provincial press throughout March, with much moralising comment. Workmen of other nationalities were also expelled or threatened with expulsion. There was a somewhat related matter: a threat – not carried out – of a takeover by the French government of railway lines built and owned by the British. Normanby received a deputation from English directors of the Orleans-Bordeaux railway and took the approach, with which Palmerston was in full agreement, that those who invested capital took the profits and must expect to bear losses. The British government would always however, agree to make unofficial representations, and in practice Normanby was vigorous in defence of British interests. He pointed out to Lamartine that the case of the British workmen had already weakened confidence and that if they carried out their threat in respect of the railways 'they created the impression that national faith was no guarantee against spoliation, they would excite such an outcry amongst English capitalists, it must affect the intimacy of the relations between the two countries': 24 March 1848, FO 146/342.

54 Normanby to Palmerston, 18 March: FO 146/342, no. 174. For accounts of these demonstrations in mid-March, G. Duveau, 1848, p. 81 ff; R. Price, The French Second Republic, pp. 127–9.

55 K. Marx, The Class Struggles in France, Selected Works, vol. 3, p. 213.

56 Palmerston to Normanby, 14 March 1848, FO 146/329, no. 106.

April

1 R. Price, The French Second Republic, pp. 110–15; P. Amann, 'The Paris Club Movement in 1848', Revolution and Reaction. 1848 and the Second French Republic, (edited by R. Price, 1975), pp. 115–32.

2 There were several Acts under which a prosecution might be laid. The Seditious Meetings Act 1817 (57 Geo. III c. 19. s. 25) made an assembly of fifty or more persons unlawful if it met within a mile of Westminster for purposes of petitioning either the King or either house of Parliament.

3 See the entry for Cuffay in Dictionary of Labour Biography (edited by J. M. Bellamy and J. Saville), vol. 6 (1982); D. Goodway, London Chartism, pp. 68–96.

4 The account in the text of the proceedings of the Convention are taken from The Times and Morning Chronicle, Wednesday 5 April to Tuesday 11 April. Both published more or less complete reports.

5 Morning Chronicle, 10 April 1848.

6 Palmerston to Russell, 7 April 1848, PRO 30/22/7B.

7 Col. C. B. Phipps to Prince Albert, 9 April 1848: RA C56/11.

8 Phipps to Prince Albert, 10 April 1848: RA C56/21.

9 Sir George Grey to Russell: 'I have had a visit from a Mr. Gurney, who tells me he had been this evening with Mr. Ernest Jones, and that the Chartist leaders were much subdued and frightened. Mr. Gurney said he urged on Jones to issue a notice tomorrow abandoning the procession: but that Jones thought this impossible, saying the leaders would gladly do so, but the people could not be controlled.' Spencer Walpole, The Life of Lord John Russell, vol. 2 (1889), p. 69. It must be added that Ernest Jones does not seem to have given the impression on 10 April of a frightened man.

10 Peterloo does not seem to have been mentioned in the manuscript correspon-

dence of ministers: nor in the public prints; but the need to avoid bloodshed was in everybody's mind. See Russell's letter to Prince Albert on the tactics to be employed in the control of the Monday demonstration. He explained that the military would only be used as a last resort: 'I have no doubt of their easy triumph over a London mob. But any loss of life will cause a deep and rankling resentment. I trust, for this, and every reason, that all may pass off quietly': *The Letters of Queen Victoria*, (edited by Benson and Viscount Esher), vol. 2, p. 198.

11 Clarendon to Sir George Grey, 7 April 1848, Clarendon Papers, Letter Book 2.

12 *The Greville Memoirs* (edited by L. Strachey and R. Fulford, 1938), vol 5, p. 460.

13 10 April 1848: 'On Saturday evening we had all been at Lady Palmerstons, when Bunsen approached the Duke of Wellington, saying, 'Your Grace will take us all in charge, and London, too, on Monday the 10th?. . The Duke answered, 'Yes, we have taken our measures; but not a soldier nor a piece of artillery shall you see, unless in actual need. Should the force of law – the mounted or unmounted police – be overpowered or in danger, then the troops shall advance, then is their time. But it is not fair on either side to call them in to do the work of the police – the military must not be confounded with the police, nor merged in the police'. *Memoir of Baron Bunsen*, vol. 2 (1869), p. 106.

14 p. 81. The memorandum of 5 April is in WO 30/81 Misc. This is a very mixed bundle from the late eighteenth century to 1873. The Wellington memorandum is part of a file headed 'Chartist Riots. Memorandum by Duke of Wellington with statement showing distribution of troops 1848'.

15 HO 45/2410 part 5, Middlesex file. This was not the first instruction to the Lord Mayor in the city of London, for on 6 April Sir George Grey sent a long memorandum on the tactics to be followed on the 10th. There was an accompanying letter from Grey, courteous but firm, which instructed the Lord Mayor on the disposition of the city police forces: HO 41/26.

16 The distribution of the troops in London is to be found in the papers of several departments. There is a convenient summary in WO 30/111, bundle marked 'Chartist Riots' and the details have been published in Goodway, *London Chartism*, pp. 134–5. Goodway also added further material from WO 30/81 and MEPO 2/65. The details of the distribution of the metropolitan police in central London are in WO 30/111. The most convincing analysis of the much disputed numbers of special constables on 10 April is in Goodway, pp. 130–1. His estimate of a total around 85,000 has been quoted in the text as an acceptable figure.

17 Letter of 5 April 1848, HO 45/2410 part 5, Middlesex file; and for aristocratic stabling, WO 30/111.

18 See the discussion above, pp. 45–6.

19 All the examples in the text come from WO 30/111.

20 There was never any serious concern about the loyalty of the Irish soldiers in the British army, although there were a few quite worrying incidents. In 1839 and 1840 it was generally recognised that the relatively peaceful state of Ireland was an important factor in allowing the British government to shift troops to the mainland of Britain – as Daniel O'Connell boasted in the Commons of 'saving' Britain from the Chartists; and it was at this same time that Sir Charles Napier was asking specifically for regiments with a high proportion of Irish troops in their ranks: for all of which see above, pp. 24, 72–4.

21 Instances in Manchester and South Wales in March and April 1848 are given below, p. 121; and see also J. W. Werly, 'The Irish in Manchester, 1832–49', *Irish. H. Stud.* XVIII (1972–3), pp. 345–58.

22 Clarendon Papers, Letter Book 2; Major-General HRH Prince George of Cambridge was GOC Dublin and District: H. G. Hart (ed.), *The New Army Annual List for 1848*, p. 321.

23 Clarendon to Grey, 10, 11, and 13 April 1848, Clarendon Papers, Letter Book 2; Clarendon to Russell, *ibid.*, 13 April 1848.

24 *The Times* was full of detailed information on all aspects of the early days of the revolution in Paris. In addition to its own correspondents it published much material from British residents in Paris or from visitors who came back to Britain. See for an example the long letter which spread over a column and a half on 1 March which was from an English resident in Paris and dated 27 February. It discussed at length the social tendencies of the Paris working classes; and, for another example, the letter from an English visitor, dated the evening of 25 February and published in the issue of 2 March which gave a long account of the shooting outside the Foreign Office; and a third example in the issue of 9 March from an English artillery officer upon the conduct of the French army in Paris in the days following 22 February.

25 HO 45/2410 part 5, Middlesex file. Part 5 includes the Middlesex file and those for Surrey and Sussex, and together with part 1 of this general class, constitute the main source of information for much of the background to the Chartist movement in London in the months from March onwards, and the reactions of the authorities.

26 There is a small file in HO 45/2410 part 1 relating to the Electric Telegraph Company. A letter dated 9 March informed the Home Office that the cost of the line between Euston and the Home Office building in Whitehall would be £1,000. Sir George Grey explained to Prince Albert (RA C56/22, 10 April 1848) that the Telegraph system was taken over 'to prevent unfounded reports being sent into the country, which might have had a mischievous effect in places where the Chartist proceedings were looked to with much expectation. I sent correct information by the Telegraph throughout the country.' The letter was written at 6.45 p.m. on the 10th.

27 Alison's reports are in HO 45/2410 part 5, Glasgow file together with some letters from the Lord Provost. There is additional correspondence between Glasgow and other towns with London in the Records of the Lord Advocate's Department, Scottish Record Office, AD 58, especially AD 58/67 to 79. The letter quoted in the text was dated 8 March.

28 Rowan to General Bowles, Master of the Queen's Household: RA J68/2 – no date, but almost certainly 9 March.

29 Mather, *Public Order*, pp. 90–7.

30 HO 45/2410 part 5, Middlesex file, has a letter dated 4 April from a Limehouse magistrate on the unwillingness of the 'shopkeeping class' to register as special constables. He called a meeting and proposed a 'Declaration' and there seems to have been a change of attitude; and he reported that he now had 'Tories, Whigs, Radicals and, I believe, one or two of these Chartists'. There were some towns where middle-class objection to serving as special constables was political: Birmingham was an example, for which see below, p. 124. A further but different example was Liverpool in the summer months of 1848 when because of the menacing situation some special constables were unwilling to patrol without arms.

31 See above, p. 75.

32 The Lord Mayor of London said in a report on the events of 10 April that his chief

embarrassment was having too many special constables: HO 45/2410, part 5.

33 Capt. H. G. Hart, *The New Annual Army List for 1848*, pp. 9, 447.

34 HO 45/2410 part 5 (Middlesex file).

35 HO 45/2410 part 1, dated 11 April.

36 HO 45/2410 part 1, dated 12 April.

37 F. Podmore, *Life of Owen*, p. 592.

38 *Nonconformist*, 12 April 1848. The *Nonconformist* went on to argue for a middle-class and working-class reconciliation and emphasised the continuing need for 'genuine reform'.

39 HO 45/2410 part 5, Middlesex file, 5 April 1848.

40 There were problems with the building workers employed by Cubitts but it is difficult to piece together the full story: HO 45/2410 part 5, Middlesex file.

41 HO 45/2410 part 1 for a letter dated 6 April from Clerkenwell police court asking for a ruling 'whether workmen and labourers presenting themselves in considerable numbers from large establishments such as Gas Works etc should be indiscriminately sworn in as special constables though at the instance of their masters without reference to such workmen being householders or to their characters as individuals'.

42 M. Dorothy George, 'The London Coal-Heavers: Attempts to Regulate Waterside Labour in the Eighteenth and Nineteenth Centuries', *Economic History*, no. 2 (May 1927), Supplement, *Economic Journal*, pp. 229–48. The Act of 1843 (6 and 7 Vict. c. 103) established an office for registration and employment. It was renewed in 1846 and again in 1851, and allowed to lapse in 1856.

43 *Hansard*, 3rd Ser. xcvii, cols. 458–9 (13 March 1848).

44 *Weekly Dispatch*, 26 March 1848. The *Dispatch* reported several letters from coal-whippers which alleged that they had been taken to volunteer by their superintendent and that 'they will not interfere to put down any meeting assembled for legal and constitutional purposes'.

45 The correspondence is in HO 45/2410 part 5, Middlesex file. The rates allotted were 3 shillings for 800 men; 1 shilling and 6 pence for 300; and 6 pence for 757. There is further material in MEPO 1/45.

46 The Home Office were always aware of the formal regulations governing the duties of special constables, and they ignored them when it suited their purpose. H. Waddington set out the legal position based on 1 and 2 Wm IV c. 41 s. 5 and 6 in an internal note dated 22 July 1848: HO 45/2410 part 5, Middlesex file.

47 This was a common enough arrangement, and there are similar comments in government files from a number of different towns.

48 HO 45/4210 part 1. Goodway, *London Chartism*, p. 132, reprinted this letter and also one in similar terms from the Marquess of Salisbury.

49 Arbuthnot to Home Office, 20 and 23 March: HO 45/2410 part 5.

50 The police reports are in HO 45/2410 part 1. The most detailed account of the Kennington Common meeting is in Goodway, *London Chartism*, pp. 129–42. Goodway also considers at length the much disputed estimate of the size of the meeting on the Common, and suggests that there is 'persuasive evidence' for numbers of 150,000 to 170,000. There is further material in his chapter on 'Turbulent London', p. 68 ff.

51 *Morning Chronicle*, 11 April 1848. Most of the London detail quoted in the text has been taken from *The Times* or *Morning Chronicle*, but the other London papers should not be neglected, especially the *Globe* and the *Weekly Dispatch*.

52 The argument was used by some contemporaries especially those of radical

persuasion. The *Manchester Examiner* for 15 April, while very hostile to the Chartists on Kennington Common, ridiculed the extensive counterpreparations by the government as unnecessary. It is an argument also used by contemporary historians: see D. Large, 'London in the Year of Revolution, 1848', *London in the Age of Reform* (edited by J. Stevenson, Oxford 1977), pp. 177–211.

53 An analytical historiography of the Chartist movement in the century which followed 1848 would be illuminating. There is the beginning of a discussion in the Introduction by John Saville to the 1969 reprint of Gammage's *History* pp. 34–47. And see Chapter 7.

54 HO 79/9 dated 11 April.

55 The correspondence between the Home Office and provincial cities is in HO 45/2410 which comprises five large boxes of files. Manchester and Liverpool are in part 2; Leicester, part 3; Bradford, part 4; South Wales, part 5.

56 HO 45/2410 part 5. Letter from Col. Love, the Officer Commanding the South Wales district to the Home Office, 14 April.

57 The poster which is interleaved with correspondence in HO 45/2410 part 2, Manchester file, was dated 15 March 1848. It was headed in large capital letters 'To the Irish Catholics residing in the city of Manchester and the borough of Salford, and the neighborhoods'.

58 For Arbuthnot see above, p. 24.

59 There is a long obituary of Armitage in *Manchester Guardian*, 27 November 1876, and it gives prominence to Armitage in 1848. See also W. E. A. Axon, *Annals of Manchester* (1886), p. 360; A. Redford, *The History of Local Government in Manchester*, vol. 2 (1940), part 1, *passim*.

60 For the general background of Liverpool in the mid-century, and especially of the Irish population, see: J. A. Picton, *Memorials of Liverpool, Historical and Topographical, including a History of the Dock Estate*. Vol. 1 *Historical* (1875) esp. p. 503 ff; B. D. White, *A History of the Corporation of Liverpool 1835–1914* (Liverpool 1951), *passim*; W. J. Lowe, 'The Irish in Lancashire 1846–71: A Social History' (Ph.D. University of Dublin, 1975), summarised in *Irish Econ. and Soc. Hist*, vol II (1975), pp. 63–5; L. R. Bisceglia, 'The Threat of Violence: Irish Confederates in Liverpool in 1848', *Irish Sword*, XIV (1981), pp. 207–15.

61 These details are taken from HO 45/2410 part 2, Liverpool file, especially the letters from the Mayor of Liverpool dated 17 and 20 March; and also from Arbuthnot's reports to the Home Office from 9 March onwards, in part 4.

62 Arbuthnot to Home Office, 4 April 1848: HO 45/2410 part 4.

63 Armitage to Home Office, 4 April: HO 45/2410 part 2.

64 Arbuthnot was always sceptical of these rumours of arms manufacture and shipments, and many that were investigated certainly turned out to have no basis in fact. But it was a common enough statement and there are a number of examples scattered through the papers of government departments in this year. For one of many from Liverpool, the Mayor to Sir George Grey, 4 April, HO 45/2410 part 2: 'I am aware that many false rumours are afloat about the manufacture of pikes.'

65 Arbuthnot to Home Office, 8 April: HO 45/2410 part 4. In this same communication Arbuthnot expressed scepticism concerning reports from his namesake, Col. Arbuthnot who was in charge of the Birmingham District, in respect of potential outbreaks and disturbances in the area.

66 Arbuthnot to Home Office, HO 45/2410 part 4, 19 April. There were other occasions when Arbuthnot made similar observations. Leicester was another town in the Midlands where the middle-class radicals were reluctant to break

sharply with the Chartists. The town was not seriously disturbed until mid-May when new regulations for the workhouse led to three days of riotous behaviour, and these continued until after the Whit Monday demonstrations. Thereafter Leicester Chartism declined quite rapidly as trade in the town just as rapidly improved: A. T. Patterson, *Radical Leicester . . . 1780–1850*, (Leicester, 1954), ch. 18; J. F. C. Harrison, 'Chartism in Leicester', *Chartist Studies* (edited by A. Briggs, 1959), pp. 99–146; 'John Skevington', *Dictionary of Labour Biography* (edited by J. M. Bellamy and J. Saville), vol. 1 (1972) pp. 300–2.

67 HO 45/2410 part 4.
68 FO 146/342.
69 Normanby, *A Year of Revolutions*, pp. 315–16.
70 T. Martin, *The Life of His Royal Highness The Prince Consort*, vol. 2 (1876), p. 31.
71 *ibid.*, p. 34.
72 Normanby, *Year of Revolutions*, p. 315.
73 Russell to Clarendon, 12 April, Clarendon Papers, Box 43.
74 Clarendon to Grey, 11 April, Clarendon Papers, Letter Book 2.
75 Both the Palmerston and Grey letters to Clarendon are in HO 79/9.
76 For a more detailed account, see below, pp. 170–1.
77 Much of the press, London and provincial, carried stories of foreigners, especially Frenchmen, flooding into London.
78 For the general background, see Nowlan, *The Politics of Repeal*, p. 193 ff.
79 Clarendon to Russell, 12 April, Clarendon Papers, Letter Book 2.
80 *ibid.*, 18 April.
81 Clarendon's personal antipathy to the Irish Catholics has been given less emphasis than is probably required in the analysis of Dublin Castle's policies in this year.
82 Nowlan, *Politics of Repeal*, p. 210 and especially the long footnote, n. 161, on this page.
83 *ibid.*, pp. 201–2.
84 Grey to Clarendon, 28 April, Clarendon Papers Box 12.
85 *Recollections*, pp. 124–5.

Summer

1 Clarendon Papers, box 12, 28 April 1848.
2 De Tocqueville in *Recollections*, ch. 7, gives his version of 15 May. For other accounts see, K. Marx, *The Class Struggles in France, 1848–1850* (various editions); G. Duveau, *1848. The Making of a Revolution*, pp. 115–28; R. Price, *The French Second Republic*, pp. 146–54.
3 FO 146/343.
4 De Tocqueville, *Recollections*, ch. 10, 'The End of the June Days'.
5 FO 146/343, no. 418. The details of the June days are set out in all the voluminous writings of this year. There is a contemporary account in A. Herzen, *My Past and Thoughts*, 6 vols. (1924–27), vol. 4; and among the secondary sources may be noted P. Robertson, *Revolutions of 1848: A Social History* (Princeton, 1952), ch. VI; G. Duveau, *1848*. p. 133 ff.; R. Price, *The French Second Republic*, ch. IV; among the periodical literature, which is also considerable, J. Vidalenc, 'La Province et les journées de juin', *Études d'histoire moderne et contemporaine*, II (1948), pp. 83–144.
6 Normanby to Palmerston, 27 June 1848, FO 146/343, no. 421.

7 Goodway, *London Chartism*, table 5, p. 15.

8 *ibid.*, '1848. Turbulent London', esp. pp. 79–80.

9 There are accounts of the discussions and deliberations of the National Assembly in all the standard histories of Chartism. See, for examples, Gammage, *History of the Chartist Movement* (1969 ed.), pp. 324–30; Goodway, *London Chartism*, p. 80. The London press covered the Assembly in considerable detail: *The Times* and *Morning Chronicle*, 2–15 May; *Northern Star*, 6, 13, 20 May.

10 Cf. W. J. Vernon who reported in *Northern Star*, 20 May 1848: 'There was no use blinking the fact, that a division existed among the Chartists as to the best means of obtaining their objects. One party thought it should be done by public meetings, lectures, and so forth, while the other considered that they should have recourse to bolder measures . . . The 10th April was not a victory, as has been asserted, but a signal defeat . . . There were many of them who did not believe that the Charter was to be got by petitioning and agitation. They knew that they would not get it without working hard for it; in fact, that they must fight for it.' Vernon had previously been a successful mesmerist: T. M. Parssinen, 'Mesmeric Performers' *Victorian Studies*, XXI (1977–8), pp. 94–5. Vernon was sentenced to two years imprisonment in July 1848 for seditious speeches on 28 and 29 May.

11 A memorandum from B division of the metropolitan police, 3 June, referred to the 'new' organisation being carried into effect: HO 42/2410, part 1.

12 Nowlan, *Politics of Repeal*, pp.186–7; Gavan Duffy, *Four Years of Irish History*, p. 202.

13 Nowlan, *Politics of Repeal*, pp. 203–6; for the details of Mitchel's trial, see below, pp. 186, 196.

14 *The Times*, 30, 31 May and 1 June gave the most detailed accounts of the demonstration although all the London press noticed them. The freelance reporter mentioned in the text was F. T. Fowler, a somewhat dubious character, whose reports were to be used as important evidence in the Fussell trial, for which see below, pp. 179–85. Fowler was a *Times* reporter of several years standing and he repeated his estimates for these late May meetings on several occasions. The best summary of the events is in Goodway, *London Chartism*, p. 80 ff.

15 Hansard, 3rd Ser. XCIX, col. 236 ff.

16 *Greville Memoirs*, vol. 6, p. 73.

17 *The Times* had been urging firmer action throughout this week. On Thursday 1 June an editorial thundered: 'Stop it at once. Nip it in the bud, or to use a more appropriate figure, crack the dragon in his skull.'

18 *The Times*, 5 June, was commenting in a short editorial on the Duke of Wellington's complaint in the House of Lords on the previous Friday (*Hansard*, 3rd Ser. XCIX, cols. 236–7) of the strain on both troops and police to be kept under arms night after night. *The Times* suggested that one of the leaders could be selected for trial, and at this point it named Fussell. Brougham referred again to the subject in the Lords on the same day, 5 June: 'It had been represented to him (and while believing it to be true, he could not wonder at it) that the greatest feeling of exasperation prevailed among the various persons interested in the maintenance of order, against those who were doing their utmost to disturb it' (XCIX, cols. 331–2). There is some scattered evidence in the HO and MEPO files of complaints from the public of rough and arbitrary treatment. John Faulk, a reporter, claimed to have been violently assaulted by the police: letter to Sir George Grey, 2 June 1848, HO 45/2410, part 1 and subsequent correspondence.

The scale of Chartist activity was well brought out by a list of meetings in the previous week which filled two and a half columns in the *Weekly Dispatch*, 4 June.

19 *The Times* was not only interested in the attitudes of London juries, but it wrote at length on the law relating to unlawful assemblies, quoting *obiter dicta* of 1820 and 1822 and then a long quotation from a recent charge to the grand jury on 2 June by Mr Justice Patterson in the Queen's Bench which was an invitation to find against those convening and participating in large assemblies of a political kind; and *The Times* then went on to suggest to Lansdowne that it was now the occasion for the government to take action.

20 RA C56/30.

21 See above, note 18.

22 The letters from which the quotations in the text are taken will be found in HO 45/2410, part 1. There are more reports in MEPO 2/66 which contain the most incriminating material against the police. Popular attitudes over this episode confirmed the general hostility towards the London police. There is interleaved with departmental material in the papers a printed bill poster headed: 'Police Tyranny and City Justice' (copied from the *Standard of Freedom* 1 July 1848) and there followed an account of 'A Respectable Person, passing through Red Cross St. on Wednesday 7th June last, saw notice about 'Brutal Outrage by Police on Sunday last', stopped to read the notice which was in the window of Cartwright's Coffee House, was ordered by a Policeman to move on, and he argued, was taken in charge, brought before Alderman Gibbs and Fined 10s. Such a monstrous act of injustice on the part of the Police, and injustice on the part of the Magistrate, is unparalleled . . .' HO 45/2410 part 5, Middlesex file.

23 The first question about the riot is in *Hansard*, 3rd Ser. xcix, cols. 337–8 (5 June) and the second and much longer statement from Grey is in xcix, cols. 502–10 (8 June).

24 Mayne's letter dated 12 June and the printed leaflet are in HO 45/2410 part 1. The signatures to the printed leaflet, most of whom were Anglican clergymen, also included two lecturers of the Episcopal Jews Chapel, Bethnal Green. The petition ended with an appeal for subscriptions for those police involved in the 4 June affair.

25 Report from Dublin dated 5 June, published in *The Times*, 7 June. The fighting was between soldiers of the 31st (mainly Irish) and the 55th (mainly English) on Saturday evening 3 June. The issue was John Mitchel and about forty or fifty were involved. There was further fighting on Tuesday 6 June when men from other regiments joined in. There do not seem to be any later reports.

26 Hansard, 3rd Ser. xcix, cols. 1153–4 (4 August); 'Lord Dudley Stuart wished to know whether it was true that certain portions of the police had been armed with swords, having saws at the back . . .', Sir George Grey: 'A larger number than usual had been armed in London, Liverpool and Manchester . . . The backs of these were serrated in the manner of a saw, as they were intended formerly for the use of troops in a bivouac, for the felling of trees and the erection of tents. They were not intended for permanent use.'

27 Russell Papers, PRO 30/22/7C (11 June).

28 It had been intended originally to hold a series of meetings on 12 June, but it was finally decided to organise a single meeting at Bonner's Fields. There is a long account in *Northern Star*, 17 June; and see also *The Times*, 13–14 June. For details of security preparations, HO 45/2410, part 1 and MEPO 7/14. Goodway, *London Chartism*, pp. 86–7.

29 Most of the information at this time came from George Davis' reports to the

police: HO 45/2410 part 1, dated 12 and 14 June.

30 The information available to the government was summarised in a long brief prepared for the Crown prosecution after the August arrests and as a background document for the trial. There is no exact date to the document: it simply says 'September Session' and it is in TS 11/138/380. Most of the information set out in this document came from Thomas Powell (alias Johnson). There is an excellent summary and evaluation of the conspiracy that was developing up to the August arrests in Goodway, *London Chartism*, pp. 87–96.

31 Mather, *Public Order*, p. 155. The details of military districts are in Hart, *New Annual Army List for 1848*, pp. 318–21.

32 Mather, *Public Order*, ch. 5.

33 The exceptions may not always have been a matter of personalities, but of the different economic and social milieux which the civil authorities represented. Birmingham, with its small-scale industry and its 'mixing' of masters and men, was an obvious example, and the magistracy there showed a good deal more reluctance to enrol special constables than the more technologically advanced factory districts, where the gap between mill-owners and operatives was much wider. Small-scale industrial organisation as such would not necessarily be the determining factor; the social recruitment of magistrates was obviously important. On 19 April Arbuthnot wrote to the Home Office comparing Manchester with Birmingham and noting that the shopkeepers and 'others of that class' had been sworn in as special constables. '. . . this, however, I feel is not the case at Birmingham when in many instances in the handicraft trades there is not much difference between the station in society of the employers and the employed, and unfortunately large numbers of the latter are now out of work in consequence of the low state of Trade': HO 45/4210 part 4.

34 Arbuthnot wrote regularly to the Home Office about the state of trade. On 2 May, for example, there was a short note from him giving brief details of employment which he prefaced by noting that matters were improving: 4,559 more hands employed at full work; 3,555 less at short time; 675 less out of employment. His figures related only to factory work.

35 Scholars have been conscious for a long time of the value of the printed ephemera interleaved with the MS material in the files of the Public Record Office; and for several obvious reasons it would be useful if listings could be made. There are eight posters from Manchester in HO 45/2410, part 2 between March and September, of different sizes, but mostly large and quite closely printed.

36 HO 45/2410, part 2, Manchester file.

37 HO 45/2410, part 4.

38 It was a large poster. Maude's letter to the Home Office was dated 30 May and is in HO 45/2410, part 2, Manchester file.

39 The account in the text of the events from the demonstrations of 31 May up to the Whit Monday of 12 June has been put together from the correspondence of the Mayor of Manchester in HO 45/2410 part 2; the reports from Northern Command to the Home Office, in *ibid.*, part 4; and the daily reports published in *The Times* and the *Manchester Guardian*.

40 The background material for Bradford is to be found in J. James, *The History of the Worsted Manufacture in England* (Bradford, 1857); E. M. Sigsworth, *Black Dyke Mills. A History* (Liverpool, 1958); A. J. Peacock, *Bradford Chartism 1838–1840* (Borthwick Papers, no. 36, 1969); A. Elliott, 'The Establishment of Municipal Government in Bradford 1837–1857' (Ph.D. University of Bradford, 1976); and

the most recent survey of modern Bradford is the excellent volume by J. Reynolds, *The Great Paternalist: Titus Salt and the Growth of Nineteenth Century Bradford* (1983).

41 Reynolds, *The Great Paternalist*, pp. 118–19. The working relationship in local politics mentioned in the text between Tories and Radicals was by no means uncommon in the late 1830s and during the 1840s.

42 There was one alderman who was a Tory, a wool-merchant by trade. More important than the aldermen were the Borough magistrates, and of the new bench of twelve, eight were Liberals and all connected with the worsted trade. The other four were two bankers, one wool-merchant and one medical practioner. The first three of this group were known Tories. The power house of Bradford Liberal Dissent, as Reynolds phrases it, was the Horton Lane Congregational Chapel: Reynolds, *The Great Paternalist*, pp. 119–120.

43 *Bradford Observer*, 10 April, 1848, quoted in Reynolds, *The Great Paternalist*, pp. 125–6. George White (?–1868): his parents were Irish and he settled in the Leicester area as a young man. He first came into prominence in the radical movement in 1837 in Leeds, and from then on was always taking a physical force line. He had two terms of imprisonment before he moved to Bradford in 1844. He was arrested again in 1848 and after his release from jail he took Harney's side in the internal quarrels after 1850. He continued some radical activity in the fifties and died in poverty in the Sheffield workhouse in 1868. A remarkable man whose career has been largely neglected. There is a dissertation by K. Geering, 'George White, a Nineteenth-Century Worker's Leader' (M. A. University of Sussex, 1973).

44 This report by a group of workers was unusual in the 1840s which saw a large number of government and private reports on the physical environments of urban Britain. According to Reynolds the Report of the Bradford Sanitary Committee was compiled by George White as secretary to the committee: *The Great Paternalist*, pp. 125–30. For the general public health background of this decade, see the introduction by M. W. Flinn to reprint of E. Chadwick, *Report on the Sanitary Condition of the Labouring Population of Great Britain . . . 1842* (Edinburgh, 1965).

45 T. Reid, *Life of the Right Honourable William Edward Forster*, vol. 1 (1888), p. 224.

46 The correspondence between Thorn and Arbuthnot, and Arbuthnot and the Home Office, is in HO 45/2410, part 4.

47 *ibid.*; for the Bingley incident see the correspondence between W. B. Ferrand and the Home Office, *ibid.* especially the letter dated 27 May which provides a full description of the rescue of the two Chartist prisoners.

48 W. E. Forster has a further passage in his diary about these events which once again illustrated the nature and character of the mainstream of Victorian liberalism. Reid visited Paris during May – his diary account is not very interesting, but he returned before the troubles at the end of the month. He enrolled as a special constable, although his biographer does not directly mention the fact, and Forster's diary entry for 29 May read: 'We had a slight Chartist fray here. The soldiers, of whom there are nearly a thousand in the town, were called out to help the specials to arrest some drillers. There were some stones thrown and heads broken but not mine, the stones flying over my head. All the inconvenience to me was patrolling till four in the morning, and being hooted by one party [i.e. the workers] and abused by the other, Joshua Pollard [Tory] attributing the row to me; but as my own conscience is clear, I care not for

that. My course is plain enough: to help the people to obtain peaceably their due, use all possible efforts to put down the rascals who mislead them and fatten on their misery, and above all to strive with all in my power to rescue them from starvation'. Reid, *Life of the Right Honourable William Edward Forster*, vol. 1, p. 247. Forster was always going on about being between 'ouvrier and bourgeois'.

49 Reynolds, *The Great Paternalist,* p. 146.

50 HO 45/2410, part 2, Manchester file.

51 There were many alarums and excursions on this matter of arms shipments through Liverpool to Ireland: one of the standard myths of this year. Most reported cases, all examined carefully, were found to be untrue or exaggerated. Examples in HO 45/2410, part 2, Liverpool file: 18 April, Rushton to HO 19 April, Mayor to Grey; 27 June, Mayor to Grey; 27 July, letter from private citizen; 29 July, Mayor to HO where a case of muskets addressed to Belfast had been intercepted.

52 For the general background to nineteenth-century Liverpool: see above, p. 260 note 60; and see also R. Lawton, 'The population of Liverpool in Mid-nineteenth Century', *Trans. Hist. Soc. Lancs. and Cheshire*, vol. 107 (1956), pp. 89–120; *idem*. 'Irish Immigration to England and Wales in Mid-nineteenth Century', *Irish Geography*, vol. 4, no. 1 (1959), pp. 25–54. There is useful material in F. Neal, 'The Birkenhead Garibaldi Riots of 1862', *Trans. Hist. Soc. Lancs. and Cheshire*, vol. 131 (1982), pp. 87–111; and an informative survey of the later growth of religious and political prejudices in P. Waller, *Sectarianism and Democracy. A Political History of Liverpool, 1868–1939* (1981).

53 All the quotations and references in the text relating to the correspondence between the Mayor of Liverpool and the Home Office are in HO 45/2410, part 2. There is, in addition, a great deal of documentary material in the *Liverpool Courier* and the *Liverpool Mercury* for the weeks between April and August.

54 Cf. White, *History of the Corporation of Liverpool*, p. 106, quoting *Reports of Inspectors of Constabulary*, 1857–8, XLVII; 'The Liverpool Police was larger in numbers than any other force in the country, and had always been recognised as efficient by the HO since the grants-in-aid of police expenditure had been introduced in 1856.'

55 HO 45/2410, Pt 2 Liverpool File.

56 Bisceglia, 'The Threat of Violence', has a useful bibliography for both McManus and Reynolds. There are only occasional references to either man in the HO papers, but there is a good deal about Reynolds in the briefs for the prosecution for the trials in the winter Assizes in TS 11/137, part 1. McManus was arrested for his part in the Ballingarry affair, convicted and transported to Tasmania.

57 *Liverpool Courier* and *Liverpool Journal* between 22 July and 2 August 1848. The Mayor of Liverpool sent full details of the numbers, and disposition, of the military forces in a letter of 26 July: HO 45/2410, part 2. The special constables numbered 12,000.

58 *Liverpool Journal*, 29 July 1848 (leading article). *The Times*, 29 July, also referred to the Liverpool petition. Its Liverpool correspondent noted that much offence had been given to the commercial community in Liverpool by the comments of certain of the London press on the habeas corpus request which, the correspondent insisted, was absolutely justified. *The Times* of this date also carried a long despatch from Manchester, noting that the Mayor and magistrates had issued a placard on the morning of the 28 July attacking the confederated

clubs and associations, and informing the public that all assemblages would be prohibited.

59 At least, there was no more correspondence in the HO files.

60 The financial economy practised all over Britain in the matter of police provision is a commonplace in historical writing on the subject. See for one example, J. Hart, 'Reform of the Borough Police, 1835–1856', *Engl. H. Rev.* LXX, no. 276 (July 1955), pp. 411–27.

61 Bisceglia, 'The Threat of Violence', p. 214; the reports of Cuddy's arrest and subsequent information are in the HO files dated 23, 24 and 25 July.

62 This was an incident which reached national headlines. The details are given in the Liverpool papers: *Liverpool Courier*, 2 August. The same issue of the *Courier* reported that the police were being drilled, in arms, every day, and that in some districts of the town they walked in pairs and were always armed. The special constables were now numbered at 20,000. The *Courier* further reported that a few days earlier large quantities of arms and ammunition had been brought into the town from Chester Castle, including cutlasses, which it was being said were for the use of special constables in an emergency.

63 Russell to Clarendon, 17 April, Box 43, Clarendon Papers.

64 *ibid.*, 3 April.

65 *ibid.*, 24 July.

66 *ibid.*, 28 July.

67 Clarendon to Russell, 15 March, Letter Book, vol. 2.

68 *Greville Memoirs*, vol. 6. p. 58.

69 Nowlan, *Politics of Repeal*, p. 303 ff. There is a useful footnote in Nowlan, 161, on p. 210, about the activities of J. D. Balfe, perhaps the most reliable informer for Dublin Castle. Box 53, Clarendon Papers, has some correspondence. His first letter to Clarendon was dated 7 April 1848. He concluded a long letter to Clarendon on 17 November 1848: 'I never was so happy as I am at present, and I say with truth that it is solely attributable in which I have been but too undeservedly treated by his Excellency that I feel a charm in life I never before experienced. I was the child of trouble and disappointment throughout life.' Balfe was never backward, however, at asking for money. There are scattered references to him in Clarendon's correspondence throughout the summer of 1848. Balfe ended up, according to Nowlan, in the prison service in Tasmania.

70 This is an interesting characteristic of the Whig leadership during this year. They were, of course, much concerned with their majority in the Commons, and before any major decisions in matters of internal security were taken, they always asked themselves what the reactions in the Commons would be. They had, of course, nothing to worry about in Parliament: support for law and order measures united almost everyone. Some sections of middle-class opinion outside Westminster were more difficult to convince, but by the summer of 1848 there were no dissenting or opposition voices of any significance.

71 Nowlan, *Politics of Repeal*, p. 121.

72 Clarendon to Grey, 28 July, Letter Book 3, Clarendon Papers. The letter was really for Russell, but Clarendon sent it first to Grey, being too tired, so he wrote, to make a duplicate.

73 This absurd statement came from another of Dublin Castle's informers, Phaire, who was always addressed as 'Colonel' Phaire, some of whose reports and

correspondence are in Box 22, Clarendon Papers, himself used a number of informants for the stories he peddled to the Castle, and that quoted in the text was imputed to one of these.

74 Accounts of the 'uprising' are in all the contemporary newspapers and journals for the early days of August 1848. Among accounts by contemporaries Gavan Duffy, *Four Years of Irish History*, p. 240 ff.; *idem*, *My Life in Two Hemispheres*, 2 vols. (1898), vol. I, chs. VII–x. The state trials of Smith O'Brien and others in the autumn of 1848 provide much background material: see below, Ch. 6.

75 Grey to Clarendon, 27 July 1848, HO, 79/9.

76 D. Goodway, *London Chartism*, 'Turbulent London' esp. pp. 89–96.

77 The Manchester authorities heard the news about Ashton – the shooting of the policeman and what was thought to be an outbreak – at 2.30 a.m. 18 August; and the Mayor wrote to Sir George Grey at 5 a.m. On the same day Arbuthnot sent his own summary of what had happened and forwarded the letter from the office in charge at Ashton, Lt-Col. Vaughan. These reports and letters are in HO 45/2410, part 2, Manchester file.

78 Very full accounts of the arrests in London appeared in *The Times* and all the London papers, beginning with the issues of 17 August 1848; and the detail can be added to by the lengthy briefs in the Treasury Solicitor's papers: TS 138/380; 139/381; 140/386; 140/387; 141/388; 141/389. The published reports of the state trials of this year offer easily accessible material; for which see below, Ch. 6.

79 The issues of the *Northern Star*, from 19 August on, are the best index to the state of mind of the Chartist movement in Britain. The *Star* always published the fullest details of all matters relating to the movement, and not least the accumulating evidence of the pervasiveness of police spies and informers. In the closing weeks of August it was beginning to warn against the 'gangs of packed jurors' in Ireland. Their reports, week after week, could only have had a depressing effect and influence upon their activists. For an example of police pressures – of which there were many – see the issue of 2 September 1848, an account of the dissolution of the 'Mitchel' Irish Confederate club which met on the 1 September at the Chartist Assembley Rooms, Blackfriars Rd. The meeting must have been advertised, or an informer was at work, for the police were out in force: 'About 50 policemen, armed with cutlasses, were on duty in Webber St' (which ran across Blackfriars Rd just north of St George's Circus). From mid-August in London the policing of all Chartist and Confederate meetings was routine.

80 Powell, the police informer, belonged to the Cripplegate locality. The following resolution was passed: 'We, the Chartists of the Cripplegate locality, solemnly declare that the man Powell was elected as a delegate by us for none other than a legal purpose, but whilst we disavow all attempts at anarchy and confusion, we declare our determination to use our best efforts to advance the cause of the People's Charter': *Northern Star*, 2 September 1848.

81 *Northern Star*, 23 September 1848.

82 *ibid.*, 11 November 1848.

83 The denunciations of Chartists during this year, while more extreme than at most times, not only made the movement the equivalent of Jacobinism and the resort of the dangerous classes, but there was also the customary anti-radical identification of the leadership with demagogues hoodwinking the honest masses. It was assumed that the leaders were doing well financially out of their roguery.

Days of Judgement

1 E. Halévy, *A History of the English People in 1815* (1924), book 1, p. 18 ff.
2 *ibid.*, pp. 23–4; W. I. Jennings, *Cabinet Government* (1947), ch. 3 and p. 425.
3 H. J. Laski, 'The Technique of Judicial Appointment', *Studies in Law and Politics* (1932), esp. pp. 168–9.
4 B. Abel-Smith and R. Stevens, *Lawyers and the Courts* (1967), p. 129. There is a defence of Halsbury's appointments in R. F. V. Heuston, *The Lives of the Lord Chancellors, 1885–1940* (1964), 'Lord Halsbury', ch. 5.
5 Halévy, *History of the English People*, p. 27.
6 W. I. Jennings, *The Law and the Constitution* (various editions, 1933–58) *passim*, esp. app. 2; A. V. Dicey, *Introduction to the Study of the Law of the Constitution* (9th edition, 1939, with Introduction and Appendix by E. C. S. Wade), esp. section 2 of Wade's appendix, 'Public Meetings and Liberty of Discussion', pp. 547–98.
7 Dicey, *Law of the Constitution*, pp. 239–40.
8 *ibid.*, p. 246.
9 Holdsworth, *A History of English Law*, vol. 10 (1938), p. 693.
10 *Reports of State Trials*, new ser. vol. I, 1820–3: The King Against Henry Hunt and Others, pp. 171–496. The words quoted in the text are at p. 435. There are slight discrepancies in the wording in other sources.
11 *State Trials*, new ser. vol. III, 1831–40, app. F, p. 1351.
12 quoted in E. Wise, *The Law Relating to Riots and Unlawful Assemblies* (2nd edition 1848), p. 87. The first edition of this most useful compilation was published in March 1848, and the second edition included a new chapter (ch. XI) which summarised the clauses of the Crown and Security Bill which became law towards the end of April.
13 *Hansard*, 3rd ser. XCVIII, cols. 6–7 (7 April 1848).
14 *The Times*, 6 June; the full statement is published in Wise, *Law Relating to Riots*, pp. 88–90.
15 *The Times*, 8 June. The reporter was Frederick Fowler. He repeated his statement at the trial of Fussell, for which see below, p. 179 ff., being asked 'what effect was produced upon the inhabitants residing in the line of march?' to which he answered: 'A great deal of fear, and terror, and surprise it appeared to me. A number of them shut up their shops and closed their doors.' *Reports of State Trials*, new ser. vol. VI, 1842–48, p. 734. The use of reporters, and their published reports, in the arrest and conviction of Chartist speakers was vigorously condemned in the radical press: for an early example, see the comment by G. J. Harney in an editorial in the *Northern Star*, 10 June 1848: 'It will not surprise our readers to find that Government spies are no longer confined to the police. Miserable wretches, calling themselves 'reporters of the press' are now seen doing the dirty work of *mouchards*.'
16 Benefit of clergy was a medieval privilege by which those in holy orders could claim immunity from trial in the secular courts. By the middle of the fourteenth century it had been extended to secular as well as religious clerks although a reading test was introduced: the so-called neck verse. It did not extend to those accused of high treason. The list of felonies without benefit of clergy, which meant that sentence of death could be imposed, was greatly extended in the eighteenth century and the practice of pleading benefit of clergy was abolished in 1827: D. M. Walker, *Oxford Companion to Law* (1980) and for a detailed history of the plea, J. Fitzjames Stephen, *A History of the Criminal Law of England* (1883), vol.

1, ch. XIII. For the law relating to unlawful assemblies: Wise, *Law Relating to Riots*, ch. 10; Holdsworth, *History of English Law*, vol. 10 (1938) p. 701 ff; *Kenny's Outlines of Criminal Law* (18th edition, 1962 by J. W. C. Turner) pp. 399–433.

17 Wades's Appendix to Dicey, *Law of the Constitution*, p. 565.

18 Draft reply from Home Office to Mayor of Birmingham who had asked for advice about whether arrests should be made. The answer was that the language spoken must be authenticated, and it was not expedient at the present time: HO 45/2410, part III, Warwick file, 12 April. On 9 June the Home Office arranged to supply a reporter from London; and on 11 June Sir George Grey, through H. Waddington, informed the Mayor that it was not advisable at present to apprehend G. J. Mantle (*ibid.*). An example of the problem that the local authorities faced was stated in a letter from the Mayor of Birmingham to HO *ibid.*, 30 July 1848: 'I have taken the best means I am able to obtain confirmation of the language used but it is very difficult, for if the purpose of the person sent is suspected he is at once hustled out of the meeting.'

19 See above, pp. 136–8.

20 This issue of *The Times*, 6 June, is especially useful for the legal background of the trials in 1848.

21 As noted above, Brougham had raised the matter of the continuous meetings in London on 2 June in the House of Lords, and there were comments from the Duke of Wellington and others. Lansdowne, in reply, said that if the meetings continued it would be necessary to seek amendment of the law: *Hansard*, 3rd ser. XCIX cols. 235–40.

22 These biographical details are taken from entries in the *DNB*; E. Foss, *Biographia Juridica. A Biographical Dictionary of the Judges of England. From the Conquest to the Present Time, 1066–1870* (1870). For an introduction to the under-researched subject of legal prosopography, see A. Dunman, 'A Social and Occupational Analysis of the English Judiciary: 1770–1790 and 1855–1875', *American J. of Legal History*, XVII (1973), pp. 353–64; and see also W. J. Reader, *Professional Men. The Rise of the Professional Classes in Nineteenth-Century England* (1966). There is a critical account of Sir Thomas Wilde in J. B. Atlay, *The Victorian Chancellors*, vol. 1, pp. 417–55.

23 Sir Thomas Platt was at the bottom end of the scale with personal estate under £16,000, while Sir William Erle was in the bracket of under £100,000: a large sum at the time of his death in 1880.

24 It is not easy to recover contemporary opinion of judges for the middle decades of the nineteenth century. J. B. Atlay, *Victorian Chancellors*, vol. 1, p. 448, has an interesting story of Maule's criticism of Sir Thomas Wilde's discursiveness; and Atlay was clear that 'Sir Thomas Wilde will not rank among the greatest judges.' Sergeant Ballantine, *Some Experiences of a Barrister's Life* (1882), wrote of Erle: 'He possessed a very judicial manner, thorough independence, and an earnest desire to secure justice in the cases he tried. He was, however, very obstinate, and once he had formed an opinion it was almost impossible to get him to change it. His experience in life had given him but little knowledge of some of its by-paths . . . his want of knowledge of the ways of the world', p. 211.

25 Originally published in two volumes in 1888, Lord Cockburn was himself one of the six presiding judges: 'This was an excellent court. Can I say more of it, than that I really believe that I was the worst judge in it. The other five, notwithstanding some peculiarities in our head, were all admirable', vol. 2, p. 228.

26 1806–76; from 1855 to his death he was both Lord of the court of Session and Lord of the Justiciary: *DNB*, v.
27 Cockburn, *Examination of the Trials*, vol. 2, p. 233.
28 *ibid.*, p. 235.
29 *ibid.*, p. 242–3. Cockburn, in this particular passage, emphasised the 'improved mode of returning the whole sixty-five jurors by the sheriff [which] made them consist of all varieties of opinion. The presiding judge no longer picked. It was a trial.'
30 *ibid.*, vol. 1, Introduction, pp. 88–9.
31 *The Times*, 8 December 1848, prints what appears to be Alderson's complete statement. His speech sentencing the accused (who included G. J. Mantle of Birmingham) is in *Reports of State Trials*, new ser. vol. VII, 1848–50, App. A, pp. 1121–3. Altogether nineteen were charged with riot and conspiracy at Hyde and sixteen were found guilty; Mantle defended himself in a speech of two hours; and the jury, 'after a brief deliberation', as *The Times* described it, found him guilty.
32 The reference is to the debate initiated by E. J. Hobsbawm, 'The British Standard of Living 1790–1850' *Econ. Hist. Rev.'* second ser. x, no. 1 (August 1957), pp. 46–68, followed by exchanges between R. M. Hartwell and Hobsbawm in the same journal. The debate has continued.
33 There is a large literature on the land question in the nineteenth century. For a convenient summary, see D. E. Martin, *John Stuart Mill and the Land Question* (1981), and his thesis upon which this monograph was based: 'Economic and Social Attitudes to Landed Property in England, 1790–1850, with particular reference to John Stuart Mill' (Ph.D. University of Hull, 1972).
34 The weekly *Economist* is a useful guide to orthodox economic thinking in mid-Victorian Britain, and it was consistently sceptical of the ideas of the land reformers and not least of the advocates of small ownership. For the latter, see C. J. Dewey, 'The Rehabilitation of the Peasant Proprietor in Nineteenth-Century Economic Thought', *Hist. of Pol. Economy*, 6, no. 1 (1974)*,* pp. 17–47; and the subsequent comment by D. E. Martin, *ibid.*, 8, no. 2 (Summer 1976), pp. 297–302.
35 *The Times*, 14 December 1848.
36 *DNB*, XIII; Foss, *Biographia Juridica*, p. 438.
37 *State Trials*, new ser. vol. VI, 1842–8, pp. 813–4. The *Northern Star*, 22 July 1848, included a tit-bit of gossip in a long editorial on the political trials of Fussell, Jones and others over which Sir Thomas Wilde presided: 'the husband of Augusta Emma d'Este, the – according to law – bastard daughter of the later Duke of Sussex and Lady Augusta Murray. There was granted to "Mademoiselle D'Este" on the 5th of March 1845 a pension of £500 yearly; and, on the succeeding 28th of July, another like sum of £500 yearly. We learn from a little book [W. Strange, *Sketches of Her Majesty's Household*] . . . that the said Mademoiselle Augusta Emma D'Este was married to Sir Thomas Wilde . . . on the 13th of August, 1845.' Very shortly after their union, Sir Thomas Wilde was raised to the Bench at a salary of £8,000 per annum. In addition to this enormous salary, the Lord Chief Justice is reported to have possessed great wealth from a lengthened course of professional prosperity, notwithstanding which Lady Wilde accepted her second pension, within a fortnight of her marriage. 'It was supposed', says the book from which I quote, 'by many, that, upon her marriage, her ladyship would have resigned the two pensions. The pensions, however, are still retained by her ladyship, and received regularly every quarter'. It should be

noted that a copy of Strange's book has not been located in any library in the United Kingdom.

38 Cockburn, *Examination of the Trials for Sedition*, comments on this problem, vol. 2, p. 227. The report of the Grant, Rankin and Hamilton trial on 13 and 14 November 1848 in the *State Trials* series (vol. VII, p. 597 ff.) was based on J. Shaw, *Justiciary Reports*. Cockburn described Shaw as 'the worst of all reporters' and offers further criticism of the *Justiciary Reports*.

39 *The Times*, 26 September 1848, p. 7.

40 *State Trials*, vol. VI, 1842–8, p. 729.

41 *State Trials*, vol. VI, 1842–8, p. 733. In the official text, after 'I have five sons' the reporter added: 'I am not positive whether it is five or four – I suppose I was knocked on the elbow at the time.'

42 Queen Victoria to Russell, RA C8/18, 31 May 1848; Russell to Victoria, RA C56/84, 1 June. In a letter to the Queen on 4 June Sir George Grey explained the problems of a successful prosecution against Fussell because of the absence of a reporter 'expressly engaged for the purpose of taking down the speeches . . .', RA C56/86.

43 quoted above, p. 135.

44 *Punch*, vol. XIV, p. 240.

45 *State Trials*, vol. VI, pp. 739–40.

46 Nor was most of the press critical. The London *Weekly Dispatch*, which in normal times was a moderately radical paper, wrote on 9 July that 'Fowler's reports were pretty warmly coloured'; and in a leading article on the front page of the succeeding issue (16 July) it underlined the point that the only evidence for the allegation about assassination was one 'jobbing penny-a-liner, swearing up the accuracy of his own report, the only means of securing his future bread and butter' as against a dozen eye-witness accounts which rejected the story. The *Dispatch* was surprised that the Lord Chief Justice did not throw out the item in the indictment relating to assassination.

47 The informer in the Smith O'Brien trial – a man called Dobbyn – was thoroughly discredited by the defence counsel: *State Trials*, vol. VII, pp. 306–16, and see below p. 192. In one of the last trials of the year, at Liverpool Assizes, an informer, Ball, was so obviously lying that he was disowned by the prosecuting counsel: *The Times*, 20 December 1848; *Northern Star*, 30 December 1848.

48 The reference is to Thomas Erskine (1750–1823) who defended, among other radicals of the 1790s, Tom Paine and Thomas Hardy: H. Roscoe, *Eminent British Lawyers* (1830), pp. 329–91; *DNB*, VI; L. P. Stryker, *For the Defence. Thomas Erskine* (1949).

49 Feargus O'Connor who, during this year, offered no serious political lead to the Chartist movement, was still as acute as he had always been concerning day-to-day politics. Commenting on the trials in Ireland and England (*Northern Star*, 29 July 1848), he wrote: 'and while you talk of the facility of packing juries in Ireland, you have never cast a thought that there is no necessity for packing juries in England, as the whole list contains a long catalogue of oppressors, whose interests are supposed to be hazarded and jeopardised by the growing spirit of Democracy'.

50 'I must own', Sir Thomas Wilde said during his summing up, 'as far as my experience goes, that if one man takes notes in ordinary hand, and another takes notes in shorthand, so far as the ordinary hand goes, it is generally the most correct, he does not take as much, but the shorthand writer has many marks and

notes. . . and, I believe, among the best reporters, it has generally been admitted, were to be found men who did not write shorthand at all', *State Trials*, vol. VI, pp. 767–8. Wilde took some time over this matter of how the reports were taken down, although, as he later emphasised, both accounts agreed on the assassination statement; but it may be presumed that Wilde was conscious of the damage that had been done to Fowler's character during cross-examination and felt it necessary to do what he could to reassure the jury on Fowler's methods of transcription.

51 p. 178; the trial of Ernest Jones is in *State Trials*, vol. VI, 1842–8, pp. 783–830.

52 J. B. Atlay, *The Victorian Chancellors*, vol. I (1906), p. 448.

53 *ibid.* Atlay adds of this group of Chartists who were tried during the same period as Ernest Jones that 'They were all convicted, and the sentences did not err on the side of leniency.'

54 *London Chartism*, pp. 87–96.

55 Cuffay's trial is in *State Trials*, vol. VII, 1848–50, pp. 468–82.

56 See note 47 above. The revelation that Powell (alias Johnson) was an informer profoundly shocked the London Chartist movement. The press carried the news first on 17 August 1848, and the columns of the *Northern Star* for 19, and 26 August and 2 September bear witness to the impact that the disclosure had upon the Chartist organistions.

57 C. Alderson, *Selections from the Charges and other Detached Papers of Baron Alderson, with an introductory notice of his life* (1858), pp. 105–6.

58 John Saville, 'The Meerut Trial, 1929–1933', *Dictionary of Labour Biography*, (edited by J. M. Bellamy and J. Saville), vol. VII (1984), pp. 84–91.

59 Nowlan, *The Politics of Repeal*, pp. 194–203.

60 *Cambridge Modern History*, vol. XI (1934), p. 13.

61 *Hansard*, 3rd ser. LXXVI, cols. 1966–8 (9 August 1844).

62 Blackburne became a King's Counsel in 1822 and was first appointed Attorney-General in Grey's ministry in 1831. Blackburne prosecuted O'Connell in the same year and their enmity lasted until the latter's death. When Derby became Prime Minister in 1852 he appointed Blackburne to the Irish Chancellorship. Blackburne retired when the ministry was defeated in the autumn of the same year, but he became Chancellor again in 1866, retiring the following year. It was said of Blackburne that 'conservatives in general placed Blackburne among the foremost judicial persons and the sagest and safest counsellors of the age'. F. E. Ball, *The Judges in Ireland* (1927), vol. 2, book VI, p. 293.

63 In Special Commissions of the kind that brought Smith O'Brien to trial, the prosecution was entitled to choose the three senior judges who would sit on the Bench: *Freeman's Journal*, 26 October 1848.

64 Sir Michael O'Loghlen was the first Roman Catholic to be called to the Bench since the Act of Emancipation. For some aspects of his career during the Melbourne administration, see above, pp. 49–51

65 The trial is in *State Trials*, vol. VII, 1848–50, pp. 2–331; and this is followed by the Report of the appeal for a Writ of Error, pp. 331–74 (21 November 1848 and concluded by the judgement on 16 January 1849); and then by the appeal to the House of Lords, 10 and 11 May 1849, pp. 375–80. The various references in the text are taken from the official report in *State Trials*, but as with the English Reports there are some discrepancies with the accounts in the press. The *Freeman's Journal* has been used for the daily reports of the trial. There is a volume by J. G. Hodges, *Report of the Trial of William Smith O'Brien* (1849).

66 *State Trials*, vol. VII, pp. 26–7.
67 *State Trials*, new ser. vol. IV, 1839–43. Sir Frederick Pollock, for the defence, made application for the jurors to be balloted and the Attorney-General announced that he saw no reason why the normal practice should not be adhered to, but that he would accept the direction of the judges. After consultation, the judges agreed to the request but made it clear that their agreement was conditional upon the agreement of the Attorney-General: pp. 105–10.
68 On the issue of the difference between high treason and petit treason the defence argued, through Fitzgerald, 'By 6 Geo. 4 c. 25 in England the crime of petit treason has been reduced to the crime of murder; and in the corresponding Act in England, which reduces the prisoner's right to peremptory challenges to twenty (6 Geo. 4 c. 50 s. 29) the word "treason" is left out' (p. 44).
69 The *Freeman's Journal*, 30 October 1848, gave an example of Blackburne's prejudice against the defence in these political trials. One day the Solicitor-General, after the defence had completed their case, said that he had a slight cold and asked for a postponement until the next day. Normally the court sat from 9 a.m. to 7 p.m., and the Solicitor-General's request was made at 5 p.m. The Lord Chief Justice agreed. On Friday 27 October Isaac Butt began his summing up in the T. F. Meagher case. After he had spoken for four hours, he asked for an adjournment until the next day on the grounds that he felt somewhat exhausted. Blackburne refused.
70 *State Trials*, vol. VII, 1848–50, pp. 203–4.
71 *ibid.*, pp. 204–5. The phrase 'on that table' has the meaning of 'in the witness box'.
72 *State Trials*, new ser. vol. IV, 1839–43, pp. 85–480.
73 Whiteside had been interrupted by the Attorney-General who protested that the letter of Russell had no bearing on the case. Blackburne also disapproved, but could not refuse to hear it.
74 *State Trials*, vol. VII, p. 222.
75 *ibid.*, pp. 304–15.
76 *ibid.*, p. 324.
77 'that you, William Smith O'Brien, be taken from hence to the place from whence you came, and be there drawn on a hurdle to the place of execution, and be there hung by the neck until you be dead, and that afterwards your head shall be severed from your body, and your body divided into four quarters, to be dispersed as Her Majesty shall think fit. And may the God of mercy have mercy on your soul.' *Ibid.* p. 331.
78 *State Trials*, vol. VII, p. 374.
79 *Hansard*, 3rd ser. XCVIII, cols. 29–34 (7 April).
80 pp. 170–1.
81 *State Trials*, vol. VII, p. 378.
82 The *Illustrated London News* had an editorial on the verdict on 14 October 1848 and was already arguing for the commutation of the death sentence. From this time the Irish press was increasingly concerned with the issue; and the general sentiment in the rest of Britain followed.
83 *State Trials*, vol. VII, pp. 379, note (a); *DNB*, XIV; Nowlan, *Politics of Repeal*, pp. 216–7.
84 *State Trials*, vol. VII, p. 1107.
85 *Dublin University Magazine*, CXCI (November 1848), p. 606.
86 *ibid.*, p. 602.

87 ibid. The *Magazine* also attacked the refusal of the Attorney-General to give the prisoners the privileges they would have had in England: of being furnished with a list of witnesses, for example (p. 605).

88 *Freeman's Journal*, 13 November, 2, 12 and 13 December 1848.

89 *ibid.*, 13 December 1848.

90 The full text of the Viceroy's statement is in *Freeman's Journal*, 13 December, and see *The Times*, *Morning Chronicle* and *Morning Post* 16 to 19 December 1848.

91 *Freeman's Journal*, 30 December 1848.

92 Clarendon to Trevelyan, Clarendon Papers, Letter Book III, 27 December 1848.

93 This was published on 2 January. The issue of 3 January quoted from the *Cork Examiner* of Monday 1 January the figures in the workhouse of the Bantry Union and of those on outdoor relief. There was no suggestion by *The Times* that the figures were exaggerated, only that they were an example of what happens when 'prudence' was not central to the affairs of daily life. Naturally, *The Times* ended: 'We deplore the catastrophe of those who will not condescend to be prudent and safe, but we cannot prevent it, and certainly are not answerable for it.'

94 quoted in C. Woodham–Smith, *The Great Hunger* (1962), pp. 375–6.

A commentary by way of conclusion

1 Introduction to *A Year of Revolution. From a Journal Kept in Paris*. vol. 1 (1857), pp. xiii–xiv.

2 *Annual Register 1848*, Chronicle. Reference to the Chartist movement are on pp. 39, 48–50, 50–4, 59, 72–4, 80, 103–4, 121–2, 137, 150, 165–6. The victory of 10 April was the product 'of the zealous and almost unanimous determination of all classes'; the demonstration on Kennington Common ended 'amidst scorn and ridicule'; the examination of the petition brought upon its organisers 'scorn and ridicule'; later demonstrations in the summer of 1848 showed that the Chartists were in a minority, and the first arrests of the London Chartists, in early June, were supported 'with the full approbation of the public', since the Chartists had proved themselves 'intolerable nuisances'.

3 For a critical review of Christian Socialism, see John Saville, 'The Christian Socialists of 1848', *Democracy and the Labour Movement* (edited by John Saville, 1954), pp. 135–59, and for a more favourable account, especially of J. M. Ludlow, see T. Christensen, *Origin and History of Christian Socialism, 1848–1854* (Aarhus, 1962). The text which follows, and also the later discussion of Feargus O'Connor, are largely taken from my Introduction to the reprint of Gammage's *History of the Chartist Movement* (New York, 1969), p. 29 ff. and pp. 62–5.

4 The most vigorous attack, from within the establishment press, was by J. W. Croker in the *Quarterly Review* for September 1951; and for other unfavourable commentaries, *The Times*, 18 October 1850; *Blackwood's Magazine*, November 1850, and *Edinburgh Review*, January 1851.

5 G. J. Holyoake was one of the few critics in the nineteenth century who properly understood Kingsley's motives. See 'The Chartists of Fiction' in *Bygones Worth Remembering*, vol. 1 (1905), ch. VIII where Holyoake sums up *Alton Locke* as a book 'written in derision of Chartism and Liberal politics . . . Alton Locke, despite the noble personal qualities with which he is endowed, was a confused political traitor, who bartered the Kingdom of Man for the Kingdom of Heaven, when he might have stood by both' (p. 90). Kinglsey was, in fact, explicit about what he and his colleagues were trying to achieve. In 1852, less than two years after the

publication of *Alton Locke*, Kingsley replied to a vigorous attack in *Fraser's Magazine* in a pamphlet whose title explained his position: *Who are the Friends of Order? A Reply to Certain Observations in a Late Number of Fraser's Magazine on the So-called 'Christian Socialists'*. 'We tell people simple to do their duty in that state of life to which God has called them . . . [the results of our work have been] to make ardent and discontented spirits among the working classes more patient and contented; more respectful to those institutions of which they have never been taught the value, and of which they have too little experienced the benefit; to turn their minds from those frantic and suicidal dreams of revolution, which have been the stock-in-trade of such men as Feargus O'Connor, to deliberate an orderly self-improvement, and the pursuit of an honourable independence; to make them aware, many of them, alas! for the first time in their lives, that there were numbers, far greater than they had ever fancied, among what are called "the upper classes of society" who cared for them, respected them, were willing to help them to the uttermost, and yet required of them no degrading counter-payment of adulation or dependence. That this has been the moral effect, and the only moral effect of our labours, I distinctly assert. Your gently implied fear that we have helped to spread destructive doctrines, is, I assure you, unfounded. Those doctrines, both French and others, were at their height among the working classes several years before we intermeddled. It was the fact of their circulation which aroused us to try if we could not supply an antidote to the poison, a true coin instead of the counterfeit; that there has been a perceptible and rapidly increasing improvement in the tone of the working-class publications of late; and men who have the very best opportunities of judging, are kind enough to attribute some of that improvement to us' (p. 16).

6 *Alton Locke*, with a prefatory memoir by Thomas Hughes (1900), ch. 34, pp. 254–5.

7 *ibid.*, ch. 40, p. 302.

8 The *History* was first published in parts: the first two parts in late 1854 and five more in 1855. The bound volume appeared in November 1855: see John Saville, Introduction to the 1894 reprint of the *History of the Chartist Movement* (New York, 1969), esp. p. 24 ff.

9 8th edition (1854), vol. vi, p. 671.

10 The *Leader* carried two articles on Chartism, 26 May and 2 June 1855, using Gammage's *History* – or the parts which had so far been published – as a peg on which to hang their own comments on the movement: 'It is a deplorable story, in many respects, but chiefly in that it exhibits "the people" taught by paltry agitators to be violent, to be suspicious, to be jealous, to doubt their friends, and to bring discredit on their principles by a rash, theatrical, and violent mode of asserting them. In substance the history is that of a vast crowd organised to follow despicable leaders, and led by them into folly, into peril, into failure' (26 May 1855).

11 vol. 2 (1876), p. 335. The section on Chartism will be found between pp. 311 and 336.

12 p. 322. Among other school texts looked at, none of which had anything but a cursory and traditional account of the Chartist movement, see: H. White, *History of Great Britain and Ireland . . . For the Use of Schools and Private Students* (1855); J. C. Curtis, *Outlines of English History, Arranged in Chronological Order* (4th edition, 1867); J. M. D. Meiklejohn, *A New History of England and Great Britain* (1st

edition, 1879); C. Ransome, *Elementary History of England* (1897).

13 vol. 1, p. 113.

14 vol. 6, p. 345.

15 W. E. Adams, *Memoirs of a Social Atom*, vol. 1 (1903), pp. 183–4.

16 W. P. Roberts, a remarkable personality, has not yet found his biographer. For his political influence on Annie Besant any of the numerous biographical studies of her will provide information: for a comprehensive bibliography, see *Dictionary of Labour Biography*, vol. IV, pp. 21–31.

17 The original request for information appeared in the *Newcastle Weekly Chronicle* 6 January 1883 (Notes and Queries, p. 2) and was republished under Unanswered Questions, 3 February 1883. The first reply was on 24 February and other letters followed in the issues of 3, 10, 17, 24 and 31 March and 7 April. The quotation in the text, from F. P (Frank Peel?) of Heckmondwike, appeared 17 March 1883.

18 *Newcastle Weekly Chronicle*, 7 April 1883. Gammage wrote: 'Since it [the *History*] was published, I have many times regretted that I did not let a few more years elapse before I wrote it. It was written under pecuniary and other difficulties which men generally are not able to understand.'

19 Among the works published before the end of the nineteenth century, see: H. M. Hyndman, *The Historical Basis of Socialism in England* (1883); E. C. K. Gonner, 'The Early History of Chartism', *Engl. H. Review*, IV (1889), pp. 625–44; S. and B. Webb, *History of Trade Unionism* (1894); J. Tildsley, *Die Entstehung und die ökonomischen Grundsätze der Chartistenbewegung* (Jena, 1898); G. Wallas, *The Life of Francis Place, 1771–1854* (1898).

20 The most comprehensive discussion is now N. Kirk, *The Growth of Working-Class Reformism in Mid-Victorian England* (1985).

21 R. A. Church, *The Great Victorian Boom 1850–1873* (1975), n. 5 p. 79, quoting data from P. Deane, 'New Estimates of Gross National Product for the United Kingdom, 1830–1914; *Review of Income and Wealth*, XIV (1968).

22 T. Tooke and W. Newmarch, *History of Prices*, vol. 5 (1857), p. 448.

23 The annual rates of growth in GNP for the United Kingdom were: 1.7 per cent for 1840–50; 2.5 for 1850–60; 2.6 for 1860–70. The lower figure for 1840–50 includes both the severe depression of the early years of the decade and the Irish famine of the middle years: Church, *Great Victorian Boom*, pp. 24–5 and n. 5, p. 79; H. M. Boot, *The Commercial Crisis of 1847* (Hull, 1984), p. 85.

24 'This phrase [the hungry forties] seems to have been coined in 1903 by Cobden's daughter Jane (1851–1949)': D. Read, *Edwardian England* (1972), p. 130. It was part of the campaign against the protectionist lobby of these years.

25 Clapham, *Economic History of Modern Britain*, vol. 1, ch. V; G. C. Allen, *The Industrial development of Birmingham and the Black Country, 1860–1927* (1929; reprinted 1966); H. L. Beales, 'Studies in bibliography. IV. The "Basic" Industries of England, 1850–1914', *Econ. H. Rev.*, V (1934–5), pt 2, pp. 99–112; C. A. W. Ward. *A Bibliography of the History of Industry in the West Riding of Yorkshire, 1750–1914*. Leeds Philosophical and Literary Society Transactions, XIII, pt 1 (Leeds, 1968).

26 The statistics in this paragraph are taken from B. Mitchell and P. Deane, *Abstract of British Historical Statistics* (Cambridge, 1962), p. 187. For the revisionist case which adopts a conservative estimate of the political activities of the handloom weavers, see D. Bythell, *The Handloom Weavers* (Cambridge, 1969), ch. 9.

27 P. Joyce, *Work, Society and Politics* (1980), and see also *idem*. 'The Factory Politics of Lancashire in the Later Nineteenth Century', *Hist. J.*, XVIII, no. 3 (1975), pp. 525–53. For a reasoned critique, N. Kirk, 'Cotton Workers and Deference', *Bull. Soc. Study Lab. Hist.* no. 42 (Spring, 1981), pp. 41–3; and *idem*, *The Growth of Working Class Reformism*, esp. ch. 1.

28 The division of the labour force into skilled and unskilled is, of course, much too simplistic. M. H. Dobb, *Studies in the Development of Capitalism* (1946), using Clapham's analysis of industrial organisation, emphasised the lack of homogeneity in the social composition of the proletariat (p. 265 ff.) and he underestimated the variety that still remained by 1900. For an introduction to the recent literature on the labour process and the divisions within the workforce in the late nineteenth century, see the essays by R. Price, A. Reid and J. Zeitlin in *The Development of Trade Unionism in Great Britain and Germany, 1880–1914* (edited by W. J. Mommsen and H-G Husung, 1985).

29 T. R. Tholfsen, 'The Artisan and the Culture of Early Victorian Birmingham', *Univ. Birmingham Hist J.*, IV (1953–4), pp. 146–66; and *idem*, *Working Class Radicalism in Mid-Victorian Britain* (1976); S. Pollard, *A History of Labour in Sheffield* (Liverpool, 1959); S. Pollard and C. Holmes, *Essays in the Economic and Social History of South Yorkshire* (Barnsley, 1976). The growth of studies in the history of the labour process has greatly illuminated the industrial structures of working-class Britain in the past century and a half. For an introduction to the subject, see: F. Wilkinson (ed.), *The Dynamics of Labour Market Segmentation* (1981); and a review article by J. Turner, 'Man and Braverman: British Industrial Relations', *History*, vol. 70, no. 229 (June 1985), pp. 236–42.

30 E. P. Thompson, 'The Peculiarities of the English', *Soc. Register*, (1965) pp. 310–62; reprinted with minor changes in *The Poverty of Theory* (1978).

31 D. Neave, 'Friendly Societies in the Rural East Riding 1830–1912', (Univ. of Hull Ph.D. 1986).

32 *ibid.*, p. 138 ff.

33 The standard history of Friendly Societies, P. H. J. H. Gosden, *The Friendly Societies in England, 1815–1875* (Manchester 1961), argued that it was the better-off workers who largely made up the membership of the affiliated Orders; and the argument is repeated in *idem*, *Self-Help: Voluntary Organisations in Nineteenth Century Britain* (1973).

34 Clapham, *Economic History*, vol. 1, p. 590.

35 C. R. Dobson, *Masters and Journeymen. A Prehistory of Industrial Relations 1717–1800* (1980), ch. 1.

36 J. B. Jefferys, *The Story of the Engineers* (1946), ch. 1; and *idem*, *Labour's Formative Years* (1948), Introduction, p. 17.

37 K. S. Inglis, *Churches and the Working Classes in Victorian England* (1963), was an important pioneering work; and for a recent survey, with bibliography, H. Mcleod, *Religion and the Working Class in Nineteenth Century Britain* (1984).

38 S. Pollard, 'Nineteenth Century Co-operation: from Community Building to Shopkeeping', *Essays in Labour History* (edited by A. Briggs and J. Saville, rev. ed., 1967), pp. 74–112.

39 G. J. Holyoake, *Self-Help by the People. Thirty-three Years of Co-operation in Rochdale*, pt 1, 1844–57 (9th edition, 1882), p. 40.

40 H. O. Horne, *A History of Savings Banks* (1940), App. 2.

41 M. Yeadell, 'Building Fluctuations and Building Societies in the West Riding of Yorkshire, 1785–1914', (M. Phil. University of Hull, 1980), ch. 4.

42 D. J. V. Jones, *The Last Rising* (Oxford, 1985), p. 226.
43 C. Driver, *Tory Radical: The Life of Richard Oastler* (New York, 1946), for the most stimulating account; and for a more traditional study, J. T. Ward, *The Factory Movement, 1830–1855* (1962).
44 quoted by J. Belchem, '1848: Feargus O'Connor and the Collapse of the Mass Platform', *The Chartist Experience* (edited by J. Epstein and D. Thompson, 1982), p. 285.
45 Conrad Gill and Asa Briggs, *History of Birmingham* (vol. 1 to 1865 by Gill, and vol. 2 1865–1938 by Briggs, 1952); and see also note 29 above.
46 J. Foster, *Class Struggle and the Industrial Revolution* (1974), ch. 4.
47 Foster's work has stimulated a considerable commentary from quite different intellectual positions. A sample includes: J. Saville, 'Class Struggle and the Industrial Revolution', *Socialist Register*, (1974), pp. 226–40; G. Stedman Jones, 'Class Struggle and the Industrial Revolution', *New Left Review*, no. 90 (March–April 1975) pp. 35–69; A. E. Musson, 'Class Struggle and the Labour Aristocracy', *Social History*, 3 (October 1976), pp. 335–56, and the reply by Foster, *ibid.* pp. 357–66.
48 T. Clarke and T. Dickson, 'Class and Class Consciousness in Early Industrial Capitalism: Paisley 1770–1850', in *Capital and Class in Scotland* (edited by T. Dickson, Edinburgh, 1982), pp. 8–60.
49 The most useful introduction to the *Northern Star* and its importance within the Chartist movement is J. Epstein, 'Feargus O'Connor and the *Northern Star*' *International Review of Soc. History*, 21 (1976), pp. 51–97. There is a shortened version in ch. 2 of Epstein's *The Lion of Freedom* (1982).
50 'There died suddenly last week a workman in Newcastle whose name revived recollections of the time when the People's Charter absorbed the attention of the entire body of the working classes in England. Feargus O'Connor Martin died at the age of 41': Robin Goodfellow's column (W. E. Adams), *Newcastle Weekly Chronicle*, 14 April 1883.
51 The above paragraph in the text is largely taken from the author's Introduction to the reprint of R. G. Gammage, *History of the Chartist Movement* (New York, 1969), pp. 62–4.
52 J. Epstein, *The Lion of Freedom* (1982) discusses in detail O'Connor's career up to 1842, but we have no overall view of his political tactics and strategy for the later years. It would seem that his own understanding of the place of the Land Plan in social reform became steadily more conservative by the time 1848 was reached: a conclusion I owe to Mlle M. T. Bodin of the University of Poitiers.
53 for which see R. Miliband, *Parliamentary Socialism* (1961).
54 There are many editions of F. Engels, *The Condition of the Working Class in England*, which first appeared, in German, in 1845. The first English edition was 1892; and the quotation in the text is taken from the Panther, London, edition of 1969, with an introduction by E. J. Hobsbawm: pp. 254, 255.
55 The definitive study of those previously described as 'Ricardian Socialists', and now more properly called 'Smithian Socialists', is Noel W. Thompson, *The Peoples' Science* (Cambridge, 1984).
56 quoted in P. Hollis, *The Pauper Press* (Oxford, 1970), p. 220.
57 The most convenient summary of the work of these middle-class educationalists and propagandists is R. K. Webb, *The British Working Class Reader, 1790–1848* (1955).
58 quoted in Belchem, 'Feargus O'Connor and the Collapse of the Mass Platform', p.

285. The quotations from Storah and Pilling are in *The Trial of Feargus O'Connor* (1843; reprint New York, 1970), pp. 256, 254–5.
59 The programme of the 1851 Convention is reprinted in J. Saville, *Ernest Jones. Chartist* (1952), pp. 257–63.
60 N. W. Thompson, *The People's Science*, pp. 219–28.
61 For the beginnings of the discussion, see 'The Owenite Legacy', J. F. C. Harrison, *Robert Owen and the Owenites in Britain and America* (1969), pp. 235–54.
62 J. Saville, 'J. E. Smith and the Owenite Movement 1833–4', in *Robert Owen. Prophet of the Poor* (edited) by S. Pollard and J. Salt, 1971), pp. 115–44.
63 G. Stedman Jones, *Languages of Class* (Cambridge, 1983), esp. ch 3, 'Rethinking Chartism'.
64 P. Richards, 'State Formation and Class Struggle, 1832–48', in *Capitalism, State Formation and Marxist Theory* (edited by P. Corrigan, 1980), pp. 49–78.
65 The literature on the Poor Law and its workings is voluminous. For a general survey, Sir George Nicholls, *A History of the English Poor Law*, vol 11 (1854), and for the Andover scandal, pp. 394–6; N. C. Edsall, *The Anti-Poor Law Movement 1834–44* (Manchester, 1971); I. Anstruther, *The Scandal of the Andover Workhouse* (1973).
66 W. M. Frazer, *A History of English Public Health 1834–1939* (1950); A. S. Wohl, *Endangered Lives. Public Health in Victorian Britain* (1983).
67 quoted by Richards, 'State Formation and Class Struggle', p. 74.
68 Stedman Jones, *Languages of Class*, 'Rethinking Chartism' p. 177.
69 *ibid.*, p. 176.
70 Above, pp. 214–15. It is worth noting that Stedman Jones omits any reference to Noel Thompson's important new assessment of the socialists of the 1820s in *The People's Science*.
71 For an introduction to Gramsci's use of the term hegemony, see the article in *A Dictionary of Marxist Thought* (edited by T. Bottomore, 1983), pp. 201–3, and the attached bibliography.
72 See above, p. 162. The changing composition of the personnel of the middle-range leadership of the Chartist movement is a subject for future research.
73 *Northern Star*, 2 December 1848. The last chance for a revival of the Chartist movement on any scale came in the two or three years after the release from prison of Ernest Jones in the summer of 1850; but the political conflicts between Jones and Harney that had developed by 1852 were a major factor in the movement's decline. The whole episode requires a more analytical discussion than is at present available.
74 K. Marx, *Letters to Kugelmann*, p. 123.
75 V. I. Lenin, *State and Revolution* (Little Lenin Library, 1933), p. 31.
76 Barrington Moore, Jnr, *Social Origins of Dictatorship and Democracy*, p. 39.
77 J. Morley, *The Life of William Ewart Gladstone*, vol. II (1903), p. 133.
78 *Trial of Feargus O'Connor* (1843), p. 283.
79 The literature on the Irish in Britain has been growing steadily. For the anti-Irish riots of the middle decades of Victorian England, there is an excellent account, and bibliography, in Kirk, *The Growth of Working-Class Reformism*, ch. 7; and see also Foster, *Class Struggle and the Industrial Revolution*, pp. 243–6; *The Irish in the Victorian City* (edited by R. Swift and S. Gilley, 1985).
80 quoted in Carol Johnson, 'Reformism and Commodity Fetishism', *New Left Review*, no. 119 (Jan.–Feb. 1980), pp. 70–96, p. 83. I have leaned heavily on Ms Johnson's analysis for my ideas on these matters.

81 This is the point made by Ms Johnson, cited in the previous reference; and also by D. Fernbach in his introduction to K. Marx, *The First International and After*. Fernbach, referring to Marx's letter to Bolte, 23 November 1871, comments: 'Despite Marx's steadfast attack on all visible reformist manifestations, he seriously underestimated the strength of reformism, and did not fully understand the nature of its roots . . . No more than in the Manifesto does Marx leave a theoretical space for the possibility of a workers' movement that is organised politically as a class and yet struggles solely for reforms within the capitalist system' (pp. 58–9).

82 G. Crossick, 'The Labour Aristocracy and its Values: A Study of Mid-Victorian Kentish London', *Victorian Studies*, XIX, no. 3 (March 1976), pp. 301–28; Kirk, *The Growth of Working Class Reformism*, ch. 5.

83 *ibid.*, p. 245.

84 *ibid.*

85 'A scab is to his trade what a traitor is to his country . . . He is an enemy to himself, to the present age, and to posterity: from *The Amended General Laws of the Amalgamated Society of Cordwainers, in Reference to Trade, Sick and Funeral Funds*, London 1867, quoted in Jefferys, *Labour's Formative Years*, p. 46.

86 The poem was originally printed in B. C. Cummings, *An Historical Survey of the Boilermakers and Iron and Steel Shipbuilders Society* (1905), p. 86; extract in Jefferys, *Labour's Formative Years*, pp. 48–9. The story of the troubles of Reed is in R. Brown, *Waterfront Organisation in Hull 1870–1900* (1972), p. 14.

87 T. Bottomore, Foreword to N. Abercrombie *et al.*, *The Dominant Ideology Thesis*, (1980), p. x.

88 The growing emphasis upon the land question in radical circles, including the working-class radicals, was an important part of the decline of a specifically anti-capitalist ideology; and it has been generally underestimated. For the land agitation of the third quarter of the nineteenth century, see the sources cited above, notes 33, 34, p. 271; and J. Saville, 'Henry George and the British Labour Movement', *Science and Society*, vol. 24 (1960), 321–33.

89 *TUC Report, 1874*, quoted Jefferys, *Labour's Formative Years*, pp. 116–17.

90 I use 'commonsense' in the Gramscian meaning of the term. For a helpful introduction to Gramsci's thought, see Anne S. Sassoon, *Approaches to Gramsci* (1982), and esp. the essays in parts 1 and 2.

91 G. O. Trevelyan, *The Life and Letters of Lord Macaulay* (popular edition, 1893), p. 507. For a general discussion, J. Hamburger, *Macaulay and the Whig Tradition* (Chicago, 1976).

92 'Vindication of the French Revolution of February 1848, in Reply to Lord Brougham and Others', *Westminster Review*, XLIX (April 1848), and reprinted in Mill's *Dissertations and Discussions. Political, Philosophical and Historical* vol. 2 (3rd edition, 1875), pp. 335–410. For a discussion of the debate, which gives it a good deal more importance than does the present writer, see F. B. Smith, 'The view from Britain 1. Tumults abroad, stability at home', in *Intellectuals and Revolution. Socialism and the Experience of 1848* (edited by E. Kamenka and F. B. Smith, 1979) esp. pp. 99–103.

93 George Eliot wrote a long letter to John Sibree on 8 March; full of interesting and intelligent comments on the revolution in France, and a comparison with the situation in Britain: 'I should have no hope of good from any initiative movement at home. Our working classes are eminently inferior to the mass of the French people . . . Here there is so much larger a proportion of selfish radicalism and

unsatisfied, brute sensuality (in the agricultural and mining districts especially) than of perception or desire of justice, that a revolutionary movement would be simply destructive – not constructive. Besides, it would be put down. Our military have no notion of 'fraternising'. They have the same sort of inveteracy as dogs have for the ill-drest canaille. They are as mere a brute force as a battering ram and the aristocracy have got firm hold of them. Our little humbug of a queen is more endurable than the rest of her race because she calls forth a chivalrous feeling, and there is nothing in our constitution to obstruct the slow progress of *political* reform. This is all we are fit for at present': *The Letters of George Eliot* (edited by G. S. Haight, vol. 1, 1836–51), p. 254.

94 S. Gilley, 'The Garibaldi Riots of 1862', *Hist. J.*, (Oxford, 1954), vol. 16 (1973), pp. 720–4; F. Neal, 'The Birkenhead Garibaldi Riots of 1862', *Trans. Hist. Soc. Lancs. and Cheshire*, vol. 131 (November 1982), pp. 87–111; P. Milward, 'The Stockport Riots of 1852', in R. Swift and S. Gilley (eds.), *The Irish in the Victorian City* (1985), pp. 207–24.

Bibliography

1. A note on manuscript sources

This study had been largely concerned with the ideas and policies of the contemporary leaders of government and with those involved in the machinery of government, both national and local. The starting point for any analysis is the collection of Home Office papers at the Public Record Office at Kew; the most useful for 1848 being HO 45/2410. This comprises five large boxes, each containing a number of files arranged by geographical location – usually by County – and which include the correspondence between the Home Office and all those involved in matters of internal security: magistrates, lay and stipendiary, Lords-Lieutenant, military commanders and members of the general public. These files also contain a large number of leaflets, posters, pamphlets forwarded to the Home Office for inspection. Much of this material, although normally described as ephemera, is unique and in urgent need of listing. Other Home Office classes that include relevant material are HO 40 and 41 (Disturbances), HO 61 and 65 (metropolitan police correspondence and entry books) and HO 79 (Ireland). The metropolitan police Records are mainly within the classes MEPO 1–8, and there is some War Office material in WO 30/81 and 111. The Lord John Russell papers are classified as PRO 30/22 and, for 1848, are disappointing. There is a full listing of relevant material for the whole period of Chartism, which includes the above as well as additional material, in D. Goodway, *London Chartism, 1838–1848* (Cambridge, 1982) 301–4. Goodway also lists the material from the Treasury Solicitor's Records at the Public Record Office, Chancery Lane.

Equal in importance with the PRO material is the Clarendon Collection in the Bodleian Library, Oxford, and in some areas it is the most useful source. The Out-Letter Books contain all Clarendon's own correspondence, and there are separate boxes for leading ministers and political personalities. The most important are Box 12, the correspondence with Sir George Grey, and Box 43, that with Russell. The latter goes a long way to make up for the meagre amount of material in the Russell papers in the PRO, at least for the year 1848. Other boxes of letters include Box 20 (Lord Normanby), Box 42 (Sir Robert Peel) and Box 45 (Duke of Wellington). The Household Accounts are in Section III A (Boxes 11, 12 and 13) and material relating to informers and agents is scattered, but includes Boxes 22 and 53. Other leading personalities of the period include Sir George Grey, whose private papers at Fallodon were destroyed by fire in 1917; and Lansdowne and Normanby, whose papers were still being listed when enquiries were made (See *Guide to Sources for British History, 1. Papers of British Cabinet Ministers, 1782–1900* (HMSO, 1982). For Palmerston, apart from the Home Office and Clarendon papers – which contain a great deal – the most important source of official papers are the records of the Foreign Office for 1848 especially FO 146/341–3. Correspondence in these Foreign Office volumes between Paris and London were copied by a clerk and then bound, and are a delight to read.

Record offices outside London vary a great deal in their usefulness for this present volume. The Scottish Record Office in Edinburgh offers supplementation to the material in London, and AD 58 Miscellaneous Papers Series, which contains a large number of sub-sections, proved the most profitable. The Records of the Lord Advocate's Department, especially AD 11, Miscellaneous Letter Books, contained useful material, and other classes, notably AD 14, 15, 16, 17, 56 and 58 were also helpful. Throughout the country in general, however, the military and police records are patchy, and only rarely – Manchester Record Office being a partial exception – do the Record offices add much to the national material in the PRO. It is possible, however, that a sustained search in what might appear to be unlikely files and repositories may bring forth new source materials.

The Royal Archives at Windsor Castle are in a different category; and for 1848 they are especially useful. C56, 'Chartists and Working Classes 1848', is a well-known file, but there is other correspondence of relevance for this year in C16, D18, F32, J67, J68 and J71.

Original source materials for the Chartist movement are scattered round the country. There is a listing, with location, in the *Bibliography of the Chartist Movement, 1837–1976* (edited by J. F. C. Harrison and D. Thompson, Sussex and New Jersey, 1978), pp. 5–25; but little has been used for this volume. One of the great strengths of Chartist historiography of the past three decades has been the development of local and regional studies, to the neglect, curiously, of some national material, notably the *Northern Star*, the exegesis of which for its later years is still incomplete.

2. British Parliamentary Papers

Return of Persons Killed or Wounded in Affrays with the Constabulary Force in Ireland, 1830–1, VIII

SC of House of Lords appointed to enquire into the State of Ireland in respect of Crime . . . 1839, XI and XII

Copy of Lord John Russell's Letter to Magistrates in Sessions, to Mayors of Boroughs in certain Counties directing them how to proceed for the preservation of the peace in disturbed districts, 1839, XXXVIII

Accounts and Papers. A Copy of the Instructions given to Crown Solicitors . . . respecting the challenging of Jurors in Crown Cases, 1842, XXXVII

SC on Railways, Fifth Report together with Minutes of Evidence, 1844, XI

Accounts and Papers. Return of Numbers of Persons who have lost their lives in Affrays with, or otherwise by, the Constabulary in Ireland . . . 1846, XXXV

Report of the Commissioners of Enquiry into the State of Education in Wales, 1847, XXVII, pt I/pt II

SC on Miscellaneous Expenditures, 1847–8, XVIII

Accounts and Papers. Estimates of Effective and Non-Effective Army Services from 1 April 1848 to 31 March 1849, 1847–8, XL

SC on Army and Ordnance Expenditure. Second Report, 1849, IX

Accounts and Papers. Army Commissariat, 1849, XXXII

Accounts and Papers. Ireland. Tables Showing the Numbers of Criminal Offenders committed for Trial or Bailed for Appearance at the Assizes and Sessions in each County, in the Year 1848, and the Results of the Proceedings, 1849, XLIV (1067)

Accounts and Papers. England and Wales. Tables showing the Numbers of Criminal Offenders committed for Trial or Bailed for Appearance at the Assizes and Sessions in each County, in the Year 1848, and the Results of the Proceedings, 1849, XLIV (1081)

Accounts and Papers. Circular Addressed by Viscount Palmerston to Her Majesty's Representatives in Foreign States, respecting the Debts due by Foreign States to British Subjects, 1849, LVI

SC on Army and Ordnance Expenditure. 1850, X

SC on Official Salaries, 1850, XV

Accounts and Papers. Tabular Returns of the Numbers of Committals for Crime in Ireland [and] . . . in England and Wales, 1852–3, LXXXI

SC of House of Lords . . . the Consequences of Extending the Functions of the Constabulary in Ireland to the Suppression or Prevention of Illicit Distillation . . . 1854, X

Reports of Committees of Enquiry into Public Offices . . . 1854, XXVII

Reports of Inspectors of Constabulary, 1857–8, XLVII

Reports from Commissioners. Constabulary (Ireland), 1866, XXXIV

SC on Jury System (Ireland) 1873, XV

SC on Jury System (Ireland) 1874, IX

3. Newspapers

London
Daily News
Globe and Traveller
John Bull
Lloyds Weekly London Newspaper
London Telegraph
*Morning Chronicle**
*Northern Star**
*The Times**
*Weekly Dispatch**

United Kingdom except London
Birmingham Journal
*Bolton Chronicle**
*Bradford Observer**
Freeman's Journal (Dublin)*
Harrogate Advertiser
Leeds Mercury
Leicester Journal
Liverpool Courier
Liverpool Journal
*Liverpool Mercury**
*Manchester Examiner**
*Manchester Guardian**
Newcastle Chronicle
Scotsman (Edinburgh)*
Staffordshire Mercury
*Stockport Advertiser**

Paris
Le Moniteur
*La Réforme**

* Most Used

4. Journals and Periodicals

Athenaeum
Blackwood's Edinburgh Magazine
Democratic Review of British and Foreign Politics, History and Literature
Dublin University Magazine
Economist '
Edinburgh Review
Fraser's Magazine
Illustrated London News
Nonconformist
Quarterly Review
Red Republican
Reynolds Political Instructor
Spectator
Westminster Review

5. Works of Reference

Annual Register
Bibliography of British History, 1789–1851(edited by L. M. Brown and I. R. Christie, Oxford, 1977)
Bibliography of British History, 1851–1914 (Compiled and edited by H. J. Hanham, Oxford, 1976)
Bibliography of the Chartist Movement, 1837–1976 (edited by J. F. C. Harrison and D. Thompson, Sussex and New Jersey, 1978)
Cockayne, G. E. *The Complete Peerage of England Scotland and Ireland . . .* New edition and much enlarged. Edited by the Hon. Vicary Gibbs, H. A. Doubleday, and others. 14 vols. 1910–1959
Dictionary of Labour Biography, vol. I, 1972–
Dictionary of Marxist Thought (edited by T. Bottomore, Blackwell, Oxford, 1983)
Dictionary of National Biography
Dictionnaire de biographie Française, vols. I–16, A–G (Paris, 1933–85)
An Encyclopedia of London (edited by W. Kent, 1937)
Foss, E. *Biographia Juridica. A Biographical Dictionary of the Judges of England. From the Conquest to the Present Time, 1066–1870* (1870)
Hansard's Parliamentary Debates, third series
Hart, H. G. *The New Annual Army List for 1848* (1848)
Kenny's Outlines of Criminal Law (18th edition by J. W. C. Turner, 1962)
Mitchell, B. R. and Deane, P. *Abstract of British Historical Statistics* (Cambridge, 1962)
New Catholic Encyclopedia, vol. 6 (Washington D.C., 1967)
Reports of State Trials, new ser. vol. VI, 1842–8
   new ser. vol. VII, 1848–50
Walker, D. M. *Oxford Companion to Law* (Oxford, 1980)
Ward, C. A. *A Bibliography of the History of Industry in the West Riding of Yorkshire,*

1750–1914, Leeds Philosophical and Literary Society, *Transactions* XIII, pt 1 (Leeds, 1968)
Warwick Guide to British Labour Periodicals, 1790–1970: A Check List (edited by R. Harrison, G. Woolven and R. Duncan, Brighton, 1977)

6. Books

(Place of publication is London unless otherwise stated)

Abel-Smith, B. and Stevens, R. *Lawyers and the Courts. A Sociological Study of the English Legal System, 1750–1965* (1967)
Abercrombie, N., Hill, S. and Turner, B. S. *The Dominant Ideology Thesis* (1980)
Adams, W. E. *Memoirs of a Social Atom*, 2 vols. (1903; reprinted in one volume with introduction by John Saville, New York, 1967)
Agulhon, M. *1848 ou L'Apprentissage de la République* (Paris, 1973)
  Les Quarante-huitards (Paris, 1975)
Alderson, C. *Selections from the Charges and other Detached Papers of Baron Alderson; with an Introductory Notice of his Life* (1858)
'Alfred' [Samuel Kydd]. *The History of the Factory Movement*, 2 vols. (1851; reprinted in one volume, New York, 1966)
Allen, G. C. *The Industrial Development of Birmingham and the Black Country, 1860–1927* (1929; reprinted 1966)
Alton Locke, with a prefatory memoir by Thomas Hughes (1900)
Anstruther, I. *The Scandal of the Andover Workhouse* (1973)
Ashley, Hon. E., *The Life and Correspondence of Henry John Temple, Lord Palmerston, 1784–1865*, 2 vols. (1879)
Atlay, J. B. *The Victorian Chancellors*, 2 vols. (1906)
Axon, W. E. A. *Annals of Manchester* (1886)
Bagwell, R. *Ireland under the Stuarts*, 3 vols. (1909–16)
Bagehot, W. *The English Constitution*. Collected works, edited by N. St John Stevas, vol. 5 (1974)
Bailey, V. (ed.) *Policing and Punishment in Nineteenth Century Britain* (1981)
Ball, F. E. *The Judges in Ireland, 1221–1921*, 2 vols. (New York, 1927)
Ball, J. T. *Historical Review of the Legislative Systems Operative in Ireland* . . . (New edition London and Dublin, 1889)
Ballantine, Sergeant. *Some Experiences of a Barrister's Life* (1882)
Bartlett, C. J. *Great Britain and Sea Power, 1815–1853* (Oxford, 1963)
de Beaumont, G. *L'Irlande, sociale, politique, religieuse*, 2 vols. (1839)
Beckett, J. C. *The Making of Modern Ireland, 1603–1923* (1966)
Bédarida, F. *A Social History of England, 1851–1975* (1979)
Belchem, J. *'Orator' Hunt. Henry Hunt and English Working-Class Radicalism* (Oxford, 1985)
Bell, H. C. F. *Lord Palmerston*, 2 vols. (1936)
Benson, A. C. and Esher, Viscount (eds.). *The Letters of Queen Victoria. A Selection from Her Majesty's Correspondence between the Years 1837 and 1861*, vol. 2 (1907)
Bernstein, S. *Buonarroti* (Paris, 1948)
Black, R. D. Collinson. *Economic Thought and the Irish Question, 1817–1870* (Cambridge, 1960)
Black, F. G. and Black, R. M. (eds.) *The Harney Papers* (Assen, 1969)
Blake, R. *Disraeli* (1969)
Blanc, L. *1848. Historical Revelations: Inscribed to Lord Normanby* (1858)

Boot, H. M. *The Commercial Crisis of 1847* (University of Hull, Occasional Papers in Economic and Social History, no. 11, 1984)

Briggs, A. *History of Birmingham*, vol. 2, 1865–1938 (1952)

Broeker, G. *Rural Disorder and Police Reform in Ireland, 1812–1836* (1970)

Brophy, M. *Sketches of the Royal Irish Constabulary* (1886)

Brown, M. *The Politics of Irish Literature* . . . (1972)

Brown, R. *Waterfront Organisation in Hull, 1870–1900* (University of Hull, Occasional Papers in Economic and Social History, no. 5, 1972)

Bullen, R. *Palmerston, Guizot and the Collapse of the Entente Cordiale* (1972)

A Memoir of Baron Bunsen . . . Drawn Chiefly from Family Papers by his Widow, Frances, Baroness Bunsen, 2 vols. (1868; second edition, 1869)

Bythell, D. *The Handloom Weavers* (Cambridge, 1969)

Carlyle, T. *Chartism* (1839)

Chadwick, E. *Report on the Sanitary Condition of the Labouring Population of Great Britain . . . 1842* (with introduction by M. W. Flinn, Edinburgh, 1965)

Chester, D. N. *The English Administrative System, 1750–1870* (Oxford, 1981)

Christensen, T. *Origin and History of Christian Socialism, 1848–1854* (Universitetsforlaget I Aarhus, 1962)

Church, R. A. *The Great Victorian Boom 1850–1873* (Studies in Economic and Social History, 1975)

Clapham, J. H. *An Economic History of Modern Britain. The Early Railway Age, 1820–1850* (Third edition, 1939)

Clive, J. *Scotch Reviewers. The Edinburgh Review, 1802–1815* (1957)

Clode, C. M. *The Military Forces of the Crown*, 2 vols. (1869)

Cobden, R. *The Three Panics* (1862)

Cockburn, Lord. *An Examination of the Trials for Sedition which Have Hitherto Occurred in Scotland*, 2 vols. (Edinburgh, 1888; reprinted in one volume, New York, 1970)

Connell, B. *Regina v. Palmerston. The Correspondence between Queen Victoria and Her Foreign and Prime Minister, 1837–1865* (1962)

Coville, A. and Temperley, A. (eds.) *Studies in Anglo-French History* (1935)

Creighton, M. *Memoir of Sir George Grey Bart, G.C.B. with Preface by Sir Edward Grey* (1901)

Cullen, L. M. and Smout, T. C. (eds.) *Comparative Aspects of Scottish and Irish Economic and Social History, 1600–1900* (Edinburgh, 1977)

Curtis, E. *History of Ireland* (Sixth edition, 1951)

Curtis Jnr, L. P. *Apes and Angels. The Irishman in Victorian Caricature* (1971)

Cusack, M. F. (ed.) *The Speeches and Public Letters of the Liberator*, 2 vols. (Dublin, 1875)

Dautry, J. *1848 et la 11ᵉ République* (Paris, 1957)

Davis, H. W. C. *The Age of Grey and Peel* (Oxford, 1929)

Delaney, V. T. H. *The Administration of Justice in Ireland* (Fourth edition, rev. C. Lysaght, Dublin, 1975)

Denvir, J. *The Irish in Britain from the Earliest Times to the Fall and Death of Parnell* (1892)

Devine, T. M. and Dickson, D. *Ireland and Scotland 1600–1850. Parallels and Contrasts in Economic and Social Development* (Edinburgh, 1983)

Dicey, A. V. *Introduction to the Study of the Law of the Constitution* (Ninth edition, 1939, with Introduction and Appendix by E. C. S. Wade)

Dobb, M. H. *Studies in the Development of Capitalism* (1946)

Dobson, C. R. *Masters and Journeymen. A Prehistory of Industrial Relations, 1770–1800* (1980)

Dommanget, M. *Sur Babeuf et la conjuration des égaux* (Paris, 1970)

Donajgrodzki, A. P. (ed.) *Social Control in Nineteenth Century Britain* (1977)

Drescher, S. *Tocqueville and England* (Cambridge, Mass., 1964)

Driver, C. *Tory Radical. The Life of Richard Oastler* (New York, 1946)

Droz, J. *Europe Between Revolutions, 1815–1848* (1967)

Duffy, C. G. *Young Ireland. Vol. 2. Four Years of Irish History* (1883)
  My Life in Two Hemispheres, 2 vols. (1898; reprinted Shannon, 1969)

Dunkley, P. *The Crisis of the Old Poor Law in England, 1785–1834. An Interpretative Essay* (New York and London, 1982)

Dutton, H. I. and King, J. E. *Ten Per Cent and No Surrender. The Preston Strike 1853–1854* (Cambridge, 1981)

Duveau, G. *1848. The Making of a Revolution* (1967)

Edsall, N. C. *The Anti-Poor Law Movement* (Manchester, 1971)

Edwards, O. D. *et al.* (eds.) *Celtic Nationalism* (1968)

Eisenstein, E. L. *The First Professional Revolutionist: Filippo Michele Buonarroti* (Cambridge, Mass., 1959)

The Letters of George Eliot (edited by G. S. Haight), vol. 1, 1836–51 (Oxford, 1954)

Emsley, C. *Policing and its Context, 1750–1850* (1983)

Engels, F. *The Condition of the Working Class in England* (various editions; 1969 with Introduction by E. J. Hobsbawm)

English, B. and Saville, J. *Strict Settlement: A Guide for Historians* (University of Hull, Occasional Papers in Economic and Social History, no. 10, 1983)

Epstein, J. *The Lion of Freedom. Feargus O'Connor and the Chartist Movement, 1832–1842* (1982)

Epstein, J. and Thompson, D. (eds.) *The Chartist Experience: Studies in Working-Class Radicalism and Culture, 1830–1860* (1982)

Fetjö, F. (ed.) *The Opening of an Era: 1848* (1948)

Finer, S. E. *The Man on Horseback: the Role of the Military in Politics* (1962)

Fisher, J. R. *The End of the Irish Parliament* (1911)

Flinn, M. W. and Smout, T. C. *Essays in Social History* (Oxford, 1974)

Forsyth, W. *History of Trial By Jury* (1852)

Fortescue, J. W. *History of the British Army*, vol. XI (1910)

Foster, J. *Class Struggle and the Industrial Revolution. Early Industrial Capitalism in Three English Towns* (1974)

Fraser, D. *Urban Politics in Victorian England* (1979)

Frazer, W. M. *A History of English Public Health, 1834–1939* (1950)

Furniss, E. *The Position of the Labourer in a System of Nationalism* (New York, 1920)

Gammage, R. G. *History of the Chartist Movement 1837–1854* (second edition reprinted with introduction by John Saville, New York, 1969)

Garrone, A. G. *Buonarroti e Babeuf* (Turin, 1948)

Gash, N. *Mr. Secretary Peel. The Life of Sir Robert Peel to 1830* (1961)
  Sir Robert Peel. The Life of Sir Rober Peel after 1830 (1972)
  Aristocracy and People (1979)

Gill, C. *The Rise of the Irish Linen Industry* (Oxford, 1925)
  History of Birmingham, vol. 1 to 1865 (1952)

Girard, L. *Le 11ᵉ République* (Paris, 1968)

Goodway, D. *London Chartism, 1838–1848* (Cambridge, 1982)

Gosden, P. H. J. H. *The Friendly Societies in England, 1815–1875* (Manchester, 1961)

Self-Help. Voluntary Associations in the Nineteenth Century (1973)

Grant, Sir A. *The Story of Edinburgh University*, 2 vols. (1884)

Gray, T. *The Orange Order* (1972)

The Greville Memoirs, 1814–1860 (edited by L. Strachey and R. Fulford), vol. v, January 1842 to December 1847 (1938); vol. vi, January 1848 to December 1853 (1938)

Gwynn, D. R. *Young Ireland and 1848* (Cork, 1949)

Halévy, E. *A History of the English People in 1815* (1924)

Hamburger, J. *Macaulay and the Whig Tradition* (Chicago, 1976)

Hammond, J. L. and B. *The Town Labourer 1760–1832. The New Civilisation* (1917)

Harrison, J. F. C. *Robert Owen and the Owenites in Britain and America. The Quest for the New Moral World* (1969)

Hedges, R. Y., and Winterbottom, A. *A Legal History of Trade Unionism* (1930)

Herzen, A. *My Past and Thoughts. The Memoirs of Alexander Herzen* (Abridged, with a Preface and Notes by Dwight Macdonald, 1974)

Heuston, R. F. V. *The Lives of the Lord Chancellors, 1885–1940* (1964)

Hobsbawm, E. J. *Labouring Men* (1964)

Hodder, E. *The Life and Work of the Seventh Earl of Shaftesbury* (1882)

Hodges, J. G. *Report of the Trial of William Smith O'Brien . . . September and October 1848 . . .* (Dublin, 1849)

Holdsworth, W. S. *A History of English Law*, vol. 10 (1938)

Hollis, P. *The Pauper Press. A Study in Working-Class Radicalism of the 1830s* (Oxford, 1970)

Holyoake, G. J. *Self-Help by the People. Thirty-three Years of Co-operation in Rochdale.* Part 1, 1844–57 (Ninth edition, 1882)

Bygones Worth Remembering, 2 vols. (1905)

Horne, H. O. *A History of Savings Banks* (1947)

Howarth, T. E. B. *Citizen-King. The Life of Louis-Philippe King of the French* (1961)

Howe, A. *The Cotton Masters 1830–1860* (Oxford, 1984)

Hyde, H. M. *The Rise of Castlereagh* (1933)

Hyndman, H. M. *The Historical Basis of Socialism in England* (1883)

Imlah, A. H. *Economic Elements in the Pax Britannica: Studies in British Foreign Trade in the Nineteenth Century* (Cambridge, Mass., 1958)

Inglis, H. D. *Ireland in 1834. A Journey throughout Ireland during the Spring, Summer and Autumn of 1834*, 2 vols. (Third edition, 1835)

Inglis, K. S. *Churches and the Working Classes in Victorian England* (1963)

James, J. *The History of the Worsted Manufacture in England* (Bradford, 1857)

Jefferys, J. B. *The Story of the Engineers* (1946)

Labour's Formative Years, 1849–1879 (1948)

Jenkins, M. *The General Strike of 1842* (1980)

Jennings, L. C. *France and Europe in 1848. A Study of French Foreign Affairs in Time of Crisis* (Oxford, 1973)

Jennings, W. I. *The Law and the Constitution* (various editions, 1933–58)

Cabinet Government (Cambridge, 1947)

Johnson, D. *Guizot* (1973)

Johnston, E. M. *Great Britain and Ireland, 1760–1800* (Edinburgh, 1963)

Ireland in the Eighteenth Century (Dublin 1974)

de Joinville, Prince. *Memoirs* (translated by Lady Mary Loyd, 1895)

Jones, D. J. V. *Chartism and the Chartists* (1975)

The Last Rising. The Newport Insurrection of 1839 (Oxford, 1985)

Jones, G. Stedman. *Languages of Class. Studies in English Working Class History, 1832–1982* (Cambridge, 1983)

[Joy, H. H.] *Letter to the Right Hon. Lord Lyndhurst on the Appointment of Sheriffs in Ireland under the Earl of Mulgrave. By a Barrister* (1838)

Joyce, P. *Work, Society and Politics. The Culture of the Factory in Later Victorian England.* (Brighton, 1980)

Kee, R. *The Most Distressful Country. The Green Flag,* vol. 1 (1976)

Kerr, D. A. *Peel, Priests and Politics. Sir Robert Peel's Administration and the Roman Catholic Church in Ireland, 1841–1846* (Oxford, 1982)

Kiernan, J. *The Financial Administration of Ireland, 1782–1817* (Dublin, 1925)

Kirk, N. *The Growth of Working-Class Reformism in Mid-Victorian England* (1985)

Lampson, G. Locker. *A Consideration of the State of Ireland in the Nineteenth Century* (1907)

Langer, W. L. *Political and Social Upheavals 1832–1852* (New York, 1969)

Lecky, W. E. H. *A History of Ireland in the Eighteenth Century,* 5 vols. (1892)
  A History of England in the Eighteenth Century, 8 vols. (1879–90)
  Leaders of Public Opinion in Ireland, 2 vols. (1903)

Lee, L. *The Modernisation of Irish Society, 1848–1918* (Dublin, 1973)

Lewis, G. C. *On Local Disturbances in Ireland, and on the Irish Church Question* (1836)

Lillibridge, G. D. *Beacon of Freedom. The Impact of American Democracy upon Great Britain, 1830–1870* (Pennsylvania, 1955)

Longford, Lady [Elizabeth Pakenham]. *Wellington. Pillar of State* (1972)

Low, S. *The Governance of England* (revised edition, 1914)

McCaffrey, L. J. *The Irish Question, 1800–1922* (Kentucky, 1968)

Macdonagh, O. *Early Victorian Government, 1830–1870* (1977)

McDowell, R. B. *Public Opinion and Government Policy in Ireland, 1801–1846* (1952)
  The Irish Administration, 1801–1914 (1964)

McKay, D. C. *The National Workshops* (Cambridge, Mass., 1933)

Mackintosh, J. P. *The British Cabinet* (Third edition, 1977)

McLellan, D. *Karl Marx. His Life and Thought* (1973)

Mcleod, H. *Religion and the Working Class in Nineteenth Century Britain* (Studies in Economic and Social History, 1984)

Maguire, W. A. *The Downshire Estates in Ireland, 1801–1845* (Oxford, 1972)

Mancuniensis. *Desultory Remarks on Ireland in 1838, Containing Reasons why an English Reformer has Changed his Opinions of the Irish Community and of Irish Politics* (1838), 38pp.

Marandon, S. *L'Image de la France dans L'Angleterre victorienne, 1848–1900* (Paris, 1967)

Marquess of Anglesey. *One Leg. The Life and Letters of Henry William Paget, First Marquess of Anglesey* (1961)

Martin, D. E. *John Stuart Mill and the Land Question* (University of Hull, Occasional Papers in Economic and Social History, no. 9, 1981)

Martin, T. *The Life of His Royal Highness The Prince Consort,* vol. 2 (1876)

Marx, K. *The Class Struggles in France, 1848–1850* (various editions)
  The Eighteenth Brumaire of Louis Bonaparte (various editions)
  Letters to Dr Kugelman (various editions)
  The Revolutions of 1848. Political Writings, vol. 1 (edited and introduced by D. Fernbach, 1973)

Surveys from Exile. Political Writings (edited and introduced by D. Fernbach, 1973)
The First International and After. Political Writings, vol. 3 (edited and introduced by
   D. Fernbach, 1974)
Marx-Engels. *On Britain* (Moscow, 1953)
   Ireland and the Irish Question (Moscow, 1978)
Mather, F. C., *Public Order in the Age of the Chartists* (Manchester, 1959)
Maxwell, Rt. Hon. Sir W. *The Life and Letters of George William Frederick, Fourth Earl of
   Clarendon*, 2 vols. (1913)
le May, G. H. L. *The Victorian Constitution. Conventions, Usages and Ceremonies* (1979)
Miliband, R. *Parliamentary Socialism. A Study in the Politics of Labour* (1961)
Mill, J. S. *Dissertations and Discussion. Political, Philosophical and Historical*, vol. 2
   (Third edition, 1875)
Mokyr, J. *Why Ireland Starved. A Quantitative and Analytical History of the Irish
   Economy 1800–1850* (1983)
Molesworth, Sir W. *History of England from the Year 1830 to 1874*, 3 vols. (1876)
Moore Jnr, Barrington. *Social Origins of Dictatorship and Democracy. Lord and Peasant
   in the Making of the Modern World* (1969)
Morley, J. *The Life of William Ewart Gladstone*, vol. 2 (1903)
   The Life of Richard Cobden (1906)
Morris, W. O'Connor. *Ireland from 1798 to 1898* (1898)
Mowat, C. L. *The Charity Organisation Society, 1869–1913* (1969)
Napier, Lt-General Sir W. *The Life and Opinions of General Sir Charles James Napier*, 4
   vols. (1857)
Normanby, Marquis of. *A Year of Revolution. From a Journal Kept in Paris in 1848*, vol.
   1 (1857)
Nowlan, K. B. *The Politics of Repeal* (1965)
Nussbaum, F. L. *History of Economic Institutions in Modern Europe. An Introduction to
   Der Moderne Kapitalismus of Werner Sombart* (New York, 1935)
Nicholls, Sir G. *A History of the English Poor Law*, vol. 2 (1854)
O'Brien, G. O. *Economic History of Ireland in the Eighteenth Century* (Dublin, 1918)
   *The Trial of Feargus O'Connor and Fifty-Eight Others on a Charge of Sedition,
   Conspiracy, Tumult and Riot* (Manchester and London, 1843; reprinted New
   York, 1970)
O'Hegarty, P. S. *A History of Ireland under the Union, 1901–1922* (1952)
O'Reilly, B. D. *John McHale, Archbishop of Tuam: His Life, Times and Correspondence*, 2
   vols. (New York, 1890)
Ormond, J. S. *Parliament and the Army 1642–1904* (Cambridge, 1933)
Parker, C. S. *Life and Letters of Sir James Graham, 1792–1861*, 2 vols. (1907)
   Sir Robert Peel, from his Private Papers, vol. 1 (1891)
Parker, G. *The Dutch Revolt* (1979)
Parris, H. *Constitutional Bureaucracy* (1969)
Patterson, A. T. *Radical Leicester. A History of Leicester, 1780–1850* (Leicester, 1954)
Paul, H. *A History of Modern England*, 5 vols. (1904–6)
Peacock, A. J. *Bradford Chartism, 1838–1840* (Borthwick Papers, no. 36, York,
   1969)
Pellew, J. *The Home Office, 1848–1914* (1982)
Philips, D. *Crime and Authority in Victorian England: The Black Country 1835–1860*
   (1977)
Picton, J. A. *Memorials of Liverpool, Historical and Topographical, Including a History of
   the Dock Estate*, vol. 1, Historical (1875)

Plummer, A. *Bronterre. A Political Biography of Bronterre O'Brien, 1804–1864* (1971)

Podmore, F. *Robert Owen. A Biography*, 2 vols. (1906; reprinted in one volume, New York, 1968)

Pollard, S. *The Genesis of British Management. A Study of the Industrial Revolution in Great Britain* (1965)
A History of Labour in Sheffield (Liverpool, 1959)

Pollard, S. and Holmes, C. (eds.) *Essays in the Economic and Social History of South Yorkshire* (Barnsley, 1976)

Prest, J. *Lord John Russell* (1972)

Price, R. *The French Second Republic. A Social History* (1972)
Revolution and Reaction: 1848 and the Second French Republic (1976)

Radzinowicz, L. *A History of English Criminal Law and its Administration from 1750*, vol. 4 (1968)

Ranelagh, J. O'Beirne, *A Short History of Ireland* (Cambridge, 1983)

Raven, C. E. *Christian Socialism, 1848–1854* (1920)

Read, D. *Edwardian England* (1972)

Read, D. and Glasgow, E. *Feargus O'Connor: Irishman and Chartist* (1961)

Reader, W. J. *Professional Men. The Rise of the Professional Classes in Nineteenth-Century England* (1966)

Redford, A. *The History of Local Government in Manchester*, vol. 2 (1940)

Redlich, J. *Local Government in England* (edited with additions by F. W. Hirst), 2 vols. (1903)

Reid, T. W. *The Life of the Right Honourable William Edward Forster*, 2 vols. (1888)

Reith, C. *British Police and the Democratic Ideal* (Oxford, 1943)

Reynolds, J. *The Great Paternalist. Titus Salt and the Growth of Nineteenth-Century Bradford* (1983)

Richards, E. *Leviathan of Wealth: the Sutherland Fortune in the Industrial Revolution* (1973)

Ridley, J. *Lord Palmerston* (1970)

Robertson, P. *Revolutions in 1848. A Social History* (Princeton, 1952)

Rogers, J. E. T. *Cobden and Modern Political Opinion* (1873)

Roscoe, H. *Eminent British Lawyers* (1830)

Russell, John (Earl). *Recollections and Suggestions, 1813–1873* (Second edition, 1875)

Ryazanoff, D. *The Communist Manifesto of Karl Marx and Friedrich Engels* (1930)

St John-Stevas, N. (ed.) *The Collected Writings of Walter Bagehot. vol. 5 The Political Essays* (1974)

Sainty, J. *Office Holders in Modern Britain. v. Home Officials, 1782–1871* (1975)

Sassoon, A. S. *Approaches to Gramsci* (1982)

Saville, J. *Ernest Jones. Chartist* (1952)

Schoyen, A. R. *The Chartist Challenge: A Portrait of George Julian Harney* (1958)

Sewell, W. H. *Work and Revolution in France* (Cambridge, 1980)

Sigsworth, E. M. *Black Dyke Mill. A History, with Introductory Chapters on the Development of the Worsted Industry in the Nineteenth Century* (Liverpool, 1958)

Smith, C. Woodham. *The Great Hunger. Ireland 1845–9* (1962)

Snell, F. J. *Palmerston's Borough. A Budget of Electioneering Anecdotes, Jokes, Squibs and Speeches* (London and Tiverton, 1894)

Sombart, W. *Der Moderne Kapitalismus*, 3 vols. (Second edition, Munich and Leipzig, 1916–28)

Somerville, A. *The Whistler at the Plough: Containing Travels, Statistics, and Descriptions of Scenery and Agricultural Customs in Most Parts of England; with Letters from Ireland . . . in 1847* (Manchester, 1852)

Southgate, D. *'The Most English Minister . . .' The Policies and Politics of Palmerston* (1966)

Spiers, E. H. *The Army and Society, 1815–1914* (1980)

Stephen, Sir J. F. *A History of the Criminal Law of England*, vol. I (1883)

Stokes, E. *The English Utilitarians and India* (Oxford, 1959)

Strauss, E. *Irish Nationalism and British Democracy* (1951)

Stryker, L. P. *For the Defence. Thomas Erskine, the Most Enlightened Liberal of his Times, 1750–1823* (New York, 1949)

Sutherland, G. *Studies in the Growth of Nineteenth Century Government* (1972)

Swift, R. and Gilley, S. (eds.) *The Irish in the Victorian City* (1985)

Thackeray, W. M. *The Paris Sketch Book. Collected Works*, XVI (1897)

Tholfsen, T. R. *Working Class Radicalism in Mid-Victorian England* (1976)

Thomis, M. I. and Holt, P. *Threats of Revolution in Britain, 1789–1848* (1977)

Thompson, D. *The Chartists* (1984)

Thompson, E. P. *The Making of the English Working Class* (1963; Second edition, 1968)

Thompson, F. M. L. *English Landed Society in the Nineteenth Century* (1963)

Thompson, N. W. *The People's Science. The Popular Political Economy of Exploitation and Crisis, 1816–1834* (Cambridge, 1984)

Thomson, D. and McGusty, M. (eds.) *The Irish Journals of Elizabeth Smith, 1840–1850* (Oxford, 1980)

Tildsley, J. *Die Entstehung und die ökonomischen Grundsätze der Chartistenbewegung* (Jena, 1898)

Tobias, J. J. *Crime and Industrial Society in the Nineteenth Century* (1972)

de Tocqueville, A. *Journeys to England and Ireland* (edited by J. P. Mayer, 1958) *Recollections* (edited by J. P. Mayer and A. P. Kerr, New York, 1971)

Tooke, T. and Newmarch, W. *A History of Prices and of the State of the Circulation during the Nine Years 1846–1856*, vol. 5 (1857)

Townshend, Charles. *Political Violence in Ireland. Government and Resistance since 1848* (Oxford, 1983)

Townshend, Charlotte. *The Case Against the Charity Organisation Society* (Fabian Tracts no. 158, 1911) 20 pp.

Trevelyan, G. O. *The Life and Letters of Lord Macaulay* (Popular edition, 1893)

Troup, Sir E. *The Home Office* (1925)

Turberville, A. S. *The House of Lords in the Age of Reform, 1784–1837* (1958)

Vigier, F. *Change and Apathy: Liverpool and Manchester during the Industrial Revolution* (Cambridge, Mass., 1970)

Villiers, G. J. T. H. *A Vanished Victorian. Being the Life of George Villiers, fourth Earl of Clarendon, 1800–1870* (1938)

Wall, M. *The Penal Laws* (1961)

Wallas, Graham. *The Life of Francis Place, 1771–1854* (1898)

Walpole, S. *The Life of Lord John Russell*, 2 vols (1889)

Ward, J. T. *The Factory Movement, 1830–1855* (1962)

Ward, J. T. and Wilson, R. G. (eds.) *Land and Industry* (1971)

Webb, R. K. *The British Working Class Reader, 1790–1848* (1955)

Webb, S. and B. *History of Trade Unionism* (1894)
    English Local Government from the Revolution to the Municipal Corporations Act: Parish and County (1906)

Wedderburn, K. W. *Cases and Materials on Labour Law* (Cambridge, 1967)

Weisser, H. *April 10. Challenge and Response in England in 1848* (New York, 1983)

White, B. D. *A History of the Corporation of Liverpool 1835–1914* (Liverpool, 1951)

Wilson, A. *The Chartist Movement in Scotland* (Manchester, 1970)

Wise, E. *The Law Relating to Riots and Unlawful Assemblies: Together with a View of the Duties and Powers of Magistrates, Public Officers, Special Constables, the Military, and Private Individuals, for their Suppression; and a Summary of the Law to Actions Against the Hundred* (Second edition, 1848)

Wohl, A. S. *Endangered Lives. Public Health in Victorian Britain* (1983)

Woodbridge, G. *The Reform Bill of 1832* (New York, 1970)

Wrigley, E. A. (ed.) *Nineteenth Century Society. Essays on the Use of Quantitative Methods for the Study of Social Data* (Cambridge, 1972)

7. Articles

Amann, D. 'The Paris Club Movement in 1848', *Revolution and Reaction. 1848 and the Second French Republic* (edited by R. Price, 1975), 115–32

Anderson, O. 'The Constitutional Position of the Secretary at War, 1642–1855', *J. Soc. Army H. Research*, xxxvi (1958), 165–9

Arnstein, W. L. 'The Murphy Riots: A Victorian Dilemma', *Victorian Studies*, xix (1975), 51–71

Bagchi, A. 'De-industrialisation in India in the Nineteenth Century: Some Theoretical Implications', *Journal of Development Studies*, xii, 2 (1976), 135–64
    'De-industrialisation of India ... A Reply', *Indian Economic and Social History Review*, xiv, 2 (1979), 147–61

Baldwin, J. R. 'England and the French Seizure of the Society Islands', *J. Mod. H.*, x, 2 (June 1938), 212–31

Beales, H. L. 'Studies in Bibliography. IV. The "Basic" Industries of England, 1850–1914', *Econ. H. Rev.*, v, pt 2 (1934–5), 99–112

Beames, M. R. 'The Ribbon Societies: Lower-Class Nationalism in Pre-Famine Ireland', *Past and Present*, no. 97 (November 1982), 128–43

Belchem, J. '1848: Feargus O'Connor and the Collapse of the Mass Platform', *The Chartist Experience* (edited by J. Epstein and D. Thompson, 1982) 269–310

Best, G. 'Popular Protestantism in Victorian England', *Ideas and Institutions of Victorian Britain* (edited by R. Robson, 1967) 115–42

Bisceglia, L. R. 'The Threat of Violence: Irish Confederates and Chartists in Liverpool in 1848', *Irish Sword*, xiv (1981), 207–15

Black, R. D. Collinson. 'Economic Policy in Ireland and India in the Time of J. S. Mill', *Econ. H. Rev.*, second ser. xxi, 2 (August 1968), 321–36

Blaug, M. 'The Productivity of Capital in the Lancashire Cotton Industry during the Nineteenth Century', *Econ. H. Rev.*, Second ser., xiii, 3 (April 1961), 358–81
    'The Myth of the Old Poor Law and the Making of the New', *J. Econ. H.*, xxiii, 2 (1963) 151–84
    'The Poor Law Report Re-examined', *J. Econ. H,* xxiv, 2 (1964)

Brock, P. 'The Socialists of the Polish 'Great Emigration' ', *Essays in Labour History* (edited by A. Briggs and J. Saville, 1960), 140–73

Buckell, L. E. 'The Surrey Yeomanry Cavalry', *J. Soc. Army H. Research*, xxviii (1950), 171–2

Burn, W. L. 'Free Trade in Land: an Aspect of the Irish Question', *Trans. Roy. H. Soc.* Fourth ser. xxxi (1949), 61–74

Cahill, M. W. 'Peerage Creations and the Changing Character of the British Nobility, 1750–1850', Engl. H. Rev., xcvi, 379 (April 1981), 259–84

Chandavarkar, R. 'Industrialisation in India Before 1947: Conventional Approaches and Alternative Perspectives', Modern Asian Studies, xix, 3 (1985), 623–68

Checkland, S. G., and E. O. A. (eds.) Introduction to The Poor Law Report of 1834 (1974)

Clarke, T., and Dickson, T. 'Class and Class Consciousness in Early Industrial Capitalism: Paisley 1770–1850', Capital and Class in Scotland (edited by T. Dickson, Edinburgh, 1982)

Clarkson, L. A. 'The Writing of Irish Economic and Social History since 1968', Econ. H. Rev., xxxiii, 1 (February 1980) 100–11

Coats, A. W. 'Changing Attitudes to Labour in the Mid-Eighteenth Century', Econ. H. Rev., Second ser. xi (1958), 33–51

Crossick, G. 'The Labour Aristocracy and its Values: a Study of Mid-Victorian Kentish London', Victorian Studies, xix, 3 (March 1976), 301–28.

Cunningham, A. B. 'Peel, Aberdeen and the Entente Cordiale', Bull. Inst. H. Res., xxx, 82 (November 1957), 189–206

Daniels, E. 'Die Engländer und die Gefahr einer französichen Landung zur zeit Louis Philipps und Napoleons III', Delbruck = festschrift (Berlin, 1908), 257–91

Deane, P. 'New Estimates of Gross National Product for the United Kingdom, 1830–1914' Review of Income and Wealth, ser. 14, 2 (June 1968), 95–112

Dewey, C. J. 'The Rehabilitation of the Peasant Proprietor in Nineteenth-Century Economic Thought', History of Political Economy, vi, 1 (1974), 17–47

Donajgrodzki, A. P. 'New Roles for Old: the Northcote-Trevelyan Report and the Clerks of the Home Office, 1822–48', Studies in the Growth of Nineteenth Century Government (edited by G. Sutherland, 1972), 82–109

Dunman, A. 'A Social and Occupational Analysis of the English Judiciary: 1770–1790 and 1855–75', Amer. J. Legal H., xvii (1973), 353–64

Epstein, J. 'Feargus O'Connor and the Northern Star', Int. Rev. Soc. H., xxi (1976), 51–97

Fasel, G. 'The Wrong Revolution: French Republicanism in 1848', French Historical Studies, viii, 4 (Fall 1974), 654–77

Field, J. 'Police, Power and Community in a Provincial English Town: Portsmouth 1815–1875', Policing and Punishment in Nineteenth Century Britain (edited by V. Bailey, 1981), 42–64

Finlayson, G. B. A. 'The Politics of Municipal Reform, 1835', Engl. H. Rev., lxxxi, 321, (1966), 673–92

Foster, J. 'Some Comments on "Class Struggle and the Labour Aristocracy"', Social History, iii (October 1976), 357–66

Fox, C. 'The Development of Social Reportage in English Periodical Illustration During the 1840s and Early 1850s', Past and Present, no. 74 (February 1977), 90–111

Garvin, T. 'Defenders, Ribbonmen and Others: Underground Political Networks in Pre-Famine Ireland', Past and Present, no. 96 (August 1982), 133–55

Gatrell, V. A. C. and Hadden, T. B. 'Criminal Statistics and their Interpretation', Nineteenth Century Society. Essays on the Use of Quantitative Methods for the Study of Social Data (edited by E. A. Wrigley, Cambridge, 1972), 336–441

George, M. D. 'The London Coal-Heavers: Attempts to Regulate Waterside Labour in the Eighteenth and Nineteenth Centuries', Economic History, no. 2 (May 1927), Supplement, Economic Journal, 229–48

Gilley, S. 'The Garibaldi Riots of 1862', *Hist. J.*, xvi (1973), 720–4

Godfrey, C. 'The Chartist Prisoners, 1840–41, *Int. Rev. Soc. H.*, xxiv (1979), 189–236

Godfrey C. and Epstein, J. 'H.O.20/10: Interviews of Chartist Prisoners, 1840–41', *Bull. Soc. Lab. H.*, no. 34, (Spring 1977), 27–34

Gonner, E. C. K. 'The Early History of Chartism', *Engl. H. Rev.*, iv (1889), 625–44

Graham, A. H. 'The Litchfield House Compact', *Irish H. Studies*, xii (1960–1), 209–25

Halévy, E. 'English Public Opinion and the French Revolutions of the Nineteenth Century', *Studies in Anglo-French History* (edited by A. Coville and A. Temperley, 1935) 51–66

Harrison, J. F. C. 'Chartism in Leicester', *Chartist Studies* (edited by A. Briggs, 1959), 99–146

Hart, J. 'Reform of the Borough Police, 1835–1856', *Engel. H. Rev.*, lxx, 276 (July 1955), 411–27

'Nineteenth-Century Social Reform: a Tory Interpretation of History', *Past and Present*, no. 31 (1965), 39–61

Henry, P. 'Le gouvernment provisoire et la question polonaise en 1848', *Revue historique*, clxxviii (Sept.–Oct. 1936), 198–240

Hill, Jacqueline, 'The Protestant Response to Repeal: the Case of the Dublin Working-Class', *Ireland under the Union. Varieties of Tension. Essays in Honour of T. W. Moody* (edited by F. S. L. Lyons and R. A. J. Hawkins, Oxford, 1980), 35–68

Hill, J. E. C. 'The Norman Yoke', *Puritanism and Revolution. Studies in the Interpretation of the English Revolution of the Seventeenth Century* (1958), 50–122

Hobsbawm, E. J. 'The British Standard of Living, 1790–1850', *Econ. H. Rev.*, Second ser. x, 1 (August 1957), 46–68

'Methodism and the Threat of Revolution in Britain', *Labouring Men. Studies in the History of Labour* (1964), 23–33

Holderness, B. A. 'Landlords' Capital Formation in E. Anglia, 1750–1870', *Econ. H. Rev.*, Second ser., xxv, 3 (1972), 434–47

Johnson, Carol, 'The Problem of Reformism and Marx's Theory of Fetishism', *New Left Review*, no. 119 (Jan.–Feb. 1980) 70–96

Johnson, R. 'Educational Policy and Social Control in Early Victorian England', *Past and Present*, no. 49 (1970), 96–119

Jones, G. Stedman. 'Class Struggle and the Industrial Revolution', *New Left Review*, no. 90 (March–April 1975), 35–69

Joyce, P. 'The Factory Politics of Lancashire in the Later Nineteenth Century', *Hist. J.*, xviii, 3 (1975), 525–53

Kirk, N. 'Cotton Workers and Deference', *Bull. Soc. Lab H.*, no. 42 (Spring 1981), 41–3

Koepke, R. L. 'The Failure of Parliamentary Government in France, 1840–1848', *European Studies Review*, ix, 4 (October 1979), 433–55

Large, D. 'The House of Lords and Ireland in the Age of Peel, 1832–1850', *Irish H. Studies*, ix, 36 (September 1955), 367–99

'London in the Year of Revolution, 1848', *London in the Age of Reform* (edited by J. Stevenson, Oxford, 1977), 177–211

Laski, H. J. 'The Technique of Judicial Appointment', *Studies in Law and Politics* (1932), 163–80

Lawton, R. 'The Population of Liverpool in Mid-Nineteenth Century', *Trans. H. Soc. Lancs. and Cheshire*, cvii (1956), 89–120

'Irish Immigration to England and Wales in the Mid-Nineteenth Century' *Irish Geography*, IV, I (1959), 25–54

Lefevre, A. 'La Reconnaissance de la Second République par L'Angleterre' *Revue d'histoire diplomatique*, LXXXII (1968), 213–31

Lehning, A. M. 'Buonarroti and his International Secret Societies', *Int. Rev. Soc. H.* I (1956), 112–40

Lowe, W. J. 'The Lancashire Irish and the Catholic Church, 1846–71', *Irish H. Studies*, XX, 78 (September 1976), 129–55

Mather, F. C. 'The Government and the Chartists', *Chartist Studies* (edited by A. Briggs, 1959), 372–405

McCord, N. 'Cobden and Bright in Politics, 1846–1857', *Ideas and Institutions of Victorian England* (edited by R. Robson, 1967), 87–114

McKendrick, N. 'Josiah Wedgwood and Factory Discipline', *Hist. J.*, IV, I (1961), 30–55

'Josiah Wedgwood and Thomas Bentley: an Inventor-Entrepreneur Partnership in the Industrial Revolution', *Trans. Roy. H. Soc.*, Fifth ser. V (1964), 1–33

'Josiah Wedgwood and Cost Accounting in the Industrial Revolution' *Econ. H. Rev.*, Second ser. XXIII, I (April 1970) 45–67

Milward, P. 'The Stockport Riots of 1852', *The Irish in the Victorian City*, (edited by R. Swift and S. Gilley, 1985), 207–24

Moore, D. C. 'Concession or Cure: the Sociological Premises of the First Reform Act' *Hist. J.* IX, I (1966) 39–59

'Political Morality in mid-Nineteenth Century England: Concepts, Norms, Violations', *Victorian Studies*, XIII, I (September 1969), 5–36

Musson, A. E. 'Class Struggle and the Labour Aristocracy, 1830–1860', *Social History*, III (October 1976), 335–56

Neal, F. 'The Birkenhead Garibaldi Riots of 1862', *Trans. H. Soc. Lancs. and Cheshire*, CXXXI (November 1982) 87–111

Newby, H. 'The Deferential Dialectic', *Comparative Studies in Society and History*, XVII (1975), 139–64

Nicolaevsky, B. 'Towards a History of "The Communist League" 1847–1852', *Int. Rev. Soc. H.*, I, pt. 2 (1956), 234–52

O'Higgins, R. 'The Irish influence in the Chartist Movement', *Past and Present*, no. 20 (1961)

Otley, C. B. 'The Social Origins of British Army Officers', *Sociological Review*, XVIII, 2 (July 1970), 213–39

Parssinen, T. M. 'Mesmeric Performers', *Victorian Studies*, XXI (1977–8), 87–104

Philips, D. 'Riots and Public Order in the Black Country, 1835–1860, *Popular Protest and Public Order* (edited by R. Quinault and J. Stevenson, 1974), 141–80

Pollard, S. 'Nineteenth Century Co-operation: from Community Building to Shopkeeping', *Essays in Labour History* (edited by A. Briggs and J. Saville, rev. ed., 1967), 74–112

'Feargus O'Connor: as Seen by a Contemporary', *Bull. Soc. Lab. H.*, no. 24 (Spring 1874), 17–27

Price, R. N. 'The Working Men's Club Movement and Victorian Social Reform Ideology', *Victorian Studies*, XV, 2 (December 1971), 117–47

Quinault, R. 'The Warwickshire County Magistracy and Public Order c. 1830–1870', *Popular Protest and Public Order* (edited by R. Quinault and J. Stevenson, 1974) 181–214

Radzinowicz, L. 'New Departures in Maintaining Public Order in the Face of Chartist

Disturbances', *Cambridge Law Journal* (1960) 51–80
Reid, C. 'Class and Culture', *Bull. Soc. Lab. H.*, no. 34 (Spring 1977), 56–61
'Middle Class Values and Working Class Culture in Nineteenth Century Sheffield, the Pursuit of Respectability', *Essays in the Economic and Social History of South Yorkshire* (edited by S. Pollard and C. Holmes, Barnsley, 1976), 275–95
Ricardo, G. C. 'Evolution of the Yeomanry', *Cavalry Journal* (1907), 21–8
Richards, P. 'The State and Early Capitalism: the Case of the Handloom Weavers', *Past and Present*, no. 83 (May 1979), 91–115
'State Formation and Class Struggle, 1832–48', *Capitalism, State Formation and Marxist Theory* (edited by P. Corrigan, 1980), 49–78
Richardson, C. 'Irish Settlement in Mid-Nineteenth Bradford', *Yorkshire Bulletin of Economic and Social Research*, xx, 1 (May 1968), 40–57
Rothblatt, S. 'Some Recent Writings on British Political History, 1832–1914', *J. Mod. H.*, LV, 3 (September 1983), 484–99
Rubinstein, W. D. 'The End of "Old Corruption" in Britain in 1780–1860', *Past and Present*, no. 101 (November 1983), 55–86
Samuel, R. 'The Workshop of the World: Steam Power and Hand Technology in Mid-Victorian Britain', *History Workshop*, no. 3 (Spring 1977), 6–72
Saville, J. 'Chartism in the Year of Revolution, 1848', *Modern Quarterly*, VIII, 1 (Winter 1952–3), 23–33
'The Christian Socialists of 1848', *Democracy and the Labour Movement* (edited by J. Saville, 1954), 135–59
'Henry George and the British Labour Movement', *Science and Society*, vol. 24 (1960), 321–33
Introduction to R. G. Gammage, *History of the Chartist Movement* (1894; reprint New York, 1969), 5–66
'J. E. Smith and the Owenite Movement 1833–4', *Robert Owen. Prophet of the Poor* (edited by S. Pollard and J. Salt, 1971), 115–44
Introduction to *Working Conditions in the Victorian Age: Debates on the Issue from Nineteenth Century Critical Journals* (edited by J. Saville, 1973), i–xix
'Class Struggle and the Industrial Revolution', *Socialist Register* (edited by R. Miliband and J. Saville, 1974), 226–40
Senior, N. 'Poor Law Reform', *Edinburgh Rev.*, CXLIV (October 1841), 1–44
Sewell, W. H. 'Corporations Républicaines: the Revolutionary idiom of Parisian Workers in 1848', *Comparative Studies in Society and History*, XXI, 2 (April 1979), 195–203
Simon, D. 'Master and Servant', *Democracy and the Labour Movement* (edited by J. Saville, 1954), 160–200
Smith, F. B. 'The View from Britain. I. Tumults Abroad, Stability at Home', *Intellectuals and Revolution. Socialism and the Experience of 1848* (edited by E. Kamenka and F. B. Smith, 1979) 94–120
Storch, R. D. 'The Policeman as Domestic Missionary: Urban Discipline and Popular Culture in Northern England, 1850–1880', *Journal of Social History*, IX, 4 (Summer 1976), 481–509
Taylor, J. S. 'The Mythology of the Old Poor Law', *J. Econ. H.*, XXIX, 2 (1969), 292–7
Teichman, O. 'The Yeomanry as an Aid to Civil Power, 1795–1867', *J. Soc. Army H. Research*, XIX (1940), 75–91
Tholfsen, T. R. 'The Artisan and the Culture of Early Victorian Birmingham', *University of Birmingham Historical Journal*, IV (1953–4), 146–66
'The Chartist Crisis in Birmingham', *Int. Rev. Soc. H.*, III, pt 3 (1958), 461–80

'The Transition to Democracy in Victorian England', *Int. Rev. Soc. H.*, VI, pt 2 (1961), 226–48

Thompson, Dorothy, 'Ireland and the Irish in English Radicalism before 1850', *The Chartist Experience* (edited by J. Epstein and D. Thompson, 1982), 120–51

Thompson, E. P. 'The Peculiarities of the English', *Socialist Register*, (1965), 310–62; reprinted, with minor changes, in *The Poverty of Theory* (1978)

Thompson, F. M. L. 'Land and Politics in England in the Nineteenth Century', *Trans. Roy. H. Soc.* Fifth ser. xv (1965), 23–44

Tilly, C. and Lees, L. L. 'The People of June, 1848', *Revolution and Reaction. 1848 and the Second French Republic* (edited by R. Price, 1975), 170–209

Treble, J. H. 'O'Connor, O'Connell and the Attitudes of Irish Immigrants towards Chartism in the North of England 1838–1848', *The Victorians and Social Protest* (edited by J. Butt and I. F. Clarke, Newton Abbot, 1973), 33–70

'Trial By Jury', *Law Journal*, 12 April 1872, 238–9

'Irish Jury Laws', *Irish Law Times*, 24 September 1881, 500–1

Tylden, G. 'Yeomanry in Berkshire', *J. Soc. Army H. Research*, XXVIII (1950), 96–101

Tyrell, A. 'Political Economy, Whiggism and the Education of Working-Class Adults in Scotland 1817–1840', *Scottish Historical Review*, XLVIII, 2 (October 1969)

Vicziany, N. 'The De-industrialisation of India during the Nineteenth Century: a Methodological Critique', *Indian Economic and Social History Review*, XIV, 2 (1979), 105–46

Vidalenc, J. 'La Province et les journées de juin', *Études d'histoire moderne et contemporaine*, II (1948), 83–144

Ward, J. T. 'West Riding Landowners and the Corn Laws', *Engl. H. Rev.*, LXXXI, 319 (1966), 256–72

Ward-Perkins, C. N. 'The Commercial Crisis of 1847', *Oxford Economic Papers*, II (1950), reprinted in *Essays in Economic History* (edited by E. M. Carus-Wilson, 1962), 263–79

Weisser, H. 'Chartist Internationalism, 1845–1848', *Hist. J.* XIV, I (1971), 49–66

'Chartism in 1848: Reflections on a Non-Revolution', *Albion*, XIII, I (Spring 1981), 13–26

Werly, J. W. 'The Irish in Manchester, 1832–49', *Irish H. Studies*, XVIII (1972–3), 345–58

Wilson, A. 'Chartism in Glasgow', *Chartist Studies*, (edited by A. Briggs, 1959), 249–87

Woodward, E. L. 'Les Caractères généraux des relations Franco-Anglaises entre 1815–1870', *Revue d'histoire moderne*, XIII (1938), 110–25

Wright, G. 'A poet in Politics: Lamartine and the Revolution of 1848', *History Today*, VIII (September 1958), 616–27

Wyatt, A. 'Froude, Lecky and "the humblest Irishman"' *Irish H. Studies*, XIX, (March 1975), 261–85

8. Unpublished theses and dissertations

Elliott, A. 'The Establishment of Municipal Government in Bradford, 1837–1857' (Ph.D. University of Bradford, 1976)

Geering, K. 'George White, a Nineteenth-Century Workers' Leader' (M.A. University of Sussex, 1973)

Kaijage, F. J. 'Labouring Barnsley, 1815–1875' (Ph.D. University of Warwick, 1975)

Keller, L. 'Public Order in Victorian London: the Interaction Between the Metropolitan Police, the Government, the Urban Crowd, and the Law' (Ph.D. University of Cambridge, 1977)

Kriegel, A. D. 'The Whig Government and Ireland 1830–1835' (Ph.D. Duke University, 1964; facsimile Ann Arbor, 1975)

Lowe, W. J. 'The Irish in Lancashire, 1846–71: a Social History' (Ph.D. University of Dublin, 1974. Copy deposited at Lancashire Record Office, Preston)

Martin, D. E. 'Economic and Social Attitudes to Landed Property in England, 1790–1850, with Special Reference to John Stuart Mill' (Ph.D. University of Hull, 1972)

Neave, D. 'Friendly Societies in the Rural East Riding of Yorkshire, 1830–1912', (Ph.D. University of Hull, 1986)

Prothero, I. J. 'London Working-Class Movements, 1825–1848' (Ph.D. University of Cambridge, 1967)

Reid, C. 'Middle Class Values and Working Class Culture in Nineteenth Century Sheffield' (Ph.D. University of Sheffield, 1976)

Rizzi, R. A. 'The British Army as a Riot Control Force in Great Britain, 1811–1848', (B. Litt. University of Oxford, 1975)

Spenceley, G. F. R. 'The Pillow Lace Industry: a Study of Rural Industry in Competition during the Nineteenth Century' (Ph.D. University of Hull, 1974)

Yeadell, M. 'Building Fluctuations and Building Societies in the West Riding of Yorkshire, 1785–1914' (M.Phil. University of Hull, 1980)

Index

Printed in the United Kingdom
by Lightning Source UK Ltd.
108698UKS00001B/151